KW-310-417

Family Offices

The STEP Handbook for Advisers

Consulting Editor **Clare Archer**
Advisory Editor **Barbara R Hauser**

Consulting editor
Clare Archer

Advisory editor
Barbara R Hauser

Managing director
Sian O'Neill

Editorial services director
Carolyn Boyle

Production manager
Neal Honney

Group publishing director
Tony Harriss

Family Offices: The STEP Handbook for Advisers
is published by
Globe Law and Business
Globe Business Publishing Ltd
New Hibernia House
Winchester Walk
London SE1 9AG
United Kingdom
Tel +44 20 7234 0606
Fax +44 20 7234 0808
www.GlobeLawandBusiness.com

Printed and bound by CPI Group (UK) Ltd, Croydon, CR0 4YY

Family Offices: The STEP Handbook for Advisers
ISBN 9781909416024

© 2015 Globe Business Publishing Ltd

All rights reserved. No part of this publication may be reproduced in any material form (including photocopying, storing in any medium by electronic means or transmitting) without the written permission of the copyright owner, except in accordance with the provisions of the Copyright, Designs and Patents Act 1988 or under terms of a licence issued by the Copyright Licensing Agency Ltd, 6-10 Kirby Street, London EC1N 8TS, United Kingdom (www.cla.co.uk, email: licence@cla.co.uk). Applications for the copyright owner's written permission to reproduce any part of this publication should be addressed to the publisher.

DISCLAIMER
This publication is intended as a general guide only. The information and opinions which it contains are not intended to be a comprehensive study, nor to provide legal advice, and should not be treated as a substitute for legal advice concerning particular situations. Legal advice should always be sought before taking any action based on the information provided. The publishers bear no responsibility for any errors or omissions contained herein.

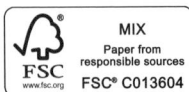

FSC
www.fsc.org

MIX
Paper from
responsible sources
FSC® C013604

Table of contents

What is a family office?

Ian Macdonald
Wright, Johnston & McKenzie LLP
Mark McMullen
Smith & Williamson LLP

1. Setting the scene

At its simplest, a family office is the structure used by a family to manage the business of the family. On that basis, every family has a family office and, although family offices are normally thought of as the preserve of wealthy families because of the resources required to manage a complex family's wealth and the costs involved, it is instructive to introduce the concept by looking at how the management of any family's affairs might develop as its wealth grows and the numbers of family members and generations increase.

At first a family office is quite simple and is usually called 'Mum and Dad'. The parents will typically set the family's attitude and values on wealth, risk and investment allocation and will select advisers to help with technical structures. If Mum and Dad are not able to deal with all the administration themselves (often because they are too busy running the family business that is generating the wealth in the first place), they will usually use the resources of the business itself or delegate it to a trusted adviser.

Such early-stage family offices tend to grow in an unplanned way without the family having a deliberate objective for the family office or a shared understanding of what it is intended to achieve. In due course, one or more of three things will happen and force the family to consider a more structured way forward:

- The family wealth will grow beyond the ability and capacity of the people involved to manage it.
- Mum and Dad will grow older and less able to manage the family's assets directly and the next generation will want and need to become involved.
- Undue mixing of family and business matters will distract those working for the business or its advisers from what should be their primary focus – the business on which the family's wealth is based.

At this point, either as part of their estate planning strategy or through their wills on death, parents often simply divide the family's assets into pots of roughly equal value and transfer these to family members. The next generation then creates its own individual family offices. This approach has, however, several limitations:

- Some assets such as land, property, valuable collections and shares in the family business itself are not easily divisible, so the family members may need to remain connected with each other through shared ownership of these assets.

- The family might want to remain connected through shared ownership of other assets that are used in common or have sentimental value, such as the family home or estate or a holiday home.
- Dividing assets into separate pots reduces the family's buying power and is likely to mean that each branch will lose potential value and incur higher costs compared to keeping the assets and management together.

If the family does decide to combine the management of some or all of its shared assets, whether by choice or because the nature of the assets effectively forces their hand, the family will need to think carefully about why they are doing this, what assets they are going to include and how the assets will be managed. We will look at this process later in this chapter but the structure that is now emerging is more recognisable as what is called a 'family office'.

Larger single family offices are likely to have a separate legal personality from the family, with all or most of the family's specialist advisers employed directly by the family office. Equally, however, a single family office may just be a place where the family administers its affairs, or it may be a network of employees and advisers in a number of different places who work together to run the business of the family.

One other point to note at this stage is that this type of family office will normally develop alongside the founding family's business, but the concept is just as valid if the family office is completely separate from the family business, if there is no longer a family business or indeed if there never was one.

2. **Is there a common understanding of what a family office is?**

It is easier to identify and agree on the definition of a family office (in the sense that most people now understand the term) when it has been created by and serves only one family. The first family offices with their own infrastructure and professional and administrative staff were created in the 19th century by very wealthy industrial and banking families, mainly in the US. The US provided us with a statutory definition of a family office when the Dodd-Frank Act of 2011 created a new exclusion under which family offices are not 'investment advisers' subject to the stringent compliance requirements of the Advisers Act.

In summary, Section 202(a)(11)(G)-1 of the Advisers Act now provides that a family office is a company that:

- has no clients other than family clients;
- is wholly owned by family clients and is exclusively controlled by one or more family members and/or family entities;
- does not hold itself out to the public as an investment adviser.

'Family clients' includes present and former family members and key employees; 'family entities' includes trusts, foundations and companies for the benefit of family members or for charitable purposes; 'family members' includes lineal descendants of up to 10 generations from a common ancestor and the spouses of those lineal descendants. Thus, the official definition of family office is a wide one but it clearly only encompasses family offices serving a single family.

This is important because some entities set up as single family offices later branched out into providing family offices for other families who could not afford or did not want to set up their own. These businesses became known as 'multi-family offices' and that model was then adopted by private and international banks, investment managers and professional firms who used their own skills, resources and compliance structures to offer multi-family offices to a wider range of wealthy families. But are all these multi-family offices actually true family offices at all? To help us answer this question, we need to consider what range of services a family office can provide.

It is generally recognised that family offices will offer most or all of the following services although which services are provided and by whom and the scope of each will vary considerably from family to family – headlines are set out below and the detailed services are listed in Appendix 1:

- investment strategy;
- financial and tax planning;
- record keeping and reporting;
- family succession and estate planning;
- trustee and company management;
- philanthropy;
- risk management;
- lifestyle (generally non-financial) services;
- family governance;
- family education.

A bank or investment manager may provide integrated investment management and reporting for all the members of a family but that is not enough to allow it to call itself a family office. Indeed some are now recognising this and have started using the title 'family investment office' which is a more accurate description of the service they provide – very valuable to the family but limited in scope.

Equally, many professional firms who now wrap up their services to families under the family office banner do not offer services that go beyond investment management and tax and estate planning. It is the non-financial services listed above which mark out a true multi-family office, particularly risk management and family governance and education, without which the family office will lack the necessary foundations.

3.   Historical development

Although there is good contemporary research, little effective historical research has been undertaken into family offices. This may be because many single and multi-family offices kept their affairs to themselves, for the obvious reason of wishing to keep the affairs of their client families confidential, and it was not possible to conduct anonymous surveys so effectively in the past as it is now.

Accordingly, a detailed historical study is not feasible; however, some broad themes in the historical development of family offices are set out below.

The very early single family offices included Joseph and his team in Egypt, offices of certain Chinese and Japanese dynasties, the heads of prominent Roman houses and some crusaders' trustees.

More recently, as described above, the single family office emerged in the 19th century in America as a natural extension of the chairman's office in many major corporations, looking after the private and family affairs of the key shareholders and their families.

In Europe, the industrial, banking and landed estate giants gave birth to a similar array of single family offices, including those established by the Medici, Rothschild and Fleming families. The chairman's office again extended into the private side, and in the landed estates the estate office adopted the twin roles of running the estate and the owners' family financial affairs.

The multi-family office is widely believed to have originated from requests to single family offices for provision of their services to other families. Sometimes this was the result of a deliberate strategy and at other times it resulted from an unsolicited approach from, usually, a contact of a satisfied family member. The main benefit to the original family was a sharing of costs, while secondary benefits included economies of scale, greater resources and an increased breadth of expertise.

More recently a new breed of multi-family offices has emerged. These provide services on commercial terms to a number of unrelated families. Some have their beginnings in single family offices and others in private banks and trust companies. There are many well-known examples, including national and multi-national names.

4.   Trusted adviser

Most ambitious advisers strive for the key status of 'trusted adviser'. This status is a natural role for someone in the family office to fulfil. The role itself has many facets, which justify a book on this subject alone, and indeed there are several of these including one leading text that is referred to below. However, the characteristics of trusted advisers in a family office context are briefly summarised in the following paragraphs.

In families without a family office, the trusted adviser is typically a lawyer, accountant, financial adviser, investment manager, family business expert or land agent.

In a family office scenario, an individual within the family office will usually adopt the trusted adviser role. Some suggest that a trusted adviser can be a corporate but the authors' view of a trusted adviser is that this is an interpersonal relationship, so it will be an individual in the family office who interacts with one or more individual clients.

This trusted adviser in a family office would typically:

put the client first and make them feel important;

- be a person who understands business and also is worthy of the client's confidence;
- behave like a fiduciary;
- look to the very long term (certainly 10 years but perhaps up to 200 years forward);
- be discreet;
- have chemistry with the client, and relate to him or her;
- deliver reliably and with the highest quality;

- be independent;
- be rounded, well read, financially mature and able to talk around the issues;
- think about the client and be proactive;
- stand up to the client and, if he or she doesn't agree, offer another solution;
- have wisdom.

The trusted adviser should communicate by using these strategies:
- connecting effectively (ie by being a good listener and responding with insight);
- being available (eg providing a mobile and home telephone number);
- understanding if the client prefers the phone to e-mail;
- speaking to each client at least every month;
- returning e-mails and calling the same day;
- remembering clients' key issues;
- remembering clients' personal details, such as birthdays.

From the perspective of the family office itself, the trusted adviser should:
- excel at client care, including outside his/her own area;
- be commercially aware;
- exceed expectations;
- manage the relationship, including fees;
- share information;
- make sure the whole team (especially the key roles of the secretary and the front-of-house staff) cherish the relationship.

David Maister (a well-known adviser to professional services firms) Charles Green and Robert Galford wrote The Trusted Adviser, which was originally published in 2000 (an updated edition was published in 2002). This book provides a very insightful analysis into the attributes of a trusted adviser and the benefits to client relationships that result.

The book's thesis is that the development of trusted adviser status follows the progression of the depth and breadth of the adviser's role in the client relationship from technical adviser to trusted adviser. The level of trust is measured by a combination of credibility, reliability and intimacy as moderated by self-orientation (ie, is the adviser looking to maximise the benefit for the client or for himself?). This measurement takes the form of an equation that adds together credibility, reliability and intimacy and divides the sum by self-orientation.

There are risks for the family office in being a trusted adviser. These include:
- failure to perform to expectation;
- having the wrong person as trusted adviser;
- loss of client relationship (if the individual trusted adviser leaves).

However, the risks are usually outweighed by the benefits which include:
- additional work from the client;
- internal and external referrals;

- high level and quick communication;
- less pretence and a more honest relationship.

5.   Single family offices

Family offices come in all shapes and sizes, just like families. They range from one-person advisers to large units. Structure and regulation are dealt with in other chapters.

In the United States, the Securities and Exchange Commission, in its notes accompanying the proposals to the Dodd-Frank Investment Advisers Act amendment mentioned above, commented that:

> 'Family offices' are entities established by wealthy families to manage their wealth, plan for their families' financial future, and provide other services to family members. Single family offices generally serve families with at least $100 million or more of investable assets. Industry observers have estimated that there are 2,500 to 3,000 single family offices managing more than $1.2 trillion in assets.

The single family office has, at least at the time of its commencement, a single family as its client. As the family grows, the single family office may find itself looking after many different family units, which usually have common ancestors. Eventually, as wealth is dissipated throughout the succeeding generations, the minor family branches may migrate to other advisers, unless new wealth can be generated, which often has the effect of binding the extended family together.

The market perception is that the number of single family offices worldwide, currently thought to be several thousand, will increase as new wealth is generated and as existing wealthy families explore the benefits that such an office can bring.

Although the Securities and Exchange Commission refers to $100m investable assets as a minimum for a single family office, other commentators believe that $30m is a more appropriate minimum.

6.   Multi-family offices

As described above, multi-family offices have many different antecedents.

Multi-family offices have their own minimum criteria for joining, which is usually in the range of $5m to $250m of investable assets.

Their major distinguishing point is that they can offer an independent and holistic advisory service which gives their clients better risk management, governance, education and financial management than alternative providers, without a product push. In part this is supplied by the availability of greater resources and in part by the exposure of the multi-family office to more different and varied scenarios.

It is estimated that there are 150 multi-family offices in the United States and in total several hundred worldwide. The total appears to be growing, albeit at a slower pace than the number of single family offices.

7.   Comparing single and multi-family offices

Each family will have its own unique set of circumstances (both financial and human) and its needs, aspirations, risk tolerance and ideas will differentiate that family from others.

Whether a family is best suited to a single family office, a multi-family office or to managing its own relationships with its different advisers will require careful thought and evaluation by the family as to how best its requirements can be met. There is no magic bullet or template providing a single solution.

A family considering setting up a single family office will usually draw up a business plan with professional help, review the feasibility of the plan and its projected outcomes and then decide the correct way forward. Examples of what might be included in a business plan are set out in Appendix 2. If it is to set up a single family office, the family would normally employ an expert in implementation in order to negotiate the complex demands, which include structuring, staffing, regulation and technology.

In a situation where a family is considering joining a multi-family office, a typical scenario is that family members will obtain names of potential multi-family offices from end-users and other contacts. A process will then commence which could involve anything from casual discussions to a full-blown tender exercise. In any event it is usual for appropriate due diligence to be carried out by the family.

8. The relationship between the family and the family office

It will already be obvious that the family is a crucial component of the family office, and not just because they are its clients. A family office is about creating, preserving and extending the family legacy, so who better to create the family office in its image and to meet its requirements? If the whole family is not closely involved in the creation of the family office (if it is a single family office) or the selection of the best organisation to provide family office services through a multi-family office, the family office is unlikely to provide the long term solution through which the family is seeking to manage and pass on its wealth.

We have already identified certain situations that can act as a trigger to the process of setting up a family office – increasing numbers of family members, ageing, ill-health or death of the senior generation, or mixing of family and business matters to the detriment of both. There are many other situations and events that can prompt discussions about a family office such as the sale of the business, retirement and other family events, or simply the broader economic situation, but the process can be started at any time the family feels ready to do the work.

The first thing for the family to consider is what the purpose – the fundamental mission – of the family office is to be. This may seem obvious, but there are many reasons why a family office may be set up and not all of them may be relevant for each family. The structure must reflect the priorities of the family. Each family has to decide who will participate in establishing the purpose of the family office, but there may be value in holding a meeting of all the adult family members whose lives will be affected by the family office. If everyone is not encouraged to participate in building the family office they are less likely to value and remain committed to it.

This approach is more likely to succeed than leaving the objectives and structure of the family office to senior family members only, far less to professional advisers who may be tempted to create the family office in their own image, emphasising their own specialisms at the expense of other functions which are equally or more important.

The family then needs to decide what assets within the family office are being managed for the whole family (so that information on these assets will be available to all) and what assets (such as individual bank accounts and investment portfolios) are to be confidential to the family members or entities which own them. Another aspect of this tension between the individual and the collective is that the family should consider not only how family members can join the family office and make use of its services and how the costs of the family office are to be allocated among them, but also how and on what terms they may be allowed to leave.

Once the family has developed the purpose, services and structure of its family office, it needs to consider what role the family is going to play in running it. Some families might want to design their family office to capitalise on the skills and interests of family members and thus ensure that the family has a prominent role in running it in order to keep as much control as possible over its own affairs. If however family members do not have the skills and abilities to manage their own family office, the family will need to engage outsiders. This is one of many areas where the lessons and techniques that have been developed over many years of advising family businesses can also be applied to the family office. Setting out at an early stage criteria for employing family members will give the family certainty for the future and influence the shape of the family office over the years.

Even if family members are not directly involved in the day-to-day running of the family office, this does not mean that they will be isolated from it and only become passive participants. Any worthwhile family office strategy should include practical advice on how the business of the family can be well-governed as well as being well-managed.

A later chapter will look in detail at governance of the family office, so here we will simply set out the building blocks that families may want to use to set up their family office system. As families grow and it is no longer possible to discuss issues among the whole family informally, a family assembly provides a forum for discussion and social interaction. In larger families where the assembly of the whole family is too unwieldy to allow easy decision-making, a family council with representatives of each branch and generation of the family can be created as the vehicle for decision-making, but still be guided by the family assembly.

Comments on a family council are included in Appendix 3.

Thus the family office and its associated bodies become the support structure for the family in the same way as the other two 'circles' of the family business system have their supporting organisations: the business has its management and technical services while the owners of the business are supported by boards of directors and committees. Just as the business and the owners will change and develop over time, so the family and the family office will change and grow. The structures, systems and people in the family office will also have to develop to address these changing requirements. Like the business, no family office can stand still, so improving and adapting must always be on the agenda.

9. Supporting the family office

Several membership organisations exist to support the family offices and their staff.

These provide a forum for confidential discussions, research, sharing knowledge, meeting peers and learning.

Some private banks run networking and educational sessions.

10.   The role of the adviser to the family office

This book is intended primarily to help professionals from any discipline who are advising family offices rather than those actually working in them, although there is likely to be a substantial overlap between these two groups, particularly as the family office market develops. Again, the subsequent chapters will develop the theme of how advisers should relate and respond to family offices, and this section merely sets out some general principles.

There are three typical structures for family offices which produce different relationships with and demands on its advisers:

- Single family offices with a large permanent staff may try to cover all the different types of professional advice which their client families will normally require. Outside advisers engaged by these offices are therefore likely to be highly specialised advisers addressing out-of-the-ordinary situations.
- Multi-family offices set up by banks and professional organisations will normally provide in-house professional advisers for the business areas covered by the host firm, but may need to engage outside advisers to address service areas which the host chooses not to cover (perhaps for financial or compliance reasons) and the wide range of specific issues which may be encountered by the multiple families the offices serve.
- Family offices of both types may take a deliberate decision not to try to provide every kind of professional advice that their client families may require, but instead to select the most suitable advisers for each category of service the families need and each type of issue they may encounter – in effect being a manager of managers.

Whatever types of advisers are engaged (and this will apply equally to the professionals employed within the family office), they will need to be truly client-centric in their approach and look beyond the technical specialism they have been asked to bring to the table. This means understanding the family dynamics, appreciating how the family and the family office operate and relate to each other and giving advice that is right not only for the individual or group affected but also for the wider family.

Outside advisers also need to take care that their duties of client confidentiality and avoiding conflicts of interest are not compromised by working within the family office structure when the client may only be one individual or a group within the larger family. Where a number of advisers are engaged, whether on specific projects or on a longer-term basis, the family office has a critical role in managing and coordinating the advisory team. In this area, as in so many others, communication is the key and the family office should encourage a collaborative approach.

11. Frequently asked questions

Why should I establish or use a family office?

- To obtain expert, independent wealth management and financial advice at a reasonable price.
- To have a dedicated family finance director.
- To delegate the administration of my financial affairs whilst retaining control.
- To simplify reporting.

What does it cost?

In the United Kingdom, the minimum cost is usually in the range of £1.5 million to £2 million per year.

With a single family office, the cost of the operation plus an appropriate profit margin is divided among the family members in an agreed way.

With a multi-family office, it depends on the level of services provided and the value of assets managed but you can expect to pay more than the equivalent private banking fee.

Are there double layers of charges?

In some cases yes, although these can usually be reduced or even eliminated by virtue of the buying power of the family office.

What are the main disadvantages?

The burden of regulation is perceived to be a significant disadvantage in many jurisdictions.

Other disadvantages include the difficulties of succession planning and incentivisation and remuneration strategies within the family office. It can be difficult to recruit and retain staff with the right skill sets. The risk of staff moving on is significant in a small office.

What is the optimum jurisdiction?

This will depend on many factors, including:

- the countries of residence of family members;
- the locations of the family assets;
- economic and political stability;
- the legal system;
- a well-established and efficient financial industry with available external advisers, especially lawyers;
- the availability of staff;
- the preferred structure (see further in the chapter on choice of structures, below);
- confidentiality; and
- taxation.

What governance structures should be put in place?
This is dealt with in the chapter on governance.

Isn't the use of the description 'family office' by single family offices, multi-family offices, accountants and others just a gimmick to mask the delivery of the same services at a higher price?
Undoubtedly this is applicable to a few situations, but in the main a well-run single or multi-family office can deliver significant advantages to its clients. In a full service scenario from a service provider, the advice would usually be better co-ordinated when delivered by a dedicated family office team.

What happens if a single or multi-family office doesn't offer the additional service that I need?
Usually family offices will have outsourcing arrangements in place to enable them to deliver any additional services the client may require through third parties if they are unable to provide such services in-house.

Appendix 1: Typical services provided by a family office
- Investment strategy
  - Investment objectives
  - Asset allocation
  - Investment vehicles
  - Choosing investment managers
  - Oversight of asset classes and managers
  - Custody of assets
- Financial and tax planning
  - Retirement planning
  - Bank financing
  - Financial analysis
  - Tax returns and planning
  - Income and cash flow
- Record keeping and reporting
  - Investment performance reports
  - Income analysis
  - Comparison with plans and targets
  - Consolidated statements
  - Personal assets
- Family succession and estate planning
  - Family objectives
  - Financial requirements
  - Estate planning strategies
  - Estate planning structures
- Trustee and company management
  - Trustee and fiduciary services
  - Selection of trustees

- Private trust company
- Corporate trusts
- Foundations
- Estate administration
- Philanthropy
  - Charitable objectives
  - Selection and training of trustees
  - Trust and foundation administration
  - Personal giving and charitable activities
  - Monitoring how donations are used
- Risk management
  - Investment and financial risk
  - Personal security
  - Personal insurances
  - Property insurances
  - Reputational risk and media policy
  - Safety of physical assets
- Lifestyle (generally non-financial) services
  - Personal employees and payroll
  - Property management
  - Travel arrangements
  - Individual cash flow and paying bills
  - Managing luxury assets
- Family governance
  - Family vision and values
  - Family structures including assembly and council
  - Regular review of structures as family grows and develops
  - Organising family meetings
  - Communication
- Family education
  - Educating the next generation
  - Career planning and monitoring
  - Leadership training
  - Trustee training
  - Beneficiary mentoring and education

Appendix 2: Contents of the business plan for setting up a family office
Firstly the family should consider:
- Why do we want to set up a family office?
- What will the family office deal with?
- How will the family office relate to the family business (if there is one)?
- How will the family office relate to other family structures?
- How will the family office relate to individual family members?
- How will the family office work?

If the family decide to proceed, a business plan will typically include the following:

- Executive summary
  - A short executive summary that encapsulates the whole plan, preferably just one page.
- Introduction – about the family
  - Describe the family, including its history, structure, strategy and mission.
  - Highlight the skills and experience of key family members.
  - Explain the rationale for the creation of a family office.
- Introduction – the family office
  - Outline the services to be provided.
  - Include an analysis of strengths, weaknesses, opportunities and threats, and don't avoid weaknesses or threats: these can only be dealt with after being identified.
- About the market
  - Analyse projected turnover.
  - If setting up a multi-family office, include information about competitors in this section, for example their strengths, weaknesses and market share.
  - Detail any major family groups that will be clients.
  - Outline marketing activities to demonstrate how you identify and develop new business.
- Financial information
  - This is normally provided as an appendix. It should include a five-year summary of profit and loss accounts, key ratios, profit and loss projections, cash flow projections, a forecast balance sheet, a detailed explanation of any assumptions, anda sensitivity analysis.
- Property plan
  - Report on your proposed business premises and outline any planned expenditure.
- Staffing plan
  - Describe anticipated personnel requirements including any training and promotion policies. Recruitment, remuneration and succession planning should be covered, and the family/non-family employees dilemma is particularly relevant here.
- IT plan
  - Describe anticipated IT requirements and costs.
- Legal structure
  - Describe the anticipated structure, including the jurisdictions to which they will be subject.
- Governance
  - Summarise how governance is to operate, including the family office's relationships with existing family structures.
- Regulatory matters
  - Summarise the regulatory environment and what will be needed to address regulations.

Appendix 3: The family council

Typically the family council will be a separate group with responsibility for running the family assembly and being the main governance link between the wider family and other parts of the enterprise, such as the board of directors. The family assembly will normally include all the members of the family over the age at which the family has agreed they should participate – usually between 18 and 25 – while the family council is a much smaller group of family members representing different generations and branches.

The illustration below shows how important a role the family council can perform in overall governance.

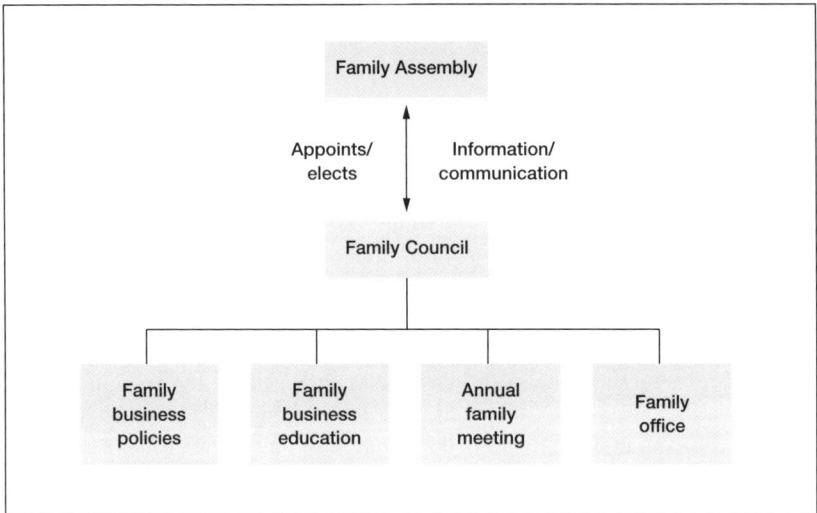

The family constitution dictates what structures will exist – family assembly, family council, family office and so on. Within that framework the family council will be subject to the governance criteria that are established.

The family council would typically have terms of reference which would include:

- purpose;
- composition;
- reporting lines (upwards and downwards) and methods of reporting;
- budget;
- frequency of meetings.

Establishing the family office

Barbara R Hauser
Barbara R Hauser, LLC

This chapter will cover the steps that a family will go through in establishing their family office. It will begin with looking at the catalyst for forming the office, and go on to cover the decisions about what services it will provide and how it will operate in a general sense.[1]

1. When does a family decide to establish a family office?

Some family offices evolve over a number of years, beginning with some simple services and growing to include additional and more complex services. At some point the group providing the services looks and acts like a family office. Other family offices are created all at once, in a deliberate act of forming a family office. The way each one operates is often based on whether they evolved or were deliberately formed. In all cases there is significant family wealth (some estimate that a family should have more than $100 million in assets to consider having their own family office).

1.1 Gradual process

Although 'family office' is a fairly recent term, which first gained popularity primarily in the United States, where it was heavily marketed in the 1990s, the services provided by a family office have been provided without using that name for centuries all over the world.

When a family is wealthy enough to pay others for services that are dedicated to that one family, they are receiving the benefits of a family office. From the old literal 'gate-keepers' in Asia to the home servant staff in English manors, the dedicated service is the hallmark of the family office.

These older models usually developed gradually: one butler would later supervise a full staff for upstairs and downstairs. This increase could take place over several generations. The main measure of a family's wealth was often in the land, the castle, the farm or the ranch. Hence portfolio management of liquid investments was a much smaller issue, and was often handled by outside advisors.

In the United States it often happened in the 20th century that the family's operating business would share some of its staff to help with the family's personal matters. This could range from help with travel plans to shopping to party planning.

---

[1] This chapter includes some portions of my article, "The Family Office: Insights into Their Development in the US, a Proposed Prototype, and Advice for Adaptation In Other Countries" published in *Journal of Wealth Management* (Fall 2001).

As the personal liquid investments would grow, often from dividends, the financial officers in the business might help out with basic investment decisions. Without conscious direction, some part of the company staff would begin to take on functions that would now be classified as family office functions. The range was as broad as the needs of the entire family: obtaining financing for an adult child to purchase a home; hiring and firing household staff; planning private business/social events; keeping bank accounts in order; paying household and personal bills; getting tax returns filed; and so on.

As the needs increased, it became increasingly awkward to fulfil all of the family services through the operating company staff. At a minimum, to preserve the tax deductibility of business salaries and overhead expenses for the company, it was necessary to maintain internal allocations of time. The personal time should have been paid for in some other way. In most cases, though, this was probably not done.

From a family perspective, it also became increasingly awkward for family members to have their personal finances scrutinised and organised by operating company staff. If one or more were actively involved in managing the company, other family members faced the additional problem of concealing confidential matters from those members who were managing the company.

The relationship between the family and the operating company was often opaque. Unsure of their rights as family owners of the company, younger family members in particular were hesitant about asking for personal assistance. The operating management team was often unclear about what, if any, involvement the family members should have in the direction of the business. Using internal company staff to handle family office functions often looked like a bridge between these two groups.

Ultimately, though, the confusion of roles, overhead allocation, and concerns of confidentiality would sometimes prompt a split. A separate family office would be created.

Another catalyst for separating the personal family services from the business would be if the family business came to a stage where it wanted to be attractive to outside investors (to go public) then the family would start to separate its services from the business. Sometimes this was done by allocating an internal charge for the family owners to pay personally for their partial use of the business executives and/or of the business's physical space.

If the family services became substantial enough, the family and business would often decide at some time to separate the family services from the business physically. This would be the birth of a family office.

It is common for the family to give a special name to its new separate family office. It might be based on a favourite vacation site or some other private family meaning. (For example, the Cargill family office is called "Waycrosse" which is a combination of two place names special to the family.) Even when they have formed a separate family office, families generally prefer to stay very private. This includes a preference not to have the family names mentioned anywhere. In some countries families are also concerned with their physical safety – another function that can be provided by the family office.

1.2 Liquidity event

The other principal catalyst for the creation of a separate family office is when the operating business is sold or goes public. This has two major effects on the family owners. First, they suddenly have much more liquid wealth than ever before. Secondly, they no longer have access to company staff to take care of their personal and family needs.

Many owners become paralysed at this point. The activity they knew so well – operating the business – is gone. The liquid wealth is not something they have had much experience with, and they do not know whom to trust. A surprising number in the United States simply put the money into ordinary Treasury bills while wondering what they need to learn about the sophisticated investment world. Their day-to-day conveniences are also gone: no more secretary, no more office to go to every day, no more staff, and so on. This sudden transition is tough.

Consultants are often hired at this stage to give advice on how to set up a family office to take care of the new financial needs. Facing the family office market for the first time can be bewildering. Other family offices wishing to expand will offer to add the new family to their original family group base. Large institutions will compete for the financial management services, and promise that they can be the family office substitute themselves.

This is a very confusing time for a family. Those who are able to speak directly to other families who have been through similar experiences are extremely grateful. Families have found particularly helpful the opportunities to participate in off-the-record small group discussions of many of the issues that need to be addressed when creating a family office.

Every family is different, and their needs and interests vary considerably. There is no one perfect design.

2. What does the family want in terms of services?

As mentioned above, there is an incredible variety of services that can be provided by a family office. A shorthand description of a family office that is primarily focused on investment services is that they "do not walk the dog". See Appendix 1 to the chapter "What is a family office" for a checklist of those services that one might expect a family office to consider.

Deciding what services should be provided is a very personal evaluation. It should not matter what most family offices provide. What matters is the unique needs of a particular family. For example, one investment professional hired by a new family office complained that this was not a "real" family office – because on the organisational chart most of the positions related to looking after six international homes and their staff, including local nannies. In that case there was still a successful operating business, with a relatively small amount of liquid investments. Nonetheless this was a good example of a real family office. The services were built to serve the current needs of the family.

Many families have a strong interest in philanthropy, and this is another area in which the family office can provide a number of services. The family office, for example, can evaluate all of the requests for charitable grants, and make recommendations to the family. If there is a family charitable foundation or trust, the family office can organise the meetings and make sure that all the records are properly kept, and that any income tax filings are properly prepared. Families that previously had operating businesses often prefer a more active role in their charitable giving. Often referred to as "venture philanthropy" the family in effect starts another venture, this one based on philanthropy. For example, a family might decide to build a school, hospital or mosque. The family office can handle the oversight and administration of such projects. This ability of the family office to help with charitable activities extends to the recent interest in 'impact investing'.

When the family has shared assets (a yacht, plane, compound, foreign vacation home, etc.) the family office can oversee their staffing, insurance, maintenance and agreements for their shared use. These assets often cause a fair amount of friction within families, so having the family office involved can be very helpful.

In terms of liquid investments, the appeal of combining their investment funds is generally that as a larger fund they will be able to pay discounted fees, can qualify to enter funds with large minimums, and can have access to top national and international managers. From time to time, one or more family members will decide that they would rather handle their investments on their own, and may leave the family office entirely.

All wealthy families are aware of the importance of the next generation in planning for the future. Some family offices will establish educational programmes to ensure that everyone has a background in the areas they think they should know (which can certainly vary by family).

As part of the family services most family offices will oversee estate planning (usually actually carried out by outside lawyers). This includes family trusts, wills, prenuptial agreements and marriage dissolutions.

Another role played by some family offices is simply to be the glue that keeps the family connected. This can be especially important when the family business has been sold. At that time many family members are anxious about losing that connection with each other.

The family office may organise regular gatherings of the entire family. In some cases the family office will hire outside advisors to help the family create its own family council, mission statement or family constitution, all of which are designed to keep the family closely connected.

3. Who will be working in the family office?

After listing and evaluating the services that the family wants to receive, the family members will have an idea of the kinds of people they should look for to staff the family office. There are several placement firms geared to the family office market (see the chapter on hiring for the family office).

One sensitive issue is whether or not any family members should also work in the family office. One the one hand, the family member is generally someone who would be trusted by the entire family to be sure that the office is well-run. On the other hand, not all family members like the idea that their individual finances (including budgets and spending reports) would be open to other family members.

In a number of family offices in the United States, one trusted family member runs the entire family office, with administrative support only, outsourcing specific services as appropriate. More common is to have non-family staff managing the family office on a day-to-day basis (see the chapter on hiring staff). The family needs to have some official oversight role, which is often provided by forming a board of directors for the family office (see the chapter on governance).

4. Where will the family locate the office?

It used to be assumed that the family office would be located in a place that is physically close to the family. On an international basis this is not always true. For example, several families in Mexico feel more comfortable if their family office is located outside the country; sometimes they choose Texas (even though that adds the regulatory complexity and related tax issues in the United States).

Today there are family offices that are split over two distant locations, neither of which is physically close to the family. For example, London is often an investment centre, but Bermuda or Cayman could be the centre for the group of family trusts. In a few cases, the family office manager may live in one city and yet all of the family members live in a variety of other countries. In one case, the family lives in Lebanon and has their family office in Switzerland, with a full-time art curator based in London. Again, what needs to be considered is how best to serve the needs of the particular family.

5. Will the family partner with a larger firm?

Due to the costs and complexity of running a proper family office, some families look at using a larger, established firm (even one as large as an international investment firm) to take care of their more tedious back office needs. The actual family office (the front office) can then have a much smaller (and more responsive) staff.

If there are a number of trust settlements in the family group it often makes sense to partner with an experienced trust company to handle the administration and filings for the trustees. In some cases the head of the family office is also named as the trustee (or protector). The appointment is often a generic one, so that if one individual is replaced as the head of the family office, the new head automatically becomes the new trustee (or protector).

Some large family offices have created their own trust companies to administer family trusts. It is even possible with a private trust company to have the family control the ownership and management of the trust company, which several families find appealing.

Another interesting option is to consider partnering with a multi-family office (discussed more below). Once a multi-family office is established, with a well-organised staff and procedures, it can offer to supply the back office services for a single family office. This compromise allows the single family office staff to continue to be the primary contact for the family, while relieving it of many of the administrative burdens.

6. Comparison of a single family office with a multi-family office

6.1 Joining a multi-family office

In the case of a newly wealthy family (eg, after a liquidity event) looking at alternatives to manage the family wealth, they are likely to consider joining an existing multi-family office. The most appealing type of multi-family office would be one that itself began as a single family office, and then grew to create a structure and staff large enough to support additional families.

The advantages of a multi-family office are a perceived reduction in operating costs, the use of qualified, experienced family office staff, increased investment capabilities and the ability to share in some areas with the other client families. As mentioned above, an increasing option for single family offices is to outsource various functions to a qualified multi-family office.

The principal perceived disadvantage of a multi-family office is that the family office staff is shared with other families. This means giving up that single dedication that is the hallmark of a traditional single family office, as well as giving up total control by a patriarch or matriarch. If the multi-family office began as a single family office, there is often a concern about whether the new clients will have an equal priority. Sometimes there are also concerns about privacy, although most multi-family offices adhere to strict privacy principles.

6.2 Creating a multi-family office

Three very different types of multi-family office exist. First, as described above, is the traditional single family office that decides to offer its services to additional families. This includes some well-known family offices like the Rockefeller office, which is now a multi-family office and has a separate public trust company, as well as a separate public company for philanthropic services. Another example is Pitcairn (a multi-family office), which began as a single family office, then added additional families. It provides a full array of services for families with "generational wealth" and has "open architecture" for investments (independent investment advice, with no internal products).

The second type of multi-family office arises when a small group of unrelated individuals (such as business partners, accountants and/or lawyers) decide to open a new family office for themselves and to take on additional members from the beginning. Often there is an expectation that they will make a profit from operating a multi-family office. It is quite difficult to rely on profitable operations if the multi-family office offers the traditional single family office services. If they decide to focus primarily on investment services, it is more accurate to call them private investment offices.

The third type of multi-family office seems to be merely a rebranding of the private client group inside a large investment firm. Even an institution as large as Citigroup has called itself a family office. The principal aim of this type of multi-family office seems to be to earn profits on the investment assets, and to use the name "family office" to attract new clients.

7. **Will the family look for a family office network?**

Once the family has created a traditional family office, they will be interested in what other similar families do and how those family offices handle similar issues. One source of information is to attend some of the many conferences that exist for family offices.

Another source of information is to join one of the several networks for family offices. Some of those networks are quite private. Others, such as the Family Office Exchange, the Family Office Association and the Family Office Network, have active marketing, menus of fees and large collections of data about family offices, in addition to putting on their own conferences.

Electronic networks (some are more networks of providers) also exist now, such as the Family Office Channel, Family Matters Online, the Family Offices Group, the Asia Family Office, the European Family Office Network, the Family Office Network India and the Family Office (Spain).

8. **Cross-border alliances**

After the global financial crisis in 2008, many family offices became more cautious investors. They have increased their interest in partnering with other family offices for direct investments in other countries. For example the Quilvest family office, owned by the Bemberg family for more than seven generations, has private equity partners in Switzerland, Argentina, London, New York and Dubai. A number of family offices invest alongside the Quilvest partners in various countries.

Another recent trend is for family offices to invest in another family's privately owned operating business, which is often a more familiar environment. The investing office will enjoy being on the board, but will not expect to control the business. One example is the organised creation of Families Investing in Families® (based in the United States and Belgium). For its part, a family-owned business appreciates the presence of investing partners who are seen as having patient capital, and who will understand the long-term nature of growing a business.

As a final example, in late 2011 the chief investment officers of seven family offices from around the world – Pitcairn (United States), SandAire (United Kingdom), The Myer Family Company (Australia), HQ Trust (Germany), Northwood Family Office (Canada), Progeny 3 (United States) and the Turim Family Office & Investment Management (Brazil) – created the Wigmore Association, which meets to review global investment opportunities of interest to the diverse families those offices serve.

9. **Conclusion**

For wealthy families who want one, and are willing to pay for it, creating their own private family office can be a rewarding solution to the many needs of the family. The secret of success seems to be a focus on the actual needs of a particular family and then finding the right staff to provide those services. To have a truly dedicated staff, who can be trusted completely, is a valuable luxury.

Choice of structures

Imogen Buchan-Smith
Ashley Crossley
Baker & McKenzie LLP

1. Classic family office structures

There is no template for family office structure, as by their nature they are tailored to the particular priorities and facts of each family. This includes the nature and personality of the family in question, the services that the family wishes the family office to perform and where the family is in its life/wealth cycle. It will also depend on whether the family office is intended to be revolutionary (in the sense that it will shape the family's structures) or evolutionary (in the sense that it will need to adapt to and complement existing structures).

There are however key themes and structures that act as a starting point, and this chapter will highlight the main options a family has.

Typically, where a family is still in business and its focus is on running that business (ie, first generation), the family office function (if any) may be performed by employees within the family's business, at the direction of the principal. Indeed, many first generation family offices may be very informal in the sense that they are solely constituted by way of the family regularly calling meetings to discuss family issues or matters as they arise, such as the family balance sheet and investment decisions regarding family assets or funds.

As mentioned previously, it is generally during the second and third generations of the family's cycle, when that business may be sold and when the patriarch is no longer around, that the family will go on to establish a more formal family office in response to the operating business transitioning to, perhaps, an investment company. However, these later generations can view the family office as an extension of the older generation and may prefer their independence; this is particularly true if a formal family office structure (operating within a clear chain of command) has yet to be implemented. An important consideration is therefore the extent to which family wealth is co-mingled or may be separated. If separation is not possible or desirable (for example, in order to preserve the family's wealth), a structure with a robust governance policy and strategy to accompany it should be established early on during the first generation in order to address potential differences of opinion and tensions among family members. This will be explored in further detail later on in this chapter.

It is important to bear in mind that the family office will have different requirements for each generation, and the original purposes and objectives for establishing a family office may change and evolve over time. It is, therefore, important to implement a structure that will retain as much flexibility as possible.

The more evolved family offices will generally fall under one of the following heads:

- Single family office – as has been outlined in previous chapters, this form of family office is independent and serves the needs of just one family. It is generally suitable only for families with significant wealth who are capable of funding this structure adequately in order for it to function effectively (one main cost being appropriate staffing) as well as those families who are concerned to maintain the maximum amount of privacy and confidentiality in relation to their personal, and indeed business, affairs.

- Multi-family office – again, as described in previous chapters, this structure is owned by and services more than one family, enabling them to pool their own staff and investment consultants as well as their resources. This form of structure may be preferable for a variety of reasons (including economies of scale as well as those factors described in more detail in earlier chapters) and may have evolved from a former single family office. However, it is important to note that the only way that this type of family office will function effectively is by it servicing like-minded families with a similar profile and investment outlook. Where a multi-family office evolves from a single family office it is often not structured appropriately to accommodate this model (for example, the shareholding or partnership may be centred in one or two of the founding family members) and for this reason, the office may need to be restructured when evolving from one type of office to another.

- Multi-client family office – unlike the multi-family office, this structure is independent of the families it services, although, as with the multi-family office, it services multiple (although often unrelated) families. This structure can therefore offer the services provided by a traditional private family office without the often challenging issues of governance and family relationship dynamics.

- Institutional family office – large institutions (for example, commercial banks, fiduciary service providers or investment houses) are increasingly providing family office services and platforms (ranging from concierge services to linking up structured finance or corporate advice for activities such as mergers and acquisitions to assist the family's business) to complement the existing investment and banking services they have traditionally provided to high net worth families. Some institutions set up a separate legal entity that provides pure consultancy services to give objective advice aside from and without involving other parts of the institution in question.

1.1 Nature of structure

The nature or style of the family office structure will mainly be determined by the resources available to the family in question (namely their ability to retain investment managers and experts on an exclusive basis) as well as the family's desire for control and privacy.

Broadly speaking, family office structures can be categorised as follows:

- Administrative – in this type of structure, advisory, accountancy, legal and investment management services are usually outsourced and managed through contracts with external service providers. The office itself will usually employ staff only to provide some level of bookkeeping, tax or administrative services (often on a part-time basis). This style of office would be suitable for families with limited resources or indeed good, pre-existing relationships with a number of service providers who can provide all the services they require but simply require a more co-ordinated approach.
- Hybrid – this structure enables a single family office to provide certain services in-house while outsourcing particular functions to other advisers or platforms. This style of office usually sees functions that are high-level or of strategic importance to the family being serviced in-house, with the non-strategic functions being outsourced. It may be that the family has particular experience in a certain area and therefore wishes to deal with these areas themselves while outsourcing where expertise in an unfamiliar area is required.
- Full-spectrum – this style of family office performs all functions and services that are required by the family in-house, although, again, (depending on the family's resources and particular expertise) specialised activities may be outsourced. This structure will only be appropriate where the family has sufficient resources as well as the commitment to a family office that is required to justify this approach.

2.   Key considerations – legal structure

Aside from an evaluation of the form and style of family office (which will largely be determined by the family's available resources), the following matters will be key in determining the appropriate legal structure for the family office.

2.1   The family's wealth and objectives

It goes without saying that the nature of a family's wealth (whether this is significant, whether it is absorbed in the family's business, which family members or structures hold that wealth, or whether a liquidity event has occurred or will occur) and the family's objectives for the functions of the family office (and how the office will function in relation to other of the family's structures) will be fundamental in determining the legal structure and the governance strategy of that office. In addition, families with significant wealth will often have different concerns to families with lesser wealth.

The extent to which the patriarch and other family members will be involved and their proposed role in relation to the family office will be the determining factor for the ownership structure and for the mechanics that are implemented in terms of governance, oversight and, ultimately, control. The provenance of the client may also dictate the preferred governance structure. For example, Middle Eastern families will be more concerned with issues revolving around *Sharia* law and multiple families, and the biggest issue for them may well be generational wealth transfer (and conflicts between generations). Therefore a separate family council may be appropriate for these families. In the United States it is common for a large family to form its own family council, as a place to resolve family-based issues. The family council may give strategic direction to the family office.

2.2   Location

The location of the patriarch and key family members, advisers and family office staff, as well as the family's assets and structures (and the consequential tax, disclosure and reporting requirements), will be of prime importance when determining the legal structure of the family office.

Proximity and accessibility to key decision makers and the people that will implement these decisions will be vital to achieve a successfully operated and run family office. The best jurisdiction in which to establish a family office company is typically dictated by the location of the patriarch, key individuals in the family and the main operating entities in the family business.

Where the family business or asset-holding structures cover a range of jurisdictions, it may be preferable to structure the family office as a holding company in a jurisdiction that suits the patriarch's location and lifestyle, where it can operate in tandem with local subsidiaries to facilitate oversight of the family business and projects.

In this scenario, care will need to be taken in relation to decision-making and the management and control of all these entities, as well as giving consideration to the functions that the family office will perform, particularly when the family office is located in a high tax jurisdiction, to ensure that structures that are located in low tax jurisdictions are not brought into the tax net of a country where the family office is sited. For example, if a family office is based in London, care needs to be taken if the family office provides investment services to offshore entities, as the investment management exemption may not be available.

If tax issues would be a negative concern, a low tax jurisdiction or financial centre may be a better option for the family in question. A number of families split the locations. The principal administrative services are based in a location that is physically convenient, and the investment activities are based in a financial centre that may also be more secure than the home jurisdiction.

The location of the family office can also be important in staffing the family office: it is vital that the location has a good local professional infrastructure to ensure that there will not be staffing issues on a short or long-term basis. The location must also have good communications and be both politically and economically stable.

3.   The governance structure of the family office

As previously mentioned, implementing a formal governance structure for the family office (and indeed any family structures/holding vehicles) becomes increasingly important when families transition from the generation that has initially generated the wealth to the next and subsequent generations. In the absence of the patriarch's direction, it is vital to have in place the principles and processes governing interactions between the family business (if this is still operational) and family asset-holding structures, the family itself and investment governance, succession and legacy planning, as well as appropriate professionally managed family office operations. Research has shown that family businesses have failed as a result of internal factors (including a failure to plan for succession and family conflicts).

Although governance will be covered in much more detail later in this book, an appropriate governance strategy must be implemented in conjunction with the implementation of the legal structure of the family office and therefore we shall also touch on this subject in this chapter.

Broadly, the family office should be governed in a similar fashion to how the family would govern a family-owned business, especially when multiple branches and generations are involved. On this basis, the family office should, for example, have a board of directors responsible for the oversight of the office. Families might also consider having a family assembly or a family council as well as an advisory board and a family policy, constitution or charter. However, a formal governance policy or charter may not be appropriate for every family and some may not wish to have such a formal statement, finding it polarising or divisive (particularly in terms of discussions between the generations). It will therefore be for the family in question to decide what will work best for them in both the short and long term. As the family and the family office evolves, the family may decide that it also needs other committees (such as an investment committee, audit committee, education committee, or indeed any committee that the family feels that it requires, although these committees should only evolve on a needs basis as opposed to having a committee purely for the sake of having one).

Example – basic governance structure

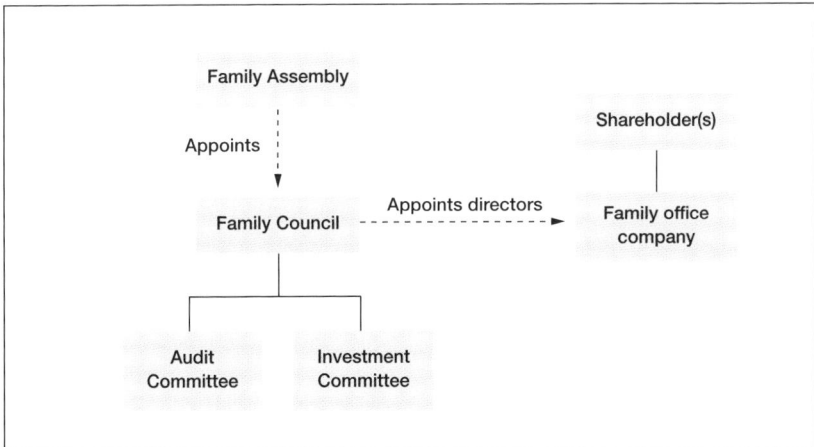

It is vital that this governance mechanism interacts and connects with the family structures, and that family members buy into it, otherwise it will be rendered meaningless and will not kick in at precisely the point at which it really comes into its own (for example, when a family conflict arises).

The family governance structure should develop in line with, and complement, the infrastructure of the family office (for example, the manner in which information is reported and communicated to the family, the services used by particular family members, the process for hiring management and decision-making processes, which we will come on to discuss in further detail) by achieving certain objectives, which may include the following:

- communicating family values, the family's mission and long-term vision to family members;
- keeping family members informed about the family's investments, business interests and strategy; and
- allowing the family to convene (both formally and informally) to make any necessary decisions and to share their ideas.

The aim behind this is to address potential issues before they arise and lead to conflict. It is important to note that privacy matters can also emerge when considering governance (for example, when one family member has authority over another, or when one family member knows the personal financial situation of another) which will need to be dealt with carefully and sensitively.

4. Infrastructure of the family office

The infrastructure of a specific family office will of course depend on the type and nature of the office. However, broadly, the following issues will need to be addressed.

4.1 Risk management/mitigation

Just as with any family structure, the management of risk is key and will therefore need to considered at every level of the family office structure.

(a) Confidentiality and security

The family office should have rigorous processes in place in relation to the hiring and vetting of employees for the family office (including full background checks) and in relation to third-party providers to whom the family office outsources work (including full due diligence). All employees should be required to enter into confidentiality agreements, as should third-party providers in relation to the information they have access to and receive as a result of their role.

The family office should ensure that systems and processes are implemented to limit access to personal data among its staff (where appropriate, it may be advisable to encrypt personal data), and should have clear policies on the disposal of information, procedures for storing data electronically rather than on paper, and a disaster recovery plan. Where information can be accessed online by employees or family members (for example, investment statements), such access should be as secure as possible.

(b) Insurance risk

The family office needs to address insurance risk as many family offices are underinsured and this represents a significant risk to the family. A family office is a business entity like any other and therefore there needs to be an insurance valuation and implementation of the full suite of appropriate coverage including, for example, business property, employment practice liability and directors and officers compensation. In the United States it is often simple to purchase a fidelity bond to insure against the risk of fraud by employees.

(c) *Investments*

The impact of the global recession and the issues that have been exposed as a result of this (such as counterparty risk) have focused many families' minds on their exposure in the market from an investment perspective. As well as the investment process and manager selection being fully documented (for example in a written investment policy), it is vital that the family office analyse the family's investment objectives and risk tolerance, and the family office should conduct a regular review of the family's investment portfolios to check the positions held, not just with one financial institution but across the full range of positions held with all institutions. To facilitate this regular review, the family office will need to consolidate all investment positions, and most of the more developed family offices have internal finance departments that will fulfil this function. However, the less developed offices, which may not have the internal capability to perform this role, should source third parties to assist them with this process or indeed perform this function outright. It is important that this information is communicated to the family in a coherent and user-friendly manner (in line with the governance strategy objectives outlined earlier).

In addition, in the context of a multi-family office, to the extent that the office is providing advice, full disclosure of the office's sources of revenue to the families it services is important to enable the families to identify potential conflicts of interest and how those conflicts are disclosed and managed.

(d) *Audit*

Just as it is important to perform an audit of the family's investments, it is also important to have appropriate systems in place to perform an audit of the family office itself (whether this is a function of a separate audit or management committee, or an independent accountant or other third party). There have been cases where family office employees have siphoned off significant amounts of money from family wealth, especially where one individual both acts as, for example, the chief operating officer and also manages most of the office's daily operations. As a result of inadequate oversight and auditing failures, such issues can go undetected, and therefore safeguards should be implemented (such as annual audits and strong internal financial controls, in tandem with screening of new hires) so that families can protect themselves against such risks.

(e) *Segregation/ ring-fencing*

In line with the family's segregation of its business from its private assets, as the family office will be acting as an employer and providing various services, it will be prudent similarly to ring-fence the family office and any liabilities that may be associated with it (such as employee claims) from other of the family's structures. We will come on to consider this issue in more detail when we consider the appropriate holding vehicle for a family office structure.

4.2 Employees

(a) *Funding*

In the case of a single-family office, the costs for staff alone can be significant: typically a fully-integrated family office would have a chief executive, chief finance officer, chief investment officer, investment analysts, accountants and administration staff, and some offices may also employ a lawyer.

In the context of privately owned family offices, it is important to establish whether:

- the office will be a self-sufficient entity generating its funding requirements by charging a commercial fee for its services. If this is the case, the fees charged should cover staff salaries, administration and running costs (for example, the payment of professional fees such as accountants') as well as any tax liabilities. The office will need to be operated on a commercial arm's-length basis. With a London-located family office, for example, this could be on a 'cost plus' basis (which would require prior negotiation with the tax inspector, the practicalities involved are discussed in further detail below); or
- the office will require external funding or capital contributions. If this is the case, the family should consider the funds used to make such contributions and whether any tax issues might arise. As the family office evolves to serve additional generations, the source of operating funds often becomes a difficult family issue. In the United States this has led a number of traditional family offices to close or merge into a larger family office.

In addition, the family's banking relationship manager will need to liaise with the family office to put in place the bank accounts and the funding structure required for the efficient operation of the family office; if there is any borrowing arrangement, this will need to be managed.

(b) *Employment contracts and employment law*

The employment relationship should be properly structured, with clear lines of authority and reporting and a clear distinction of roles in contractual terms. The family office should employ its staff under properly drafted employment contracts and make sure that it adheres to any other employment-related legislation (for example, working time regulations, minimum wage requirements and grievance procedures). Performance insurance coverage, like a fidelity bond, should be considered

(c) *Incentivising employees/staff retention*

The employment and retention of the best staff is a key issue for family offices, and families should therefore carefully consider the strategies they implement to achieve these objectives, maybe including flexible working hours and ensuring that a full pensions/benefits package is available, as well as adequate levels of support.

4.3   Tax compliance

It is important that a suitable accountant is employed to ensure that tax obligations of both employees and the family office vehicle are met. For example, in the case of the family office company located in the United Kingdom, Pay As You Earn and National Insurance obligations will be in point, as well as a consideration of the company's Corporation Tax and Value Added Tax (VAT) profile and status: as it will be providing services to the family, fees for services would usually be subject to UK VAT. In the United States, the tax compliance function often includes the administration of family trusts that are overseen by the family office.

4.4   Service agreements

It may be appropriate to put in place service agreements (upkeep, maintenance etc) between the family office structure and asset-holding structures for use of assets such aircraft, yachts and properties. These agreements would need to take into account transfer pricing regulations (and, where appropriate, VAT or purchase tax) in the relevant jurisdictions.

4.5   Technology

Having the appropriate technology to support the family office operation is essential to ensure a well-managed family office. Depending on the services that the office performs, this can include anything from account aggregation, customised accounting and reporting of all family office investments costs, to systems assisting office management, family connectivity and communication. Ensuring security of information was flagged earlier in the context of risk management and confidentiality.

5.   Family office vehicles: ownership structure

There are a variety of ways in which the holding vehicle for the family office can be structured. This section will focus on the most common ways of structuring a private family office and the main advantages and disadvantages of each of these structures that will need to be considered by the family in question.

In the United Kingdom, the most common vehicle used for holding a family office company seems to be a private trust company (PTC). Provided that it is structured and administered correctly, a PTC can provide continuity of family trust administration over multiple future generations and reduce the liability of family members who may wish to act as trustees (subject to tax and management/control considerations, it should be possible to have family members and trusted advisers on the board of the PTC), as well as formally providing fiduciary services directly to the family as opposed to simply supporting the family's trustees.

5.1 Establishing the family office within an existing structure

Example – family office within an existing structure

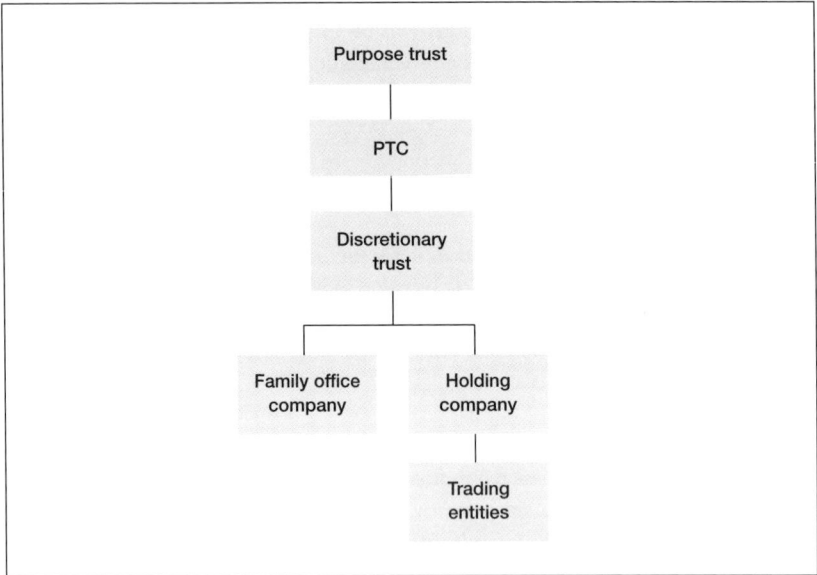

```
                    ┌──────────────┐
                    │ Purpose trust│
                    └──────┬───────┘
                           │
                    ┌──────┴───────┐
                    │     PTC      │
                    └──────┬───────┘
                           │
                    ┌──────┴───────┐
                    │ Discretionary│
                    │    trust     │
                    └──────┬───────┘
              ┌────────────┴────────────┐
      ┌───────┴───────┐        ┌────────┴───────┐
      │ Family office │        │    Holding     │
      │    company    │        │    company     │
      └───────────────┘        └────────┬───────┘
                                        │
                               ┌────────┴───────┐
                               │    Trading     │
                               │    entities    │
                               └────────────────┘
```

Depending on the services to be performed by the family office and the available resources of the family, the family may wish to consolidate the family office in an existing structure. This approach would result in a simpler structure from an administrative perspective and a reduction in administration and legal costs. However, it is important to note that any cost-saving will be restricted to only the top level of structure, as the costs associated with the family office company will be the same as the costs that would be incurred if the office was held in a separate structure.

The other advantage of consolidation would be centralised control, as the family office and other family assets would be under the control of the board of directors of one PTC in the case of an existing PTC structure. In this scenario, this would mean that the patriarch would only need to identify trusted advisers/ key personnel to act as directors of one company rather than of two.

However, such consolidation may result in the exposure of the family (and more valuable) assets to increased risk of investigation and claims. Again, taking the example of a PTC structure, while having a PTC as trustee of the top holding structure enables the family office to be held in a separate trust structure from other assets, having the same legal registered owner may increase the risk at the top of the combined holding structure. For example, in the event of an investigation into the family office or in the event of claims or proceedings brought by third parties (such as employees), the PTC could become the subject of such investigations, claims or proceedings, and by having the same legal entity and name as a party this could potentially implicate other assets of which the PTC is the registered owner. For this reason, it is not advisable to have the family office held within an asset-rich structure.

In addition, the existing structure may be inconsistent with the operation of a family office business (especially if the family office becomes multi-family), and the consolidation of the family office in an existing structure may lead to the need to disclose the entire structure to various regulators, thereby undermining the confidentiality that the existing structure may enjoy. For example, the family office may (depending on its location and the location of the holding vehicle) require a licence to conduct trust company business (unless it can fall within certain defined exemptions or delegate those activities that require a licence to a licensed service provider). The licensing process for the family office may involve disclosure of the ownership chain of the family office to the relevant regulator, and therefore may also involve disclosure of family assets that would not otherwise be required if the family office is held in a stand-alone structure with no assets.

5.2   Establishing the family office as an independent stand-alone structure

Another option is to establish the family office in a structure separate from the family's existing structure. Broadly, this strategy mitigates the risk of cross-contamination between structures. It is preferable for private assets to be kept separate from business assets, and structures that provide services in potentially numerous jurisdictions and entities that employ staff should not be held in the same structure as those that hold assets. The following strategies can be adopted, again, dependant on the particular family's aims and objectives.

(a)   *Direct ownership of the family office company by the patriarch or a family member*
This approach may keep the family office structure straightforward as well as minimising costs. The shareholder (who may also be the patriarch) would have control over the board of directors of the family office, which would give the necessary safeguards in the event that he wishes to replace the directors for any reason. Direct ownership would also eliminate the need to involve third-party service providers (at least at the holding level) and would provide flexibility, for example, if the shareholder wishes to move the family office to a trust structure at some point in the future, which could again be relevant if, for example, the family office became a profitable multi-family office business.

However, the shares and interests in the family office company would form part of the shareholder's personal estate, which could pose risks during his lifetime (for example, in the event of divorce or claims by third parties), and there would be a need to consider succession and devolution of shares on his death. Indeed, if the family office became a profitable business this structure would not be advisable. In addition, from a confidentiality perspective, the shareholder may not wish to hold the shares in his own name or that of a family member (although this could be addressed by a nominee).

(b)   *Ownership of the family office by a purpose trust*
A purpose trust could be formed, in those jurisdictions that recognise such a trust,

for the sole purpose of owning the family office. This structure would again have the advantage of simplicity and cost-efficiency, as it would keep the day-to-day control at the level of the family office company with the directors of that entity and the trustees (who could be trusted advisors or family members), conferring a top layer as a check and balance. The patriarch could have the power to replace the trustees at any time, thereby having ultimate indirect control over the structure. In addition, this structure would confer flexibility as it should be possible (subject to local law advice) for the shares and interest in the family office company to be appointed out of the purpose trust into a discretionary trust holding structure at a later stage if the family decides to operate the family office as, for example, a multi-family office business. Furthermore, if the family office is run as a self-financing cost centre, a purpose trust could be a suitable structure as there would be no need for extraction of significant surplus funds. Again, a PTC can act as trustee of the purpose trust.

(c)   *Ownership of the family office by a discretionary trust with a PTC acting as trustee*
Alternatively, if, for example, the family office will be providing services to other families, it may be preferable for the shares and interest in the family office to be held in a discretionary trust with a PTC acting as trustee (in this scenario, the shares in the PTC are usually held by a purpose trust of which key trusted personnel would act as trustees, again subject to tax advice). If the family office is run as a business, a purpose trust is not a suitable entity for the distribution of surplus assets to beneficiaries (as it will typically not have beneficiaries) and the holding of what should at that stage be a valuable asset, whereas a discretionary trust can have the patriarch and his family as beneficiaries of the profits from the business.

Example – family office within a stand-alone structure

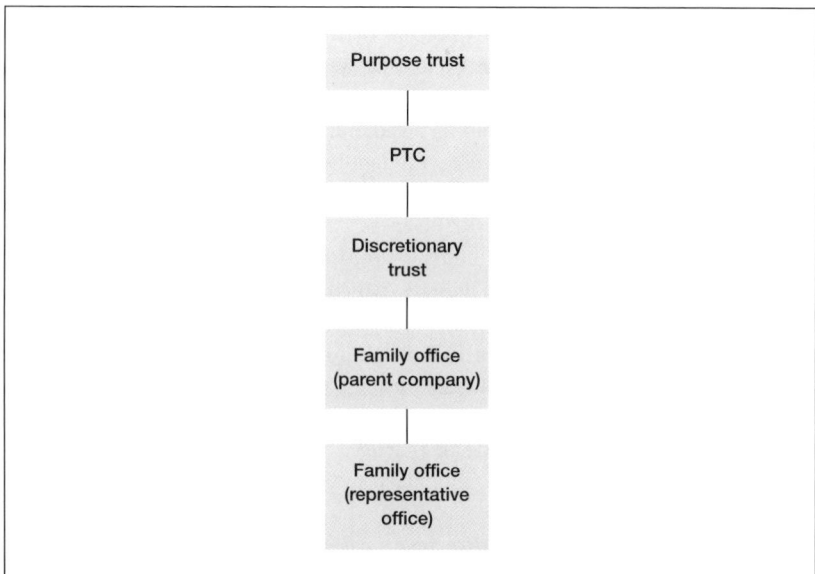

Purpose trust

|

PTC

|

Discretionary trust

|

Family office (parent company)

|

Family office (representative office)

6. Case study

The example of an evolving family office structure we will look at is that of a wealthy, entrepreneurial, international individual. This individual moved to the UK a few years ago with his family and implemented a formal family office platform soon after arriving in the UK.

The family office is held in a stand-alone structure, comprising an offshore discretionary trust with a parent company incorporated and managed outside the United Kingdom that, in turn, is the sole shareholder of a UK-incorporated and managed subsidiary. The UK company is authorised by the Financial Services Authority to provide certain regulated functions (such as acting as an investment manager in relation to a diverse pool of investments) as well as a variety of other roles, including providing estate management (including the management and refurbishment of certain projects), accounting and auditing functions and a variety of more *ad hoc* tasks (including concierge services), while outsourcing certain advisory functions. The family office is run on a cost-plus basis.

The family office interacts with certain other family structures to provide a holistic and coordinated approach to the management of the family's wealth and investment strategy. As well as more formal, regular meetings with the patriarch, contact between the patriarch and key employees in the family office is also on an ad hoc and informal basis.

The key challenges for the family office team are formalising and regulating the various investment relationships, ensuring that the family office company operates within the parameters of its licence and risk management, while also delivering the service that the principal expects and requires.

The family office may offer services to a wider range of carefully selected families in the future, developing into a multi-family office, as a result of the experience it has gained. However, the main focus during the patriarch's lifetime is on how to ensure the transition of the structure (which will be facilitated by formalising the governance strategy) to ensure that the office continues to service the second and indeed subsequent generations of the family.

7. Key recommendations

It is important to keep the family office structure under constant review to ensure that it adapts to the needs of the family in question in order to:

- remain relevant in fulfilling the family's objectives;
- operate efficiently;
- keep abreast of the constantly changing legal, tax and regulatory environment; and
- adapt to the geographic dispersion of family members.

With this in mind, any family office structure should be kept as flexible and as straightforward as possible: simplicity and transparency are key. A structure should not be implemented if it will only work on paper and not in practice: the family needs to be on board, and to achieve that the structure needs to operate and reflect the way in which family assets and structures will be dealt with in reality (albeit being mindful of the consequential tax, reporting and regulatory requirements). As any family office structure will be bespoke, it is vital that legal and tax advice is taken at every stage in the process to ensure that what works from the family's perspective will also work from a legal, regulatory and tax perspective.

The authors would like to thank Phyllis Townsend for her assistance in the preparation of this chapter.

Recruitment and talent management strategies

M J Rankin
The Rankin Group LLC

Conducting a search for quality talent that will meet your expectations for performance in any industry can be an excruciating process. It is even more complex for a family office. It takes a major commitment of time and resources to find a short list of top candidates that have the unique skills, experience and background to work successfully with wealthy families in a family office structure. Since each family office situation and the family clients it serves is distinctly different from other family offices, finding candidates that transition well into these roles is challenging.

Another challenge is getting family members to recognise that their family office is a business that not only helps manage their assets and lifestyle issues, but also helps them become better stakeholders and risk managers of their family wealth. Consequently, the question of who should they employ and how should the family office be managed going forward are closely intertwined with the family's goals and their vision for how the family office can help them accomplish those goals.

Additionally, the culture, values and behavioural DNA of family members and employees is a critical element in making these unique relationships work.

## 1.	The one-page business plan

Like most businesses, starting with a business plan provides the clarity needed to define the purpose and expectations for the family office. This leads to the development of job descriptions and skills/experience criteria for prospective candidates. It can also help determine governance structures that guide the roles of the family office professionals.

Investment in the time required for a discussion about how best to manage the family's wealth for today and future generations is critical to defining the role the family office will play in assisting family members with the challenges and complexities of wealth management.

The skills and experience of the family office professional should complement the skills and experiences of family members with regard to the in-depth, technical knowledge of the financial services (investment, tax and wealth transfer planning and philanthropy) needed to grow the family's financial capital, along with business management, leadership skills and the emotional fortitude to achieve success, however defined by the family clients.

Since each family is unique and, therefore, each family office is unique in how it is structured and staffed to meet the needs of the family members it serves, success may be measured against performance expectations in terms of either tangible or intangible benchmarks. For example, it can mean asset growth or preservation of capital; enhanced communication between family members; business succession; establishment of philanthropic goals; or family continuity.

The following is an example of a one-page business plan that can be used to guide discussions about what you are creating in the family office and how it will ultimately relate to the people you empower to accomplish your goals and objectives – whether they are family members, external advisors or family office executives.

Family office business plan

Vision
Describe what this family office will look like in three, five or 10 years.
    Include nature of business, service offerings, description of family clients served, geographic scope, and what the family is passionate about.
        Vision = Graphically describes the business of the office.

Mission
Describe why this family office exists in one sentence or less.
        Mission = Purpose
        Why the family office exists from the family's point of view.

Objectives
List between four and eight goals that this office must achieve to meet clients' expectations
        Objectives = Measurable results.

Strategies
Describe between five and eight things this office must do extremely well over time.
        Strategies = Define how the office will be built and managed.

Action Plans
What are the six to eight specific business building or infrastructure projects this office must successfully complete to implement the strategies listed above.
        Plans = Work or tasks to be completed.

©The Rankin Group, Ltd.

---

2.   Search process based on risk management

Selecting and hiring professionals to work in a family office requires discipline, patience, and a commitment to completing the appropriate amount of due diligence that controls the risk of making a bad hire. A successful search does not mean just hiring people to staff an office, it means hiring the right people, who will be with you for a long time. You are making a substantial investment that deserves the same attention you give to evaluating your money managers.

Executive due diligence can make or break the search process. It involves more than finding an impressive résumé. It requires digging deeper to assess if a person is a good business risk for the long-term.

A poor investment in human capital can become a major expense financially and emotionally. In today's market hiring the wrong person will cost between three and 14 times their salary and benefits, plus potential family conflict and untold personal anxiety.

3. Success factors for better hires

Here is where we circle back to the family office business plan. Once you clarify your family mission, goals and purpose of the family office, along with the values statements that define your culture, you can begin translating that into job profiles and performance expectations. As examples:

- do you have an operating business that your family office executives will help manage?
- do you seek guidance on philanthropic initiatives or assistance in educating future generations? or,
- are your needs focused on the more traditional aspects of wealth management relating to financial and investment expertise?

The key to a successful hiring process is to provide a clear definition of responsibilities for the job as well as the personality characteristics required for communication and success. The next step is to take the time to profile your goals in ideal candidate terms, whatever your strategic vision. Determine which skills, experience and personal characteristics will complement your family's level of expertise, culture and unique family dynamic.

This goes beyond the development of a traditional job description, which typically focuses on the candidate's background and experience, not on the job. In contrast to outlining experience, duties, tasks and responsibilities, a more comprehensive job profile will detail the results expected in the successful execution of the position, emphasising outcomes that this specific job delivers that no other job can do. The objective is to 'let the job talk' describing what this job does, what the successful candidate will be held responsible for, and how their performance will be measured at review time.

The job analysis process is the most essential and most neglected aspect of hiring because most people don't want to dedicate the time. In the long run, however, this initial effort saves valuable time, money and misunderstandings when it comes to screening candidates.

If you already have an existing family office and are replacing someone, do not just recycle their job description. Chances are the role has changed based on the family's changing needs. A fresh look will help you determine what the job needs now and what new skills and experiences you would like to add to the team. You may also discover that parts of the job should be outsourced or handled by someone else in the office.

- Know what you want – invest the time to develop the one-page business plan and determine what the job needs.

- Create a comprehensive job profile – focus on outcomes and competencies that are required for success. Develop a scorecard and candidate criteria to screen candidates against. This helps to eliminate unqualified candidates more quickly.
- Look for the intangibles – a candidate's success goes beyond their functional abilities and includes soft skills such as leadership, communication, work style, personality, fit with culture and values. Consider using behavioural assessment tools to look beyond the résumé.
- Organise the interview process – agree on an approach that will objectively and systematically evaluate prospective candidates. Consider things like who will be involved in the interviews, how impressions and information gathered during the interviews will be collected and interpreted, and who will make the final hiring decision.
- Look for reliable resources – take advantage of human resource experts to help you with job profiles, development of screening tools and appropriate interview practices. Look to your advisers and colleagues for candidate referrals. Work with a search firm that specialises in family offices.
- Be competitive – set a realistic compensation package for the job. Determine market value standards for the job and for the types of people that qualify for the job. Structure a package that makes sense for current market demands and sets reasonable precedence for your own organisation and family expectations.
- Be patient – hiring the right candidate takes time. Develop a comprehensive hiring plan and stick to it.

4.   Candidate screening that looks beyond the résumé

A person's behavioural style, values, and attitudes play a major role in determining not only whether they fit in a family office environment, but whether their style fits the job, the culture and the dynamic of your family. We are all hard-wired to work a certain way that plays to our strengths and personal satisfaction. Behavioural profiling helps you look beyond the résumé to assess which candidates are a good business risk in terms of personal and professional fit with the job.

The number one reason for resignations or terminations is that the job or workplace was not the right fit.

For example, in many family office jobs career growth is restricted, leaving limited opportunity for upward mobility. The job challenge comes from the variety of the work; the job satisfaction comes from helping others attain their goals. This means looking for people that are motivated by serving others rather than climbing the corporate ladder. By screening for an individual's motivations, maturity and emotional intelligence you can ensure a better fit with the unique roles for family office professionals, as well as lower hiring costs and reduced turnover.

Today more than ever we are faced with the challenge of screening candidates with vastly different generational talents and very different value structures. Additionally, candidates are better prepared for the interview process, making it more difficult to determine their innate abilities from their prepared performance for what they think you want them to say in order to land the job.

A good interviewer can uncover a candidate's skills, educational background and employment history. The challenge is determining if their soft skills and judgment ability mesh with the requirements and expectations of the job and the organisation. Behavioural-based assessments and interviewing techniques help you with this.

It should be noted that one of the key concerns in using assessments is the risk of discrimination litigation. You should never use an instrument that does not meet all the stringent requirements of the Equal Employment Opportunity Commission. You should also engage the services of an expert who is trained in the use of the assessment tools and knows how to conduct the interviews and interpret the results.

5. The screening and interview process

Most employers have not been trained to interview well. Consequently, they tend to overlook key points that should be covered in discussions with candidates. The process of screening candidates takes time and effort. There are no real shortcuts. There are, however, some techniques and pointers that can make the process go quicker and reveal the candidates that most closely fit your criteria.

There are three steps in the candidate screening process that sets you up for personal interviews and behavioural assessments: reviewing résumés and cover letters; phone interviews; and sorting for the top candidates. There are a number of approaches that can be used, but we suggest doing whatever makes sense for you and the level of the position. Your time is valuable. Finding the most efficient way to identify and screen candidates is important, which is why contracting with outside experts when you don't have an internal recruiting and human resources staff can be the best approach.

5.1 Résumé review

The most efficient process for reviewing résumés is to scan for keywords that relate to skills and experiences you have identified in your job criteria and to read over the last three to five years of job duties. Look for long gaps in employment, stability and tenure with employers and progressively more responsibility. You can examine cover letters and letters of reference along with the résumé to give you an overall impression of the candidate. This will give you a sense of their writing style and how they are perceived by previous employers and colleagues.

5.2 Phone screen

For candidates that make it past the résumé review, many times the next step is a quick phone screen. This serves two purposes: first you can use it to verify that the candidate is active and available for new positions; secondly you can find out how the candidate presents themselves to prospective employers and gauge verbal communication skills. If you like what you hear during the phone screen, you should set up a time for a phone interview.

5.3 Phone interview

You should have a plan for what you want to accomplish during the telephone interview. With some well-thought-out questions, you can often gauge quite a bit on this call with regard to practical experience that meets your needs, motivations for career moves, expectations for their next job choice and ability to transition into your job for the right reasons.

Part of your focus should be to fill in any information that is missing on the résumé and to gauge interest and fit with the position and your expectations for someone working with your family. Before starting the phone interview, you should have a copy of the candidate's résumé, the job description and screening criteria in front of you. You can make notes or jot down questions on the résumé, referring back to items in the job description that need clarification. For example, you may look at a résumé and not see where the candidate has the requisite 10 years' experience but you think that is because it is wrapped up in parts of two different jobs.

It is also appropriate to ask questions about salary and other requirements of the job. For instance, you can make sure the candidate understands the salary range and that the job requires travel or relocation.

Anything that is not clear should be addressed at a preliminary level before the candidate is brought in for a personal interview. You do not want to spend unnecessary time with someone that is not right or shows no potential as a fit for the job.

5.4   Sorting for top candidates

This is a not as much a scoring exercise as it is a chance to find the top candidates from your phone interviews that should move to the next level. You should identify at least five, if available, for the initial selection. Next have two or three other people review them (ie, your family search committee) and select the ones that will move to personal interviews.

5.5   Personal interviews

Before the personal candidate interviews, you should transfer the most important candidate criteria into a candidate rating chart that is weighted on a scale of one to 10 in importance. After candidate interviews, each interviewer can rate the candidates according to the weighted criteria. This tool helps to compare candidates objectively and quantitatively and allows you to arrive at a sound hiring decision.

One of the best approaches to conducting candidate interviews is to use behavioural based interviewing techniques. The goal of the interview process is to predict future job performance based on examples of previous specific behaviours, which illustrate the desired competencies through tactful probing and diagnostic evaluation of a person's personal style, values and motivators. The interviewers are looking for behaviours in situations similar to those that will be encountered in the new job. By relating a candidate's answers to specific past experiences, and determining their behavioural DNA, you can develop much more reliable indicators of how the individual will most likely act in the future. Behavioural questions ensure more genuine spontaneity than traditional questions since candidates cannot practice as easily for them in advance.

Past behaviour in past situations will more accurately indicate a candidate's attitudes and behaviours. A person can have the knowledge and the competencies to do the job, but they may not have the desire to do it. The behaviour-based interview incorporates structured questions on the candidate's past behaviour in situations similar to those that will be encountered in the new position. It goes beyond determining whether a person can do the job. It determines if a person will do a good job: how it will be done and to what extent.

To ensure that the candidate you wish to hire has represented themselves accurately, it is important to utilise the services of an investigative agency to conduct a thorough background, criminal and credit check on finalist candidates. You should also complete extensive reference checks by talking with previous employers, colleagues they have worked with and people they have managed.

6. Designing a retention plan

After you have invested considerable time and money recruiting and training your employees, it is important to design a plan that will make sure those valuable employees are productive and remain loyal to the family office. Losing experienced employees results in significant costs to the family office and the family emotionally.

As stated earlier in this chapter, one of the main challenges for retention of employees within a family office is the static nature of the jobs relative to upward career mobility. If they are not people dedicated to serving others and who thrive on the ever changing agenda of tasks in any given day, other attempts at keeping them in the job long-term will be ineffective. Their work environment and the nature of interaction they have with family members is another key factor. Make note, however, that there is a fairly common burn-out rate in these jobs of between 12 and 14 years. This is a good reason to do some succession planning for the office early on.

The keys to employee satisfaction and retention are founded on strong leadership and sound management practices, along with good operating systems and providing the tools to allow staff to do their jobs well. We know that in most cases families hire family office executives to run their family office and take over the leadership and management role of the other employees. However, the engagement of family members through a family committee or board is essential to ensuring that the family office executive receives the leadership that he needs.

The following paragraphs consider a few basic talent-management practices that will provide a strong basis for building a retention plan.

6.1 Compensation

As in any job, compensation is a critical factor in driving performance and loyalty. The structure and level of compensation relates directly to the overall success of the family office and the motivation displayed by its employees. Due to the diverse nature of the jobs performed by family office employees, it has been difficult to create compensation standards like those in other segments of the wealth management and financial services industries. Titles and responsibilities do not correlate as easily to responsibilities and duties performed as they do in other industries. Compensation and benefits vary considerably in terms of the type of family office, the degree of direct interaction with family members, and where the family office is located. Additionally, compensation in family offices is noticeably less in many cases than that found in the wealth management professions they draw talent from.

There are a number of compensation surveys available from organisations such as The Family Office Exchange (Chicago), Rothstein Cass (New York) and Campden FO/Sulger Buel & Company (United Kingdom), but each provides only a snapshot of the real picture and admits that its validity is limited to an inconsistent sample of the market. What they do show as a consistent trend is that most family offices structure their compensation plans on a traditional model that is based on salary and benefits more than on a performance bonus approach.

Our approach when consulting with clients is to help them focus on the perceived internal value for the position and the true market value. Salaries are measured against industry standards for similar positions with similar responsibilities and current salary for prospective candidates. Most comparable salary levels are found in privately-held small businesses, boutique wealth management firms and other family offices.

Performance measurement generally includes evaluation against tangible financial achievements and intangible (subjective) measures, such as the effectiveness of the executive director's style of leadership, management, communication and influence on the success of the family office. Maintaining a report card of accomplishments that helps family clients understand what employees have achieved can be beneficial in supporting bonus pay-outs.

6.2 Orientation and motivation

A thoughtfully planned orientation and welcome for new employees helps set the stage for a positive experience in their new workplace. First impressions are lasting, and a positive initial impression can be highly motivating to a new hire, reinforcing the decision to accept the position. In this way, it can directly reduce turnover. By personalising the process, a new employee can become acquainted with key leadership, his or her manager and other employees as well as the values of the family that carry over into the family office.

As in any small company, the key to keeping your employees engaged is to remember that when the employee's career goals match what the family and family office is trying to achieve, they stay and contribute effectively to the team effort. As soon as they diverge, they become dissatisfied and may look for another option.

Here are a few things to consider:

- challenge them – most employees want to be challenged: as you raise expectations, performance levels and job satisfaction also increase;
- empower them – Give employees the ability to make their own decisions and be responsible for their outcome. Many human resource articles and surveys indicate that employees who have control over their daily environment have a higher level of job satisfaction and stay longer;
- communicate with them – listen to your employees and let them know that they can talk with you without fear of judgment. Also clearly define your beliefs and values so they know how to act relative to your goals and objectives.
- recognise them – when you recognise an employee's good work by appraisal or acknowledgment he or she gets motivated to do the work with more

sincerity. A few words of praise can have a greater effect that rewarding with money.

- evaluate them – it is often easier to avoid the discussion about how well or how poorly someone is doing in their job against your expectations. However, by consistently assessing an employee's skills and performance, you have the opportunity to reward the stars and identify those that are not doing their jobs. There is nothing more debilitating to hard-working employees than a peer that is not doing their job. Non-performers should be weeded out quickly and replaced by contributing members of the team.
- respect their personal goals – always remember that your employees have personal goals that are as important to them as your goals are to you. Find ways to help them accomplish their goals while helping to fulfil yours.

7. Running the family office as a business

All family offices no matter their size should put in place effective and efficient human resource practices and procedures. These should include:

- establishing overall guiding principles for the family office:
  - overview of strategic goals;
  - overview of disaster plan;
  - procedures for office closure;
  - office appearance;
  - working hours expectations;
  - computer policies;
  - travel/cell phone policies;
- describing benefits and policies for benefits usage:
  - holiday and paid time off;
  - eligibility;
  - procedure for requesting time off;
  - types of paid time off;
  - leave balances at end of year and termination;
  - voluntary benefits;
  - educational benefits;
- retirement plans:
  - eligibility;
  - company contributions;
- healthcare and insurance:
  - eligibility;
  - types of insurance;
  - annual window for changes;
  - other employee benefits;
- setting up appropriate record-keeping systems:
  - insider trading policy;
  - disclosure of employee trading activity (quarterly);
  - U4 disciplinary proceedings (annual);
  - non-exempt employees (Fair Labour Standards Act);

- number of hours worked day by day;
- employee résumés;
- initial job applications;
- job descriptions;
- acknowledgement of corporate code of ethics;
- confidentiality agreements;
- minutes from ongoing employee reviews;
- any disciplinary actions;
- special recognitions;
- developing termination procedures:
  - interview in person;
  - provide reason for termination;
  - prior documentation helps;
  - document final interview to personnel file.

Although all of this may seem a bit overwhelming, it is required to protect you and your employees and to meet human resource fair employment practices.

8. Summary

The family office is an important business that manages the personal financial and lifestyle affairs of its wealthy clients with confidence and discretion. To be successful it should apply certain basic business principles. There is significant risk if you get it wrong through poor planning, hiring the wrong people and taking the wrong approach to retaining and managing them.

Family office environments are often unstable, which makes them less attractive as a career. Consequently, finding people who will remain long-term is difficult. These are very unique jobs because of the emotional aspects rather than the business functions performed. For this reason, you need to evaluate prospective employees carefully against realistic expectations for personality, style, values and professional experience.

Additionally, you need a clear vision for why and how establishing an office accomplishes your desired goals and objectives. Once you establish your vision, it is important to tie job functions to your goals and objectives, which in turn help to define the recruiting plan that manages your risk of making a poor hire. Hiring the wrong people can be very expensive mistake financially and emotionally.

You also need to set realistic compensation based on the market value of the person you want to hire and the value they will deliver in the job. In a single family office, combat pay should be considered in view of the emotional and sometimes irrational aspects of the job.

Building a quality personal services firm, which a family office is, requires motivation and drive to harness your employee's individual skill-sets and motivation. Optimising the family office's service offering requires focus on optimising the individual strengths of the family office team.

It is important to pull together people with complementary skills and styles to get things done – whether they are direct employees or outside advisers. A lot can be gained by understanding and appreciating the value of individual styles, and where an individual's strengths reside. That is why we encourage our clients to look beyond the résumé and assess behavioural styles as well as technical credentials when conducting a search. Look for people that fit your culture, mesh with the team and family member clients, and are prepared from the beginning to interact effectively.

Finding people to apply for a job is not the hard part – using the right criteria to select them is.

Carefully define your screening criteria. Determine who should be part of the interview process. Organise your thoughts around specific issues and observations to be addressed in the interview. Organise your findings so that you remember what you liked and did not like about each candidate. Compare notes with the other members of the interview team.

Finally, address the need for human resource policies and procedures, employment contracts and effective leadership and management techniques.

Appendices

1. Ten tips for long-term hires

- Develop a formal hiring process. Commit necessary time to define your culture and success criteria for prospective candidates.
- Write a well-defined job description that relates to the company's goals and objectives and expectations for the person in this role.
- Set a competitive, market-valued compensation for the job.
- Interview more than one candidate and look beyond the résumé to determine cultural and behavioural fit with the organisation and other members of the team.
- Hire candidates who are not just like you, but complement your skills, experience and style.
- Follow through on background and reference checks. Be sure you know who you are hiring.
- Promise a candidate only what you can deliver.
- Have others in the organisation/family interview the candidate(s).
- Don't rely on classified or internet advertising.
- Network to keep tabs on the hiring pool in anticipation of future needs; develop internal bench strength when you can.

2. Organising and interpreting your findings

Balance sheet

Applicant _____ Position _____

Interviewer_____ Date _____

Recommended _____ Not recommended _____

Résumé

| Strengths | Limitations |

Education/experience
Degree
Certification
Related experience

Intellectual
Analytical ability
Problem-solving skills
Written/verbal communication skills
Judgement
Logic
Organisational skills

Interpersonal
Leadership skills
Team player
Training skills
Self-confidence
Extrovert/introvert
Persuasive
Patient

Motivational
Interests
Energy
Salary expectations
Hobbies

Cultural fit
Evidences benefits and values similar to ours
Service oriented
High work standards
Technical competence

While listening to the applicant, the interviewer should be getting some good answers to the following questions:

- Is he interested in ....Did he take the time to prepare for the interview?
- Does he show effort ....think before he speaks.......... Is he thoughtful?
- Does he show sincerity ....get to the point.........avoid ducking or evading the questions?

- Are his answers appropriately matched to questions......Does he avoid canned answers?
- Does he lead with benefits.........distinguish between features and benefits.......highlight the facts that favour his being hired?
- Does he communicate effectively........ stick to the point without over-elaboration?
- Is his expression clear, precise?
- Does he show confidence..........commit to an idea?
- Can he spar........maintain composure in stressful situations?
- Am I enthused.........would I want this candidate working for me?

To assist in your objective evaluation, the following check list may be considered:

Work attitudes and habits
- How does he work.....what is his style.............results?
- Why does he work......what does he like about work?
- Can he take broad, general assignments?
- Does he need emotional support...........Is he independent?
- Will he follow through on action?
- How will he respond to pressure?

Drive and ambition
- How energetic is he... How does he use energy?
- Will he take initiative...start things on own.....broaden assignments?
- What are his career goals and ambitions?
- What does he want from life and work.......What motivates him (money, status, power)?
- Do his aspirations appear to be realistic?

Intellectual ability
- What is his overall level of intelligence when compared with other candidates?
- Does he have any special talents?
- How well does he communicate?
- How would you describe his thinking (colourful, dull, dramatic, pedestrian)?
- How does he approach problems (impulsive, deliberate)?
- How about his judgement?

Emotional resources
- How would you evaluate his overall stability (mature, sound, spontaneous)?
- What is his confidence level?
- Can he see own strengths and weaknesses?
- What is his reaction to conflict and aggression?
- What are his major characteristics (passive v active, dependent v independent)?

Interpersonal relations

- What was his general impact on you (pleasant, remote, cool, sociable, aggressive)?
- Does he understand and interpret interpersonal situations (perceptive, sensitive, oblivious)?
- Can he adjust to different social levels (snobbish, intolerant, humane, flexible)?
- How will he operate with superiors (rebellious, resentful, cooperative)?
- How will he operate with subordinates (push or lead, friendly or remote)?
- How will he operate with peers (friendly, distant, competitive)?
- How will he get along with outside advisers and family members......if there is customer contact involved.......service oriented v exploitative ....relies on logic or charm......hard sell or soft sell?

Management of the family office

Sandy Loder
AH Loder Advisers Ltd

It requires a great deal of boldness and a great deal of caution to make a great fortune: and when you have got it, it requires ten times more wit to keep it. – Nathan Rothschild

Family offices come in many different shapes, sizes and locations, and each with its own unique and specific purpose. Given the significant variations between each, there is no typical family office, and the best approach is to ensure the functions of the office are in alignment with the purpose for which the family office was created. In the following chapter, we will explore the management of the family office and the guidelines it would be best to take into consideration.

The creation of a family office normally occurs when a considerable amount of wealth has been created, either by an individual or a family as a result of a transaction or a liquidity event, or from dividends from a family business or enterprise. The nature and function of the office is generally shaped by the original founder, with a specific reason or purpose in mind. These can range from a need to have an office to administer or manage the family's assets to one that just provides concierge services. The services of the family office can change over time, as the family unit grows in size or as the assets change hands and dissipate, or as the family's needs change over generations. The predominant function of the family office is to preserve the family wealth. However, every family office has its own culture, values, vision, personalities and working practices.

Managing a family office is nothing like managing a corporate entity. When a family office is created, it often takes on the role of managing a complex web of intra-family relationships. As with most families, an overarching ingredient is emotion, which unfortunately in some cases can include greed, fear and jealousy. This is a predominant reason why 90% of families do not see their wealth going beyond the third generation. Hence, the chief executive/head of the family office becomes a strategist, confidant, business adviser, investment adviser, nanny, carer, counsellor and administrator, to name just a few of the roles likely to be taken on.

1. Types of family office

Humans like to place things in boxes as part of their mental filing system. But this approach does not work when it comes to family offices. Just as every individual and family is different, so too is every family office – each with its own vision and objective. With every family office managing different amounts of wealth, and each looking after different quantities and generations of people, how does one determine the ideal manner in which to manage the family office? The best family office for the family is the office that fulfils its functions to achieve the family's objectives and vision. If it can do that, then it is the right type of family office. As opposed to a 'one size fits all' solution, family offices are all different in their own unique ways and they fulfil the function for which they were set up and have adapted accordingly.

Whether you are looking at establishing a new office, enhancing operations of an existing set-up or transforming the operations of a family office, it helps to take a closer look at some examples of various types of family offices.

A family office can range from an office on an estate, looking after the estate's assets, whether that is farming, forestry or sport, to an office based in one of the more glamorous and expensive streets in London, Switzerland or New York, looking at different possible private equity investments. There are all types of family offices that fit in between the two. There are offices run by one person and there are offices with up to 50 people in them.

We have listed below some examples of different family offices:

- estate office – an office on a landed estate or farm that looks after the assets as well as the affairs of the family;
- investment office – an office that is purely focused on investing in different assets on behalf of the family. This office might also act as an advisory office to another office based in a different jurisdiction;
- administration office – an office that purely deals with the administration needs of the family;
- multiple family office – an office that looks after the affairs and investments of more than one family, but is not a commercial business looking for new clients;
- legal office – an office set up for tax and legal reasons, run by the family or a set of trustees. There is a small number of staff which runs a small number of services and most functions are outsourced;
- general office – where there are more in-house staff to manage a number of limited functions but also to monitor the outsourced functions;
- comprehensive office – this office runs a broad set of functions, both in-house and outsourced.

## 2.	Size and wealth

When setting up a family office, one needs to ascertain some key criteria:

- the current and future size and dimensions of the family;
- the assets that the office will look after;
- the number of generational members currently alive who might use the office;
- the number of dependents the funds must support;
- the domicile of all relevant family members and the country in which they currently reside;
- the total size of assets/wealth of the family and of the individuals;
- whether the wealth is equally spread across the family or is in one branch of the family. And if the latter, whether that branch has more influence;
- what the average wealth is of each individual.

How the family office is organised and managed will vary quite considerably, depending on which generation or generations the family is serving, the size of wealth and the structures surrounding it.

3. Vision/objective

Figure 1: The process of establishing a family office

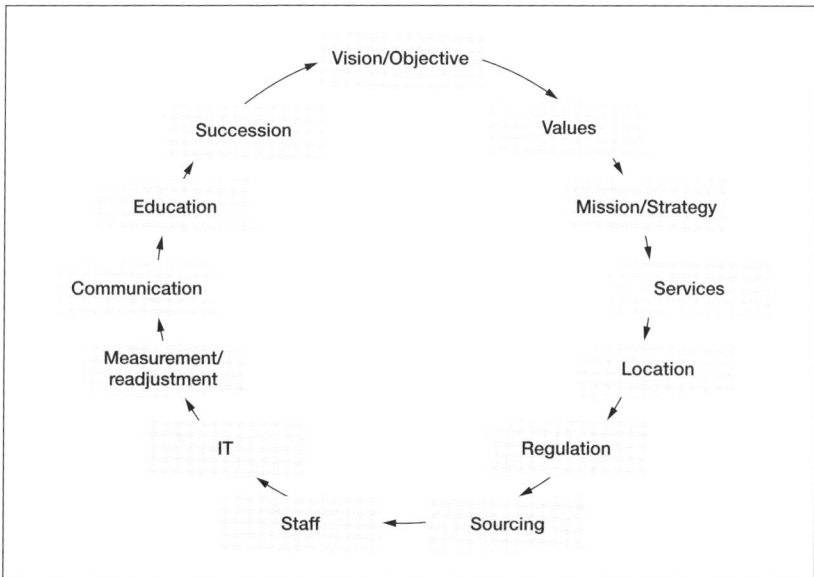

The first step in managing a family office is to establish a clear vision or objective for the office. Why is the office being set up in the first place? In some cases the family office will have emerged naturally out of a family business, or it could be in existence already as an estate office. What functions does it fulfil? What functions does it need to fulfil? Are the current needs in alignment with the original purpose?

It is a good idea to have a vision statement that defines the mid to long-term goals of the family office. It should contain:

- a stretch goal that might seem impossible at the present;
- how it is going to be achieved; and
- over what time period.

Without this vision, it makes it almost impossible to manage a family office efficiently. Most family offices are set up with the intention of preserving the wealth of the founder and family. Having a family office allows greater control and flexibility of the family's affairs. But just as with the progression of time, events can change the underlying purpose and vision, and therefore the function of the family office. So it is always good to review and adjust, to ensure needs are met through the appropriate structure, services and operations.

Figure 2: Single family office objectives

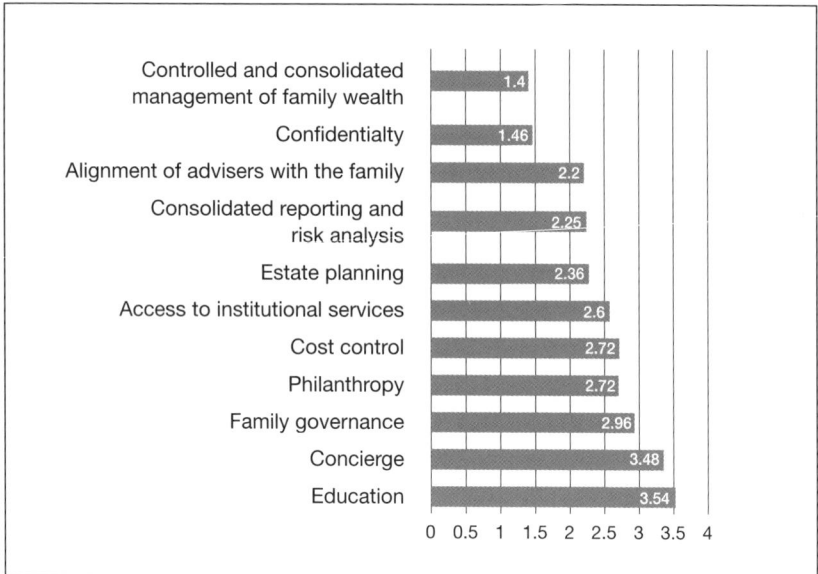

Objective	Value
Controlled and consolidated management of family wealth	1.4
Confidentialty	1.46
Alignment of advisers with the family	2.2
Consolidated reporting and risk analysis	2.25
Estate planning	2.36
Access to institutional services	2.6
Cost control	2.72
Philanthropy	2.72
Family governance	2.96
Concierge	3.48
Education	3.54

0 0.5 1 1.5 2 2.5 3 3.5 4

Source: UBS/Campden Research European Family Office Survey 2011.

A clear vision for what the family office has to achieve makes the next steps much clearer for those establishing and managing a family office. In planning the vision, it is a good idea to look forward two or three generations, and to try to predict the size and needs of the family. If thought can be given to that and to what sort of structure would function then, bringing it back to the present will lead to much better strategic planning.

The most common objective for family offices in Europe in 2011 was the control and consolidated management of the family wealth. The second was confidentiality, followed in third place by the alignment of advisers with the family. It is clear that family offices want to retain control of their assets, and want to be sure that the advisers they use are aligned with their interests. Surprisingly, the least important objective listed was education. Education and entrepreneurship are possibly the two most important functions of a family office.

4. Alignment of values

Every individual within a family has his or her own values. It is important that these values are aligned into one common set of values that the whole family buys into. It may be necessary to do the same exercise with the family office and the family business, but only after the individual family members have established what their values are. Values are the bedrock of human society and it is upon these values that the family, its wealth, its health and its business flourish. So if we see the vision as the compass setting, the values would be the guiding principles that steer the direction to get to the vision. The vision and the values bring together the various members of the family, uniting them to a unified underlying purpose. Most people assume they know what their values are, and yet experience has shown that only after reflection and inner knowing can they truly understand and vocalise them. Not meeting one's values is what typically creates disharmony and discord, both within an individual and the family unit. Hence, an understanding of and respect for one's own and others' values is essential for the overall success and longevity of the family members, the family unit and the family wealth.

Figure 3: An example of an individual's values after a values exercise

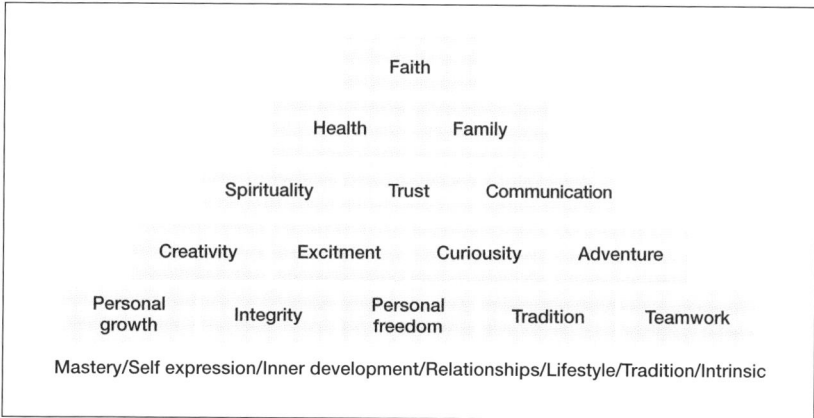

```
                              Faith

                    Health          Family

            Spirituality      Trust      Communication

        Creativity      Excitment      Curiousity      Adventure

    Personal                    Personal
    growth      Integrity       freedom      Tradition      Teamwork

    Mastery/Self expression/Inner development/Relationships/Lifestyle/Tradition/Intrinsic
```

5.   Mission/strategy

Strategy without tactics is the slowest route to victory. Tactics without strategy is the noise before defeat. – Anonymous

In the process of starting a family office, you should have defined your objective and understood what the family's unified values stand for. The next step is to decide how you will execute a strategy that will lead the family and the family office to achieving its set objectives. In October 2007, Tony Hayward, the chief executive officer of BP stated: "Our problem is not about the strategy itself, but about our execution of it." This is also relevant for family offices.

To quote Robert Kaplan from his very good book, *The Execution Premium*:

Managing strategy differs from managing operations. But both are vital and need to be integrated. Companies generally fail at implementing a strategy or managing operations because they lack an overarching management system to integrate and align these two vital processes.

Michael Porter, who invented the five forces strategy noted: "Operational effectiveness and strategy are both essential to superior performance ... but they work in very different ways."

It is important to have an effective strategy that is not lead by any financial budget. The danger is that the budget ends up co-ordinating, forecasting and evaluating the performance.

The family office needs to address three questions initially:

- What is the office for and why?
- What are the key issues?
- How can the office best perform?

The next step is to plan the strategy. A very good tool to use is a strategy map, which shows on one page a visualisation of how the strategy is to be executed, integrating the various components of the family office. This allows the office to build a plan around a collection of strategic themes. However, all are coherently linked to achieving the objective.

The strategy can be summed up in a mission statement. This is a brief statement that defines why the family office exists. It should describe the purpose of the office and what it provides to the family. It can also inform the family and office about the overall goal that the family office has been created to pursue.

How do you measure that strategy? It is important that the strategy has some measurables and targets, to check that what is being implemented is working and that the family office is on track. We talk about measuring and readjusting below.

The office needs to decide on the funding of the strategy and the allocation of assets to each of the different elements of the strategy. What are the sensible weightings? After that, there needs to be a person made responsible for the execution of each element of the strategy. In a small office that may well be the same person. Finally, there needs to be a person or team responsible for checking that the targets are being met.

Once the strategic plan is defined, it is important that all parts of the office are aligned and clear about the objective and the strategy. The staff should also be motivated correctly to be able to execute the strategy. We talk about that below in the section on staffing.

At defined times, the strategy needs to be tested and adapted. The world and the economy are constantly changing, as will many internal factors within the office. It is important to be realistic and open, and to be prepared to be flexible to changing situations and needs.

6. Services

Once a clear vision or objective has been decided, then it is important to decide what services the family office will carry out. As mentioned earlier, family offices are primarily focused on preserving the family's wealth. However, there are a number of other services a family office will carry out. Three of the most popular services provided by the family office are:

- tax planning;
- financial planning;
- trust monitoring and management.

However, as you can see from the table below, there are a number of other services that family offices may provide.

Figure 4: Services typically provided by a family office

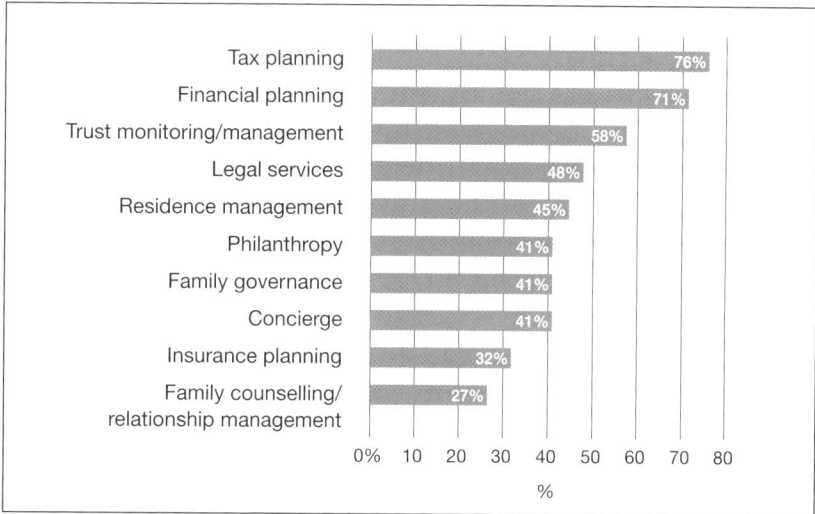

Source: UBS/Campden Research, European Family Office Survey 2011.

Although the above chart highlights the current focus of services provided by family offices, it is also worth noting that in 90% of cases, the wealth does not survive beyond the third generation. Hence, given that the primary function of the family office is to preserve and maintain wealth for current and future generations, one would be well advised to look at the above chart only as a guideline into what services should be provided, as opposed to viewing it as a prescriptive approach. Adjusting the focus on each service according to the needs and outlook of the family will in turn improve the continuity of the family's wealth and therefore, the success of the family office.

6.1 Key services

We have listed below the key services provided by a family office:

- tax planning – in-house tax planning will involve ensuring the family's wealth assets are placed in the most tax-efficient structures for the individuals' situation. It can also involve the filing of tax returns for family members;
- financial planning – the office will often take a top-down strategic approach to financial planning for the family members. As it has the full picture of every individual's position, it is able to structure the financial plans of every family member accordingly;
- trust monitoring/management – it is quite common for a family's wealth to be placed in a trust structure. The office will not only monitor the performance of the trust or trusts, but can administer them as well. In some cases the family office will create a trust corporation for the underlying trusts and act as trustee;
- legal services – quite often, a family office will have a legally trained person in the office who provides 'tax light' advice for the family. The more complex

and sophisticated legal issues will commonly be outsourced to specialist law firms, reducing the liability of the family office in providing complex legal advice and ensuring the best legal advice.

- insurance planning – the family office is able to provide cost-saving efficiencies for the family. It is able to consolidate all the various different insurance policies for the individual family members and negotiate a larger bulk discount for the family. It is also able to align all the insurance policies to renew at the same time in the year.

6.2 Other services

The family office can also provide other services such as:

- concierge;
- family counselling;
- family governance;
- philanthropy;
- property management.

7. Location

Where should one locate a family office? This will depend on a number of factors:

- where the family members live;
- where the family business or family enterprise offices are located;
- where the functions of the office are best fulfilled;
- where the best jurisdiction is in order to fulfil its services in a tax efficient manner.

8. Regulation

Regulatory issues are dealt with elsewhere in the book.

9. Sourcing

In order to be able to manage its duties efficiently and effectively, a family office will divide its services between those that are dealt with in-house, within the family office, and those that are outsourced to external service providers.

In deciding whether a service should be in-house or outsourced, one should take the following factors into consideration:

- skills of the family office staff;
- security of information;
- complexity of the service required;
- cost;
- security of assets;
- size of the family;
- wealth of the family;
- regulation;
- rate of change within that service, whether it be technological change or regulatory change; and
- sensitivity

Families are taking more control of strategic asset allocation decisions and are becoming more active. – UBS/Campden report, 2011

9.1 Possible in-house services

Listed below are some services that family offices have a tendency to keep in-house:

- administration of assets:
- bookkeeping/accounts;
- basic tax computation;
- budgeting and cash planning;
- oversight of custody services and banking services;
- delivery of consolidated financial reporting;
- paying bills;
- personal security;
- investment:
- strategic asset allocation – family offices tend to take control of the strategic asset allocation of the family wealth, including both liquid and illiquid assets;
- advice on or oversight of the assets;
- selection of wealth/investment managers;
- investment performance measurement;
- risk management;
- concierge services;
- succession planning;
- philanthropy:
- administration;
- grant making;
- trustee responsibilities.

9.2 Possible outsourced services

The following services are likely to be outsourced:

- tax advice;
- legal advice;
- accounting advice;
- banking arrangements;
- Education and training of the next generation;
- Advice on philanthropy.

9.3 Combined services

Some of the above services will either be carried out in-house or could be outsourced. This comes down to the size of the family office, the skills of the family office staff, and concerns over confidentiality and security.

Whatever sourcing route is taken, it is always important to remain flexible, balancing out cost, quality and effectiveness. And of course, one needs to measure these against the backdrop of the vision and purpose, readjusting as and when necessary, to ensure alignment between the service and the objectives.

10.   Staffing and running the office

Attracting and retaining talented staff to run the family office is always a challenge. Finding the right staff whom the family trust and like, as well as being able to carry out the specified tasks, is a time-consuming task. A family office, on the whole, is generally quite small and fulfils a broad spread of services within it. Therefore, finding, motivating and retaining staff who are capable of managing all or some of those services is difficult.

In the table below, we have shown from least important (larger number) to most important (smaller number) the main reasons that staff are attracted to working in a family office. The most important being an attractive working environment that provides job stability but rewards them with performance or incentive bonuses when they do a good job.

Figure 5: Important factors for recruiting and retaining senior family office staff

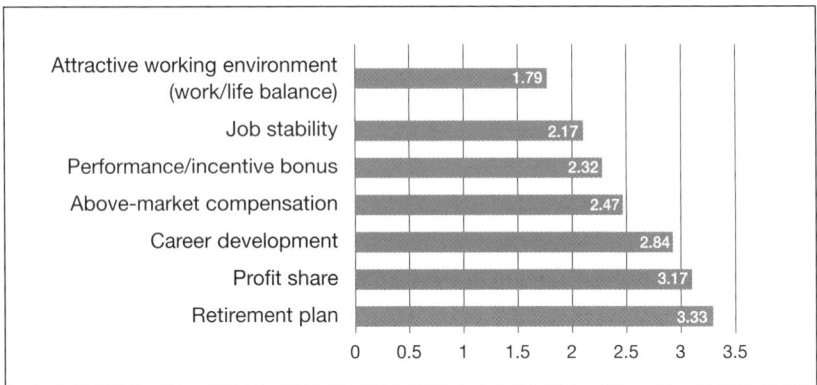

Source: UBS/Campden Research, European Family Office Survey 2011.

There is such diversity in the services of a family office that, naturally, every office varies in terms of size and number of people employed. In general, a family office will employ an average of 15 salaried staff, with the smallest employing just one person and over 40 in the larger offices, depending on the circumstances. In most cases, the majority of the staff will be focused on the investment side, be it the investment, legal, tax or accounting aspects.

Finding good, and more importantly trusted, family office staff is challenging, since they are highly sought after. Because of this, it is quite common to find staff transferred over from the family business or enterprise, with families gaining comfort and peace of mind from their first-hand knowledge and experience of the individual's track record, level of relationship and trust. In the case where a business is sold, some families choose to retain some senior executives as confidants and use them to help establish an office. In other cases, external candidates are recruited for their specific skills. In all cases, it is imperative for families to ensure the right calibre of people are chosen, both from a skills perspective and cultural fit, since these largely impact on and determine the success or failure of the family office. Just because someone was successful in the family enterprise does not mean they will fit in and thrive in the family office environment, and due care should be taken in ensuring the right people are on board.

10.1 External directors or advisers

Quite often family offices will appoint external advisers, directors or trustees, who provide impartial advice to the family and/or the office. They will either be selected to act as the family's business adviser or to bring a certain expertise to the proceedings. The important point to remember is whether they bring value to the organisation, and are not just shirt-tailing on the strength of being a close family friend. It is important that they remain impartial to all generations of the family and do not necessarily favour the founder. It is their independence that will help transition a family office from start-up to success. They must have the courage to ask difficult questions if they see something wrong, tackling things as they are presented, as opposed to letting them fester for someone else to deal with when their time is over.

10.2 Family members working in the family office

In determining who should work in the family office, the question arises of whether or not family members should do so.

Figure 6: A vision of the family future – scenario 1

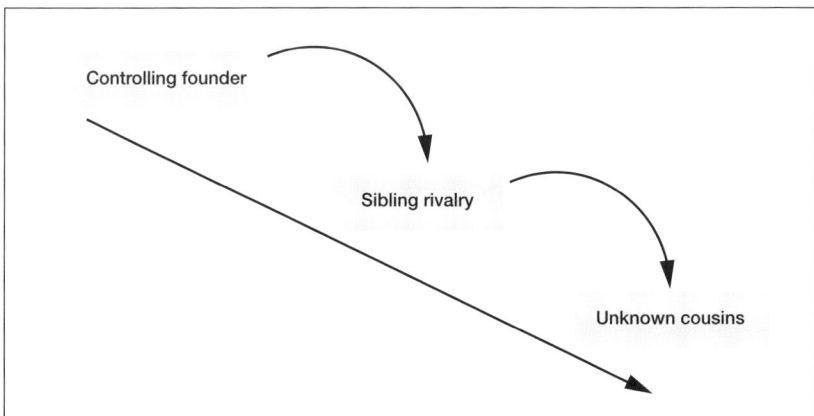

There appears to be a longer-term decline in the numbers of family members working full-time in their family offices. In some respects, this is healthy, in order to reduce conflicts of interest and to bring some semblance of impartiality to the office. Overall, it is the general view that it is probably preferable that family members work for the family business or enterprise rather than in the family office. This is especially the case when one considers the ever-present contentious issue of whether nepotism is encouraged or meritocracy is preferred.

When setting up and running a family office, the office will automatically take on the role of managing a group of intra-family personal relationships and characteristics. These will become more diverse with each generation, as close ties start to break down. If not managed carefully, greed, fear, jealousy and emotion can start to arise. If not handled carefully and fairly, then this can lead to a split within the family. It can lead to disputes, which can lead to more drastic action, such as litigation or contentious legal action against the trustees. Is having a family member working in the family office the right thing in those circumstances? The answer will only be known to those in that particular family and those working in the family office.

On the positive side, family members can bring quite a lot to the family office. They can take a long-term view of the strategy and success of the office. They are naturally aligned to ensure the office functions correctly and efficiently. They are also knowledgeable about the customer base: the family.

Figure 7: A vision of the family future – scenario 2

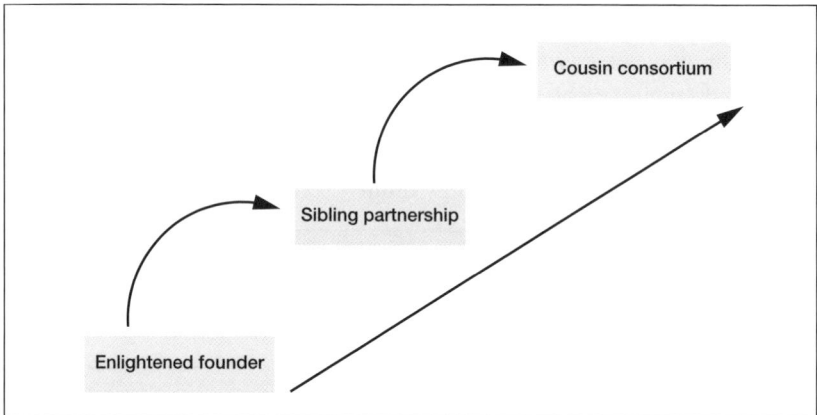

10.3   Providing a service to the family

It is important that the family office seeks to provide the very best service to the founder and the family. As the family grows generation by generation, this becomes much more pertinent. The loyalty that ties the family together in the early days can diminish as cousins do not know other cousins and their requirements start to differ. They could start to question the services being provided by the family office and the costs associated with that. They might not want to be controlled by other family members or the family office, nor might they want other family members having access to their personal financial affairs. Although the family office might, in some cases, hold the purse-strings, customer service becomes increasingly important by each generation. The office must be aware of the generational transitions and the differing service required by each generation. It must also be impartial in its service, and provide an equal and honest service to all family members, regardless of wealth or influence. If not, then other family members will start to question the function of the office.

The office may end up looking after the affairs of the spouse of a family member. It is at this point that the office must be professional, impartial and provide the service the spouse requires.

It may also be important to family offices that spouses are not privy to certain matters involving family members. The family office will have to manage that aspect of the client relationship so that the spouse does not feel like there is a 'them and us' approach.

10. 4   Disputes and conflict resolution

Disputes over inherited assets have always been a threat, and there are many instances of their having torn families and friends apart. The global credit crisis brought about a new level of potential turmoil, with lawyers indicating a 152% increase in the number of beneficiaries suing trustees for mismanagement.

Trusts are widely used in the United Kingdom to hold an individual's assets tax-efficiently for the benefit of third parties, usually family members, but the collapsing value of many of those assets, including shares and residential property, means more cases than ever are being brought to the High Court in London, with potentially ruinous consequences.

Disputes launched in the High Court over property held in trust jumped to 111 in 2010, up from 44 in 2009 and 13 in 2008. In 2007, before the credit crunch took hold, there were just three such cases. But with many cases settled out of court, these figures are likely to be the tip of the iceberg, according to the city law firm Wedlake Bell.

The trustees being sued are often family friends and relatives who may have taken on the unpaid role as a favour to the family. Fay Copeland, head of private client team for Wedlake Bell was cited in an article in The Independent on October 29, 2011, as saying:

The extreme volatility of the stock markets and other asset classes will have created a lot of big investment losses. Beneficiaries will want to recoup that lost money and suing the trustees is seen as one solution.

A lot of trustees are amateurs or 'lay' trustees, possibly a member of the beneficiaries' family, but unfortunately that doesn't provide them with a great deal of legal protection. Trustees have a duty to their beneficiaries which includes ensuring that the trust assets are properly managed.

10.5   Costs and pricing

How much does it cost to run a family office? How much should it cost to run a family office? Who pays for the family office and its services?

According to a survey carried out by Campden Research in 2011, the actual cost of running a family office is around 63 basis points of assets under management, with the average being around 73 basis points. This does not include the start-up cost of an office. Investment costs generally account for less than 50% of the office's total costs.

At the current time, a family would need above £50 million of investable assets to consider starting a family office, but it really depends on the family's situation.

Initially if there is a first generation founder, then the costs can sometimes be borne by them. However, as the family grows, the issue of how the office is funded will arise.

It is important at this point to remember the earlier point about service. Is the office providing value for money?

What are the most common costs:

- managing the family business holdings;
- managing liquid and illiquid assets;
- operating expenses of running the office, including salaries;
- fees and commissions of any external providers such as investment managers, banks, lawyers, accountants, insurance and IT support.

10.6 Should the family office be run to make a profit?

As a general rule, the office should be run efficiently, cost-effectively and to the highest possible standard in order to achieve the set objectives. Initially, it might not be a profit centre in the first generation or in the initial start-up phase. The profitability of the office is a decision that the family and executives of the office need to take. Obviously, it does not make too much sense if the office runs at a huge loss, but at the same time making money from the family is slightly unethical. If that is the case, then it would be worthwhile examining what services are provided to the family and where they are sourced from. As the family grows, this could become more of a concern.

11. IT

Information technology requirements in a family office are not much different from a normal business office – secure server (although this is often being replaced by cloud services), email, Word, Excel, PowerPoint and maybe an accounting package. The office may have extra news feeds from Bloomberg or Reuters. What differs from office to office is that the family may require a consolidated reporting and monitoring platform, in which case it will look to buy an off-the-shelf product. If it has some quite sophisticated investments or is a large family office, it may look to develop some bespoke software. If it is a regulated office, it will have much more onerous requirements, depending on the regulator of the jurisdiction in which the office is based.

12. Measurement and readjustment

Once the family office has been set up, the objectives have been set, the values defined and the strategy deployed, the next step is to monitor, learn, evaluate and measure in order to improve the performance of the office in meeting the objectives.

How do you measure the performance and effectiveness of the office and the strategy?

On the investments side, there are a number of ways of measuring performance, relative to a benchmark index or absolute performance. Some investments will only be valued at infrequent intervals, such as private equity investments. The office should be able to define what investment performance measures best suit the family members and how frequently they are used.

As regards the actual office, a useful way to measure it is to create a dashboard of key result indicators (KRIs) and key performance indicators (KPIs). These will tell you what to do to increase performance dramatically, and measure the key drivers from parts of the family office. The key differentiator between a KRI and a KRP is this: if it has a $ or £ sign in it, then it is a KRI and not a KPI. There should be between 10 and 20 indicators, and all should be associated with achieving the objective or vision set by the family and the office.

KRIs might include:

- client satisfaction – the clients in this case being the individual family members who use the services of the office;
- net profit before tax;
- profitability per family member;
- employee satisfaction;
- return on capital employed;
- cost to net assets ratio.

These will give a clear picture of whether the family office is doing the right thing. They do not, however, tell you what you need to do to improve those results.

These can be measured over a monthly or quarterly period. The office might consider using a balanced scorecard to measure performance. The balanced scorecard might be used for teams within the office if it is a large office, otherwise there are other tools that are effective in measuring and growing effectiveness.

KPIs represent a set of measures focusing on those aspects of the family office performance that are most critical for the current and future success of the family office. It is up to each family office to define what their KPIs should be, but their characteristics should include:

- non-financial measures;
- frequent measures;
- to be acted upon by the office's chief executive;
- all staff understand the measure and the action taken to correct it;
- ties responsibility to an individual or team;
- significant impact;
- positive impact;
- continual professional development.

KPIs should be measured daily, weekly or monthly as they measure what is key to the success of the family office. The KRI shows what has happened, but the KPI shows what is happening and how corrective action can be taken immediately. A KPI should tell you what actions need to take place and should be linked to a specific individual or team.

The balanced scorecard, created by Kaplan and Norton and shown below, is a useful tool to use within a family office. It helps with strategic mapping and is more satisfactory than the normal budget process. There are six different measures.

Figure 8: Adapted from Kaplan and Norton, The Balanced Scorecard – Translating Strategy into Action

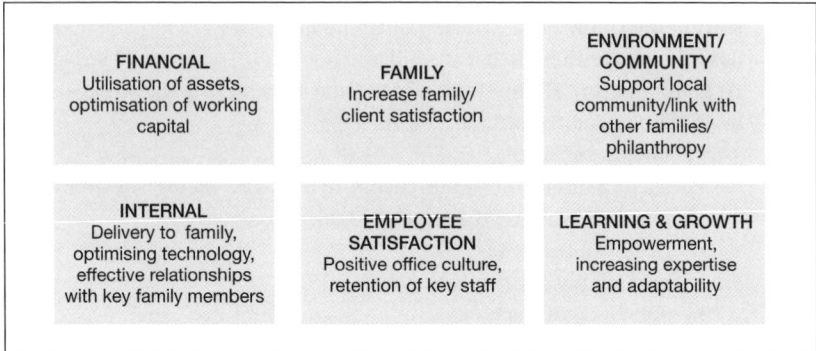

FINANCIAL Utilisation of assets, optimisation of working capital	FAMILY Increase family/ client satisfaction	ENVIRONMENT/ COMMUNITY Support local community/link with other families/ philanthropy
INTERNAL Delivery to family, optimising technology, effective relationships with key family members	EMPLOYEE SATISFACTION Positive office culture, retention of key staff	LEARNING & GROWTH Empowerment, increasing expertise and adaptability

Performance measurements are meaningless unless they are linked with the family office's vision/objective (which of course has to be aligned with the family's overall mission), the strategies (issues and initiatives) to achieve the objective, the balance scorecard and the critical success factors as outlined in the figure below.

Figure 9: Alignment of measurements

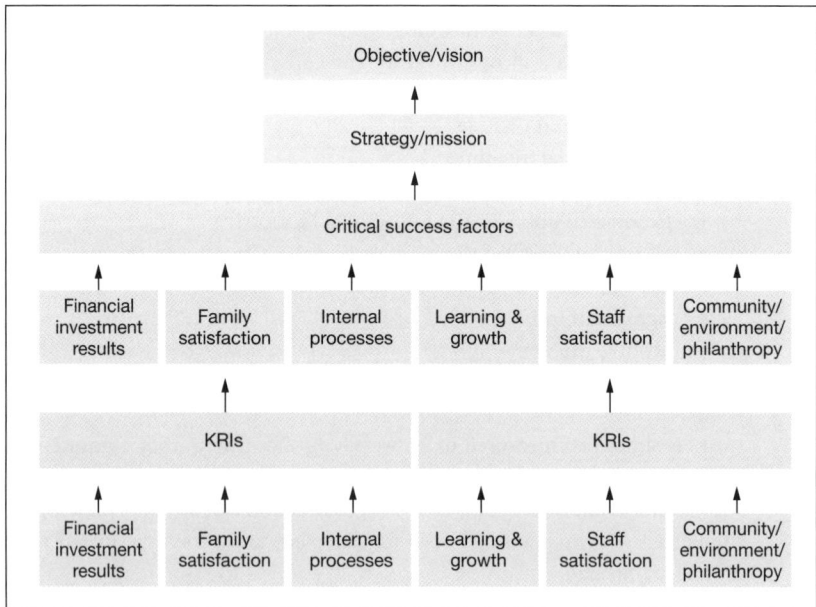

12.1 Leadership

No ship can be steered without a captain, and strong leadership is necessary and essential within a family office. A passive or absent leader will not be able to execute a successful strategy for the family office. The leader needs to be present. Moreover, the nature of the family office requires the leadership to be diverse and flexible in its strengths and capabilities. The office's leaders initially need the skills to harness the support and backing of the whole family. Then they need the leadership skills to define a strategy that will reinforce and meet the objective, mission/strategy and values of the family and family office. They then need to be able to lead, earn the respect of, and motivate the office staff to execute the strategy. The majority of leaders have a preference for a specific leadership style. Developing and deploying the flexibility required for the scenarios depicted above will determine the success or failure of the leader, and subsequently, the family office.

A lot of offices will feel more comfortable with committees or a board of directors. The board or committee format provides a more democratic and partnership-based forum in which to make decisions and review progress.

12.2 Fees

How do you charge the family for the services the family office provides?

Whichever method is chosen, the aim should be for it to be:

- fair;
- simple;
- transparent;
- competitive;
- tax-efficient;
- scalable.

The family office usually charges in two ways:

- asset-based fees;
- hourly or flat fee.

Let us initially take the first method: asset-based fees. This is probably the most common method used for charging, and it is very similar to how banks and wealth managers charge. Given that family offices tend to have a significant percentage of investment-related staff, this will be a model with which they are more familiar, and hence perhaps, more comfortable.

Asset-based fees probably work well in the early stages. However, as the family becomes multi-generational and the wealth starts to vary between individuals, some members of the family might use the office services a lot more than another individual. This could lead to accusations of unfairness from factions of the family who hardly ever require the family office's services.

There is also the issue of cost/income for the family office to consider. As a family expands from one generation to the next, so does the number of family members with each additional generation. At the same time, the wealth is dissipating, placing greater stress on the accumulated assets.

Hence, the issue of costs versus income arises. The family office needs to cater to and look after more and more family members whose net assets are worth less and less. One can see how the costs and number of administration people in the office potentially starts to rise, taking up a larger percentage of the underlying assets, which in turn are dissipating. This then would take us back to analysing whether the fee structure is right for the family, or whether the in-house services provided are correct. Ultimately, this would be a good time to review the purpose of the family office since, if it is the preservation of wealth, having a team of people to administer as opposed to growing wealth seems counter-productive.

If we look at the hourly fee charge, then this charging method, compared to the one above, looks as if it is probably more scalable over time, since it does not matter how many members of the family there are or what their net assets are worth, but rather what service is being provided to what family members.

Above all, members of the family must feel that they are getting value for money and a good service. If that is not happening, then there could be the potential for family members to become unhappy and a potential for splitting, seeing family members starting to break away from the family office.

12.3   Rewarding staff in the family office

Compensation, which is still a bit of a taboo for confidentiality reasons, is now more discussed by families and their family offices. – Christian Sulger Buel

Rewarding staff in the family office has traditionally been fairly opaque and secretive, with few guidelines that can be used. However, a survey conducted in 2012 found that pay varies considerably depending what type of family office it is and where it is situated geographically.

Figure 10: Family office salaries

	UK wealth[1]		International wealth[1]	Swiss-based wealth[2]	US[3]
	London	Regional	Switzerland	Switzerland	
CEO	£150,000 to £390,000	£110,000 to £175,000	CHF400,000 to CHF600,000 (£594,000 to £890,000)	CHF200,000 to CHF500,000 (£297,000 to £743,000)	$300,000 (£187,000)
CFO/ COO	£70,000 to £230,000	£75,000 to £85,000	CHF300,000 to CHF600,000 (£446,000 to £890,000)	CHF200,000 to CHF400,000 (£297,000 to £594,000)	$340,000 (£213,000)
CIO	£100,000 to £250,000	£80,000 to £250,000	CHF400,000 to CHF500,000 (£594,000 to £743,000)	CHF250,000 to CHF450,000 (£370,000 to £6668,000)	

Source: CampdenFO/Sulger Buel & Company survey over 25 single family offices in the UK and Switzerland, 2012.

1 plus bonuses. 2 optional bonuses. 3 Source: Prince & Associates, 2009.

The table shows the wide disparity in pay depending on the country, region and type of wealth being looked after. According to Russ Prince, President of Prince & Associates, "top people are not interested in downsizing and they want to earn more money, not less."

Figure 11: Family office bonuses (% of base)

	UK wealth[1]		International wealth[1]	Swiss-based wealth[2]	US[3]
	London	Regional	Switzerland	Switzerland	
CEO	20% to 50% Performance based	10% to 50% or none at all	Up to 50% of base	20% to 40% of base	$2.6 million Performance bonus
CFO/ COO	15% to 20% Discretionary	15% to 20%	Up to 40% of base	Discretionary	Participant model
CIO	Discretionary or benchmark index performance	Discretionary or benchmark index performance	Can be rate-of-return spread over several years	Discretionary	Participant model

Source: CampdenFO/Sulger Buel & Company survey over 25 single family offices in the UK and Switzerland, 2012.

1 plus bonuses. 2 optional bonuses. 3 Source: Prince & Associates, 2009.

12.4 Managing external providers and contacts

Some family offices will not provide all their services in house. This is either because they are not big enough, do not have the skills or it is too complex and too expensive. So these services are outsourced to external providers.

Quite often, the family office will oversee and monitor the external service providers to the family. They will take responsibility for negotiating the fees or rates, as well as monitoring the performance of these providers.

Once a family office becomes well known, it can start to suffer from spam. In this instance spam could include cold calls from fundraisers for charities, fundraisers for financial products or services, begging letters for donations and enquiries from the media. In these cases, the family office acts as the barrier between such people and the family. In order to determine who gets through and who does not, there are a number of different strategies family offices deploy to ensure the right level and quality of filtering. These can range from a systematic approach based on pre-defined criteria, established in alignment with the family office's and family's vision, mission and objectives, to something as simple as only dealing with people or businesses that were referred to them via people they know. As long as the right approach is adopted, the family office can become a very useful filter to the family.

13. Communication

60% of why families fail is due to lack of communication and trust. 25% is due to unprepared heirs. Only 3% is of failure is due to failures in financial planning, taxes and investments! – Williams and Pressier.

Communication is one of the most vital tasks that both the head of the family and the head of the family office must undertake. They must be able to communicate clearly, accurately, impartially and regularly with the different members of the family, including spouses and siblings. A breakdown in communication could lead to a breakdown in the family, the family business and the family office.

In today's world there are more and more platforms to use to communicate with the family: having a dedicated and secure website for the family to log into; producing a regular newsletter that covers both soft and hard issues; emails; mobiles; landlines; skype; apps; investment letters; and finally the family gathering. If this is done well, it will help act as the glue that keeps the family together over many generations.

13.1 Decision-making/governance

The family office will need a clearly defined mechanism of decision-making, especially once the office is managing multi-generations. Decisions are being made on behalf of family members and maybe even their spouses, on behalf of the office and with outside advisers. It is critical that whatever method is used, it has the full backing of the family and staff. This is even more important if there are spouses working in the family business or family office.

Above all, strong leadership is important in order to drive through both easy and difficult decisions, especially if the economic environment is very volatile.

14. Education

We would rate education as one of the most important pillars of a family office. Although not ranked highly by many family offices, it is without doubt a vital service for the family. Education of the family members should cover a number of areas. These could be:

- history of the family and family business;
- understanding the investment process;
- understanding what the family office does;
- understanding their personal financial situation;
- entrepreneurship;
- leadership;
- learning to work with their siblings or cousins;
- career mentoring;
- philanthropy.

Human capital is one of the main sources of the family's future wealth and success. One could go as far as saying that it is part of the family's overall wealth, the family members being assets themselves. Therefore it is important to invest time and money in them, and that does not just include academic education. The family needs to be supporting and encouraging the next generation of entrepreneurs and leaders from within the ranks. A future leader will be required to lead the family, family business and family office going forward. Support and encouragement from an early age will boost children's self-esteem and belief. It is very difficult for a subsequent generation to follow a successful entrepreneur. There are all sorts of issues that need to be overcome.

Philanthropy is a great education tool if used and handled correctly. Even better is the use of social enterprises for the next generation to practice their decision-making, investment, management and entrepreneurial skills.

15. Succession

In many respects, the family office is fulfilling the function of succession if you look at the services it provides. However, the future survival of the family, and therefore the family office, depends on the succession of the following:

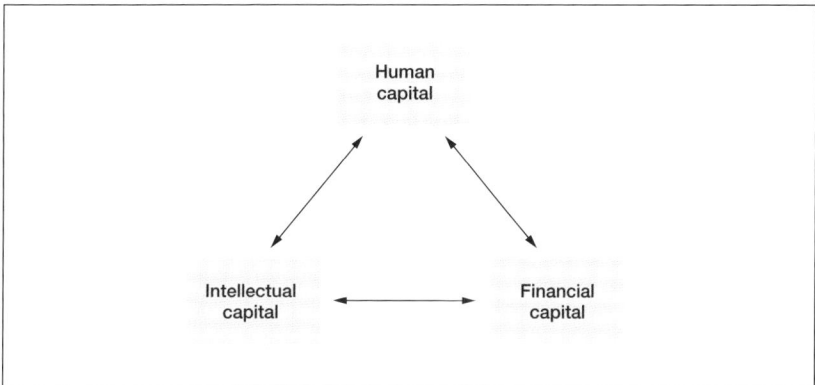

It is essential that the founder, the leader, the head of the family, and the head of the family office all address the issue of succession. There are three parts of succession (as shown above) and all need to be addressed individually and revisited regularly as the world's economic and social environment changes. The odds are stacked against both the family wealth and the family business surviving multiple generations, so a well-planned succession strategy is an essential task of the family office.

16. Future family office vision

Based on the current projection, what could the future family office look like in the next 30 to 50 years?

Over the past 50 years people have begun to live longer. Current life expectancy in the United States is 80 years. This century, we will regularly start to see four generations alive at one time, and possibly working in the family business together. However, we are starting to see fewer children per family as more and more people move into cities and become wealthier.

If everybody is living longer, there will be a greater call on income, as there will

Life expectancy in the United States

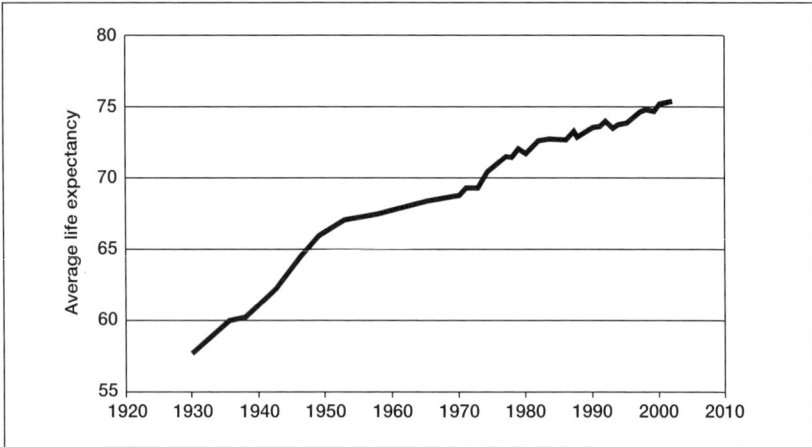

be more mouths to feed in a family unit. Where will this income come from? Possibly income will come from the dividend of the family business. This will put pressure on the family business to produce increasing dividends. Does the family business have a strict dividend pay out policy? It is sometimes a good idea to have it documented in the family constitution, if the family has one. The other source of income will come from investments – liquid and illiquid. The family office of the future may well require higher returns, which will involve it being tempted to take greater risks. This is especially so in an environment where markets could become even more correlated, due to computer technology monitoring market differentials much more than has ever been done before.

Investment strategies will become much more short-term than they are now, as the markets become more volatile. This volatility will be driven by the micro-managing of news events. Computers will be programmed in a more sophisticated way to read potential risks or market moving events. High frequency trading in 2012 make up a third of all trades in the United Kingdom and 60% in the United States. Humans will become less important in the process. Family offices will have an overall long-term vision or object but will use short-term strategies to achieve that objective. What is driving this? It is the exponential rate of change.

We are seeing an exponential rate of change in the word around us. Humans see everything in a linear way, but the rate of change of technology for instance, is measured against Moore's Law and it is increasing at an exponential rate.

Technology will continue to develop at a rate not seen before. It will make its way into every part of our lives, including the human body. Our knowledge bank will get broader and thinner until we have a built-in Wikipedia in our brains. Also many services currently provided by the family office will be replaced with technology.

There will be many more family offices. Technology will lower the entry cost to set up a family office as well as the day-to-day running costs. It will be economical to have a family office with just $20 million despite the increasing size of families.

More and more families will have more than one business in order to drive the desired investment returns. We call this a family enterprise.

What could stop the exponential rate of growth of new family offices is regulation. We have started to see this with the introduction of the Dodd Frank Law in the United States. Across the world, regulations will make the services of a family office more onerous and restricted. This could in turn restrict the ability to make the necessary returns to prevent wealth dissipation.

It will become ever harder to preserve wealth. Tax evasion and tax exiles will virtually disappear as more loopholes are shut down. The returns in the global stock markets will become more correlated, and any movements watched more carefully by computers. Great risks will have to be taken in order to make the necessary returns, but regulation will make it harder.

We have already seen the creation of trusts in the United Kingdom decrease as new tax laws affect them. This could spread across other jurisdictions as governments seek ways to raise money. So it will be hard to preserve wealth for the next generation.

The next generation will be more knowledgeable than ever before. They will also ask more questions and expect more answers. And if they do not get answers, they will take more legal action. Recent years have seen an increase in litigation and contentious trust issues.

With a move away from the financial markets and a desire to build stronger enterprises to produce increased income streams, more families will be looking to collaborate with other families.

The banks' business model for servicing family offices will change. They will have less discretion over the family office's assets and will instead execute the office's strategies.

Family offices are taking more control of their service provision.

So the future looks mixed, with added complexity. Recent years have already left an indelible mark on some families, and navigating the road ahead will take tenacity, courage and strength of character. This is not necessarily about taking high-risk decisions, but rather about having the courage to ignore the cacophony, and instead lead through strong principles, shaping values and executing a strategy that leads to achieving the family's objectives.

17. Other matters to consider in managing a family office

There are a number of other issues that may well arise in managing a family office, that are considered elsewhere in this book:

- succession planning;
- conflict resolution;
- disaster recovery;
- family governance/constitution;
- philanthropy;
- security;
- reputation management.

Investment

Charles Peacock
Alex Scott
SandAire

---

1.   Management

While the term 'family office' can incorporate multiple forms of business and services, the core function of the great majority will be oversight and management of the financial assets of one or more families. In this chapter we will address the investment and associated activities that are central to the fulfilment of this responsibility.

The management of assets, rather than oversight (a role that could simply involve receipt, consolidation and analysis of reports from one or more investment organisations) provides the greatest scope for interpretation and management in each office. Families that have decided to incur the cost and complexity of choosing to have a family office have done so because they believe that the outcome of this decision will be a better response to the family's investment requirements than that of a third party bank or investment manager (though the services of external financial institutions are likely to be employed via delegation).

Having concluded that a family office is the right route to pursue (as examined further in the chapter on establishing a family office) the choice lies between an office dedicated to one underlying family (the single family office) or one serving the needs of many families with similar investment requirements (the multi-family office). Both forms are likely to be dedicated to serving families rather than institutions, and the key differences are likely to be those of the size of resource that can be applied to management of a family's financial affairs and the fact that a multi-family office's services are not delivered exclusively.

The costs of running a single family office will need to be paid for by one family, so the asset base under management needs to be sufficiently large to ensure that the annual compensation bill is proportionate to the value that the family office is capable of adding. The fact that it is increasingly expensive to build and run a financial services business with appropriate skills and competencies has led to the emergence of multi-family offices as an alternative to the single family office.

The key roles and responsibilities that the employees of the family office are likely to undertake can be described under three main headings:
- investment (responsible for investment strategy, asset allocation, portfolio risk management and all investment related functions, e.g. safe custody);
- operations (responsible for reporting investment performance and the management of the investment office); and
- finance (responsible for financial reporting, operational cash flows and risk management).

For the purposes of this chapter, we will focus on the first two. The smaller the office, the greater the chance that more of these functions are part of the chief executive's remit, and herein lies one of the most important decisions facing a family setting up a single family office: is the size of our liquid portfolio sufficient to warrant the recruitment of one or more experts to deliver the services outlined in this chapter? Can we recruit appropriate talent to deliver what we need? If the costs of fulfilling the responsibilities to the level of professionalism required are greater than approximately 0.75% of the value of the family's portfolio, the impact of such costs compounded over many years will be significant. The family (and their trustees and advisers if appropriate), must believe that the value thereby created is sufficient to warrant the cost. This cost/value trade-off will be on the minds of those establishing a single family office: if we must limit numbers of employees to ensure that costs are appropriate to the size of our portfolio, are we putting too much responsibility on the shoulders of too few? Will we sleep at night if the resulting office is so small as to be vulnerable? The challenge of acquiring appropriate expertise at an appropriate cost is one of the drivers behind some families' decisions to appoint a multi-family office rather than create a single family office. The bigger the family balance sheet, the less sensitive the cost/value decision.

The breadth and depth of skills available in-house to a family office will be of a different scale in comparison to most financial institutions, and it is for this reason that many of the functions necessary for the effective management of the portfolio will be sourced externally. Most family offices will choose to retain control only over those functions that they feel are necessary to the successful execution of their (or their clients') strategies. Their capacity to source appropriate external skills, to manage the resulting relationships both directly and as part of a wider web of interrelated relationships, to integrate the results of these external providers into a coherent strategy for the owners, to report on the outcomes and to deliver the family's financial strategy will be a fundamental factor in determining their success.

2. Asset allocation

As is discussed in the chapter "Setting an investment strategy", we anticipate that all family offices will take a multi-asset class approach to the management of the wealth for which they are responsible. At a minimum, there are likely to be three asset classes, namely equities, fixed income and cash. More likely, a family office will also consider property, private equity, commodities and possibly collectibles (eg art, wine and cars). Hedge funds are sometimes cited as a separate asset class, although we would argue that most are essentially a style of management of the assets listed above, whether in equity or fixed income. An example of this would be a 'long/short' equity manager, who essentially merely takes a different approach to managing the risk in a portfolio, compared with a 'long-only' equity manager.

The importance of asset allocation lies in the fact that research[1] has shown that

---

1   See, eg, Brinson, Singer and Beebower, "Determinants of Portfolio Performance II: An Update", *Financial Analysts Journal* volume 47, number 3 (May/June 1991); Ibbotson and Kaplan "Does Asset Allocation Explain 40, 90 or 100 Percent of Performance?", *Financial Analysts Journal* volume 56 number 1 (January/February 2000).

asset allocation explains about 90% of the variability of a fund's returns over time. It follows that this is the most important decision that a family office will take both at outset and as the portfolio grows and changes.

Investment returns vary across asset classes predominantly in accordance with economic conditions. While it is possible to have a view as to the likely relative performance of asset classes, accurately forecasting the magnitude of the returns in either nominal or inflation adjusted terms has proved to be elusive.

Empirical observations tell us something about very long-term returns for asset classes. Investors in equity, for example, seek a premium over the returns on bonds to compensate for the associated additional risk. Looking back at historical returns shows that these have varied between markets and over different time periods. Nonetheless, by way of example, Dimson, Marsh and Staunton of the London Business School calculated in their paper "Global Evidence on the Equity Risk Premium"[2] that the geometric mean equity risk premium, relative to government long bonds, was 4.8% for the United States and 4.2% for the United Kingdom.

The variability of returns over the short term is, however, so large and persistent that the simple rules-of-thumb described above are blunt instruments for the real world task of meeting a family's financial requirements and objectives. By way of illustration, the table below shows the volatility of annual total returns for UK gilts (government bonds), sterling corporate bonds and five major equity indices over the past six years.

Annual returns (%)	2008	2009	2010	2011	2012	2013
UK gilts	13.0	-1.3	7.6	16.9	2.8	-4.3
Sterling corporate bonds	-9.9	15.1	8.7	5.4	15.6	1.9
FTSE All Share	-29.9	30.1	14.5	-3.5	12.3	20.8
S&P 500	-14.2	14.1	19.2	2.7	10.8	29.8
FTSE Europe ex UK	-27.1	23.4	7.0	-15.2	17.3	23.8
Japan	-2.7	-4.5	19.5	-13.1	3.2	24.8
FTSE Emerging Markets	-35.8	64.8	24.1	-18.5	12.6	-5.4

Note: UK gilts – ML UK Gilts Index; Sterling corporate bonds – iBoxx GBP Corporate Bond Index

---

2   Available at: faculty.london.edu/edimson/assets/documents/Jacf1.pdf (September 2002).

Assuming sensible diversification within a portfolio, the impact of weaker performing investments can be offset, or at least moderated, by better performing ones. Nonetheless, the allocations that are adopted will clearly determine the eventual return achieved by the portfolio. As no asset class consistently outperforms, investors need to consider carefully the weightings they adopt for each.

There is, however, no single approach to asset allocation, although most family offices will adopt a strategic asset allocation, as discussed in the chapter "Setting an investment strategy". This strategic asset allocation may be expressed as a benchmark, which sets out default weightings for each asset class within a portfolio. Commonly, there are a number of different approaches to managing the allocation to the different asset classes over time:

- an allocation that is rebalanced at set time periods through the sale/purchase of investments;
- an allocation as above but where rebalancing takes place not on a periodic basis but as and when the percentage represented by a particular asset class varies from the default position by more than a certain amount;
- active allocation, whereby the default or neutral position represents the spread of investments where the manager has broadly equal conviction on the prospects for each asset class.

Under this last approach, the family office takes a considered view of the stages of the economic cycles in major economies around the world, political issues, the state of financial markets and valuations to assess the prospects for returns from each asset class. Typically, if wealth is to be managed along these lines, minimum and maximum asset class limits and drawdown risk tolerance are agreed with the client and provide clear parameters for the manager of the assets.

Whether changes to asset allocation are semi-automatic, by way of rebalancing in the first two approaches above, or tactical, by active management, the frequency with which they are done is an important decision since all will involve cost. The costs may include the difference in the bid-offer price spread, brokers' commission or managers' upfront fee, duty or tax and possibly the exchange rate spread if the investment is not in the portfolio's base currency. These costs may add up if rebalancing is frequent, and weigh on the returns. In the case of some individual or one-off transactions, such as those involving property, the associated transaction costs can be very considerable.

Where an active tactical allocation approach is taken, the frequency in trading will also be influenced by the philosophy of the family office or wealth-owner with regard to market timing (the timing of investment purchases and sales with reference to the level of state of financial markets). This is notoriously difficult, particularly at times of instability and limited investment visibility. A decision needs to be taken whether the focus should be on the longer (multi-year) investment cycles, shorter-term movements resulting from volatility or, to some extent, a mix of the two.

A final point is that the liquidity of investments (the ability to sell them quickly at a not significantly discounted price) will also influence the scale of rebalancing or the frequency of change in asset allocation. Investments in property and private equity can require multi-year commitment and hedge funds often have a minimum investment period followed by a rolling lock-up period. Consequently, rebalancing over shorter periods will be limited to the more liquid investments, a consideration when seeking to manage the level of risk carried in a portfolio.

While asset allocation is a critical element of investment management, it is equally important to understand and manage the risks associated with each asset. We expand on risk later in the chapter but would note here that risk is a more controllable element in portfolio management than the returns are. This proved particularly important in the immediate aftermath of the financial crisis that broke in 2007/2008, when market volatility was often at elevated levels.

Consequently, risk should sit at the heart of the investment process, and the family office should seek clear agreement with the wealth-owners as to the limits or guidelines on the level of the downside (or drawdown, a measure of the change in values from the peak to trough) risk that they are prepared to accept. The level of risk that wealth owners can tolerate will depend on a host of factors, including the quantum of their wealth and of their investible assets (recognising that much may be tied up in a family estate, company or other businesses), the time horizons over which they will judge performance and the purposes for which they wish to use their wealth.

While historical returns are not a reliable guide to future returns and risks will vary over time, influenced in part by asset valuations, there is great value in a process in which the family office and wealth-owners consider together the risk associated with generating returns. It helps to ensure that there is a clear understanding that returns are rarely generated without risk, and allows wealth-owners to review and align their financial objectives and expectations with their attitude to risk. There should consequently be less scope for (unpleasant) surprises, even in the event that financial markets develop unfavourably.

3.   Investment

After asset allocation has been determined, the focus switches to portfolio construction: selecting the assets that best meet the investment strategy. The family office will need to have regard for a number of what we might call operational issues that will impact on the population of possible investments. These may include the style of returns, investment restrictions or stipulations.

The family office will need to have regard to whether a particular style of return is required. For example, there may be a need for a certain level of income, which will produce an income bias to the investments that a manager may select – that is to say that only investments that produce an interest, dividend or rental yield may be eligible for such a portfolio. This may particularly be the case where there are life interests or restrictions on the distribution of capital. Alternatively, the portfolio might be run on a total return basis, where the manager seeks the optimal (risk-adjusted) overall return from both income and capital, and any shortfall in required income can be distributed from capital. A total return approach provides a much greater range of potential investments to select from. Examples include many hedge funds that have 'non-distributor' status (ie, they do not distribute income), property development where capital gain is the goal, commodities, gold and collectibles.

Taxation may also influence selection, for example if investors are subject to different effective rates of tax on capital gains and income. Particular care, for example, needs to be taken for UK investors with funds that do not have distributor status due to the unequal treatment of gains and losses.

The family office will also have to take account of any restrictions or stipulations imposed by the wealth-owner. It is not uncommon to find that wealth-owners have a bias towards sustainable businesses and investments, and want to avoid those involved in, say, the armaments industry or businesses that are viewed as unethical or environmentally unfriendly.

These criteria apart, the family office will be faced by a number of decisions. Should it, for example, invest directly into individual company shares or bonds? The answer to this will be partly influenced by the resource issues mentioned at the start of this chapter. Does the family office wish to recruit staff to research satisfactorily individual investments across the public equity and bond markets? Besides that, will individual share investments make a great enough impact on performance to warrant such a resource?

The family office can, alternatively, make investments through passive funds (eg, exchange-traded funds) or draw on the expertise of third-party managers, either through collective investments (funds) or segregated accounts. Exchange-traded funds have become increasingly popular among investors, since they represent a low-cost way of accessing certain asset classes, such as equities. Exchange-traded funds are now available that offer high liquidity for investing in many of the indices of the larger equity markets around the world.

In some more developed markets, such as the United States, exchange-traded funds are also available for particular sectors, facilitating investment in industries that are perceived to outperform at different stages of the economic cycle. As mentioned above, exchange-traded funds are generally low cost, particularly in comparison with managed funds, are simple to trade, and provide an effective way of increasing or reducing exposure to the market. Consideration should be given to counterparty risk if derivatives are used to replicate an index in an exchange-traded fund.

While funds offer the opportunity to access expertise of specialist managers, many fail to outperform their benchmark index consistently over the longer term and across the economic cycle. It is not unusual to find that new funds start strongly but, over time, show a tendency to trend towards tracking the benchmark index. It is also worth remembering that, due to management fees and other costs, a manager will normally have to outperform the index in gross terms to deliver a performance equal to the benchmark or the slightly lower (compared with the benchmark) return of the exchange-traded fund.

An additional point of consideration in the choice between exchange-traded funds and managed funds is how quickly one can make or realise an investment. While exchange-traded funds normally have real-time pricing and allow intra-day trading, the ability to reduce exposure in a managed fund can be constrained by them only having daily, weekly, monthly or less frequent trading. Furthermore, certain funds, especially hedge funds, impose longer fixed initial investment periods, and retain the right to gate investors to prevent a significant outflow of funds. They may do this at times of heightened uncertainty or risk in the markets, to prevent forced selling of underlying investments at discounted prices due to limited liquidity, which would prejudice the interests of continuing investors.

All that said, managed funds may well be the investment of choice for many family offices. They may be the only effective way of accessing a particular asset class or investment strategy. They may also be favoured where the chief investment officer or portfolio manager anticipates that deriving returns on an asset class will be less reliant on beta (the returns delivered by investing passively in a market) and more on alpha (value added by skill of a manager in making investment decisions).

The key question then is how to choose from the vast array of collective investment vehicles. A rigorous approach to selection is recommended. From the asset allocation process, there should be a clear idea of the style of investment sought in each asset class. Specialist fund databases (such as Morningstar) allow screening for investment candidates meeting specific criteria. At this stage the process really involves removing those that are not of interest, because, for example, their historical performance has been relatively weak. While it is certainly true that historical performance is no guarantee of future performance, it does provide some insight into a manager's ability to add value.

Other factors that should be considered include the following:

- Volatility – how much risk has been taken on in delivering the returns, and is that consistent with the investment strategy of the fund?
- Fees – high fees provide a drag on performance, so care should be taken to look at the net total return after all costs. There are different levels of fee payable in many funds and care should be taken to ensure that a family office is paying the fee appropriate for the level of investment they are likely to make.
- People – the individuals involved are key, although the level of their importance will vary, depending on whether the fund management firm's structure is along the lines of a star manager or a team/process approach. Continuity and a break therein might have a dramatic effect on future performance compared with the past. If the family office wishes to have access to the fund manager on a regular basis to receive reports first hand, this is also something that should be established at the outset.
- Liquidity – how quickly can the investment be sold to raise cash or execute an asset allocation change?
- Operational aspects – a family office is likely to make fairly meaningful investments in funds. The greatest concern is that the capital should be safe and not subject to loss through fraud, as happened with Madoff's infamous fund, a one-time darling of the asset management industry. Two particular points to focus on are whether the performance reported is consistent with what is understood to be the investment strategy and approach, and whether there is proper risk management and governance. Any material variance, or indeed resistance from the manager to providing information, should set off alarm bells. Where there is inadequate governance, separation of responsibilities and other risk management procedures in place, there is a heightened risk of fraud or other irregularity.

Once managers have been selected and investment made, the family office will monitor the performance of the funds to ensure that it is both satisfactory and in line with what was expected. We will return to this later.

There are consultants who advise on manager selection and to whom a family office could outsource this part of the investment process. Similarly, there are the organisational aspects of dealing, settlement, record-keeping and custody to be considered, and a decision to be made as to whether to keep these functions in-house or outsource. For a family office, the question of custody is likely to be a straightforward decision to use one or more third-party custodians. The strength of the custodian's balance sheet and availability of segregated accounts for clients are key considerations for clients of a multi-family office (as they have delegated responsibility rather than building their own family office) because a multi-family office is likely to be more thinly capitalised than the major banks offering such services. The advantage of third-party custodians is also that they have the resources and systems to deal with the regular flow of activity associated with holding investments, be they dealing with dividend receipts or payments in response to calls from private equity funds in relation to commitments made.

As noted earlier, risk is inextricably linked with investment. Some of the main risks that investors are concerned about are the following:

- Counterparty and credit risk – for example, in the case of investment in a bond, investors are exposed to the risk that the bond issuer (borrower) defaults and is unable to pay the interest or repay some or all of the principal, resulting in loss on investment.

- Interest rate risk – if interest rates rise, values of fixed interest bonds are likely to fall so that their yields are aligned with then current rates. This may make no difference to the overall return if an investor holds them to maturity but the decline in capital value will be reflected in the shorter-term performance reported.

- Inflation risk – we touched on this above but, more generally, inflation undermines the preservation and growth of wealth by or for family office clients.

- Custody risk – also noted above, this is an important consideration, since the custodian is the legal owner of the assets. Much can be done to reduce the risks associated with a custodian failing by insisting on segregated client accounts (assuming that the custodian's systems and controls ensure this is done in practice).

In moving from the asset allocation decision to asset selection, there are still many factors to consider in choosing which investments offer the appropriate, or at least most acceptable, risk/reward balance. In brief, we would highlight the following.

Cash and money market funds: Counterparty risk is an important consideration here. For most family offices, the amounts being dealt with mean that government compensation schemes to protect retail investors will offer insufficient recompense in the event of failure. Banks used for deposits must be selected with care, and similar issues lie behind the use of money market funds, even if the risk exposure is reduced through a greater spread of underlying institutions. Higher interest rates will generally not compensate for even a partial loss of capital from what should be the safest part of a portfolio.

Fixed income: This is a huge and diverse market worldwide, and ranges from government bonds, debt instruments issued by supra-national institutions (such as the World Bank) to corporate debt. Investors can choose between investment grade, high-yield and distressed debt, their decision influenced by their outlook for the economic cycle, interest rates, corporate profitability and an assessment of default risk specifically or more generally. There are agencies (such as Standard & Poor's, Moody and Fitch) that produce ratings and research on issuers of debt, denoting how safe they view them to be. Ratings are based, however, on the interpretation of information relating to the issuer and also on anticipated macro-economic conditions. The start of the financial crisis in 2007/2008 demonstrated that the creditworthiness of quite a number of issuers was less robust than their respective ratings had previously suggested. It is also worth remembering that the ratings agencies are not completely free of potential conflicts of interest in that they are paid by the issuers.

Public equity: The outlook that determines the tactical asset allocation will also inform the profile of exposure sought through public equity. Consideration will be given to where in the world to invest and what exchange rate risk is appropriate. This is less straightforward than simply looking at the different countries' equity markets and assuming that each will produce outcomes similar to the underlying economy, since global markets have become more correlated over recent years. Nevertheless, volatility varies between markets and some offer greater liquidity than others. For a UK investor seeking international exposure, a consideration may be the extent to which it gets this, *de facto*, by investing in the major UK-listed companies, since many of these are either foreign companies or derive the majority of their revenues and profits from countries other than the United Kingdom. Similar considerations will apply for some of the other major stock markets.

Another variable in the equity sphere is the degree to which the investor favours large or small cap (capitalisation) companies and, from a style point of view, value or growth (mature businesses more able to deliver dividends or those at an earlier stage in their evolution). Having considered this, the next decision is whether to invest in individual stocks, through exchange-traded funds for low-cost broad market exposure or through managed funds. As noted before, liquidity is a consideration, but funds may well be the only cost-effective route to access the desired strategy or market with the required expertise. If the investment environment is one in which markets overall are not expected to deliver real returns, concentrated stock-picking funds and long-short funds may be favoured in a search for alpha.

Private equity: There are a number of routes into private equity, the main two being by direct purchase of an interest in an unlisted company (or partnership) or by investment in a private equity fund. Perhaps the most important feature of this asset class is the acceptance of significantly reduced liquidity and, if directly investing in a company through a minority shareholding, fewer investor protections than are typically enjoyed with listed companies. Directly investing into an unlisted company provides a concentrated exposure, but may also offer the investor a seat on the board of the business and other involvement or influence. The period of lock-up in the company and prospect of dividends is clearly dependent on the performance of the company and, at an extreme, the investor carries the risk of total loss if the venture is unsuccessful.

The fund route provides reduced risk of total loss, since a fund diversifies the risk by investing in a number of opportunities and can offer access to experienced private equity investors/managers with the resources to carry out in-depth due diligence. At the same time, funds normally carry an extended lock-up, generally at least 10 and sometimes up to 15 years, and relatively high management fees during the life of the fund. Given the length of this relationship, investors should be satisfied that the manager has the process, contacts and capability to deliver on their promise, since evidence of success takes time to show. One further important feature to bear in mind is that the full investment commitment is not normally drawn down immediately but over a number of years. Adequate cash resources or liquid investments need to be maintained within the portfolio to meet unexpected calls, some of which could come at a time when financial markets put investment portfolios under pressure.

Property: The principal decision here is whether to invest directly in property or to go through funds. Other important decisions include: whether the purpose is to invest for income/yield or capital gain; what type of property, for example, commercial (office, industrial etc) or residential (for lettings); and where in the world to invest. Many family offices tend to favour their own country as their underlying families have the comfort of greater familiarity and a better understanding of their home market.

These choices will be affected by the amount of money available for investment in the asset class and what is viewed as being an acceptable level of concentration or exposure in individual properties. Where direct investment is concerned, instead of going it alone, a family office may prefer to club together with other families or investors.

If investment is through funds, this could be done through listed property companies or real estate investment trusts, or unlisted funds and limited partnerships. While shares in real estate investment trusts can normally be readily purchased or sold, the related share price movements will often be more volatile than the underlying net asset values. Unlisted funds, by contrast, tend to come with a multi-year commitment, and the ability to exit early is severely restricted. As a consequence, investment in property will frequently involve a degree of illiquidity. The reduced frequency and speed with which an investor can trade these investments will mean that, along with private equity, property will often represent a less variable element of an investment portfolio. Investment choices on property will accordingly be influenced more by the longer-term strategic asset allocation and less by shorter-term tactical weightings.

Commodities: Unless one has or can readily arrange storage facilities, investors will mostly access this asset class through specialist managed funds or derivatives. For certain commodities, namely precious metals such as gold, exchange-traded funds are available and provide investors with an ability to trade in the metal in a similar way to equities.

Other: In addition to the main financial asset categories above, family offices may look to invest in other assets, including wine, art and other collectibles. The extent to which they do will most likely be influenced or directed by the underlying families. These other assets will typically require specialist knowledge or skills (particularly for selection and authentication) and services (such as storage, security and insurance), and the family office will need to decide whether it wishes to build in-house expertise or rely on third-party advisers. Traditionally investment in such assets has been direct, but a growing number of specialist funds have sprung up to meet investor interest.

4. Compliance

Compliance is a wide-ranging subject and is important at different levels. At a high level, the decision whether to be a single family office or operate as a multi-family office will have significant implications for whether and how both the office and its staff are regulated. As a broad generalisation, single family offices are not regulated, nor are their direct employees. Multi-family offices, on the other hand, which seek to provide advice and services to a number of families, will likely be required to register with a supervisory body and be subject to regulation, especially for their investment activities. The regulations with which a multi-family office must comply will vary according to the jurisdiction within which it operates.

The compliance issues that we concern ourselves with here are those more narrowly related to investments, operations and the associated risks. There are two main elements in addressing the compliance issues: organisation and reporting.

As noted earlier, the size of family office and whether it is a single family office or a multi-family office will dictate the level of resources within the office and the extent to which there is a proper division of responsibilities and checks and balances within the business. For example, it is desirable to have proper segregation of duties between trading and settlement functions, to ensure that positions can be independently reconciled and cash payments authorised. If resources permit, separating portfolio risk analysis and reporting from investment selection and day-to-day portfolio management should also strengthen decision-making and risk management.

Reporting should fulfil two primary purposes: the periodic reporting to wealth-owners, which we return to later, and the normally more frequent and detailed reporting that facilitates day-to-day portfolio management and compliance with the investment mandate. In both cases, it is preferable for reporting to require little manual intervention, to reduce the risk of human error. The complexity of the systems required will depend on what functions are retained in-house. For example, an approach that focuses on asset allocation and manager selection requires investment management systems that are less complex than those needed for one that has a greater emphasis on individual stock selection, which brings with it a requirement for greater amounts of data and analysis.

At a portfolio level, day-to-day investment management reports should provide information on:

- what positions are held, so that the actual asset allocation can be monitored and managed in line with strategic and tactical allocations, as appropriate;
- volatility/value at risk, showing how much potential volatility or risk of loss exists at any point in time;
- liquidity in the portfolio, to ensure that funds are available to meet any commitments to invest, such as may arise with private equity funds, or margin calls, if required for derivatives positions;
- investment concentration and counterparty exposure, to enable monitoring of risk of capital loss from poor underlying performance, default or insolvency.

Even where third-party investment managers or managed funds are used, the family office remains responsible for the decision to invest with them and, accordingly, for the performance that the portfolio returns. As noted earlier, there are various reasons for replacement of a manager, the most obvious of which is that they underperform. It may also be that asset allocation decisions dictate that a different investment style is required. Even where there has been no such change, it is not unheard of for a manager to move away from their original strategy because it is no longer investible or the scale of opportunity alters, and this may nullify the decision to invest with the manager in the first place.

A final point with regard to compliance is that, where structures such as investment trusts, unit trusts and open-ended investment companies are used, there are often restrictions that must be complied with. By way of illustration, in the case of such structures in the United Kingdom, there are limits on the levels of cash that can be held, concentration limits for individual positions and outright bans on certain types of investment.

5.   Reporting and review

Clients understandably expect to receive regular reports on how their investments are doing. In our experience, in the case of a multi-family office the level of detail and the frequency with which it is provided will vary by client.

One of the benefits of a family office is, or should be, that a complete picture of a client's wealth can be provided, even where it is divided up into multiple portfolios. This crucial role of integration and interpretation allows the client to understand their total asset allocation, their risk exposure, how it has changed over time and what strategic initiatives are possible or desirable.

If appropriate investment management systems are in place, the family office should seek to report performance on a consistent basis across all investible assets. This allows a more ready comparison of different assets and managers, something that is not necessarily possible where a number of investment managers or private banks have been appointed and only a collation of reports from them can be produced.

As we suggested much earlier, risk sits at the heart of investment and should be a key feature in the investment reports. Without this, the returns achieved will tell only half the story. By reporting on and reviewing both the risks taken and returns generated, the investment circle can be closed. Family clients will gain a better understanding of the relationship between the two, and this allows a regular review to be undertaken to ensure that the portfolio is achieving its purpose. Where circumstances, financial objectives or risk appetite have changed, the family office can return with the client to the start of the investment process and review whether the investment strategy and asset allocation is still appropriate or needs revision.

Families working (well) with outside lawyers

Joe Field
Withers Bergman LLP

One of the biggest issues facing a family that is considering creating a family office is defining what they mean by a 'family office'. The issue seems straightforward on its face, but it is not. This is a field that has attracted a great deal of attention over the last few years, and an outside lawyer who has worked in this area can often be of great help in helping a family shape what kind of entity they may want.

1. Some preliminary issues

Often, the family office is an outgrowth of the family business and in its initial phase is there to deal with family issues of the owning family, rather than dealing with matters specifically related to the family business. However, this often creates a variety of issues.

1.1 Who runs the office?

In many cases, it is the person who runs the business that initially runs the family office. This can create major tensions, in that the objective of a business is to make profits every quarter, whereas the goal of a family office is to preserve its financial and social capital over a very long term. An experienced law firm can work with the family in sorting out who should be the initial head of the family office, and what its objective may be. As the structure may change over time, to the extent that there are written guidelines, flexibility should be built into the structure.

While a family member may or may not actually run the office, outside counsel can perform a useful function not only in helping set up the initial composition and structure of the office, but also in providing guidance as to how the office leadership should be perpetuated. Clearly, the composition of the board governing the office should be defined, but in most cases this board is composed of family members. Their replacement is an issue that needs to be examined critically.

1.2 What is the function of the office?

This is also an area where the focus may change over time. The outside lawyer can be of great help in defining initial objectives and providing for the flexibility of the office moving forward. It is important to point out to a wealthy family that the costs of running a family office can be very high, and that this cost is often in direct proportion to the range of services that are offered. Here, a lawyer can be helpful and provide guidance as to the experience of other families, and can also help in assessing what the cost of initial operations might be. By way of example, many of the functions of a family office can be outsourced, and deciding how and what can best be insourced (rather than outsourced) is often a delicate topic.

A related topic would be what form the office should take. Some offices are structured informally, some are corporations, some are limited liability companies (LLC's) and a few are structured as limited partnerships. Sometimes multiple structures and entities, including family fund structures, are needed. One of the key issues where a legal adviser can perform a very useful function is in setting up the office, planning for its possible taxation and giving guidance with respect to how its form may relate to its operation.

In this vein, an experienced adviser can look at the exposure that family members may have with respect to officers' and directors' liability and help the family in dealing with an issue that can create real problems later on.

One area where lawyers are absolutely necessary is where a family acts as its own investment manager and may be in danger of running afoul of the relatively new Security and Exchange Commission rules in the United States on the registration of investment managers, which would also apply to US investments by international families. The sanction for running afoul of these rules may include posting of the family's investment strategy and all of its holdings in a publicly accessible website.

1.3   **What is the role of family members?**
This is an issue that arises at the formation of a family office, and remains relevant throughout its existence. Here, an outside counsel is important not only in defining the role of family members, but also in defining the way in which family committees are created and appointed or elected, as the case may be.

An important question, often overlooked, and where a lawyer can provide a real service to the family relates to anticipating situations in which family members may be dissatisfied with the operation of the office, or their role in its functioning. Prior to this becoming an issue, and indeed some would suggest from the outset, it is important to raise the point and suggest some options for future dispute resolution and indeed for an exit plan for family members who do not, or do not any longer, wish to associate themselves with the family office.

2.   **Some ongoing issues**

2.1   **What does the family do?**
If it is still in business, it becomes increasingly important to differentiate between the functions of the family business and the family office. Here, the question of conflicts of interest may arise, and it is important to insure that the family understands these issues and that neither family members nor the legal adviser has problems in this area. Another area where a legal adviser can perform an important service is in creating an understanding as to how family members employed in the family business (if there are any) are compensated, and making sure that all family members understand this and subscribe to the policy.

If the family has had a liquidity event and is an investor family, rather than a business family, the most serious issue is often who decides investment policy.

Lawyers can be useful in framing the issue, but ultimately the family has to make this determination. Again, the issue of succession may be very important. Another area where counsel may be of importance is structuring both direct investments and, increasingly, investments in other family businesses.

Hybrid family offices are an increasingly prominent phenomenon. Here, a family may be in business and also have a significant portfolio of non-business interests. The problems are parallel, but the scale may be much greater as the investment portfolio grows.

An increasingly important issue for family offices is the role of charity, philanthropy and, more recently, socially responsible (and impact) investing. While the lawyer may play only a limited role in the operation of such activities, the use of an adviser in setting up family charitable foundations and related structures can help ensure that such structures not only serve to fulfil family objectives, but also provide a significant degree of tax savings or relief, as well as protection from family and third-party liability.

Another area where a lawyer's input may be vital is with respect to deciding whether to invest in or operate through a multi-family office, or when to try to convert a single family office into a multi-family office. Definitions of aspirations with regard to the types of structures available are often illusory, and a lawyer's experience may give some guidance to a family anxious to embark on this process.

3.   Some issues for reflection

One of the most serious issues that needs to be addressed in the relationship between the family (or family office) and the lawyer is the question of conflicts of interest. Specifically, a lawyer has a duty to his or her client. In a family office situation, who that client is or may be should be carefully considered at the outset and on a continuing basis. Where the family begins to have internal friction, it is the duty of the lawyer to raise the issue and make sure that parties at odds are separately represented, or if the situation becomes substantial the lawyer may have to withdraw. Indeed, even when there is no confrontation, the interests of family members may be sufficiently divergent to require the lawyer to raise the issue on his own.

Another area where thought should be given and where the issue is not readily apparent relates to international families with family members, investments, assets or residences outside their home country. Today, this area is fraught with compliance issues, complex legal structures and serious potential personal liability for which an outside lawyer can be essential. Also, for those who undertake a multinational charitable programme, the lawyer can be very helpful in assisting in crafting an appropriate structure.

In today's world, confidentiality is an increasingly rare commodity. In a number of cases, using the lawyer as a tool to hire outside advisers can often be an effective way to protect family secrets. An example of this would be where tax-sensitive information needs to be analysed by a family accountant. In the United States (and indeed in most countries), accountants' work is not privileged. However, if the accountant is providing information at the instruction of an attorney, they may well fall within the ambit of legal privilege. Also, the lawyer may be well versed in what sorts of structures will be open to disclosure as opposed to those which may be more opaque.

This note is clearly not all-encompassing, but is meant to underscore some basic issues in the relationship between a family office and its legal adviser. Indeed, even in a statement as simple as this, it is necessary to point out that the larger the family and the more diverse its interests, the more likely it is that family legal adviser may in fact encompass several lawyers, either representing divergent family views, or advising on different aspects of family investment or management.

An adviser's view – private banker

Samy Dwek
JPMorgan Chase NA
Paul Knox
JPMorgan

As private bankers, we have a long history of dealing with family offices in their many shapes and sizes across the globe. In this section we share both our experience and our observations of the issues facing this sector at the current time.

1.   Definitions

'Gatekeeper' or 'advisor' – this is normally the chief financial officer, lawyer, best friend or confidant of the principal of a family. In most cases they have an understanding of financial affairs but this may not be their area of expertise.

'Single family office' – this is predominantly a family office that has been specifically created by the principal to manage his or her financial assets and those of his or her heirs. In some cases, the family office goes beyond managing liquid assets and will manage the principal's business assets too. Generally, this type of family office is headed by financial professionals.

'Multi-family office' – this is a common model we work with as private bankers, where the office manages the assets of multiple unrelated families. In many cases these are run by ex-bankers. A multi-family office model may be the evolution of a single family office, which we will review later in this section.

2.   Family office or not?

The first question to ask a principal or family on the creation of a family office is why they feel they need a family office and what activities they want the family office to execute. Family offices sometimes fail as insufficient attention is given to these basic questions at the outset. One of the key triggers for a principal to create a single family office is either a transition event, such as selling a portion or all of the family business, or the accumulation of liquid wealth that requires a more focused approach to managing it. In most cases, the principal either does not have the private wealth management expertise or does not have the time to focus on managing this wealth.

In our opinion, the single family office structure makes sense for those managing liquid assets in excess of $400 million. This size of assets under management usually ensures that the cost of maintaining such a structure is both cost-effective and adds significant value. For those principals with fewer assets to manage, the option of a multi-family office will be attractive. Multi-family offices generally do not offer tailored services for the family, but one can benefit from their due diligence processes and relationships with multiple institutions ensuring some pricing efficiencies. As an alternative to a single or multi-family office, one should not rule out the option of a gatekeeper who coordinates with the different banking providers.

In all the options shown above, the family needs to determine their long-term goals and have a plan in place for the next generation and potential transition events. Many of the single family offices that do not have a long-term plan in place cease to operate once the assets transition to the third generation.

3.   Family office services

So this begs the question: what services do single family offices offer? There is no simple answer as the services are made-to-measure based on the principal's objectives and values. Some of the typical services offered by single family offices are discussed here.

3.1   Asset management

The main focus of a family office is usually asset management and the ongoing due diligence of their underlying investments and money managers. In March 2012, JP Morgan conducted a global survey of 125 single family offices managing in excess of $100 million to gain insight in to how they invest, govern, and manage risk. More than 70% of those who responded selected wealth preservation as the most important aspect of managing their investments, and not wealth creation.

The same survey established that the majority of respondents' offices are staffed with between one and 10 people, but many of those stated that only one or two people on their staff are dedicated to managing the assets; hence their scarcest asset is time. Due to capacity constraints most family offices outsource the function of managing assets to financial institutions using discretionary mandates.

There is a correlation between the number of employees in single family offices and the number of financial institutions used by such offices; the more advisors they have to focus on particular asset classes, the greater the number of financial institutions they contract with.

3.2   Asset aggregation

Another key function of the family office is asset aggregation and performance reporting/tracking. Family offices have three options available to them:

- in-house asset aggregation;
- use of a global custodian;
- use of a third-party asset aggregator.

Newly established single family offices typically choose in-house asset aggregation, as it is considered the least expensive option and provides privacy of data. This option does provide a potentially higher risk of error due in part to the lack of data feeds and lack of understanding of the different banks' systems, which often leads to much unnecessary frustration.

The alternative solutions (ie, global custody or asset aggregation) are often preferable. If data privacy and flexibility are key concerns, the third-party solution ensures no one bank will have access to the entire data of the family, and flexibility is maintained in terms of foreign exchange trades and leverage.

In terms of flexibility, when choosing a global custodian the single family office should be aware that their assets will be held in one institution, therefore choosing a third party for leverage becomes more expensive and complicated or may require moving assets away. Additionally it is common practice that all foreign exchange transactions and deposits are only done with the global custodian.

3.3 Due diligence on funds

Due diligence on invested funds (ie, mutual funds, hedge funds or private equity), is usually outsourced. Again, this comes back to the discussion on the size of the family office and its ability to conduct the due diligence in-house. In our experience this responsibility is often delegated to external providers such as banks and other due diligence firms.

3.4 Concierge services

It is becoming increasingly common for single family offices to avoid the provision of concierge services as this is can easily become a contributor to dissatisfaction with the principal. The car being late or the wrong kind of hotel room may be more disruptive and annoying to family members than financial performance. When outsourcing is not an option, it is often preferable to have concierge services provided through a dedicated person sitting outside the family office.

3.5 Miscellaneous

There are a few other services that some single family offices overlook for the family that we have not touched upon, they are: philanthropy, investing in art and real estate. These are areas of growing importance and in most cases are either outsourced or are managed by the family with family office oversight.

4. Transition events

There are a few key transition events in the life cycle of a family; such as the creation of wealth, the partial or total exit from the family business, and succession to the next generation. The exit scenarios are normally the trigger for the creation of a family office. However, the next generation can be the cause for either the office's demise or its evolution.

Anticipation and management of transition events is one of the reasons why addressing family governance issues at the outset is so important. This can ensure that the right structures and processes are in place to allow key decisions to be made in the right way. Education of the next generation in the responsibilities of inheriting and managing wealth and gradually involving them in the decision-making regarding the family wealth are also key factors to ensure long-term preservation of the family wealth.

5. Evolution

What drives a single family office to become a multi-family office? There are three principal reasons:

- Costs – in some cases the family does not anticipate the cost of setting up and running a family office. One way to reduce their running costs is to open their services to other friends and families.

- Success – due to the successful management of the founding family's assets, they agree with the family to open their doors to other families.
- Next generation – as mentioned above, the move from one generation to the next will reduce the size of assets under management, as some family members may wish either to create their own structure or to manage the assets themselves. When either of these occurs, this may force the single family office to become a multi-family office in order to continue operating.

6.   Final thoughts

In dealing with family offices, the key role for us as bankers is to understand the specific needs and dynamics of the family and the family office, and to be flexible in tailoring a service to meet their specific requirements. With the complexity of tax, legal and regulatory issues in the modern world, it is also essential that private bankers work and liaise closely with lawyers, accountants, tax advisers and other professional advisers to ensure that the advice provided is coherent and cohesive.

An adviser's view – accountant

Jonathan L Sutton
Dixon Wilson

Professionals from different disciplines and technical backgrounds, including lawyers, accountants and investment managers among others, may be involved in the operation of a family office for clients.

The job of professionals in this capacity is to sit at the shoulder of their client in the management of the family's affairs. Different family offices will inevitably have a slightly different focus that will be driven by both the client's requirements and the technical background of the professionals at its core. Nevertheless, the office will need to address all of the usual tax, legal, financial, cross-jurisdictional social and communication issues affecting a family with complex assets. Therefore, notwithstanding the differences between one office and the next, successful family offices share common attributes. In this article I have attempted to draw out some of these attributes that I have observed. There are no doubt others.

I have referred to these common attributes as management of:

- process;
- risk;
- relationships;
- priorities;
- communication;
- decision-making; and
- cost.

To these I would add three further points. These are to understand properly the purpose and role of the office, not to be afraid to advocate simplicity and to be mindful of the need to manage a family's privacy.

1. Process

In my opinion, among the most important of the attributes of a successful family office is process.

At one end the family office can be deeply involved in high-level strategic thinking, but at the other it is immersed in the detail and implementation of compliance, governance and reporting. This is not the high-end, complex advice for which professionals are often applauded or work that gives an opportunity to showcase their technical talents, but without good process the day-to-day work that all clients require becomes disproportionately complicated. Only by tackling these less glamorous tasks well does the office have the foundation it needs to deal with the more complex and out of the ordinary.

Good process is therefore at the core of delivering effective and efficient family office services on time and at reasonable cost. This requires planning and capable personnel.

2.   Relationships

The office will do much in-house but there are inevitably boundaries on the internal skill sets. The family office must therefore be capable of identifying and cultivating a good working relationship with the external professionals involved while policing cost and quality of service from them.

3.   Priorities

Far-sightedness can remove many potential issues from a family's path. Issues should be anticipated and they, or the risk of them, should be put firmly on the table in a manner that provokes a sensible debate.

The successful office will have procedures to deal with events, whether those that are outside the family's control such as fiscal changes or financial crisis or those within their control such as a change of residence or marriage. Addressing these issues at the right time can necessitate raising matters with which the family are uncomfortable or which are outside the immediate skill set of the professionals in the office, but it is nevertheless vital.

4.   Risk

In the current economic environment there is a great value attached to the management of the risks that can destroy established family wealth, and the family office must be central in managing increasingly complex risks. Normal commercial risks aside, the potential vulnerability of the family wealth to a further banking crisis and a collapse in market confidence has had particular attention in recent years.

Other common risks are illiquidity, poor personal investment choice and divorce, all of which are well reported. To those can be added the risk of over-spending.

These risks and many more are greatly magnified if there is not a clear framework and a clear set of objectives for identifying and addressing them. The family office should encourage safety-nets to protect against these events, and should coordinate and direct the decision-making process to anticipate or address them.

5.   Communication

One of the prime causes of family difficulty is a breakdown of communication and cohesion within the family. This can result from a failure to plan – for instance, for passing on the wealth from one generation to the next – but it is often unrelated to a particular task or event. The office must, through its internal and external professionals, be able to manage matters such as communication between the family, to address questions of fairness and equality, and to work with family members' different interests and agendas.

6. **Decision-making**

The processes by which decisions are made are almost always critical to the future wellbeing of the family. The office must help govern and direct the overall objectives and decision-making processes within a fair framework.

7. **Costs**

Professional costs are significant for most families with a family office; in absolute, even if not in relative, terms. Further, they have been rising sharply. The office must be capable of controlling costs and ensuring value for money. Insofar as possible there should be transparency. Clear metrics are required to measure performance against goals and achievement.

8. **Purpose and role**

To act in context the advisor requires a clear understanding of the objectives placed on the office. These include the sometimes difficult question of what is the purpose of the wealth: purposes might include enhancing the quality of life of the family, avoiding inheritance without responsibility, preservation of a business or philanthropy. Without a guiding philosophy any decision can potentially create conflict.

9. **Simplicity**

If advisers can address something simply then the benefits of a more complex solution must always be weighed against the costs and risks that come with it. Where complexity is necessary then the exit strategy or ability to unwind the structure must be examined at the outset, with those that are difficult or expensive to break being considered very carefully before being adopted.

10. **Privacy**

My final point is privacy. The world is increasingly hostile towards wealth, and information is more publicly available than ever before. The result is that managing privacy will become increasingly important and requires more active attention than in the past.

Family offices and technology: the challenge, approach and opportunity

William S Wyman
Summitas

1. Introduction

Everyone deals with issues in his business and personal life that did not exist a few short years ago, particularly due to the Internet's rapid and pervasive growth. The challenge is to reconcile a few seemingly incompatible objectives that are important to family offices: the need and desire for privacy; the benefits of universal access to information; and the advantages of collaboration.

Family offices confront the same information technology challenges as other sectors, but for these entities it is different in a few key ways:

- The information managed is dense, diverse and private;
- The families supported span multiple generations, each with its own level of comfort with technology and how it should be applied or avoided;
- Most individuals probably lack the breadth of expertise and technical infrastructure available in large organisations.

If the right decisions are made, technology can be harnessed in ways that bring advantages to both family office professionals and the family members they serve. What are some examples? Families are about legacy, continuity and culture; using private collaboration tools can keep family members connected but ensure that family matters are kept private. Family members want timely information about their portfolios and resources; using a secure digital vault can provide easy access to personal information. Now more than ever, family office professionals can avail themselves of technology's advantages while protecting themselves and their clients from risks.

Before considering various technology solutions, a family office should think about a few important questions. First, where is the balance point between ease of access and sharing on one hand, and digital privacy and securing sensitive information on the other? Second, how can one keep current when one may not be a technology specialist, and innovation outpaces the ability to evaluate its risks and benefits?

2. The challenge

Family offices and their clients are desirable targets, and the entry point for hackers is often an internet-connected user. Why? As bank robber Willie Sutton once said when asked why he robbed banks: "Because that's where the money is." New technology can help families communicate, but everyone needs to understand the implications and implement appropriate safeguards.

An example is pretexting, which is when a scammer gains unauthorised access to a person's email account under false pretences. Once the scammer has access to a client email account, he can send a message instructing a family office to wire funds. The family office professional might receive what looks like a valid email and then inadvertently execute a fraudulent transaction.

In another example, a client might use a non-secure public wireless network – commonly accessed at coffee houses or airport lounges. A hacker sitting nearby might gain entry to the person's device to find her user IDs and passwords. At a later time, those credentials can be used to gain access to online banking accounts that do not offer additional protection through two-factor authentication or dedicated internet addresses.

Family office professionals have a mandate to provide first-rate support in everything from planning to portfolio management, to concierge services. This requires an infrastructure that supports each family office's particular culture and business model.

Most family offices do not have the necessary resources to build and maintain a platform required to safeguard information. Professionals develop a sense of what a person can be up against when hearing about security breaches at major corporations and government agencies; all with huge technology budgets and staffs. The bad guys are smart, they are nimble, and they are increasingly well-funded and organised.

Criminals will always be with us. While individuals cannot completely eliminate the potential for harmful activity, each person can take a number of behavioural and process steps that, when combined with a solid technology infrastructure, will mitigate much of the risk. Most burglars, given the choice of breaking in to a well-guarded home with electronic surveillance will opt instead for the equally large home with minimal security. In the 21st century, especially for custodians of private financial and family information, family office professionals need to understand the risks and take the required steps to increase control of the existing environment.

2.1   Cost

Ignore the risks, and it will open individuals up to outsiders gaining access to personal information and accounts. Consider this actual event: On December 24, the patriarch of a family office used his free email account to send instructions to wire money. Without realising that his account had been compromised, the family office processed nearly $100,000 in wires before they decided to phone and confirm the validity of the instructions. For the family office, this was an expensive lesson in the use of unsecured email platforms, and it led to major changes in controls and procedures.

The cost and ramifications go beyond financial loss. A security breach can tarnish a person's professional standing or a family's reputation. There have been several recent high-profile resignations of esteemed C-level executives and managers due to data break-ins and failure to protect private information.

2.2   Change

Keeping track of investments, estate planning and other family office activities is challenging, but now there is another important task that must be added: understanding and leveraging continual technological change. Since individuals cannot specialise in everything, the smart professional must rely on experts, particularly ones that have enough knowledge of his domain to identify the right tools and communicate effectively with family office professionals.

To drive the point home about the pace of change, it was reported at a recent technology conference that computer processing power has grown exponentially since the 1970s, and the smartphone used today is about as powerful as a circa 1980 supercomputer.

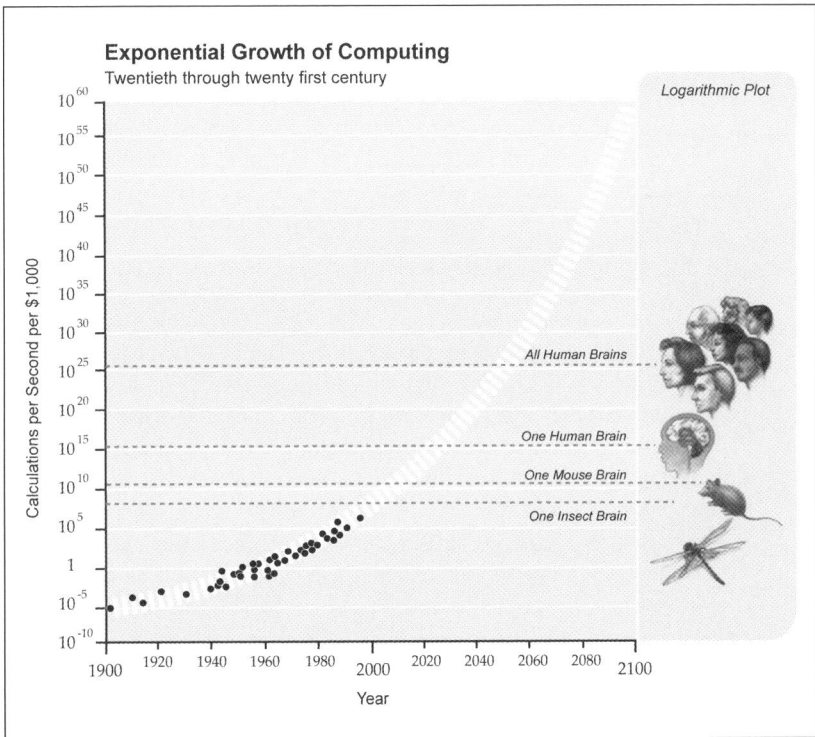

Exponential Growth of Computing
Twentieth through twenty first century

Logarithmic Plot

Source: Kurzweil, The Singularity is Near *(Viking Press; singularity.com)*

This trend will continue, and each person will need a plan to select the most effective solutions for his family office in an ever-expanding field.

Complacency in computing is the enemy. There are otherwise sophisticated professionals who think that because their system has been working for years, it will continue to do so indefinitely. The reality is that the world around those systems changes all the time, so unless attention is placed on upgrading the environment, updating tools and managing user behaviour, the tech platform will become vulnerable.

2.3   Expertise

There are knowledgeable professionals and firms that provide technology reviews and advice that can help one understand the risks and how to address them. An independent review of an office's tech environment can provide valuable insights, including areas of concern, recommendations and a clearer understanding of costs and benefits. Armed with this knowledge, those in charge can now make informed decisions about what needs to be done, and can evaluate the costs and benefits of any changes that should be made.

Think about it. Do you remember when the latest products had names like Netscape, WordPerfect, and Lotus 1-2-3? How long ago was it that no one had ever heard of Facebook, Twitter, Instagram, WhatsApp, Tumblr, and Pinterest. How many fully understand the benefits and risks of using these technologies? Who has thought about the 'map' of a person's or his family's lives that are shared on social networks: his friends, locations, hobbies, plans? Cybercriminals can target individuals and companies more easily when this kind of information is posted and shared. If a person does not have the expertise to navigate these waters, hire someone who does.

How can one find the right expert? Ask a professional network. This includes other family office professionals, service providers, and industry networking groups; all great resources to help the concerned person find the right professional.

2.4   Education

When someone is old enough to use technology, they should start learning how to protect personal identity and private information. A family's business and its personal information are only as secure as the weakest link, and it is not just the young that need help; many older people are technology novices too.

Here is an example where proper planning and communication worked: a father discussed technology risk with his children when they were young. Years later, when his daughter was in her teens, she raised concerns about a possible phishing situation when checking her email. (Phishing is the process of obtaining personal or sensitive information about a person by sending them what looks like an official email from their financial or other institutions. The email usually contains genuine logos and professional copy that attempt to get the recipient to log in to a false web address in order to capture usernames, passwords, and answers to security questions.) In this case, the daughter was concerned about the validity of the email and knew not to access any of the email's links. Instead, she decided to validate the details with the banking institution and found out it was a newly discovered phishing scam.

2.5   Responsibility

Finally, everyone in the family office and every family member must accept personal responsibility for protecting information. Why? Because the entry point for hackers is often the online user. Would a person speak in a crowded elevator about something personal or private? Probably not. Using standard or free email services is akin to talking aloud where others can hear a private conversation.

There are email service providers that can encrypt email and attachments based on rules set by the user. For instance, if an email subject line contains a special keyword, or if the email body includes dates of birth, social security numbers, account numbers and so on, those emails and attachments could be automatically encrypted.

What about passwords? Does the family office have a policy to ensure passwords have sufficient complexity to reduce the chance of discovering them using brute force techniques? Does the office require that passwords be changed on a periodic basis? Is there a requirement to verify compliance? Do policies extend to family members?

3. The approach

With a goal of having an efficient, secure and effective technology platform for the family office, the manager may ask: "Should we build, buy and integrate multiple platforms, or outsource our technology?" There is no one technology model, just as there is no one model for a family office.

Buy versus build? With so much talent, innovation and growth within the tech sector, family offices should be careful before choosing the build option. The obstacles to success are many:

- hiring and retaining the right tech team;
- establishing an effective project manager;
- taking on the risk that proprietary and custom technical solutions will isolate the environment; and
- managing 'scope creep' and the 'never-ending project'.

Family offices should first look to the outsourced model. Companies specialising in software know how to build quality teams comprised of project managers, analysts, designers, architects, developers, database administrators, data centre specialists and customer care representatives. They understand the technical minutiae and keep abreast of innovation within their areas of expertise. The best partners can hide complexity, provide reliable service, secure the information, respond to the outlined needs and help the user adapt to an ever-changing technology ecosystem.

3.1 Questions and answers

What are some of the factors a professional should consider when evaluating solutions and potential partners? The following matrix puts questions in a form that can be used to gauge risk in the areas most important to the organisation and how it operates.

Some questions and comments to consider

Risk area	Questions	Comments
Operations	Does the solution lead to more efficient execution?	Make a laundry list of the areas of chief concern: • wealth management and financial planning (eg, asset allocation model, what-if portfolio analysis, lifestyle planning); • investment management (eg, portfolio management, trade order management, rebalancing model portfolios, client reporting at the account and aggregate levels); • accounting (eg, tax-lot accounting, tax processing, cost basis reporting); • account reviews (eg, rules-based compliance, trust reviews, *ad hoc* queries); • performance reporting (eg, asset classification, internal rate of return or time-weighted returns, benchmarking); • data aggregation.
	Does the team have the skills to help implement then administer the system?	Do not go it alone. The industry is littered with failed technology projects that ultimately could not deliver. The cost in wasted time and family capital can be huge.
	Are all the decision-makers committed to the project? In the absence of buy-in and leadership, most technology projects are doomed to failure. New technology can seem threatening when in most cases it provides opportunities for career advancement. When people feel uneasy they will not be committed, and may subconsciously sabotage the effort. Make sure buy-in is based on understanding and supporting the anticipated benefits.	It happened – there was a family office that was planning to implement an outsourced reporting package. In the middle of the project, the patriarch decided to fire the head of the family office (he had asked for a raise). The new person in charge had not supported the project so within a few months it was killed.

continued on next page

Risk area	Questions	Comments
Planning	Does the vendor's development roadmap make sense?	Look for vendors that actively seek input from their customers. Those roadmaps will reflect communication with real life family offices that ring true. Do not be sidetracked by too many 'perfect system' discussions. An easy way to derail a tech project is for users to start asking for features that are either not available (eg, after tax performance reporting), never used in the regular workflow (eg, wouldn't it be nice if X, Y, or Z were available) or are well outside the identified scope. 'Feature creep' reduces the probability of success because it impacts on one or more of the three metrics a family or family office needs to control: time, quality, and cost.
Security	Was strong security and privacy added later, or was it part of the core architecture of the vendor's solution?	This will often determine how well family office and client information will be protected. Bolted-on security, by definition, is an afterthought. Modern systems should address security during the design phase.
	Does the solution provide end-to-end encryption?	Sensitive information needs to be encrypted at the source, then stay encrypted during transmission and while being stored (ie, 'at rest').
	Are encryption standards, like transport layer security (TLS), advanced encryption standard (AES), and triple data encryption standard (triple DES) employed?	Encryption algorithms that have become standards are published for all to see. Seeing how they work does not jeopardise their effectiveness. Home-grown solutions will not have undergone the same level of scrutiny by mathematicians and security experts.
	Does the solution provide two-factor authentication, or restricted internet addressing, during the login process?	Two-factor authentication, such as receiving an SMS/text message from the bank's tech platform that one must enter before completing the login process, provides additional protection. Restricting logins to known IP addresses can also enhance security.

continued on next page

Risk area	Questions	Comments
Reporting	Is there a way to demonstrate that information being reported is correct? Ask about the vendor's testing and quality assurance process. Are there test cases that validate computations and detect errors in data?	It happened – a mid-size wealth management firm implemented a new system. They found out that for the first year, statements sent were incorrect. It took them a great deal of time and effort to get the reporting right. They were lucky. The firm's clients never noticed!
	Do the graphs, charts and reporting make it easy to understand the information?	It also helps if new graphs, charts, and reports can be created to meet the specific needs of the entity.
Access	Can one obtain the information needed when it is required?	This implies that the system is running 24/7 and that it's accessible from anywhere on both mobile and desktop devices.
	Can the vendor enable customisable levels of access to the users of the information?	How do the users define what they need?
	What is the vendor's history with respect to system outages?	If one lives in a storm-prone area, like the Outer Banks of North Carolina, what are the things that can be done to ensure the user can access her critical information during an emergency?
Reputation	What is the impact to the family and the office if private information gets disclosed?	It is probably anywhere from bad to worse. This has been discussed above, but people positively need to make sure this is extremely unlikely to happen.
Compliance	The family office has various accounts and structures, like trusts, that require compliance reporting. Does the vendor's solution support those activities?	Some types of compliance are useful during day-to-day operations (eg, year-end reporting). Other types are meant to protect individuals when something goes wrong. Pay close attention to the second type as those are usually not centre stage during evaluations even though they are critically important.

continued on next page

Risk area	Questions	Comments
Going Concern	Find a vendor that is stable and has the financial backing to continue operations. Will they be acquired and integrated, never to be seen again? Will the organisation be partnering with a firm they do not even know?	Do not shy away from asking potentially difficult questions. If the evaluator is not satisfied with the responses, trust the instinct and challenge the firm. No organisation wants to be going through the same effort in one or two years. It happened – an East Coast family office contracted with a technology firm that had generated a great deal of industry buzz. The firm professed to have a robust offering that provided everything that the family office needed, and more. The buzz had the effect of shortening the evaluation period and skimming over a few critical issues. The family office also too readily accepted answers such as "We can build that for you." After 18 months of effort, and at great expense, the family office was forced to terminate the relationship. (Three years later, they still have not found a replacement.)

3.2   Next steps

What are the next steps to consider, once a project manager has decided upon the strategy, approach and finalists? The informed person should:

- Hire a technology expert with experience in the family office segment – the individual can be an 'outsourced chief technology officer' or brought on board for specific projects. He will be the project manager and will be well positioned to work with existing service providers to get what the family office needs, make final recommendations, negotiate fees and manage implementations.
- Execute a mutual non-disclosure agreement – as a family office, there will be the sharing of private details and the tech firm will be outlining proprietary information about its platform; Getting a non-disclosure agreement executed is in the best interests of both parties;
- Have the providers respond to a 'response for proposal' (a response for proposal contains the questions of greatest interest to each project). If the reviewer is not sure what questions to submit, ask the tech firm to provide a sample response for proposal. Once received, it can then be assessed and reviewed to determine which questions are applicable to the overall analysis;
- Talk to existing clients – professionals managing the project will learn a great deal and, based on the answers received, be better prepared should the

organisation adopt that firm's technology. Questions to ask include ones concerning time to implement, post-implementation support and the stability of the platform;

- Visit the tech firm's main offices – during such a visit, the professional will gain unique insights into the firm's people and operations. Look at their offices (eg, are they shabby, do they look state of the art), sense the energy, and look for happy motivated employees who will actually deliver what the organisation needs;
- Try before buying – ask for test accounts where users can enter their own data, see results and explore the solution outside the constraints of a sales demonstration. Who would buy a car without driving it? Without testing the technology, the family office and its broader community may not get what they think they are buying;
- When comfortable with a particular vendor, ask if they will help build a high-level implementation plan that includes key milestones and costs – this will set expectations prior to signing an agreement, and will help the process of managing the project once it is underway. If they baulk, consider paying them.

4. The opportunity

For family offices and the families they serve, the solution lies in simple, reliable systems and tools that navigate the challenges and opportunities inherent in the technology now at everyone's fingertips. With some planning and engagement of the right support, managers and their users will soon be supporting growth, improving communication and securing peace of mind for years to come.

Family office risk management and insurance

Linda Bourn
Crystal & Company

Family offices are established to centralise wealth management services to the extended family group they serve. As such, the family office should play an important role in establishing an approach to risk and insurance management practices that serves both the office and the family itself.

Family offices that have good risk management practices have been proactive in establishing risk management objectives at the highest level of management and have taken steps to fund, operationalise and monitor their risk management practices. Accordingly, these offices evaluate risk management exposures for the family office at an enterprise-wide level, and are not limited by boundaries such as the family office, a department, or family branch when determining priorities or processes.

With all this in mind, family offices benefit from having these three objectives as they evaluate risk and insurance management:

- knowledge – understand good risk management practices within family offices;
- implementation – compare good practices implemented among the best family offices;
- effectiveness – measure the effectiveness of implementing good practices and understand how to monitor them.

Practical risk and insurance management practices should be applied to both the family itself and the family office, and should be able to address exposures as they change over time. Jonathan Crystal, executive vice-president and a third generation family business executive of Crystal & Company, has offered this thought: "The family has to be an integral component of family office risk management. It's impossible to divorce the activities of the individual family members – and their attendant risk exposures – from the family as a whole."

1. Challenges for family offices

To have a sense of perspective, it is important to acknowledge the obstacles faced by family offices that hamper their ability to establish good practices:

- no full-time risk manager – most family offices do not employ a full-time risk manager, and as a result the responsibility for identifying and managing risk or purchasing insurance usually falls upon someone who wears multiple hats and may not have time or experience to address all areas of risk adequately;

- you've seen one family office, you've seen one – because family offices tailor services to meet the unique needs of the family who founded the office, they vary in ownership structure, size, and complexity. Staffing also varies from smaller offices of three or four staff members working with a founder to those offices with over 30 staff and several departments providing services to over 100 descendants. The impression that a small family office does not need a risk management programme or that a large family office has too much to address, leaves some family offices trapped by inertia – they will not do anything until something happens and they need to react;
- lack of family participation – the family itself is frequently not a partner, though it should be, in identifying a point person or in establishing a risk and insurance management committee to work as a partner with their family office. If it is not, the best wealth planning on the part of the family office will be for naught. If the family has not taken steps to identify risk, family members could be impacted by an unforeseen event that could have been prevented, or the family could suffer a financial loss that is not insured and therefore needs to fund it from its personal holdings;
- silos – the temptation to limit risk and insurance management within certain boundaries, such as the family office, a department within the office such as investment management, or to a family branch, such as the senior generation only, may miss the opportunity properly to address risks that impact more than one of these areas.

2.   Risk and insurance management for the family office
Good family office risk and insurance management practices begin with understanding risks impacting on leadership, services delivered and the management of employees.

2.1   Leadership
In establishing an organisational chart for the family office, directors and officers and their board illustrate what services will be provided to the family with clarity about the relationships among employees overseeing the services. Clarity about roles is important since family members are often part of the management team of their family office.

Directors and officers oversee the range of wealth management services delivered by the office staff and also the selection of outside advisers such as law firms, accounting firms and advisers who deliver specific asset management needs. They have a strict fiduciary duty to family members and family operating entities. Through this fiduciary duty they have standards of care and legal liability exposures similar to their counterparts in large corporations.

To mitigate potential liability associated with their decision-making and fiduciary duties, directors and officers should follow the business judgment rule:
- loyalty – the general duty of undivided loyalty to the entities they serve;
- diligence – the duty to exercise the same care as would a reasonably prudent person in the same circumstances;

- obedience – the duty, in addition to legal requirements, to conduct business within the powers of the corporate charter.

Long-standing family offices that have been in service to multiple generations have professional staff and a board of directors who have demonstrated a record of making strategic decisions and establishing priorities as the family grows in number and develops increasing complexity in its needs.

Any documentation of decision-making should exist to demonstrate that the business judgment rule was in place and was followed. In larger decisions that could significantly impact on family owners, documentation should include the use of an independent outside party to validate those decisions.

As a consequence of their leadership role, directors and officers of family offices may be named as parties to litigation, regardless of the merits of the claim. Examine these three areas to maximise indemnification protection for family office executives:

- Review the corporate charter of the family office with legal counsel to ensure that the indemnification provisions provide the maximum protection permitted by law, whether under corporate charter or by employment contract;
- Obtain indemnification and incorporate hold-harmless agreements into contracts with outside service providers to shift the responsibility of risk away from the family office;
- Ensure that the indemnification is backed with sufficient financial resources.

2.2 Services delivered

The family office has a responsibility to define the relationship that family members (as clients) have with the family office (as a service provider). Family offices that have good risk management practices usually have client service agreements in place with each family member that clearly describe the services provided and the associated fees that apply. This approach manages the accountability of both parties and provides transparency. This also contemplates the ability to tailor services and fees to family members based upon complexity.

Common services agreements can include the following areas and examples:

- investment management:
- investment policy;
- asset allocation;
- consolidated reporting on all assets;
- complex financial planning:
- tax and estate planning;
- partnership accounting;
- budgeting and bill-paying;
- insurance oversight;
- trustee:
- administration of trusts;
- quarterly financial statements;
- trust distribution decisions;

- preparing and filing annual tax returns;
- philanthropy:
- managing the family's philanthropy through various family foundations and funds;
- foundation compliance, including legal oversight of grant-making activity, revision and updating of bylaws as directed by the foundation board;
- miscellaneous services:
- family education;
- household staff management;
- concierge services.

Even where there is accountability, including service agreements, exposure to professional liability exists. Potential allegations can come from clients, regulators or other third parties. Allegations usually involve a breach of fiduciary duty such as:

- breach of duty of care for failing to diversify trust assets;
- failure to act impartially to certain beneficiaries;
- mismanagement and negligence in the selection, oversight or supervision of outside money managers;
- negligence in tax planning or performing other services.

Be aware that centralising services for the family can also mean that family office services are delivered from a business team within a family operating company or family holding company. Directors, officers and trustees should develop a policy to centralise accountability in delivering these services so that standards of care, including service agreements, are maintained.

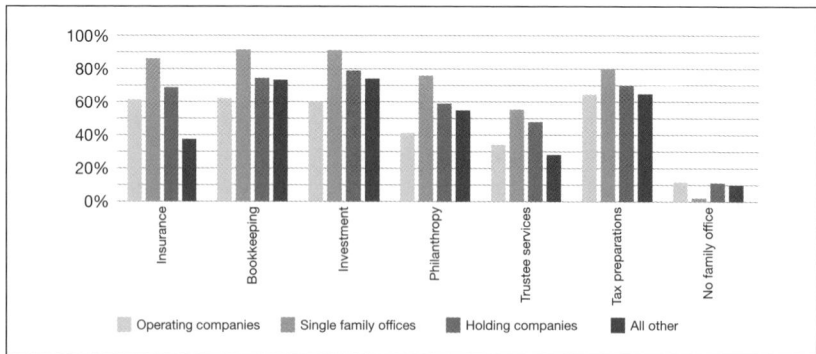

Source: 2015 Crystal & Company family enterprise risk index study N=159

As an example, in a 2014 survey of over 159 family enterprises, respondents indicated what family office services they provided to family owners by type of company they worked within. It was surprising to see that similar services are delivered to family owners whether the entity was a family business (operating company), a single-family office or a family holding company (where the family owns multiple operating entities).

2.3   Managing employees

People are the most important asset in a family office. Professional staff have access to confidential information, are keepers of institutional knowledge, know the family tree and culture of the family, and have access to a range of data about the family they serve. They are often on call 24/7 to ensure that the family owners can rely upon them. Family office professionals are on the front line of recognising potential liabilities of the family office or family members.

Because family offices do not typically employ a full-time human resources manager, they generally consult an employment practices law firm to help craft good human resource policies to prevent:

- wrongful termination;
- discrimination;
- harassment; or
- retaliation.

Mature and well-managed family offices have the following in place through consultation with their legal advisers:

- organisational chart – describes the family office governance and ownership structure, roles and relationship to one another in decision-making and in the delivery of services to the family members;
- employee handbook – describes in detail the family office's general rules and regulations, day-to-day job policies including the range of compensation, employee benefits and procedures from hiring to progressive disciplinary action. It also may provide details about the history of the family office and confidentiality controls that apply. It is usually updated as needed;
- job descriptions and performance appraisal process – job descriptions are in place for all employee roles, including those of domestic staff employed by the family members. Additionally each staff member understands how they will be evaluated annually in their role;
- structured communication: – a weekly or monthly staff meeting and regular staff discussions to share top-down information and hear from staff about day-to-day operational challenges as they serve the family group and work with outside advisers are recommended. This approach can mitigate future liability issues.

3.   Risk and insurance management for the family itself

3.1   Who is managing the family's risk?

Because they serve the wealth management needs of the extended family group, family offices should evaluate the risk exposures of the family they serve. The best trust and estate planning is inadequate if it does not address the potential financial impact of liability exposures on their family owners, security risks and the protection of wealth through the purchase of insurance.

Consider implementing a structured and recurring process for identifying family risk exposures (see below). Once that is completed, utilise the process for aligning risk exposures with an insurance strategy. This approach will enable the family office to keep pace with any changes and to address issues proactively.

3.2   Risk exposures

Identifying family risk exposures for high net worth families requires a holistic approach across many areas. Some of the key areas to consider when thinking about the family structure and culture and how it relates to risk are:

- roles:
- evaluate the roles family members fulfil and any associated liability;
- understand who surrounds the family and what role they play. This is especially helpful to know in security planning and in controlling confidentiality;
- locations:
- review where the family lives, both in primary and secondary residences, including any yachts or sailing boats that are open-ocean residences;
- understand travel for philanthropic activity, vacations, business ventures and the mode of transportation and associated services (eg, private aviation, crewed yachts, outfitters utilised during safaris or other tours or expeditions);
- understand what happens in the geography where they reside and where they will travel in order to plan for security and emergency preparedness;
- ownership (what they own and the type of ownership entity):
- understand the type of asset owned and entity ownership structures. Know how family members are protected against potential liabilities;
- review small business start-ups and when insurance should be considered for liability protection;
- review specialty assets that require understanding the scope of operations such as farms, ranches and operating businesses that generate cash flows.

The chart on the right provides a more detailed look at these core risk consultation areas that should be part of an annual discussion with family members in order to keep pace with any changes.

3.3   Other considerations

High net worth families are typically in the public domain where information is available on the firm they founded and on individual family members. The Internet has created a way to search and find all sorts of information. This area is often overlooked when it comes to risk planning, and it is crucial to integrate it into the insurance and risk discussions for the family.

If there isn't currently a policy developed for evaluating security, it is always a good time to begin. Family offices and family members should consult with a security expert. Security firms will usually include the following areas as part of their assessment:

- personnel security – employment practices should include employee background checks conducted by a reputable specialist firm, for all family office staff but also for all domestic staff employed by family members.

Risk consultation areas

Roles	
Family member roles	Influencers: external advisers
<ul><li>Beneficiary</li><li>Board member (private or publicly traded firm, non-profit)</li><li>CEO</li><li>Employer</li><li>Family business shareholder</li><li>General partner</li><li>Limited partner</li><li>Philanthropist</li><li>Trustee</li><li>Venture capitalist</li></ul>	<ul><li>Art consultants, curators, appraisers</li><li>Drivers</li><li>Pilots, yacht captains, property managers, farm/ranch managers</li><li>Residential staff</li><li>Travel advisers (outfitters, local tour guides, local drivers)</li><li>Professional advisers (accountants, attorneys, asset managers)</li></ul>
Locations	
Locations	Global travel profile
<ul><li>Multiple residences/multiple states/multiple countries</li><li>Remote locations: islands, mountains, deserts</li><li>Natural hazard areas: hurricane, typhoon, seismic activity, wildfire</li></ul>	<ul><li>Global: ecotourism and adventure travel locations</li><li>Known piracy regions (oceangoing vessels)</li><li>Political and terrorism risk areas</li><li>Remote areas</li></ul>
Ownership	
Ownership	Ownership Entities
<ul><li>Closely held business</li><li>Collections: fine art, wine, jewellery</li><li>Farms or ranches: vineyards, cattle ranches, horse breeding farms, horse stables, field crops</li><li>Land for development</li><li>Mineral rights</li><li>Private aircraft or yacht ownership/charter/leasing</li><li>Real estate</li></ul>	<ul><li>Trusts</li><li>Private trust companies</li><li>Limited liability companies</li><li>General partnerships and limited partnerships</li><li>Family foundations</li><li>Operating companies (S corporations, C corporations)</li></ul>

Security firms also recommend the same for vendors providing services to the family office and to the family members;

- emergency preparedness – scenario planning can help the family office and family members understand what to do, and who will respond in case of emergency:
- medical – understand medical emergency responses domestically, including during global travel. Very often this may include enrolment in a membership organisation providing global response and evacuation if needed;
- threat assessment – kidnap and ransom can be a threat domestically, as well as abroad depending on the country visited and the mode of travel. Security experts can conduct a threat assessment to identify risk exposure specific to each family member's routine and global travel plans;
- internet security – this is a challenging area since smart phones and social media create transparency and access to information. Education usually results in understanding privacy controls, identifying phishing e-mails, and what is trustworthy in navigating a virtual world;
- physical security – hiring security staff should be done in combination with a security expert to evaluate needs and recommendations from a firm specialising in providing this service;
- training and awareness – family offices and family members would benefit from ongoing education and training, similar to any other corporation as part of their preparedness planning.

4.   The benefits of an integrated insurance programme for the family office

Insurance companies perceive family offices as a niche market. It is vital for your insurance adviser to understand the complexity of your office, and to be able to articulate your risk profile to insurance underwriters. If insurance policies are not tailored to specific needs, gaps in coverage will occur. The loss of wealth due to unforeseen circumstances is an increasing concern to families, and family offices have the opportunity to play a key role in helping their clients manage personal insurance needs in a strategic and comprehensive manner.

The benefits of having a management and professional liability programme structured for the family office includes, but is not limited to, the following:

- qualified individuals can be recruited to the family office board;
- the personal assets of the individual directors and officers can be protected;
- the family office can be reimbursed for the costs of defending lawsuits against the company; and
- protection is provided against lawsuits alleging breach of fiduciary duty of directors and officers that negatively impacted on family member finances or family office operations.

In addition to maximising the protection of indemnification through contractual language, the other means of managing liability is the purchase of insurance. The best risk management programme involves doing both. Typical insurance programmes for family offices include insurance in the following areas:

- directors', officers' and private company liability;
- errors and omissions: family office and trust services liability, including vicarious liability;
- employment practices liability;
- personal insurance and life insurance;
- kidnap and ransom;
- fiduciary liability;
- cyber Liability;
- fidelity and US Employee Retirement Income Security Act (employee benefits plans) bonds, which can include coverage for funds transfer fraud, subject to confirmation of required operational controls in place at the family office;
- professional and management liability coverage, which can include:
- hedge fund and private investment fund coverage;
- pension and welfare benefits plans;
- outside directors' liability.

5. The benefits of an integrated insurance programme for the family

To help understand insurance as a strategy, the chart on ther next page illustrates common shortfalls in insurance programmes for family members, as observed over the years in advising family offices.

A group purchasing strategy for the family itself may make sense. Family offices can utilise the strength of the family buying group where insurance companies would be willing to provide group policies, or to provide insurance solutions for difficult risk exposures. Examples of group and master insurance policy concepts include:

- group personal excess liability – a group policy can provide a flexible and cost-effective approach to obtain high limits of worldwide personal excess liability protection for each family member of the designated group programme. The coverage would be excess over existing underlying personal insurance coverage. The family office defines the group, then selects a liability limit that meets the needs of individual family members (example $20,000,000). Limits up to $50,000,000 or higher are available. Additional family members can be added to the programme during the year or upon policy renewal with minimal underwriting considerations. Legal entities with insurable interests (such as trusts) can be added for liability protection;
- family valuable articles and collections – a master policy approach can enable family members to receive favourable coverage and rates for fine art, jewellery, silver, antiques or other valuable articles. Flexibility exists to issue individual policies or a group policy;
- kidnap and ransom – group programmes can include the family office staff and the family members when the programmes are structured. In addition to broad policies with favourable rates, insurance companies are partnered with global security firms who would conduct a threat assessment and assist the family with education about this risk area;

- unique assets – master and specialty policies are also available for ownership of unique assets or challenging insurance risks. These include: luxury yachts, private aviation, high valued and collectible automobiles, farms/ranches, international properties, island properties and special events.

Observation	Potential implication or risk
Lack of a structured and recurring risk identification process	• Unidentified risks, risk perception may not match actual needs • Poor alignment between risk exposures and insurance programmes • Changes to insurance programme lag family changes
Limited use of group purchasing	• Paying too much for insurance • Administrative costs of maintaining numerous policies • Uncoordinated approach to insurance, susceptibility to gaps or duplications in coverage
Infrequent or inconsistent inclusion of younger family members in insurance delivery	• Increased risk exposures • Evidence of a narrow perspective – no risk awareness • Uncoordinated approach to insurance, susceptibility to gaps or duplications in coverage
No family risk manager	• Lack of coordination of business and personal risks • Inefficient premiums, inadequate programme structure • Wealth being compromised

Source: Insurance Matters: The Case for Strategic Insurance Planning (Family Office Exchange and Crystal & Company, 2010).

On the right is a sample scorecard to help a family office assess how effective this strategy might be.

Overall, it is important to look at risk across the family enterprise. Putting in risk management processes and insurance policies that address risk in an integrated fashion is not only a good way to protect family wealth, it is becoming essential.

Should your office consider a group purchase strategy?

	Score		
Family dynamics	◄—— Disagree Agree ——►		
There is a collaborative family dynamic	1	2	3
The family office directs the purchasing strategy for the group	1	2	3
Risk issues and priorities	◄—— Disagree Agree ——►		
Uniform coverage levels for all family members are important	1	2	3
A cost-effective method for purchasing insurance is important	1	2	3
Reducing the number of policies maintained by each family member is important	1	2	3
Offering family members higher limits of excess liability is important	1	2	3
Complexity factors	No ◄————————► Yes		
Aggregate family premiums exceed $250,000	1		3
Properties are located in several geographic locations	1		3
High value collections: fine arts, jewellery, silver, etc.	1		3
Total points			

22+ High Potential   16-21 Moderate Potential   9-15 Low Potential

Source: Insurance Matters: The Case for Strategic Insurance Planning (Family Office Exchange and Crystal & Company, 2010).

Family values, mission and vision and the family office

Kirby Rosplock
Tamarind Partners Inc

Defining the shared values, mission and vision of the family office, particularly those that continue for several generations, is an exercise often overlooked or underappreciated by family owners, advisers and operators. This chapter explains the concept of values and why the importance of understanding the shared values a family identifies with its wealth is pivotal. Next the chapter reveals how values influence a family's mission and vision for the way in which its wealth will be managed by the family office and discusses the development of statements of those values. Finally, the Sample family case study is shared and their experience of engaging in a family visioning retreat.

1. Introduction to values

Values reflect our innermost principles and beliefs, providing behavioural guidelines that inform how we behave and what we do. Values shape significant moments in our lives and help us discern our priorities consistently over time.[1] Brian Hall, a values expert, explains that there is a hierarchy to our values based on how we prioritise them. In a way, values are the 'soft side' aspects that mould one's belief system and help one to understand what is a treasured and significant experience as opposed to an everyday experience. As a result, our individual values inform our choices and the decisions we make on a regular and often unconscious basis. Formative values, those that we develop early in our lives (around the childhood to young adult timeframe) tend to be the foundational values we hold dear for our entire lives. However, a shift in wealth and status can influence and impact how we perceive those very core values. A well-respected Canadian family business coach, Franco Lombardo, admits that families often get distracted by placing more importance on their valuables, or what they have, than on their values.[2] As a result, children growing up in this environment can mistakenly place more importance on the financial value of objects and material trappings than on their self-worth (how they perceive their own value). But wealth and material goods are void of values and empty when it comes to significance; thus, assigning a base of positive values to how to perceive wealth and relationships is key. Values are the constants in our lives, and no amount of financial wealth can buy one's values; they are simply part of one's DNA as one grows and evolves.

---

1 Brian P Hall, *Values Shift: A Guide to Personal and Organizational Transformation* (Twin Lights Publishers, Rockport, MA, 1994), p21.
2 Franco Lombardo, *Great White Elephant: Why Rich Kids Hate Their Parents!* (Roper House Publishing, 2012).

The experience of more deeply understanding and identifying shared family values is powerful. Providing a chance to reflect on the importance and meaning of those values in conjunction with wealth, business, family and relationships may illuminate new, unfamiliar and sometimes unexpected realities of our behaviours and lives. And for many, embarking on a journey to explore the soft stuff may be far more scary and daunting than figuring out the technical nuances and structures of their wealth and enterprise.

One family wealth expert, who has done significant work in the arena of family wealth and values, is Ellen Miley Perry. Author of the book *A Wealth of Possibilities*, Perry clarifies the need for family members to have these important conversations in order to build trust and connections with one another. In her book, Perry explains that "To earn trust, one must be vulnerable. It is the only path to real intimacy."[3] However, the challenge with values is that most people operate unconscious of them, and the experience of talking about values may be off-putting or make individuals feel vulnerable. However, for those families who endeavour to go down this path, there is a chance to break down old mental models, dated constructs, and negative behaviours that may have damaged relationships or jeopardised fostering a family bond. A simple conversation around values can bridge many communication divides and encourage togetherness in a family.

2.   Sharing family values

There is virtually no wrong way to have a values discussion, and there are many aids and tools that can help foster this dialogue. Some families are comfortable discussing their values openly and informally; however, most families prefer to work with a third party adviser or facilitator to guide them through the process. There are several talented consultants and advisers who may aid families down this path. Dennis Jaffe is one such adviser who has been working with families for years to discover their values through a deck of values cards that he developed. Engaging family members to associate personal experiences and stories to various values, the family may link together their core shared values and create an open dialogue on what those values mean to the family. For families with a wide age range, a values discussion is a means to link generations to a core thread of values that may impact their family office, their lifestyle, their giving and their impact in the community. Jaffe indicates that developing a shared purpose around their values motivates the next generation to stay together. By working together on family values, they can combine the legacy of the founding generation and what they stand for with the concerns and ideas of the newer generations.[4]

Another values expert, Gunther Weil, is a leading organisational consultant, coach and educator. His company, ValueMentors LLC, aids individuals, families and organisations to discover their values. Weil describes how values provide a deep sense of inner meaning and establish a sense of actionable priorities. Utilising a values inventory, Weil has worked with a number of families and their family offices, and

---

3   Ellen M Perry, *A Wealth of Possibilities: Navigating Family, Money, and Legacy* (Egremont Press, 2012).
4   Interview with Dennis Jaffe, 2012.

helps individuals appreciate their unique set of values. Based on 25 years of academic research and studies with more than 20,000 people, the survey tool has been used around the world. But it is not just the list of values the report provides, rather the wisdom and insight that Weil and his trained coaches reveal through the facilitated discussion. Not all families will want to take this approach, so the question becomes, how can families explore their values on their own? First, consider asking family members to ponder what values are most important to them and why. Make the experience fun and interactive by asking them to provide an experience or memory where that personal value was demonstrated or tested. If you have a very large family, consider breaking into pairs or small groups and have them share their greatest lesson learned from the experience or memory and why it is important to them today. This exercise may give you a head start to understanding shared values among the family.

3.   **The purpose of a values statement**

Once a family identifies their family values, the list of values can be memorialised in a values statement. A values statement is simply a short summary of the central values that matter the most to the family and those with which the family most identifies. These values inform and anchor the family's belief system, and ultimately guide their behaviours. Having the family group come to consensus on the values that should be a part of the family's values statement is an important element of the process. Only the shared values the family believes are important to the family's identity and culture need to be included. The values statement is often the preamble to the family's mission statement. Figure 1 presents an example of a family values statement.

Figure 1. Masterson's family values statement[5]

We hold dear the family's shared values and recognise that these values guide our family's actions and behaviours, and reflect our heritage and legacy. They are the guideposts for our future generations to honour, uphold and cherish. Those values include:

- *Truth and honesty – integrity, trustworthiness and transparency are pivotal values for each and every family member to uphold. The family values behaving in a manner that lives up to the family's honour, character and esteem.*
- *Caring, nurturing and kindness – the family is encouraged to be modest and humble both with the family wealth and their individual successes. Being dutiful, appreciative and sensitive are enduring qualities of the Masterson family.*
- *Ethics and responsibility – the Masterson family values being accountable and responsible. Having a strong moral code and compass help guide the family's enduring ethics.*
- *Family unity – the Masterson family revels in family togetherness and cohesion.*

---

5   The following is a fictionalised representation of a family office's actual values statement. The name of the family has been obscured to protect the privacy of the family on which it is based.

We encourage a culture of inclusivity and believe our greatest family capital is our combined knowledge and wisdom from our family's ancestors.

4. The role of a mission statement

Once the shared family values have been identified, the mission statement shares the family's goals, objectives and intentions for keeping the family connected with its wealth and/or enterprise. A family's mission answers two important questions:

- Why are we together?
- What are we going to achieve as a family?

The mission grounds the family with the governing principles (or values statement) by which family members will abide. Therefore, the family's values statement is positioned just before the mission statement in most cases. So, how does the mission statement get crafted?

In a similar vein to how there is no one way to explore a family's values, there is really no one way to create a mission statement. Some families employ a facilitator on staff who can provide advice regarding the values and mission process, while other families look to a consultant or a multi-family office that has these types of capabilities. If outsourcing this exercise is the path chosen, then involving the family office leadership and advisers to the family can be very insightful for all parties. The purpose of developing a values and mission statement is to articulate the principles that will inform the leadership, operations and advice given by the family office to the family. The experience and timing with regard to creating the shared values and a mission varies; for some it may take several weeks and for others it may take several months. There is no prize for finishing these statements the fastest; rather, it is about the experience of co-creating it with your fellow family members.

Once completed, presenting and sharing the finished values and mission statement with your advisers and any family members involved in creating it and those who may have missed the process is important to reinforce and reiterate the prominence of these statements. Furthermore, these statements will help validate the behaviours of those family office executives and set a proverbial high bar for the behaviour of the rising generation of family members. Several family offices indicated that they routinely read and revisit the family values and mission statements at off-sites, family meetings and retreats.

5. The importance of a vision statement

Developing a family's vision statement helps bridge any divide between the current family reality and the preferred future state. Although no-one has a crystal ball that can discern what the future will bring, a family may set its intentions, desires and dreams for what the future may hold for it as a whole. This notion encapsulates the vision concept. By imagining where the family may be in 10, 20, 50, even 200 years into the future, the family begins to vision:

- What would life be like for the family in this perfect future world?
- How do family members work with one another?
- What is the family culture like and what are its enduring values?

- How does the family stay connected and establish a sense of togetherness?
- What is the state of health and well-being of each individual family member and of the family collectively?
- If you were to walk into the family office of the future, what would it be like?
- What has stayed the same for the family and family office and what elements have changed?

These questions are at the heart of the visioning process, which is designed to inspire the preferred future for the family and the family office. The process of developing a family vision as well as a family office vision is an exciting journey; nevertheless, some families may think that it is not all that important or does not apply to them.

If the family pushes back with the idea that a vision does not apply to them, consider the outperformance by visionary firms from their counterparts with similar attributes in the same industries but without a vision.[6] In his paper "Demystifying the Development of Organizational Vision", Mark Lipton found that visionary companies with an established mission statement far outperformed their contemporaries by more than 15 times since 1926. In another research study, firms having a long-term vision were most identified as an important criterion by shareholders for selecting companies in which they would invest.[7] Simply put, vision and mission matter to shareholders and appear to have a direct benefit on a firm's long-term performance. Therefore, applying these principles to family offices is only logical.

As with the values and mission development process, there is a wonderful opportunity for families that engage family members in the visioning exercise. What are the critical components that enhance a family's ability to follow through on their vision? The following three tenets enhance a family's success rate when crafting a vision:

- having strong family engagement and commitment to the family clan – in other words, getting family members to the table to create an atmosphere of inclusivity where all voices will be heard;
- embodying a strong sense of stewardship and fostering an ethic of responsibility and accountability around the wealth, which helps the family take into consideration the needs of future generations in addition to the needs of the current generation;
- the principle of 'hastening slowly', – going more slowly at first in order to move more quickly later on and taking the time to consider systematically the consequences of each decision, which allows the process to move along faster in the long run.

---

6   Collins and Porras, as cited in Mark Lipton, "Demystifying the Development of an Organizational Vision", *Sloan Management Review* Volume 37, Number 4 (1994), pp83–92.

7   *Ibid.*

6.   Sample family case study: building a family office vision[8]

The Sample family was in the midst of transition. Unsure if it would continue the family office for a third generation, the family was at a major inflection point. Several dramatic changes had occurred in the family over the last decade that forced the family members to re-examine their commitment and desire to perpetuate the family office. First, a core legacy business that had been a centrepiece of the family's financial holdings was sold. With the sale of the business, increased liquidity for the family members presented each of them with more options for wealth advisory and investment services coupled with growing autonomy. Secondly, one of the key family members, who had retired as chairman to the family office just the year before, unexpectedly passed away. His death signalled a sea change in the generational leadership of the family office, with the remaining senior leaders being non-family key executives. Finally, the third generation, whose ages ranged from teenagers to adults in their 40s, was increasingly expressing a desire for their voices to be heard. Despite having several governance forums, such as a board, family council, shareholder assembly and semi-regular family meetings, many in the third generation were asking why they should hold fast and dear to the family office construct?

As a result, several members wrote letters to the family council expressing a desire to meet and discuss the future of the family office. Knowing that this was a daunting request, the family council set to work to identify a series of consultants to interview who might be able to lead the family through this process. Facilitating a discussion of the vision of the family office was not something that the non-family CEO felt he could undertake, as he aptly noted: "I am biased. I have my ideas of where this family office could go, but it is not up to me. I am merely the conduit, the implementer of the strategic plan. It's really up to the family." Therefore, the family council identified a list of top three candidates and had each family branch identify one family member to interview and assess all three candidates. The votes from the family council coupled with the outside family members helped them to decide on their choice of consultant, whom we will call Sally.

Sally met with the family council to hear as a collective the core issues that were at the top of the agenda for the family and the family office. She considered a range of issues, from how the family office was operating to what was happening on an individual level with family members and with the family as a collective. With a fairly comprehensive picture of the family and the family office, Sally met with key family members from various branches and generations in order to garner a broader perspective, but also to create a sense of buy-in, trust and belief in her abilities to facilitate a visioning experience.

Next, Sally outlined a process whereby some of the family council and those members who interviewed her became her visioning subcommittee. She explained her approach, the logistics and each detail of the proposed process to ensure the

---

8   The following is a fictionalised case study built on a family office's experience in defining its vision. The names and identifying information have been obscured to protect the privacy of the families on which it is based.

committee was comfortable with the idea and accepted it. At times, family members would push back and Sally would challenge them to consider the consequences of their suggestions. For example, one family committee member indicated that he did not think it was right that the family office should pay for the travel expenses of family members to participate. Rather, they should pay to get to the retreat on their own. Sally directed the subcommittee to their established values and mission statement that identified inclusivity and supporting the family collectively, asking if this suggestion was aligned with that value in the values statement. The other family members on the committee out-voted him, and it was determined that in order to garner the greatest participation, the family office would cover travel expenses for the two-day retreat.

The sub-committee drafted a communication that was reviewed and approved by the family elders and disseminated to all 50 plus family members in 12 states. The retreat was positioned as an opportunity to discuss the future of the family office and its vision. The letter discussed the importance of the collective involvement of family, and paraphrased a statement from leading organisational development thinker, Peter Drucker: "If you want to know what the future is, be part of its development."[9] Giving family members nearly a year's worth of notice, and with the commitment to house and cover travel expenses, the response was positive. Promoting the retreat as mechanism to harness the collective wisdom of all generations, the subcommittee garnered the commitment from the majority of family members to attend and to give the requested feedback, ideas and suggestions to personalise and bring a sense of family community to the two days together. The family office executives were also prepared to present operational and performance data as well as to participate in parts of the vision building process. If the family office is the metaphorical bridge that helps link one generation to the next, then involvement from the family office executives in developing the vision for the future of the family office is instrumental in crafting the ideal future. However, it became clear from the initial feedback from family members, that not all family members were exactly clear on the role, responsibilities and actions of the family office. Therefore, Sally and her subcommittee set to work on having the first half day focused on educating family members on the roles of key family office executives, the organisation of the family office, the services offered and the expectations that the family office had of family members. They labelled this exercise 'know your family office'.[10]

Next, the family recognised the importance of building family cohesiveness among branches of family who may not have regular contact with one another. Accordingly, over lunch the family orchestrated tables of different family members of different ages and from different branches, who had to discover the unique stories, experiences and talents of each family member at their table with a modified scavenger hunt list of characteristics, values, experiences and talents.

---

9   "Inspirational Quotations", Appreciative Inquiry Commons: www.appreciative inquiry.case.edu
10   This is a riff on 'know your client', which is commonly used in the financial industry typically from a risk and compliance standpoint.

The following afternoon the family members broke into a series of education forums led by different family office executives and family members on aspects of the family office's investment approach, the accounting and aggregated reporting functions, the wealth advisory services, including 'refreshing your financial plan' and discussing wealth transfer, gifting and philanthropic goals. These working sessions were designed to inform the following day's sessions which were all about the vision of the family office. But first, that evening a special dinner was hosted by the widow of the deceased chairman of the family office, and she identified a lauded author and inspirational speaker to discuss the importance of finding meaning and passion in one's life. This lifted the family's spirits and also set the tone for the importance of finding meaning and passion in each family member's life. Following dinner the family met under the stars to release paper lanterns into the sky to honour and remember their loved ones who had passed before retiring for the evening.

The next morning, Sally and the subcommittee welcomed the family members into a room with several tables and surrounded by flip charts. For the first couple of hours the family focused on what they had learned from the family office executives the day before, and identified those aspects of the family office that were working well and those opportunities for change. Each table had a different family office focus and one family member facilitated the table discussion for each topic, in which different groups of family members mixed and matched with other family members, before addressing all the various table topics. This data was then reviewed as a family group before the family broke for a casual, informal lunch.

Meanwhile, the consultant and the committee members reviewed the headline findings and reframed some of the aspects of the family office that they wanted to stay the same and the areas for change. The afternoon session focused on the family office vision and family members were asked to reflect on the feedback from the morning and what it meant for the future vision of the family office. Small group discussions ensued on several key questions:

- What are our collective objectives for the family wealth?
- How will it enhance responsibility of each family wealth owner?
- What roles and responsibilities belong to the owners and what to the family office executives?
- How will family governance evolve with our family office?
- What are the core services that the family office should provide and what will they be in the future?
- How will we measure the success of the office? How will we keep the family office accountable?

At the end of the small group discussion, Sally facilitated a large group dialogue on the various responses and to debrief from the questions. Capturing the feedback on flip charts that were then posted around the room, Sally condensed the collective thoughts at this stage. Following an hour-long discussion, family members were asked to walk around the room and place a star next to the points that they believed were most important to the vision of the family office. The family's hard work of the morning and afternoon was rewarded with a little friendly family competition in the form of tennis, lawn bowling and volleyball. That evening there was a closing ceremony to review the work that had been accomplished and to commit to the work ahead. Sally had each of the family office executives internalise the visionary elements of the different areas of the family office and provide their commitment to figure out an action plan that incorporated the family's feedback. Finally, Sally had the family also commit to establishing a post-vision retreat committee to articulate several of the ideas expressed in the form of a draft vision statement that could be shared with all family members before it was ratified at the following year's family meeting. Concurrently, the family office executives realigned the strategic plan for the family office to reflect the core tenets in the family's vision statement. The retreat was just the beginning of a new chapter for the family and their family office.

7.   Conclusion

Shared values, mission and vision provide the foundation that guides the family and the family office both day-to-day and for the long term. Without defining these elements, a family may have greater difficulty inspiring commitment, creating continuity and building cohesion across different branches and generations of the family. In order for the family office to be successful, a family has to articulate its preferred future, being clear on who they are, what the purpose of staying together is and why having a family office is important. If the family is not clear on their shared values and mission, assigning a vision to the family office becomes less impactful. In closing, the process of aligning the family's vision with that of the family office is empowering, liberating and may provide inspiration that will guide the family for generations to come.

Culture, communication and conflict

Ian Marsh
*Family*dr Limited

1. Introduction

In *Preparing Heirs*,[1] Williams and Preisser report research which suggests that, of the 70% of wealth transition plans that fail (you may want to rewind and read that statistic again if you're not familiar with it), 60% of those failures are due to a breakdown of trust and communication within the family, and a further 25% to a failure to prepare the next generation for what is to come; itself, I would suggest, a symptom of failed communication.

Numbers of studies confirm that one of the keys to the successful management of family wealth across generations is to "communicate, communicate, communicate"[2] and some suggest that without good communication, governance structures can provide a false sense of security, with predictable results.[3]

I would just add that, in my experience, the difference between conflict managed constructively (which can be a powerful agent for invention and innovation) and conflict managed destructively (which is utterly corrosive of everything it touches) is the effectiveness of the communication between those involved.

This chapter examines why we find effective communication so difficult, and considers what we might do to improve the situation.

2. We are family[4]

Speaking at a conference recently, Ken McKracken[5] referred to the "natural governance" that keeps families and their enterprises functioning as "the way we do things around here". That struck a chord with me because Joanna Kalowski,[6] who first taught me intercultural mediation, uses exactly the same phrase to define 'culture', and I have long believed that every family has its own (micro) culture. If you don't believe me, think about the first time you celebrated a significant festival

---

1   Roy Williams and Vic Preisser, *Preparing Heirs: Five Steps to a Successful Transition of Family Wealth and Values* (Robert D Reed, 2003).
2   See, for example: JP Morgan, *Effective governance: The eight proactive practices of successful families* (2004); Coutts *2005 Family Business Survey*; G Gordon, "It's Good to Talk", *Families in Business*, Sept/Oct 2005; S Barimo, K Rosplock and J Shipley, *The 25 Best Practices of Multi-Generational Families* (GenSpring Family Offices, 2007); and, most recently, D Jaffe with J Flanagan, *Three Pathways to Evolutionary Survival: Best Practices of Successful, Global, Multi-Generational Family Enterprises* (www.dennisjaffe.com, 2012).
3   SandAire Ltd, *Family Wealth*, Issue 3, Spring 2005.
4   Lyrics by Bernard Edwards and Nile Rodgers, recorded by Sister Sledge, the Pointer Sisters and, no doubt, others.
5   Co-founder, Withers Consulting group; www.withersconsulting.com.
6   Mediator, judicial trainer and cross-cultural communications expert; www.jok.com.au.

with someone else's family (I suspect that of a first serious girl, or boy, friend); didn't they do everything wrong? Sorry ... differently?

So, if 'we' are those who do things in a particular way, how do we define our family 'in-group'? Who is family?

For some, it is the nuclear family (parents and children) that is most important. For others it is the extended family, and that can extend a very long way indeed, perhaps taking in all blood relatives, however remote. I almost used the term 'me and mine' in relation to the nuclear family, but that would be wrong; to those whose concept of family is extended, 'mine' inevitably includes all of those relations. Indeed, it is interesting that some ethnic West African languages, and perhaps others, have no words for 'auntie', 'uncle' or 'cousin', using 'mother', 'father', 'brother' and 'sister' instead.[7]

What of marriage? In some cultures it is a joining of families so that, where extended family is the norm, each marriage may increase family size by an order of magnitude. Elsewhere, marriage means a change of family, generally for the bride who may leave her parents' family (physically and economically, if not emotionally) and join her husband's, likely taking on the care of her in-laws in place of that of her parents.[8] For others, bloodline is all, and in-laws are not really regarded as family proper.

Religion too may play a part, with conversion, apostasy or 'marrying out' potentially having an impact on family membership as witness, for example, the UK's Act of Settlement 1701 (an early family constitution?), which provided that the English throne would pass to the Electress Sophia of Hanover and her Protestant descendants who had not married a Roman Catholic.

All of which is to say nothing of the interesting consequences of divorce and remarriage and the relationships that result; same sex relationships; or the impact of adoption – not least the Japanese practice of adult adoption, sometimes credited for the longevity of Japanese family businesses.[9]

The point is that there is no one fixed meaning of 'family', no Platonic ideal form of which the families we deal with are mere shadows. Each family defines its own in-group, its own 'way of doing', and those of us who work with them must take care not to assume that our clients share our sense of family, or to project on to them the expressed norms of the broader society in which we live.

3.   **Who's there?**[10]

We are each the product of our genes, of our environment, of our experience and, seemingly, of an element of randomness.[11] Does nature or nurture predominate? Perhaps inevitably, it is not that simple.

Our genes, our DNA sequence, is fixed, but how certain genes express themselves, whether they are switched on or not, turns out to depend on our experience[12] and,

---

7   Thanks for this to Adjoa Tamakloe, mediator and founder of CLASS™ Resolutions; www.classresolutions.co.uk.
8   Thanks to Dr Xiaohui Yuan of Nottingham University for this, illustrated by the Chinese proverb: "When a daughter is married, she is like the water poured out of the door".
9   Freakonomics.com.
10   Shakespeare, *Hamlet*, Act 1, Scene 1.
11   That is, changes that happen which we cannot currently explain or predict.

in no small part, on our interactions with one another (particularly those with our primary carers during our formative years – typically up to the age of seven), and that state of expression can be passed on to our children.

Research by Nisbett and Miyamoto[13] suggests that we acquire our initial attentional patterns, the way we see the world, through those early socialisation processes, which both reflect the norms of the culture in which we grow up and, in turn, contribute to the 'default' neural firing patterns that are characteristic of that culture; a positive feedback loop.

Those patterns reflect in our personality traits. Siegel and colleagues[14] suggest that each of us tends to focus predominantly on one of the following aspects of new situations and relationships:

- right versus wrong, errors and mistakes;
- other peoples' needs and desires;
- tasks, goals and achievements;
- that which is missing or longed for;
- potential intrusion by, and demands of, others, especially regarding time, space and knowledge;
- potential hazards and worst case scenarios and how to deal with them;
- positive or pleasurable options and opportunities, with a general emphasis on planning;
- injustices and the need for control or assertiveness; or
- maintaining harmony with one's physical and social environment.

Those traits, in turn, reflect in our learning preferences (do we tend, for example, to ask why? how? what? or what if?);[15] in our communication styles (are we high or low context communicators, literal or metaphorical; are we visual, aural or kinaesthetic?); in our approach to conflict (do we tend to compete, appease, walk away or mediate?); in our priorities when faced with conflict (substance, process, relationships or identity/face);[16] and so on.

Moreover, our attentional patterns appear to determine not just how we perceive the world, but what we perceive. Nisbett & Miyamato note, among other things, that:

> People in Western culture have been found to organise objects by emphasizing rules and categories and to focus on salient objects independent from the context, whereas people in East Asian cultures are more inclined to attend to the context and to the relationship between objects and the context … [Research] suggests that participating in particular social practices leads to chronic differences in perceptual processes.[17]

How we perceive the world also determines how we describe it to others, as witness, for example, the West African use of the word for 'mother' to refer to a

---

12 The process of epigenesis: D Siegel, *The Developing Mind: How relationships and the Brain Interact and Shape Who We Are*, second edition (The Guilford Press, 2012).

13 R Nisbett and Y Miyamoto, "The influence of culture: holistic versus analytic perception", *TRENDS in Cognitive Sciences*, Volume 9 Number 10, October 2005.

14 As reported in D Siegel, *The Mindful Therapist*, first edition (WW Norton & Co, 2010).

15 B McCarthy, *About Learning*, first edition (About Learning Inc, 2000).

16 W Wilmot and J Hocker, *Interpersonal Conflict*, seventh edition (McGraw Hill, 2007).

17 Nisbett and Miyamoto, *op cit.*

biological aunt, referred to above, and the fact that: "Russians find it odd that an Englishman uses the same basic term for light blue (Russian: *golubuy*) and dark blue (*siniy*)."[18]

Having said all that, it is also now clear that our brains retain their plasticity, and continue to be rewired by our subsequent experiences, throughout our lives,[19] and it appears that individual attentional patterns may be temporarily affected by "priming with different cultural cues,"[20] such as by living, studying or working abroad.

Since no two of us have identical life experiences (even identical twins are treated differently by their parents), it would seem to follow that no two of us see – or describe – the world the same way, which might at least begin to explain why we sometimes find it difficult to communicate as well as we would like.

4.   Life itself is the most wonderful fairytale of all[21]

If we are all so different, how does a family (any group for that matter) become a cohesive whole?

To borrow from Iain McGilchrist,[22] families are not utilitarian relationships but are "based on felt connection and cultural continuity". According to Geert and Gert Jan Hofstede,[23] culture manifests itself in shared symbols (words, gestures, pictures or objects that carry a particular meaning only recognised as such by those that share the culture, here family members), heroes (whether living or dead, real or imaginary, who possess characteristics prized in the culture and so serve as role models), rituals (collective activities that are superfluous to reaching desired ends but which the family regards as socially essential) and, at its core, values (broad tendencies to prefer certain states of affairs over others).

Peter Leach[24] says that:

Families learn to build a shared vision by aligning individual and family values and goals, and that vision becomes a guide for planning and action ... Values are what a family and its business stand for; vision is a shared sense of where each is heading.

and Jay Hughes[25] uses the term "family of affinity" to refer to a family that sees itself as linked by affinity and a common mission rather than simply by genetic lineage, and which he sees as: "A family system that declares that anyone who loves its stories and embraces its value system is welcome to join."

Storytelling, it seems to me, is key to all this, for it is primarily through the rituals of storytelling that we share our symbols, heroes and values. Indeed, neuroscientist Antonio Damasio[26] suggests that storytelling evolved from the inner storytelling we

---

18   P Ball, "Riddled with irregularity: why are languages so different – and disorderly", *Prospect*, September 2012.

19   N Doidge, *The Brain that Changes Itself*, first edition (GB) (Penguin Books, 2007).

20   Nisbett and Miyamato, *op cit*.

21   Hans Christian Andersen.

22   I McGilchrist, *The Master and his Emissary: The Divided Brain and the Making of the Western World*, first edition (Yale University Press, 2009).

23   G Hofstede and GJ Hofstede, *Culture and Organisations: Software of the Mind*, second edition (McGraw Hill, 2005).

24   P Leach, *Family Businesses: The Essentials*, first edition (BDO Stoy Hayward LLP, 2007).

25   J Hughes Jr, *Family: The Compact Among Generations*, first edition (Bloomberg Press, 2007).

26   A Damasio, *When Self Comes to Mind: Constructing the Conscious Brain*, first edition (William Heinemann, 2010).

all do to create our very sense of self as a means of making our shared cultural norms "understandable, transmissible, persuasive and enforceable"; in other words, to give culture its continuity.

McGilchrist[27] goes further and suggests that language itself may have evolved, not merely to allow us to communicate (which, he argues powerfully, we are well able to do without language), but to allow us to memorialise our experience of the world, to give it fixity – in effect to create stories – to enable us to collaborate more effectively in solving mutual problems.

Fivush and Nelson[28] also conclude that:

Through the creation of a shared past, individuals gain a sense of who they are in relation to others, both locally within their family and community and more generally within their culture. They also attain a shared perspective on how to interpret and evaluate experience, which leads to a shared moral perspective.

I learned the practical power of storytelling in my own mediation practice and soon began, wherever possible, to structure mediations to ensure that all parties had the space to tell their own stories, in their own words and in their own time – if only to me.[29] I now adopt a similar approach in all my work with families, whether they are in conflict or not. It is amazing just how many people tell me that it is the first time anyone has really listened to them. And, feeling heard, they become much more open to hearing what others have to say and, through that, to finding common cause with them.

What fascinates me more, though, is the extent to which, in the course of telling their stories, people become aware of what is most important to them, and why. It is almost as if they are listening to their own story themselves for the very first time; perhaps they are.

Storytelling, however, is not just a unilateral act of the speaker. Walter Benjamin[30] described it as "the ability to exchange experiences". More recently, Siegel[31] put it this way:

The storytelling and story listening process often involves the essential features of social interaction and discourse. The teller produces verbal and nonverbal signals that are received by the listener, and then similar forms of communication are sent back to the teller. This intricate dance requires both persons to have the complex capacity to read social signals, to share a subjective experience of mind, and to agree to participate in culturally accepted rules of discourse. Stories are thus socially co-constructed. *[emphasis added]*

5. The best mirror is an old friend[32]

Those non-verbal, social, signals involve posture, gesture, eye contact, facial

---

27   McGilchrist, *op cit.*

28   R Fivush and K Nelson, "Culture and Language in the Emergence of Autobiographical Memory", *Psychological Science*, Volume 15 – Number 9, 573-577 (American Psychological Society, 2004).

29   I Marsh, "Mediating Families at War", *Asian Dispute Review*, January 2011, 24 -27; www.familydr.co.uk/articles/6.

30   W Benjamin, *The Storyteller: Reflections on the Works of Nikolai Leskov* (1936); http://slought.org/files/downloads/events/SF_1331-Benjamin.pdf.

31   D Siegel, *The Developing Mind, op cit.*

32   Peter Nivio Zarlenger.

expression, prosody (the rhythm, stress and intonation of speech), and the timing and intensity of response. Reading those signals appears to involve specialised brain cells, mirror neurons which, working with other structures in the brain, seem to be designed to allow (to cause?) us to mimic one another, which seems in turn to allow us to understand the actions, intentions and emotions – if not the words – of another.[33] Try it yourself: mimic someone else's (a consenting adult's, in private, is probably best!) body language – particularly their facial expression – as closely as you can, and then see how you (and they) feel. Try doing it again, this time with a pencil between your teeth.[34]

One of the things I sometimes do in mediation is to ask people to reframe their grievance in the form "When you did ... , I felt ... , because ...". I started doing it largely for pragmatic reasons: it isn't accusatory, so it is less likely to put the listener in defensive mode, and is more likely therefore to be the beginning of a dialogue; and it cannot be denied, so the easiest of parries is barred. (Some might respond "well you shouldn't", but that has never seemed very strong to me.) In the event, most acknowledge the emotion – and are often shocked to find themselves the cause of it. (Interestingly, research shows that just naming an emotion tends to reduce it,[35] which itself can be very helpful. Again, try it with yourself sometime.)

But there is much more to it than that. When Mary told her son, David, that she felt ashamed and humiliated when David suggested to his siblings that it was time they took over looking after the family wealth from their parents, because such behaviour was clear proof that she was an appalling mother (in Mary's world view, no well-brought-up child would have suggested such a thing, so she had clearly failed to teach him right from wrong), David could, and did, try to argue with the words, but her body language was unmistakable to everyone including him, as was his to her (one of the reasons I try to avoid having desks or tables in such meetings is to ensure that all body language is fully on display); whatever David said, Mary knew that he knew. If feeling heard is powerful, feeling felt is positively profound and in that case, as in so many others, it provided a breakthrough.

Done as a regular part of family life, it need not (always) be quite so dramatic. Indeed, I believe that regular storytelling within the family is one of the best ways to breathe real life into "regular extended family gatherings and interaction"; to build "a climate of family openness, trust and communication"; and to develop "sharing and respect for family history and legacy", three of the five practices identified by Dennis Jaffe in his "Three Pathways to Evolutionary Survival".[36] It is also one of the best ways of creating "binding social ties", securing the "emotional attachment of

---

33   M Iacoboni, *Mirroring People: The Science of Empathy and How we Connect with Others*, first edition (Picador, 2008); G Rizolatti and C Sinigaglia, *Mirrors in the Brain: How Our Minds Share Actions and Emotions*, first English edition (Oxford University Press, 2008); J Decety and W Ickes (editors), *The Social Neuroscience of Empathy*, first paperback edition (MIT Press, 2011).

34   The pencil stops the micro-muscles in your face mimicking the other's, which are probably the biggest tell.

35   D Creswell, B Way, N Eisenberger and M Lieberman, "Neural Correlates of Dispositional Mindfulness During Affect Labelling", *Psychosomatic Medicine* 69: 560 – 565 (2007), confirming what had previously been intuited by the proponents of nonviolent communication (M Rosenberg, *Nonviolent Communication: A Language of Life*, second edition, Rosenberg, 2003).

36   D Jaffe with J Flanagan, *Three Pathways to Evolutionary Survival, op cit.*

family members", and the "renewal of family bonds", three of the five dimensions of socioemotional wealth described by Pascual Barrone and colleagues.[37]

6.   A tribe of one?[38]

Telling and listening to stories. That shouldn't be so difficult, should it? So why is it?

Walter Benjamin[39] suggested that the art of storytelling was coming to an end, not least because "experience [had] fallen in value"; he felt that the rate of change in life had become so fast that experience of the past was no longer useful in trying to deal with the future – and that was in 1936! But if families are to achieve the cultural continuity they seek over generations, they must find ways of ensuring that their stories, their myths and legends, their symbols and heroes, their rituals and their values will always have relevance to the rising generations.

Benjamin felt that true storytellers passed their wisdom "from mouth to mouth". Stephen Porges[40] suggests that "To develop a social bond, individuals have to be in close proximity". Yet, in the West at least, we seem to spend less and less time together as families. That may be because our families are spread around the country, or around the world. Or it may be that we have, as Sherry Turkle[41] puts it "sacrificed conversation for mere connection", preferring texting (SMS), e-mail and social media to conversation, even when we are physically gathered together, something which Turkle says has got us used to the idea of "being a tribe of one, loyal to our own party"; the antithesis of the cultural continuity families need to succeed.

7.   Everyone hears only what he understands[42]

But if story *telling* has become harder, listening is harder still.

At one level, there are many obstacles to effective listening, born of our individual temperaments and the various cultures to which we all belong (family, of course, but also ethnic, gender, faith, workplace, and so on). In the short term, these can be bridged with the help of a skilled facilitator, but that is like using an interpreter and, however good the interpreter, it is never as good as knowing the language; which means looking deeper.

It turns out that we have the means to engage in collaborative, empathic, contingent communication, curious as to why the other experiences the world differently than we do, open to whatever may come out of our dialogue, accepting of whoever the other turns out to be, and compassionate towards the other. That is indeed the way to truly listen; to make the speaker feel both heard and felt. Sadly, it is much easier said than done.

37   P Barrone, C Cruz and L Gomez-Mejia, "Socioemotional Wealth in Family Firms: Theoretical Dimensions, Assessment Approaches, and Agenda for Future Research", *Family Business Review* 25(3), 258-279 (2012).

38   S Turkle, *The Flight From Conversation* (2012); www.nytimes.com/2012/04/22/opinion/Sunday/the-flight-from-conversation.html.

39   W Benjamin, *The Storyteller: Reflections on the Works of Nikolai Leskov, op cit.*

40   S Porges, "Social Engagement and Attachment: A Phylogenetic Perspective", Ann. N.Y.Acad.Sci. 1008: 31-47 (2003); www.somaticpractice.net/trainings/touch_skills/resources/articles/polyvagal/Porges-2003-Social_Engagement_and_Attachment.pdf.

41   S Turkle, *The Flight From Conversation, op cit.*

42   Johann Wolfgang von Goethe.

First, we have to do battle with the oldest part of our brain, the brainstem (inherited from our reptilian ancestors), which manages our fight/flight/freeze response. It is quite crude, but very fast (waiting for a reasoned analysis of whether that is a fallen tree branch or a poisonous snake would likely not enhance your chances of surviving and breeding, which is the primary driver in all of this!). If the brainstem perceives a threat, it may get you ready to fight, or to run away: your pulse and blood pressure increase; you start to sweat; your libido disappears, and you may feel a strong urge to go to the toilet. If the threat is existential, it may do the opposite – freeze – causing a complete shut down,[43] though whether that is a defence mechanism or to make for a cleaner, quicker kill appears unclear. Either way, it is not setting you up to ask your brother (with curiosity, openness, acceptance and compassion) to tell you more about the nervous breakdown he has just told you your mother had shortly after you were born, and of which you were previously unaware.

Then there is the brainstem's mammalian upgrade (a bolt-on rather than a replacement version), the limbic system, which works with and in parallel to the brainstem, deciding what we should pay attention to, deciding whether it is good or bad, and driving us towards pleasure and away from pain. Of course, we may not always experience it so: how often do we try to avoid the difficult conversation, telling ourselves that we are doing so to avoid causing pain to the other (so giving ourselves pleasure), when it is really our own pain we fear for.[44]

Indeed, you may get both signals at the same time when, say, your father, who provides for you materially and whom you love dearly, denigrates everything you do (perhaps by comparison to your sister's near perfection). The effect is a bit like getting into a Ferrari and stamping hard on the brake and the accelerator at the same time – very uncomfortable, and something is likely to get broken!

The good news is that the middle pre-frontal cortex has direct connections with both the limbic area and the brainstem and can modulate their effects, giving us (among other things) what Siegel[45] has called "response flexibility", what Puddicombe[46] calls "headspace"; that is to say the ability to take a mental step back, pause, and consider and weigh the available options, before acting.

The bad news is that excessive states of arousal appear to shut down this process and, in this situation: "People don't think; they feel something intensely and act impulsively."[47] So, fear, anger, or other strong emotion may leave you at the mercy of impulse. Alcohol and narcotics, it seems, can have the same effect.

Even if we can keep these higher brain functions online, that is not the end of our challenges. Our brains are highly adaptive. We use our previous experience to predict the future, and act accordingly. Great music, and comedy, tend to play on that: creating expectation and then teasing us by sometimes fulfilling it, and sometimes not. But our experience often gets the better of us. It becomes

---

43   S Porges, "Social Engagement and Attachment: A Phylogenetic Perspective", *op cit.*
44   What Brooks calls "the dishonesty of niceness": D Brooks, *The Social Animal: A Story of How Success Happens*, second edition (Short Books, 2011).
45   D Siegel, *The Mindful Brain: Reflection and Attunement in the Cultivation of Well-Being*, first edition (WW Norton & Company, 2007).
46   A Puddicombe, *Get Some Headspace*, first paperback edition (Hodder & Stoughton Ltd, 2011).
47   D Siegel, *The Developing Mind, op cit.*

assumption, prejudgment or prejudice, and we act on it regardless of what our bodily senses are telling us, our "gut reaction". We may rationalise this as "not letting our heart rule our heads".

When we prejudge a conversation, we need no input from the other, so we stop listening and spend our time rehearsing our own speeches in the privacy of our own minds. When we feel hurt, we jump to conclusions: you spoke; I hurt; therefore you intended to hurt me. And so on.

On the other hand, when we are too much "in the moment", whether it is a musical reverie, the sight of a gorgeous boy or girl walking down the street, or just lost in our own mental chatter, we may find ourselves hitting the wall of the garage we have driven into without incident thousands of times before.

8. Remembrance of things past

A word or two about memory is appropriate here.

As Proust surmised, "remembrance of things past is not necessarily the remembrance of things as they were."[48] First, it appears that what you remember depends (in part at least) upon why you are trying to remember it (not good if you are preparing a witness statement in a dispute over the family trust), and that your recollection of any event may change with each remembrance.[49] This is not recalling a read-only file from a hard disk. It is, perhaps, more like taking a paper file from the draw, taking out the bits that do not meet your present need and then putting back the reordered file.

Second, only things that we focus on get incorporated in our autobiographical – explicit – memory, which is all we can consciously recall. Ever worried about whether you turned the gas off, or put out that last cigarette, or locked the door when you left home? They are things you do so often that you no longer pay attention to them, so they never get stored in explicit memory. Here again, intense emotion, alcohol and narcotics can also rob us of the ability to process memories in this way; the route from last night's party may be something you know well, but the walk home may never be!

But the overwhelming preponderance of our experience[50] goes into what is called implicit memory. Inaccessible to conscious recollection, it is implicit memory that accounts for our mental chatter; for those inexplicable changes in mood that come when (consciously or not) we hear a tune, or smell a scent, with some strong emotional tag that never made it into explicit memory; and through which our immediate sensory experience is filtered even when our so-called higher functions are online.[51]

And when there is a gap in our explicit memory, we generate a script that suits, typically one that fits well with our worldview, one that tends to make us feel better, and it becomes part of our reality; a process psychologists call *confabulation*.

---

48   Marcel Proust, *À la recherche du temps perdu*.
49   D Schacter, *Searching for Memory: the brain, the mind and the past*, first edition (Basic Books, 1996).
50   It is estimated we take in around 11 million bits of data per second but can only process consciously around 15 bits per second: T Nørretranders, *The User Illusion: Cutting Consciousness Down to Size*, first English edition (Penguin Books, 1998).
51   D Siegel, *The Mindful Brain, op cit*.

9. The story so far ...

To recap: we each experience the world differently; how we experience it plays a huge part in who we become as individuals, but most of that is not accessible to us in memory; we tend to react, rather than respond, not only to events around us, but to our own thoughts and emotions (a double whammy: you get upset, then you get upset that you are upset!); when there is a hole in our personal story, we make it up and believe that is the unalloyed truth; blessed with affluence and technology, we choose to live apart from one another (whether physically or mentally), losing both proximity and shared experience; we have come to prefer connection to conversation, the exchange of information to communication; ... and we wonder why we do not always communicate well!

10. The mindful brain[52]

Fortunately, we can learn to listen deeply, empathically, to what others have to say. We can learn to be open to whatever we hear, and accepting of others whoever, or whatever, they turn out to be. We can learn how to make others feel both heard and felt. We can learn not to react, but to respond to events appropriately and proportionately.

Our ability to attune to others, to balance our emotions, to be flexible in our responses, to soothe our fears, to create insight (my sense of me), empathy (my sense of you), moral awareness (my sense of we), and intuition are all key to this learning, and all appear to be mediated by the middle pre-frontal cortex of the brain.[53] Research shows both that the practice of *mindful awarenesss* (paying conscious attention to our inner sensations, images, feelings and thoughts) tends to increase neuronal growth and speed of function in that area of the brain, and that more mindful people show less reactivity when presented with threatening emotional stimuli.[54]

Those practices have their origins in religious observance,[55] and for many the element of faith is important, but it is not necessary to achieving the results we seek here. Tai chi chuan, chi kung, yoga and a variety of mindfulness meditation techniques have all been shown to be equally effective.[56]

A number of these techniques are based on simple breath awareness. We breathe continuously, but are rarely aware of it. Mindfulness practice trains us to be conscious of our breath for minutes at a time. We also learn to notice when we are distracted from that and, when we are, simply to bring our focus back to the breath. This seemingly pointless exercise trains the mind to be more generally aware, increasing our awareness of our thoughts, feelings, emotions and bodily sensations; and it empowers us to choose whether to act on them, or just to let them go.

---

52   Daniel J Siegel.
53   D Siegel, *The Mindful Brain, op cit.*
54   D Creswell, B Way, N Eisenberger and M Lieberman, "Neural Correlates of Dispositional Mindfulness During Affect Labelling", *Psychosomatic Medicine* 69: 560 – 565 (2007); and see also Mental Health Foundation, *Mindfulness Report* (2010), www.livingmindfully.co.uk/downloads/Mindfulness_Report.pdf.
55   Notably in the Buddhist tradition, but similar practices are also found in contemplative Christianity, Judaism and Islam.
56   D Siegel, *The Mindful Brain, op cit.*; A Puddicombe, *Get Some Headspace, op* cit. Mental Health Foundation, *Mindfulness Report, op cit.*

As long ago as 1891, William James, the father of American psychology, said that an education which would improve "the faculty of voluntarily bringing back a wandering attention, over and over again ... would be the education *par excellence*."[57]

Further description of such techniques is beyond the scope of this chapter, but guides can readily be found on line.[58]

As we become more mindful, and learn to listen (both to ourselves and to others) with curiosity, openness, acceptance and compassion, we can become more adept co-constructors of our family stories and, through that process, cement the felt connection and cultural continuity that I believe is key to cohesive, multi-generational, family prosperity.

11.   Great stories happen to those who can tell them[59]

Of course, how and when we do our storytelling will vary from family to family. It generally begins as we reminisce to our infants and young children. Fivush and Nelson[60] suggest that the more elaborative that reminiscing is, the more effectively past events are set in time and place and in emotional and personally meaningful contexts, and the more the child too is encouraged to talk about his experiences both as they occur, and in reminiscence, the more coherent and evaluative the child's own narrative will become.

Our symbols, heroes, rituals, and values are all passed on through these exchanges, and reinforced over time through the sharing of nursery rhymes, fairy stories, folk tales, songs, and so on.

For some, their family stories will be factual, full of historicity. For others, they will be more mythic, full of metaphor. Neither is right, or wrong, but simply reflects the family's cultural and communication norms.

For some families, particularly those who remain geographically close, this process develops naturally through daily interaction, birthday and other celebrations, a regular round of breaking bread together. In some faiths and cultures the regular cycle of feasts and festivals provides a natural framework for that.

Others, for whatever reason, never develop that way of doing. For those families, a facilitated discussion of "who are we as a family?", "where do we come from?" and "why do we choose to manage our capital collectively?" may provide a useful starting point. A genealogical exercise may be an interesting project for a younger generation.[61] Which branches they choose to research, and the individuals they most connect with, let alone the discovery of how "we" used to live in different social, political and economic times, can be a great stepping off point for further conversation.

It is important that our shared stories look forwards, as well as backwards. Our dreams and aspirations – our memories of the future if you will – are just as much a

---

57   W James, *Psychology: Briefer Course* (Harper Torchbooks, 1961).
58   See for example: drdansiegel.com/resources/everyday_mindsight_tools/; www.getsomeheadspace.com/.
59   Ira Glass.
60   R Fivush and K Nelson, "Culture and Language in the Emergence of Autobiographical Memory", *op cit.*
61   I start all my work with families by compiling a *genogram*, a stylised form of annotated family tree developed by family therapists, which forms the heart of my file; M McGoldrick, R Gerson and S Petry, *Genograms: Assessment and Intervention*, third edition (WW Norton & Co, Inc, 2008).

part of our personal and family narratives as how we come to be where we are; a shared sense of "where we are heading" just as important to our sense of continuity.

Nor should we expect them to be fixed, constant. All culture is dynamic, and families are no exception. People come (birth, marriage) and go (death, divorce), levels of affluence wax and wane,[62] we change with experience (physiologically, as we have learned), and so on. The value of our stories is that they memorialise our symbols, heroes, rituals and values. They will, inevitably, change over time, and our stories must change too. That is not to say that we should consciously edit them, but nor should we be overly resistant to their evolution over time; a changing story may be a clue that other things too are changing.

While the power of the story may be, as Damasio[63] suggested, to make our chosen values "persuasive and enforceable", we should not be too dogmatic about that. The aim is cohesion, not homogeneity. To quote Siegel again:

> [It] is more like making a fruit salad than a smoothie: it requires that the elements retain their individual uniqueness while simultaneously linking to other components of [the] system".[64]

To paraphrase McGilchrist,[65] without difference there can be neither harmony nor counterpoint.

Technology has a great role to play in all this, not least in memorialising the family story, creating a dynamic, living and interactive archive, including music, pictures and videos, particularly of family members telling their personal stories while they are still around to do that. Technology allows us to keep in touch in circumstances where we never could before, but being in touch is no substitute for touching, for physical and mental presence which, as we have seen, is crucial to building and maintaining the bonds between us.

12. Conclusion

So, to summarise, I am proposing that:

- The biggest threat to a family's capital (be it financial, human, intellectual, social or spiritual) is a breakdown of trust and communication within the family;
- To minimise the risk of such a breakdown, families need to pay attention to the glue that holds them together, to their *felt connection and cultural continuity*;
- To do that, we need to spend time together creating, nurturing, and recording our evolving family story, through which we pass on our shared symbols, heroes, rituals and values and win the commitment of the group to them;
- The listener is as important to that process as the teller, and we each need to learn to listen deeply to the other with curiosity, openness, acceptance and compassion;

---

62   See, for example, Hofstede and Hofstede (*op cit.*) for the impact of changes in affluence and other factors on various cultural metrics.
63   A Damasio, *When Self Comes to Mind: Constructing the Conscious Brain, op cit.*
64   D Siegel, *The Developing Mind, op cit.*
65   I McGilchrist, *The Master and his Emissary, op cit.*

- We each need to learn to assess, not assume; to respond, not react;
- Ancient tradition, the recorded experience of many, and modern neuroscience all tell us that the practice of mindful awareness improves our facility to do all of these things.

There is, of course, much else that any family must do if it is to succeed in developing its capital (in all of its forms) harmoniously and cohesively over generations, and about which others have written in this book. This, however, I believe offers a sound foundation to all of that.

Thanks to Roselyn Fell, Cinnie Noble and Martin Stepek for their thoughtful comments on a draft of this chapter. Any remaining errors are mine.

The journey towards governance

Dennis T Jaffe
Independent adviser

In addition to legal, financial and business advice, advisers are increasingly asked to help the family create policies about personal relationships, conflict and differences in an increasing pool of relatives, aligning goals and values, learning to work together as a cross-generational family team, and making fair and effective decisions that serve the long-term interests of the family. In accounts of family feuds and lawsuits, we observe the great personal and financial losses that arise from seemingly minor disagreements, and the great passion aggrieved family members bring to a dispute about inheritance or control.

Legal and financial advisers are increasingly called upon to help families anticipate needs and prevent or head off future conflicts. Advisers not only have to work with legal and tax structures, but also the personal relationships that exist between family members who share assets as business partners. While an agreement can be legal, the family must also see it as fair, and understand how it works and why is it there, or conflict will ensue. A growing wealthy family must help all family members understand and deal with the dual aspect of their relationships – as family members with a shared history, and as business/financial partners. The structures and practices set in place must serve both sets of interests, which can sometimes seem divergent and incompatible. This is not the kind of work that the adviser anticipated or learned about in professional school, but it is what the family wants and needs in order to make use of some aspects of professional advice.

This chapter reviews concepts and activities that define the best practices of relationship management and governance of the wealthy global extended family. It is based upon several articles written by myself and my colleague James Grubman, building upon the important work of many colleagues, our experience with families, and the tools, models and practices emerging in family business and wealth consulting. These concepts are being incorporated more and more into the holistic practices of financial, legal and accounting firms who serve the global ultra-wealthy.

1.   Acquirers and inheritors: from founder to successors

We have defined a common process of social adaption as a family acquires wealth and passes it to the next generation.[1] While there are cultural differences, wealth

---

[1]   See Jaffe, D and Grubman, J, "Acquirers' and Inheritors' Dilemma: Finding Life Purpose and Building Personal Identity in the Presence of Wealth", Journal of Wealth Management, Fall, 2007, and Grubman, J, "Strangers in Paradise: How Families Adapt to Wealth Across Generations", Family Wealth Consulting, 2013.

acquirers in all cultures tend to have certain character traits that suit them for the risks of starting a company, such as a deep reservoir of self-confidence and passion about what they are doing. Stylistically, they tend to keep their own counsel and keep control over as much of the business as they can. They are adaptive and improvise, taking advantage of opportunities. They often come from modest or even poor backgrounds, and their motivation is less to create wealth than it is to actualise their dream. They want to make a difference, and they see their business as the centre of their lives. Family plays a lesser role.

Coming from mostly modest backgrounds, they are in a sense immigrants to the lifestyles, habits and world of the wealthy. They know very little about how to live with wealth, and nothing at all about how to prepare their children to inherit wealth. This challenge has led to the homily "from shirtsleeves to shirtsleeves in three generations," and the observation that most family wealth is dissipated by the third generation.

The wealth acquirer is therefore not the type of person who makes a good teacher, or a patient and understanding parent. Creators are proud of what they have done, which is expressed in part by their wealth and power, and they want the best for their children. But they may also lack understanding of the experience or needs of their children, and tend to deal with the future by trying to control it. This can present a challenge to their children as they pursue their own independence amid family wealth and privilege.

Inheritors, especially those who inherit great wealth, report contrasting experiences, again across cultures and nations. Unlike their parents, who remember not having wealth, the next generation grows up around wealth; the culture of wealth is natural to them. But they frequently report that their parents, especially wealth-creating fathers, are distant or even absent from their lives. 'Having the best' means going away to schools, rooms full of luxury items, and servants doing many tasks that would otherwise fall to parents. Being special means that they grow up in enclaves of wealth, often isolated not just from ordinary people but also from learning how to meet demands or take care of themselves; this has been called the 'gilded ghetto'. Money is frequently a substitute for contact and intimacy, and they may grow up feeling peculiarly deprived even amid all their riches.

The greatest challenge is for the inheritors to develop as people, figure out what to do with their lives, and find ways to experience a sense of personal fulfilment, self-worth and accomplishment. This is difficult. As offspring of well-known and powerful parents, how can their actions compare with the achievements of their parents? Their parents can make things even more difficult, with high but unclearly defined or unrealistic expectations. They are protected from failure and from learning from adversity, but they face a web of expectations and pressures to perform.

As we see in the comparison in Figure 1, acquirers and inheritors, while they grow up in the same household, have very different life experiences that may put them at cross-purposes. While the parents are concerned about their wealth being spent by their children, the children are concerned about finding their place in the world.

Figure 1: The realities and concerns of acquirers and inheritors

Acquirers	Inheritors
• immigrant to land of wealth • passion for control and autonomy • business is centre of life • remember not having financial security • enter new social reality, want to fit • self-confident risk-takers • improvisational, thrive on crisis • not good listeners or teachers	• grow up with money • anxiety about sustaining it • stewardship and entitlement mixed • desire continuity, tradition • familiar with financial resources • risk-averse, prudent investors • not conscious about financial affairs • delegate wealth management • searching for life purpose, meaning
Concerns about their wealth	**Concerns about future wealth**
• effect of wealth over generations • what to pass on to heirs? • raising happy, productive children • fear of spoiled, entitled kids • making mark after parents have done so well	• getting motivated to discover their life passion • anxiety about failing family, making mistake • being credible to the older generation

Parents may not fully understand how to help them develop themselves, and by creating trusts and other vehicles to manage family wealth, may keep them feeling like dependent children far into adulthood. As a family, they ought to send a clear message to their heirs about what is expected, and how they are expected to relate to the family resources. If there is a trust or a family board with outside advisers, it may not be clear how or when the next generation can become involved in governance or participation, even if they are expected to be ready to do so, which may feel frustrating or even demeaning. They can feel that the trust's very existence into adulthood means that they are not trusted to take care of the family's wealth.

Each generation of the family adds inheritors who grow up in a world of wealth, developing particular expectations of what is theirs, what they will have to do, passions, skills, capabilities and willingness to be part of the extended family. The challenge for each offspring is to what degree they feel entitled to a certain level of wealth and lifestyle, and what they are willing and able to do for the family to help preserve its wealth and develop other forms of family capital; to become stewards rather than merely consumers of the family wealth. Clear family values, messages and policies about this must guide them.

The older generation wants their children to become stewards and take good care of what they inherit. The wealth creators worry about what will happen to the wealth when it gets into the hands of the next generation. How will the kids use it? If simply preserving the money is the goal, then it is prudent to put it in the hands of financial professionals who can invest wisely. Make the professionals responsible, so the kids are passive heirs who can enjoy their gift. Mission accomplished: the wealth is preserved. Or is it?

What is the underlying message given to the (now) adult children when parents take control and responsibility for the family wealth out of their hands in this way? On the one hand, elders want their children to be responsible and not squander their inheritances. Yet they frequently create trusts and layers of professional management that deny them this opportunity. Being a 'trust fund baby' means a life of affluence and continued dependence well into adulthood, which is not an adult role. This conundrum – wanting to share the benefits of money with children, but wanting to control how the children use the money – causes confusion. How can parents trust their adult children to use the wealth responsibly? When can they risk giving up control, and how can they best prepare the next generation to take control?

Their children have almost the opposite worldview. They grow up as 'natives' in a culture of great comfort, where they are treated as special because their families are wealthy. They may never realise that other people do not have what they have. They have never been without wealth, but they don't really know where it comes from or very much about the skills they would need to earn such wealth. Unconsciously, they may project arrogance or exhibit incompetence in daily activities. They assume and expect that their lives will continue to be privileged. They may think that the money is, or should be considered, theirs, although in fact it is not. Because they have so much, they may experience anxiety about what would happen if it were gone.

It is hard for them to prepare to work, assuming that an inheritance awaits them. Why work? What will it mean for them and their family? They may fear making choices and not being good enough, especially when compared to the outsized achievements of their parents. So, while they may want to work, they find it hard to take the first steps successfully. At the first sign of difficulty, they may pull back. Because they have a nice cushion, they don't feel pressure to push through adversity as they start careers. This dynamic explains the chequered work careers of some heirs – they don't have the incentive or the skills to put up with adversity or take risks. This may puzzle their parents, who have taken great risks in their lives. Why are their children so different from them?

Growing up in the very narrow world of wealth, privilege, fine houses, grand vacations, and private schools (living, as Robert Frank put it, in the country of "Richistan") they often have a very naïve view of how the world works and what real effort and achievement looks like. For example, young people from wealthy families who get into highly competitive colleges may feel (reasonably) that family connections – not personal efforts – are responsible for the accomplishment.

When they get to school, their allowances and their names may lead to distractions they are not prepared to overcome. Young people coming from such circumstances need to grow and develop their own sense of what to do with their lives, and the credibility and capability to achieve it on their own. To do this, they need to become independent of the role their parents have set out for them.

Young people from wealthy backgrounds frequently begin this journey when, often for the first time, they get the message that they can't do anything they want.

Figure 2: Inheritor's developmental journey in a wealthy family

Stage	Life stage	Outcomes	Activities
Teach children about money	Childhood to pre-teens	Acquisition of values about money and basic understanding	• Talk about money in family • Saving, giving, spending • Share money values • Work within family
Develop positive wealth identity	Late teens to young adulthood	Development of personal sense of who one is and what one wants to do	• Leave family home • Make personal financial choices • Find passion, develop skills • Develop close relationships outside family
Encounter the family enterprise	Young adult	Understanding of nature, responsibilities, and opportunities of the family enterprise	• Attend family enterprise briefings • Develop functional skills to understand the enterprise • Explore career options
Participate in a social mission	Young to mature adulthood	Development of commitment to improving the world	• Active involvement in a social cause, service • Define personal, family philanthropic mission • Participate in family service, philanthropy
Become a family citizen	Adulthood	Taking an active role in family estate and enterprise activities	• Participate in activities to develop family connection • Take contributing role in family enterprise • Engagement in succession dialogue

They get poor grades, get cut from a sports team, or have difficulty in a relationship. Others struggle with drugs, alcohol, eating disorders or behavioural addictions, which they have to solve on their own. Some heirs do not emerge well from these challenges; for others, these challenges provide a wake-up call that guides them to personal responsibility, self-confidence, and capability. Parents must hang back but provide appropriate emotional support and show children that they have faith in them. That often is a hard balance for any parent to find.

To grow up in a wealthy family, a young person will have to go through several life stages that are somewhat unique to families of wealth, all over the world, in that they have different challenges than young people from more modest circumstances.

In Figure 2, I define the key stages, challenges and activities a wealthy family faces to help their children become stewards. This progression outlines the multiple tasks that a wealthy family must engage in to educate and support its heirs. Due to the family wealth the young person faces added responsibilities and threats, which the family must actively confront.

2. The challenge of crossing generations

The problem of crossing generations has another wrinkle that makes it difficult to sustain a family over time: the family by nature centres power and control in the older generations. Their past success leads them to avoid, resist and find it difficult to consider any sort of change, especially change that affects the way they have always done things or threatens their continuing control. A family thus has a natural tendency to resist change and maintain what has been successful in the past, even though this tendency can lead to difficulty in innovating and adapting.

Change, however, is going on both within the family and outside, whether the family chooses to deny it or not. The challenges facing a family are tremendous, and to succeed a family must actively adopt and respond to them:

- Internally, it faces growing numbers of family members, diverging interests, the limitations of the family's talent (its gene pool) as regards duplicating the skills of the wealth creator, and a family culture that may not support the values and behaviour needed to sustain wealth.
- Externally, the family business faces forces of growth or decline, market pressures, globalisation and the need for capital and business reinvention in order to survive.

Over generations, the family enterprise evolves in a biologically determined pattern. The first generation has a single wealth creator, with children growing up together in a single household, with the consequent family dynamics and rivalries. Even though one may be designated as the next leader of the family enterprise, no sibling can have the same credibility in the family as the wealth creator, and, therefore, as heirs the siblings have to form a team and learn to collaborate,. The other siblings have their own needs and sensitivities, which can lead to conflict and the need for clear rules and policies for how to manage them.

With the emergence of the third generation, each sibling has married and formed another family. Third generation cousins grow up in separate households and may know little about each other, and hold very different values, expectations and desires for the family wealth. Hence, by the third generation, the lack of family intimacy must be recognised as the family partners develop clear and explicit governance for how they make decisions. As new members join the family by marriage, and new cousins grow up and are introduced into the extended family and its business/financial entities, they often express new and different values and needs that must be taken into account. Also, with each generation, more family members means the family wealth will have to go further. Without clear processes to limit spending, preserve wealth and add to it with entrepreneurial ventures, the wealth will dissipate – as predicted – by the third generation.

3. Best practices that develop all types of family capital

Families that have acquired wealth are not only concerned with passing the money on to their children. They are also concerned with other aspects of their legacy: keeping united as a family, sustaining their business and financial enterprises, their standing in the community, the well-being and livelihood of their children and grand-children.

Specifically, to be successful over generations, a wealthy family must balance goals from three major pathways.

- Pathway I – Nurture connection as a family. The first pathway is about how the family actively builds connection and shared purpose over generations, fighting the natural tendency for family members to move into separate worlds and greater disconnection.

For a multi-generational family to remain together as a financial or business entity, the family members in several generations must find a reason for them to remain together as partners. They must create an inspiring and motivating common vision as an extended family that makes them want to work together. In addition, as partners and shared owners, they need to develop trust in each other, spend time together, develop personal relationships across families, and develop common values they stand for in the community.

- Pathway II – Steward the family enterprises. The family must organise itself for the business of the family, and these are the practices of the second pathway. It contains practices by which the family has a voice in the management and oversight of its business and financial enterprises, which are applied transparently and clearly to all family members.

The extended family has not just a family legacy of values, but a shared family business or several family financial enterprises, which they own together. The business can be large and public, employ many people and have a high profile in the community. As owners who are personally involved and accountable, they are identified with the business, with personal expectations of what the business will provide and their role in and relationship to it. As more family members expect to become owners, there must be clear rules for how to make decisions, work together, and operate their financial and business entities. The family needs a plan for growth and diversification, and how the rewards and resources of their family enterprises will be distributed. It needs to create an internal market for buying and selling shares of family enterprises, so that family members can choose whether to remain together or leave. The roles, responsibility and authority of each person should be clear, so that each family member feels that he or she is treated fairly.

Often a first or earlier generation had a single benevolent leader, or a simple structure that will need to be adapted to deal with the new realities of the second or later generation. As the family moves across generations, it must organise to anticipate the challenges it will face. Family members have also to deal with any conflicts and differences they have as family members, who share a tradition that does not exist with owners who are not related. Many families have good intentions, but they do not go so far as to define how they are to be put into practice. Therefore, different interpretations of what ought to be done can lead to conflict. The practices in this pathway help the family anticipate or avoid conflict, and help it make decisions that preserve both family harmony and financial returns.

- Pathway III – Cultivate human capital for the next generation. The third pathway defines practices that are unique to a family enterprise: how they will prepare and develop the next generation to take over control of the family wealth.

The most unique element of a multi-generational family enterprise is that a new generation of young people grows up in the family, feeling a connection and an expectation of sharing in its legacy. The young people are in a new category of potential and expected owners-to-be, which need to be prepared for this role, and to learn how to work with each other. As inheritors of family wealth, they need to learn how to deal with their inheritance responsibly, and have a clear pathway outlining how to move into responsible family roles. The successful multi-generational family enterprise must actively, even pro-actively, develop the next generation. It must create clear, explicit and active steps for the next generation to emerge into full citizenship in the family. Developing the next generation involves governance and family activities that are unique to a family enterprise – a shared concern with the development, roles and responsibilities of a new generation of family members.

A successful family must create practices along each of these three paths. Emphasis on setting up family activities to support only one element of this trio, for example to support anything that young family members want uncritically, risks undermining other elements, such as effective business practices. Alternatively, an emphasis on controlling the business may interfere with the healthy growth and development of the next generations, who remain dependent and find it difficult to grow and thrive. Finding structures that balance and support all three of these is a large challenge, and often a family is divided with some wanting to emphasise one above the others.

How common are such practices in successful families? A sample of nearly 200 wealthy, multi-generational family enterprises (families who had either a family business or family office), most of them moving into the second, third or even fourth generations by the Family Office Exchange and Family Business Network, were asked whether they used the 15 practices listed in Figure 3. We found that these families all used a large number of these practices to organise their family governance. They also intended to develop many of these practices further in the near future. These findings suggest that the use of these governance structures is an important element in becoming one of the few families that sustain themselves over generations, and continue to generate additional wealth (see Jaffe, Three Pathways to Evolutionary Survival, fully cited in references below).

Figure 3: Best practices of multigenerational families

Pathway I: Nurture the family
1.1 Clear, compelling family purpose and direction 1.2 Opportunities for extended family to get to know each other 1.3 Climate of family openness, trust and communication 1.4 Regular family meetings as a family council 1.5 Sharing and respect for family history and legacy 1.6 Shared family philanthropic and social engagement
Pathway II: Steward the family enterprises
2.1 Strategic plan for family wealth and enterprise development 2.2 Active, diverse, empowered board guiding each enterprise 2.3 Transparency about financial information and business decisions 2.4 Explicit and shared shareholder agreements about family assets 2.5 Policies that support diversification and entrepreneurial ventures 2.6 Exit and distribution policies for individual shareholder liquidity
Pathway III: Cultivate human capital for the next generation
3.1 Employment policies about working in family enterprises 3.2 Agreement on values about family money and wealth 3.3 Support and encouragement to develop next generation leadership 3.4 Empower individuals to seek personal fulfillment and life purpose 3.5 Opportunities to become involved in family governance activities 3.6 Teach age-appropriate financial skills to young family members

Another way to conceptualise the multiple tasks of cross-generational family governance, as suggested by Jay Hughes in his seminal book, Family Wealth: Keeping it in the Family, is to consider the family as generating both financial and non-financial 'capital' (sources of value) for succeeding generations.

These forms of capital represent the types of value a family creates and can then pass on. The foundation and starting place is legacy, or spiritual capital. This refers not to religious faith, but more broadly the values, meaning and core purpose that motivates and inspires a family to see itself as a meaningful entity and to have pride in what it can do. Every generation needs to replenish and develop its spiritual capital, before it can develop other areas. Then, elements of financial, family, human and social capital can be developed by the family.

To do this means that the family has to see itself as a dynamic, active operating group beyond its various business and financial entities. As a family sets up trusts, foundations, new businesses and investment entities, they must be organised to reflect the meaning and values of the family as a whole. In addition to its businesses, the family will want to undertake other activities to further its goals and values. These will entail meeting and working together as an extended family team. These are described in Figure 4.

4. Governance, constitutions and the family council

I have suggested that families, perhaps because of their refusal to face the need for change, tend to avoid or deny the need to prepare for the next generation. But even families that prepare with a good legal and financial structure tend to put off, or not understand the need for active engagement in, planning for the future as a family. The family looking at future generations must set up more than just a legal financial structure for inheritance. It must also consider how it will sustain and preserve a family connection, make family decisions about governing its shared wealth, and develop and empower the next generation. Activities to achieve these goals go beyond the usual legal agreements, into informal and formal family policies and agreements.

As a family becomes involved in more complex family investments and businesses, the need for new policies increases. The structure and agreements that worked for an earlier generation may not take into account the added size and complexity of the future. For example, as a new generation takes control over assets, and new family members have less informal contact, the need to share, reassess and revise operating agreements arises. A sibling team that worked together seamlessly and never had to vote on decisions will find that the next generation may need to develop a more formal process.

'Governance' is a word for the sum total of the agreements about how the family owners set priorities, define goals and values, and make decisions about their shared assets. In a family enterprise, governance covers a lot of ground, in terms of all of the possible activities that a family can engage in. Governance is not just about financial decisions, regulations and business oversight; it also encompasses decisions on roles and activities to prepare the next generation, to convene family activities and to set up philanthropic and charitable activities. Some elements of governance are defined in legal agreements; others can be based on custom or what are termed morally binding policies, that are known and adhered to by all family members. For example, a family can invite all family members to an annual family gathering, even support it financially, but family members are expected, not compelled, to attend. If they are present, they can then express opinions and participate in the work of the family.

Family governance can only be understood in relation to the unique nature of family enterprise; the family owners include people who have a deep and shared history (and set of values and expectations) as a family, and include not only the actual owners but also a group of people who expect to obtain ownership, and as potential owners have their own expectations and assumptions. Unlike strangers who are shareholders in a venture, family shareholders care about their children, and want to prepare them ultimately to take their place in decision-making and control. The complex nature of family governance for a global family arises because it must be set up to govern both personal and business/financial relationships, and to balance the multiple priorities of each.

Figure 4: The five dimensions of family capital

Capital	Definition	Expressed as
Legacy	Spiritual mission, values, core purpose and shared meaning – the foundation of the family, its approach to wealth and to relationships with each other	• Understanding the deeper meaning and purpose of family wealth • Family mission and values statement • Telling the family story to the next generation • Talking together about values and what is really important, including faith-based values
Financial	Resources to manage and sustain over time support for a comfortable lifestyle for the family – partnership between the family and the family's wealth management/ family office	• Choosing and implementing good wealth management, with appropriate oversight and collaboration by the family • Creating clear and realistic expectations among all family members and generations • Teaching heirs values, responsibility and skills about managing wealth • Generating a sense of responsibility and stewardship • Creating trusts and financial entities that coordinate with overall long-term wealth management
Family	Ability to develop structures to make decisions, manage family capital, maintain connection, compromise, manage conflict and create caring positive and productive relationships	• Creation, maintenance and ongoing adaptation of family councils, boards and assemblies • A written family constitution • Accountability and clear communication to beneficiaries • Generating respect, caring and trust by communication • Develop family social networks
Human	Fostering development of the character, skills and identity of each family member for managing self and wealth; encouraging purpose through paid or unpaid work; guidance for a complex, demanding global environment	• Initiating age-appropriate discussions about money with heirs and those entering the family from the outside (in-laws, stepchildren) • Building self-esteem and identity independent of having money • Helping heirs develop a sense of purpose for their lives • Developing skills and capability for heirs to make their way independently in the world
Social	Commitment, respect, compassion for suffering and concerns of others, service within one's community for the future of the planet.	• Expressing individual and collective family values in the community through action and/or investment • Involving family members in service and philanthropy • Socially-responsive investing, micro-loans, etc.

However, we have seen that a growing set of practices is being used by global families to achieve these goals (Figure 3). These practices are often organised and integrated into a set of family agreements that has been called a family constitution. This is a master agreement that covers all of the activities and policies of the family. Some families call upon a legal or governance expert to draft or propose such an agreement for a family. But, looking at families that have successfully created and used constitutions, a different picture of where they come from, what they look like and how they are used emerges.

Keeping in mind the three key pathways for a thriving cross-generational family enterprise, we view the successful evolution of a family enterprise as the development of a set of governing agreements, policies, practices and activities that help the family act as a coordinating entity for many kinds of family capital. To develop them, the family must begin to work together not just in the financial and business arena, but in social, educational, recreational and philanthropic activities. As the family numbers grow, and disperse to many different communities, active maintenance of family connection and oversight is an increasing challenge.

While the family finances and legal agreements are centred on either a trustee or board of directors, the role of family governance expands to include how the family defines and communicates its intention to the trustee or board, and also the ways in which the family members decide that they have shared interests and a desire to conduct other activities as well.

While the business of the family is under the direction of the board or trustees, the other activities must be set up by an organisation of the family. While this organisation has many forms, the term that has grown to describe it is a family council. The intention of gathering family members to define shared values, interests and policies is a clear one, but putting it in place is a challenge. First, all members (though some may choose not to participate) must agree to set it up, and the family elders must support this activity. For the first two generations, membership in the council is clear and manageable – it contains the founding parents, their children, and often, but not always, their spouses who have married into the family.

By the third generation, the adult membership expands; the council contains more people. At this point, a family may elect a smaller steering committee or executive council for this purpose, holding annual or semi-annual meetings for the whole family. But the purpose and nature of the family council is unchanged. The role of the council is to unify the family, define its operating values and principles, communicate them to the board or trustees, and set up activities to deal with shared family investments like vacation property, to create recreational activities, to oversee the growth, development and education of new family members into the family enterprises and, finally, to deal with conflicts that arise in the family in order to make sure that they do not escalate or affect the business or the wider community.

The council begins in the form of a single family meeting. If a family decides to continue to meet regularly, and begins to take action and make decisions, it can then be considered a family council. This entity creates the family constitution. While the council may have an adviser, and may draw on legal and trust agreements for parameters for how decisions are made, the task of creating the constitution is one the family has to do itself. If an outside person draws it up, the family members who are closest to the adviser may understand and agree to it, but the whole family will not. An adviser can help a family create agreements, but the family must define the specifics. As we have seen, the policies and practices often go beyond the legal, to set up family task forces that, for example, plan vacations or work on a family mission and values statement. In order for the agreements to work, the whole family must be engaged in creating them. They will often go through several drafts, and evolve over a year or more.

The activities undertaken by the family council and included in the family constitution include those that deal with each of the pathways defined earlier. They begin by working on the legacy capital, defining what the family is and stands for, its mission, vision and values. These values guide the family not just in its personal relationships but also in the directions it goes as an investment or business partnership. Then the family defines its goals and activities in each type of capital.

While it may be argued that many of these activities are under the control of a trustee or governing board, the family council's activities create a formal two-way communication vehicle for the family to make its intentions known and to learn about the family's investments and business activities. The family, not the business, has to define how it wants or expects family members to participate. If there is a family employment policy, whereby family members are expected to adhere to certain policies if they want to work for the business, this is a family, not a business decision. As a business, the board is concerned that family members are competent and accountable. As a family, it can decide what family members can do to prepare for work in the business – for example educational expectations or work outside the business. The family, or the sub-group of shareholders, may also decide who to appoint to the board, or what level of risk and return it wants from investments. It may also add ethical or social impact values for investments.

A major focus of the family council is to make sure that the new generation of adult family members, who grow up in different households and environments, develop the commitment and capability to make sure that the business continues to thrive. The greatest hedge against having spendthrift or thoughtless inheritors is for a family to develop not just a set of policies, but some clear ways that the next generation can become educated, can learn about the family legacy and businesses, and can begin to get involved and demonstrate their ability to become shareholders and leaders in the family enterprises. Many family councils develop family educational programmes, briefings for family members about the business, hands-on philanthropic programmes, and family social networks that engage family members in productive pursuits. These are also active ways that the family can actualise its values and mission together, so that the inheritors will have the desire to continue the family as a shared entity over one more generation.

5. Final thoughts

This article offers a brief overview of the family dimension necessary for a family that owns a business or multiple enterprises if it is to survive and thrive over several generations. Only a few families are able to combine business and financial success with success at sustaining cross-generational connection and engagement as an extended family. While a good trust agreement and a strong business can be helpful, I have suggested that a family must become aware of itself as a network of personal relationships, and begin to work together actively on both a personal and a business/financial level.

Family office governance

Håkan Hillerström
Independent family business adviser
Ken McCracken
Amelia Renkert-Thomas
Withers Consulting Group

As outlined earlier in the book, a single family office is a private company of dedicated professionals devoted exclusively to the investment, personal and legacy needs of one family.

A number of wealth management firms have created multi-family offices to provide a range of services beyond investment management to their client families. While these multi-family offices are a widespread trend in the wealth management marketplace, this chapter focuses on governance for the single family office – a privately-owned and run wealth management entity operated for one family.

Each single family office is as unique as the family who founded it – as the saying goes: "If you've seen one single family office, you've seen one single family office." Nowhere is that statement more accurate than in the area of single family office governance.

Some single family offices are substantial wealth-management institutions, with teams of experienced investment managers overseeing fully diversified portfolios, and providing extensive services to the family. Other single family offices are smaller, managing more limited assets. Some oversee operating businesses. Almost all single family offices share the following features:

- Clients of the single family office typically go beyond individuals to include trusts, foundations, holding companies, and partnerships;
- The single family office manages a complex pool of investment and personal assets;
- Investments are selected and managed with a long-term focus (typically, for multiple generations of the family);
- The creator of the single family office wishes to play an active role in overseeing investment management.

For the family that creates it, an effective single family office can provide:

- control, coordination and integrated management of investment, business, philanthropic and personal services;
- privacy and confidentiality;
- dedicated focus on the needs and requirements of the family;
- coordination and management of outsourced providers;
- purchasing leverage, fee minimisation and cost savings;
- management of tax and reporting obligations;
- fiduciary administration;

- risk management;
- alignment with the family's legacy, vision and values.

1. Single family office governance

Governance has long been a focus of corporate investors, but until recently less attention has been paid to how single family offices are governed. For a single family office intended to serve a family for generations, taking time to develop and implement an effective and appropriate governance structure can significantly improve the longevity and success of the office.

Some families shy away from the term 'governance', which can bring to mind dark and musty legislative chambers and mind-numbing rules, regulations, policies and provisions. At its core, however, governance is really nothing more than a set of rules that define how a family or organisation will make decisions, large or small. For governance to be effective, the owners, the board of directors and management need to be informed, understand their respective roles, rights, and responsibilities, and operate the organisation accordingly.

As mentioned at the outset, single family office governance is particularly challenging because every single family office is different, making oft-cited best practices so general as to be useless. Single family office governance is a creature of its environment – it typically arises spontaneously as a natural response to the specific circumstances faced by the founder and office's staff. This 'natural', or 'organic' governance is a collection of understandings, assumptions and expectations that comprise 'the way we do things around here'. Organic governance often works well for a period of time, but as the family and the single family office's clients grow, there is a real risk that understandings, assumptions and expectations will become misunderstandings, mistaken assumptions and unfulfilled expectations.

To see how organic governance might arise, consider the typical forms single family offices take:

- Embedded single family office – an embedded family office is one that exists within an operating business and is managed by the family business's management team. The result is that the perspective, priorities and values of the business, not the family, drive decision-making in an embedded single family office. The management team is loyal to the chief executive officer and may treat some of the family office's clients – such as trustees of family trusts, or individual family members who do not work in the business – differently from others.
- Liquidity single family office – a liquidity family office is one that was created by a family following the sale of a business. A liquidity family office is often run by the financial team that served the business, making it very like an embedded single family office in terms of its perspective, priorities and values. The difference is that the work of the family office, not the family business, is now the centre of the team's attention. However, old lines of command and ways of doing things often linger on, whether effective or not.
- Investment single family office – an investment family office is one that has been created by an investor to organise and run an investment portfolio for

the benefit of a group of family members and affiliated clients, such as investment partnerships, trusts, and/or foundations. Investment family offices have no operating business legacy, so there is no 'shadow governance' carried over from a business. However, the perspective, priorities and values of the founding investor will generally dominate decision-making by an investment family office.

- Philanthropic single family office – a philanthropic family office is one that has been created to manage the affairs of a substantial foundation or family-controlled charitable organisation. In this case, the mission of the foundation may drive all decision-making.

- Multi-generational single family office – A multi-generational family office is one that has survived its initial founders and is now run for the benefit of a group of family members. Very often, a multi-generational single family office will arise unexpectedly, as a result of a death or illness, and the clients and staff of the office find themselves without any clear procedures for decision-making. Such a situation can breed anxiety and launch a power struggle within the family office. Multi-generational single family offices can therefore be highly fragile organisations, held together by history but without a common vision for the future.

By way of example, consider the governance of a liquidity single family office founded by a successful entrepreneur following the sale of his business. The founder will have built the family office structure to suit his own needs and interests as the proceeds of the liquidity event are invested. As with any business run by a controlling owner, there isn't a great need for formal governance at this stage of the office, because the entrepreneur-investor is fully informed, understands the goals and objectives of the office, and handles all three of the critical roles – ownership/stewardship, oversight and management – himself. Unless the entrepreneur-investor has a formal governance mind-set, he generally will prefer to run the family office 'lean and mean', without a lot of staff or formal structure, making decisions on the fly in accordance with the his intuitive assessment of what is needed now. He will often rely on a key advisor or staff member who 'gets it' and knows how to implement the entrepreneur-investor's plans – who understands what is needed, and does whatever is necessary to make that happen.

It's critical to recognise that this sort of organic, first-generation governance generally works quite effectively, at least for the time being – the office runs, investments are made, tasks are completed. However, when the single family office comes to be managed for a wider group – typically, upon the entrepreneur-investor's death, when the assets pass to descendants or trusts for their benefit – the absence of established, articulated policies will create a power vacuum. Suddenly, no one really knows who is in charge, what needs to be done, who is responsible for doing it, or how that performance will be measured or compensated. If the next generation has not been prepared for their new roles, there may be a struggle for dominance, or the opposite: fearing conflict, family members may feel powerless and simply abdicate any role in the family office. The family office may slowly collapse, one family may seize power, or a non-family member may come to fill the vacuum – for good or for ill.

3. Building better governance structures

Successful single family offices have strong governance structures to ensure that the organisation is operated in accordance with the family's mission, vision and values over multiple generations. These governance structures must be robust yet flexible enough to withstand family conflict, generational transitions, cataclysmic changes in the environment, both anticipated and unanticipated. The following are key elements of a good governance structure:

- The family has articulated its mission, values and vision for the future, and the strategic plan of the family office is built around that core;
- The powers, rights and responsibilities of owners, board and management are clearly spelled out and followed;
- The owners have appointed a board of directors or advisers to provide perspective, access to specialised experience/skills, and to set strategy and investment policy. The board includes individuals who are not members of the family, members of the management team, or paid advisors;
- Management is free to implement the family office's strategy, without interference or meddling from the family or the owners;
- There are regular owners' and board meetings, with written agendas and complete minutes. Information necessary for effective decision-making is distributed well in advance of voting, and there is adequate time for discussion;
- Family office performance reports are clear, comprehensive and timely, so that decision-making can be based on accurate and complete information;
- The family office's strategic plan goes beyond investing to include education of family members to promote effective stewardship over the long term.

An effective governance process for a single family office can do much to align its operations with the family's interests, particularly in times of generational change. For instance, family office leaders may find that meetings become a venue for family members to air family grievances that have little to do with the family office's work. To prevent this problem the family office might encourage and support the development of a family council, to provide a forum for discussions of family issues separate and apart from the family office. Single family offices can play a key role in family education, modelling best practices, training next generation family members, and fostering an attitude of stewardship.

Single family offices are typically designed to serve multiple generations of a family, but a family office is not eternal. Over the past decade there have been well-publicised stories of substantial single family offices that crumbled under the conflicting demands and high costs of serving tens or hundreds of family members, each with comparatively modest holdings. Other single family offices, recognising that they could no longer achieve the family's mission and vision, or that the mission and vision had changed in such a way that the family office's activities were no longer cost-effective, have undertaken carefully orchestrated dissolutions. Families should recognise that dissolving a single family office is inevitably a complex, expensive and time-consuming process, and seek the advice of families and consultants who have navigated this experience successfully.

4.   Developing more formal governance: case study – the Santos family

To illustrate better the governance issues that can arise within a single family office, meet the Santos family:

Born in 1938, Pepe Santos grew up in a family in Barcelona, where his father was a teacher and his mother worked in a pharmacy.

Pepe's upbringing was rather strict and times were tough following the Spanish Civil War. However, following his school studies, he got the chance to work as an apprentice. He learned a lot and was gifted with understanding figures. Soon Pepe became responsible for a small subsidiary of the industrial conglomerate in which he was working.

In 1962 the conglomerate decided to refocus its efforts and chose to close and sell off a number of the subsidiaries. Pepe was given the opportunity to cheaply buy out the small company he was running (80 employees), and thus the Distro Group was born. Distro concentrated initially on food distribution but later expanded into a larger distribution chain, selling everything from hardware to inexpensive clothing and toys. With the profits made from distribution, Pepe expanded into real estate and later trading.

In 1962 Pepe married Maria. They had had three children: Pablo (1963), Pedro (1965) and Conchita (1968).

Pepe worked hard and Maria looked after the household and the children.

Around the dinner table, Pepe spoke regularly to his children about his vision for the future – work hard and you will succeed, get a good education, be honest and never give up. Maria had a very good sense for people and helped her husband to select good managers, which proved to be one of the key ingredients for the success of the fast growing Distro Group.

In the late 1970s and early 1980s Distro Group encountered cash-flow problems due to its rapid expansion, the Arab oil embargo, and soaring inflation rates. Pepe had to tighten his belt and slow down expansion, but by 1990 the business was back on track and doing well again. During this time he had started to show his children the different parts of the business. The cash-flow difficulties he had encountered in the 1970s and 1980s reinforced Pepe's resolve to reinvest as much as possible, and he constantly urged his children to live simply and save money.

By the end of the 1990s, Pepe had sold one of the subsidiary distribution companies, and due to political and economic uncertainties had decided to move his family to Switzerland. That same year, he opted to diversify his family's investments further and started a small family office. The cash from the sale of the subsidiary division was invested in a very conservative portfolio.

Pepe and Maria had, by this time, made it clear that they wanted their children to join the business but not before gaining a university exam and at least three years of work experience outside of the family business.

By this time the Distro Group employed some 5,200 people spanning three businesses. Pepe, who still owned all the shares of the Distro Group, put cash-flow not needed by the businesses into their family office operation, which by the end of the 1990s had reached a considerable size. The family office continued to invest in only the most conservative investments.

Pablo joined the family business and worked both in Mexico and Argentina. He married Ana, a girl from Argentina, and had two boys, Severiano in 2000 and Raphael in 2002.

After graduating in London, Pedro worked in Spain and Germany, and during one of his holidays in Mallorca met his future wife Nancy. They had three children: Carlos (2004), Juan (2005) and Rosario (2007). Conchita has not married and instead has had a few very close female friends, which is not to the liking of her parents.

Early on in 2005 Pepe suffered a heart attack and Maria pushed him into making two major decisions. One was to sell off their distribution and trading businesses and the other was to start his succession planning. The Distro Group businesses were successfully sold off to a major competitor in early 2007 and the family office fortune substantially increased. Because such a substantial part of its assets were in cash or extremely conservative investments, the Santos family office did not lose any money in the 2008 stock market crash.

Today, Pablo and Pedro, who each have watched their friends make considerable money investing in alternatives, are pressuring their father to expand into new types of investments and give them bigger roles in the strategy and operations of the family office.

Pablo and Pedro have different ideas about how the family office should be run and they are not happy with the family office's ultra-conservative investment policy. They were shocked when they uncovered the carry trade business that the family office staff had been operating, which had not been fully divulged to Pepe. They also criticise their father for mainly employing staff from Distro Group, who have no training or expertise in investing. Pablo and Pedro, who are facing tuition fees and other expenses for their growing families, want to increase the distributions to family members, but Pepe, remembering his cash-flow problems in the late 1970s and early 1980s, insists that distributions will lead to financial ruin. (While he will not say this to his children directly, Pepe is also struggling with how to treat his children fairly, given that Conchita has no family and Pedro's wife Nancy has a significant inheritance of her own.) The Santos children have also requested that the family office should provide more common concierge services in the family office, such as tax filings, insurance contracting, and travel planning, which Pepe thinks are not necessary.

Succession has not been an easy issue as the in-laws: Ana and Nancy are both pushing their husbands to take prominent roles. In addition, it has become clear that Pablo, the eldest son (pushed by his wife Ana), wants to assume the leading role in the family and the family office once his father retires. This in itself is a problem as Pepe, who is back to full health and has become bored since the sale of Distro Group, has no desire to retire.

The chief executive officer of the family office, Rodrigo Torres, was formerly the chief financial officer of Distro Group. He has suggested to Pepe that he create more formal rules for the family office. Rodrigo, a straightforward, honest person with a lot of common sense, has spoken at length with Pepe about his future plans for the family and the family office. Pepe has several wishes, one of which is that he wants the children to continue the family office with equal ownership, making sure that each has their own clear responsibility without stepping on each other's toes. Pepe has also urged Rodrigo to keep distributions at a minimum, to avoid his grandchildren becoming 'entitled'.

Rodrigo is becoming frustrated trying to run the family office according to Pepe's wishes and with increasing interference from Pepe's children, which has made his task more and more difficult.

Last week, Rodrigo issued Pepe with an ultimatum and said that if the family does not create proper rules for the future and does not unite over a common vision, he will resign.

As the case study shows, the Santos family is facing at least three major transitions:
- from being a single family office embedded in the Distro Group to becoming a stand-alone entity;
- from being wholly owned and controlled by Distro Group's founder, to becoming owned and managed by a family group; and
- from a system of organic governance to more formal governance.

If the Santos family can develop better governance, decision-making will be improved, more effective policies will be developed and implemented, and as a consequence much of the current tension among family members, and between the family and the family office, may be reduced.

5. Developing more formal governance: the process
How can a single family office move from natural or organic governance to more formal governance? The following steps outline a process to guide the work of the family office's clients and staff.

5.1 Determine the purpose and create a mission statement
What will be the purpose of this family office? To manage liquidity generated by the sale of a business? To oversee a portfolio of direct investments? To fund family lifestyles? To serve as a safety net? To preserve a family legacy? And why does the family want to manage assets collectively?

Every family office is different, but the key point is for the clients of the single family office to articulate its purpose and its role within the family.

A critical early task in setting up a single family office is defining the mission, vision and values of the family office. Developing a short, focused mission statement to guide the work of the family office will help to avoid 'mission creep' in future years. The founders should avoid drafting a mission statement that is vague and high-minded but short on specifics. A family office consultant can help the family mould their vision and values into a practical and useful tool to guide the work of the single family office.

The Santos family office embodies many of the values Pepe Santos and his family cherish most. While the children disagree on some of the policies of the family office, it is likely that their attitudes align with their father's in many respects. Investing time in articulating mission, vision and values will help the Santos family office plan and carry out its work more effectively – and will also serve to frame the intergenerational discussion that must happen for succession to take place. To accomplish Pepe's vision for the future and to manage the family's legacy, the children will need to learn to communicate clearly and work together effectively.

5.2   Assess the needs and objectives of the single family office

(a)   Who are the clients?

At the outset, make a list of all the individuals and entities to be served by the single family office, and their specific objectives in joining the family office. Individuals, family branches, investment entities, businesses, trusts, trust companies, foundations – the design of the single family office should take into account each client's unique needs and requirements.

For the Santos family, it will be critical for the family office to understand Pepe's estate plan and to take into consideration any new entities that will be created under it. New entities will bring new participants, such as trustees or directors, new investment policies, and new reporting requirements. Timing will also be an issue – will Pepe transfer assets at pre-established times during his lifetime, or will transfers occur on his death (or the death of his wife, Maria)?

(b)   What assets will be managed by the single family office?

The family and staff will need to draw up a list of all the types of assets that the single family office will be responsible for managing: marketable securities, hedge fund interests, master limited partnerships, direct investments, operating businesses, residential real estate, commercial real estate, farms, collections, yachts, horses, sports teams and so on. The single family office will need to hire or outsource the specific expertise needed to oversee and manage each different segment of its particular asset pool.

(c)   What services do the clients of the single family office need and want?

Families with extensive investments, or with liquid capital to be invested, will need investment management services, including development of investment policy statements and asset allocation plans, manager due diligence, and investment reporting. All the single family office's clients will need comprehensive and accurate performance reporting, accounting and tax return preparation. Coordination of risk management, such as insurance, security and reputation management, is also a nearly universal need of single family office clients. Furthermore, individual family members are likely to develop different risk profiles over time, and the family office may therefore need to adjust investments from being collective to being more individual over time. Development and coordination of estate and tax planning, possibly including management of a private family trust company, is an obvious need of a multi-generational client group, but can be equally critical for a first generation entrepreneur who wishes to perpetuate the family's legacy over the long term. Other possible needs include property management and staffing, bill payment and concierge services.

The Santos family office has to-date made conservative investments (for the most part!) but it is clear that the children will push for a less conservative investment policy. The family and the family office staff would benefit from a facilitated discussion about investments, grounded in the mission and values of the family office. The Santos children have requested more extensive concierge services, and the discussion should include these issues as well.

5.3   Establish appropriate policies and procedures

To go beyond governance based on understandings, assumptions and expectations, the single family office will need a more formal approach to governance based on clear policies and procedures, with a goal of achieving organised accountability among the family office's clients and staff. Such policies might include:

- asset allocation policy, appropriate to each separate client;
- investment policies, detailing what types of investments may be made and what due diligence should be undertaken before an investment may be made;
- reporting policy, detailing the contents, timing and recipients of financial and other reports;
- distribution policy, detailing how distribution amounts will be determined and when distributions will be made;
- fee policy, articulating how the costs of operating the family office will be borne by its clients;
- collective use policy, for a joint asset such as a ski home, detailing how, when and by whom the property may be used, and how costs for such use are paid for;
- exit policy, detailing how a client may withdraw from the single family office;
- dissolution policy, detailing the circumstances under which the single family office should be dissolved (for example, upon withdrawal of more than 50% of the assets of the family office). Some single family offices provide for automatic dissolution after a term of years; the family office may then be continued only on the affirmative vote of its clients;
- client satisfaction policy, providing for regular and detailed surveys of the family office's clients to ensure that services and service levels are appropriate and adequate.

The Santos family office clearly will need policies in a number of areas, including an investment policy, fee policy, and most especially a distribution policy. The carry trade investments made without Pepe's knowledge suggest that there has been insufficient guidance and oversight, and inadequate reporting. Pepe's long-standing policy of reinvesting all proceeds and profits may need to be adjusted to reflect the financial needs and circumstances of each of the children and of the family as a whole. Here again, the policies should be grounded in the specific mission, vision and values of the Santos family office.

Developing policies should be a collective effort, with open discussion among Pepe and his children. Facilitation by an experienced family office consultant may be useful, as a facilitator can help to make sure that a full range of policy options are considered, that difficult issues are aired constructively, that all family members have a chance to speak, and that the final policy reflects consensus among family members. Without facilitation, there is a significant risk that one voice – likely Pepe's – will dominate, silencing the children's opinions. If that were to happen, disagreement might be forced underground, with the risk that it would resurface upon Pepe's death or retirement, when children might be less inclined to participate in a facilitated process, and more inclined to attempt to seize control.

Pepe envisions a future where his children work together peacefully and collaboratively within the family office, each with his or her own area of focus. While such a vision is lovely indeed, it may not be realistic. Articulating the policies of the family office – and then acting in accordance with those policies – will be important steps for the Santos family office. The Santos family would be well-advised to develop a clear exit policy, so that in the event one (or more) of the children is unable or unwilling to participate, his or her share of the assets may be distributed from the family office without destroying the office in the process. Parents in particular may wish for eternal peace and goodwill among their children, but families would be wise to plan for acrimony.

5.4   Develop a business plan

Once the mission has been articulated and the clients, assets and needs have been itemised, and policies and procedures established, single family office leaders can begin the process of developing a business plan. A business plan is essential to good governance because it defines the scope and parameters of the office's work.

A key objective in developing a business plan should be to determine a budget. Typically, single family office budgets are defined as a percentage of assets under management. Single family office operating costs vary widely – smaller family offices, or those managing complex assets, tend to cost more to operate than larger family offices, or those managing a simpler portfolio, because there are fewer economies of scale to exploit. The budget of a single family office managing an extensive portfolio of alternative investments and commodities for three generations of family members, all of whom also share a passion for modern art and house their collections in in multiple homes around the world, will necessarily be larger both as an absolute number and as a percentage of assets under management, than the budget of a single family office managing a portfolio of publicly-traded securities for a single family unit. Family office consultants can be very helpful in determining a reality-based budget for a single family given a specified clientele, asset pool, and service requirements. Single family offices are not inexpensive to operate, and the future clients may balk at the projected cost at first. However, when compared against the current expense of managing the family's assets – taking into consideration all costs, fees and expenses – the expense of a single family office will likely be lower. Certainly, because the single family office will be custom-tailored to the family's needs, the return on that expenditure will be higher.

The budget will in turn drive creation of benchmarks to set expectations for the performance of the single family office.

Budgeting will be an important process for the Santos family office, particularly if the family adopts new, broader investment policies. The family and the family office team will need to consider whether additional investment managers should be brought in or whether the investment function should be outsourced to one or more outside managers, and in any event how managers will be overseen. New reporting protocols will need to be developed and rolled out. New benchmarks will be necessary to set expectations and measure performance (and avoid unpleasant surprises like the carry trade investment). All of these will have an impact on the budget for the office.

How will the cost of the single family office be funded? Particularly when the goal is to create a family office to serve the needs of a multi-generational family, it is important to consider how the costs will be allocated and charged to individual clients of the family office. Tasks classified as 'needs' by a client may slip to the category of 'nice to have but not necessary today' when that client finds he must bear the cost. Future conflict between family office clients or between the family and the office can be avoided if the method of allocating expenses and the expected contributions by each client are made explicit from the outset.

Given the different financial positions of the three Santos children, it is likely that each will require different services from the family office. Developing an à la carte system for charging services to family members may be useful, so that the expense for a particular service is borne by the family member using it. The system for allocating costs and expenses should be made clear to all clients of the family office.

5.5 Create an effective organisation chart: leadership, staffing and oversight

The business plan for the single family office should identify the expertise required to meet the specific needs of the its clients, given the specific assets to be managed and the available budget. The plan should also specify whether such expertise will be provided internally – via the family office staff – or outsourced. It should also be clear which issues should be handled by management, and which must be brought to the board or to the clients. The plan should include clear job descriptions for each position in the single family office, and all staff members should receive training on its mission, policies and procedures.

The single family office should be overseen by a board of directors, which will meet regularly and be responsible for setting strategy and overseeing the chief executive officer. Most families control the board of their single family offices to ensure that its strategy is in line with the family's mission, vision and values. Many single family offices are following the lead of private businesses and bringing independent advisers onto the board to provide outside perspective and expertise.

Who will lead the Santos family office? Since its inception, Pepe has led the office with Rodrigo's assistance. Given Pepe's age and health, his wife's pressure, and the children's increasing involvement, it is likely there will be a change of leadership in the reasonably near future. If planned for and implemented with care, there will be a greater likelihood that the transition can be accomplished smoothly and without excessive turmoil. If planning for the transition is deferred or ignored, there likely will be chaos!

The family will need to decide whether family members will run the office on a day-to-day basis, or whether the office will instead be operated by non-family executives overseen by family members serving as directors. Do the children, individually or as a group, have the skills, interests, experience and availability needed to operate a family office of this size and scope? The process should include a realistic assessment of each child's capabilities and willingness to serve.

Whether or not one or more of the children ultimately serve as executives, the office will in the future be run for the benefit of three children and their descendants, and a board of directors should be implemented to increase transparency, provide for greater oversight, and ensure that the office is run for the benefit of all of its clients. Including outsiders – perhaps as non-voting advisors, rather than voting directors – will bring wider perspective and access to skills and experience the family and staff do not possess. The respective powers, rights and responsibilities of the family office clients, board and management should be carefully thought through and articulated to avoid gaps, conflicts or ambiguities.

Staff should receive training in the specific mission, vision and values of the Santos family office, as those tenets will guide their day-to-day work. Educating the grandchildren and further descendants about the family office, its purpose and its work will also be critical.

Will Conchita participate? If her brothers crowd her out in their haste to control the office, they may find that she opposes many of their decisions and thwarts their plans. They would be wise to cultivate her participation and bring her into their decision-making. Given her training, they may find that she brings valuable skills and perspective heretofore unavailable to the office.

6.   Conclusion

At its core, governance is really nothing more than a set of rules that define how a family or organisation will make decisions, large or small. Single family offices that invest time and energy in developing effective governance policies and processes are most likely to survive and thrive through complex transitions.

Philanthropy and the family: improving social equity and creating family legacies

Gina M Pereira
Dāna Philanthropy

1.   Introduction

To give away money is an easy matter and in any man's power. But to decide to whom to give it, and how large and when, and for what purpose and how, is neither in every man's power – nor an easy matter – Aristotle

Philanthropy is ever evolving, and this has become especially evident in recent decades. Globalisation and the international mobility of individuals and businesses have led to a rise in global giving, while increased awareness, networking and collaboration have inspired more strategic giving.

Driving this evolution is a younger generation of high net worth individuals who are insistent on accountability, focused on impact, and passionate about finding solutions to social inequities within and across borders.

While these developments are positive, they also make planning more complex, necessitating increasingly sophisticated advice from a variety of professional advisors.

Given their holistic perspective of, and intimate connections to, high net worth families and their wealth, family offices are uniquely positioned to support family philanthropy. Family philanthropy helps to build family legacy. It honours the founders and creators of wealth, and inspires future generations. Families that embrace a philanthropic agenda build and strengthen familial bonds across generations, based on shared goals and commitment. Philanthropy provides an opportunity to work together, and include those not involved in the family business.

Philanthropy can be a powerful means of educating the next generation. The older generation's active commitment to giving sets a positive example, and can foster a sense of ownership and responsibility in offspring who did not earn their wealth and often struggle to establish their own identity. Through philanthropy, younger generations are exposed to realities beyond their privileged experience, and develop empathy and compassion. They also learn vital skills around governance, fiscal responsibility, decision-making, teamwork and accountability as they carve out their niche within the family unit.

Private client advisers have more opportunity than ever to develop stronger, long-term client relationships by offering philanthropy services. But in order successfully to help clients implement their philanthropic goals, advisers must stay abreast of developments within the industry.

2. The state of global philanthropy

Myriad factors influence philanthropy, including religious traditions, political histories, immigration and the strength of the economy. But in general, cultural influences drive behaviours and attitudes toward philanthropy, while the regulatory environment impacts scale.

While some countries have relatively favourable environments that encourage giving, others maintain multiple legal, regulatory and tax impediments and cumbersome bureaucratic processes that inhibit private giving. Indeed, registration processes, permissible legal entities, government intervention and tax policies are the most pressing policy issues limiting philanthropy across nation states.[1]

The relationship between the roles of the state, markets and civil society is being challenged, especially in countries where government cannot provide adequate social services and support – and where confidence in the government to resolve societal problems has faltered.[2] Favourable regulatory environments are vital to developing an impactful and scalable giving strategy. Governments struggling to maintain their role as primary service providers can be reluctant to give too much leeway to private giving.

China maintains tight controls over private giving. Stringent restrictions on operations and fundraising mean most contributions go to government-affiliated organisations. And yet, observers have described the existence of a competition for public favour between the government – which has historically been perceived as the sole social service provider for the people – and the private philanthropist.

The availability of tax incentives related to charitable giving across nations varies from attractive to negligible. Common tax incentives for charitable giving include exemptions from income tax, estate tax or inheritance tax, and capital gains tax. Income tax incentives (deduction or credit) are the most common form of tax incentives. Certain jurisdictions cap eligible deductions or credits, although they may allow donations exceeding the deductible limit to be carried forward into subsequent fiscal years. While estate tax incentives are less common, some countries offer an incentive for bequests to registered charities. In jurisdictions that impose a capital gains tax, contribution of appreciated securities can be a highly attractive and cost-effective way of donating.

Despite discrepancies in philanthropic practices across nation states, private philanthropy and social investment is growing on a global scale. The increase in wealth, the opening of the political space, markets and civil society, the growing visibility and influence of philanthropists, as well as the move toward privatisation, are all factors influencing growth. Where government is unable to provide a sufficient level of support, private philanthropists have greater opportunity to step in and address social disparities.

Developing economies have proven fertile ground for private philanthropy. China has observed strong annualised high net worth individual population growth

---

1 PD Johnson, *Global Institutional Philanthropy: A Preliminary Status Report,* Part I (Worldwide Initiatives for Grantmaker Support (WINGS) and The Philanthropic Initiative, Inc (TPI), 2010).

2 *The 2012 Bank of American Study of High Net Worth Philanthropy: Issues driving charitable activities among wealthy households,* (Bank of America and The Centre on Philanthropy at Indiana University, 2012).

of 15.8% between 2008 and 2013.[3] Despite a recent decline in economic growth in India, this demographic grew by 21% between 2009 and 2010, compared with 8% in the United States, and 6% in Brazil.[4]

Global high net worth individual financial wealth is expected to reach new records by 2016, led by Asia-Pacific with a projected annual growth rate of 9.8%, followed by 7.1% growth in Europe, 6.6% in the Middle East, 6.4% in North America, 6% in Africa and 2.3% in Latin America.[5]

Individual philanthropy has corresponded with economic growth in developing markets, and in some instances has become a social norm and expectation.[6] Given the recent accumulation of wealth by individuals in developing markets, it is anticipated that private giving will continue to increase, and that governments will respond accordingly, updating legislation and regulations to create a more supportive environment for giving.

Philanthropic practices are also evolving in developed economies. In Germany, where public financing supports the majority of the charitable sector, there was a 9% increase in private donations between 2009 and 2010.[7] In France, changing patterns of giving amongst the elite have been observed in recent years: family philanthropy is emerging as a trend, the size of bequests are on the rise, and successful entrepreneurs are devoting a portion of the next chapters of their lives to philanthropic pursuits.[8] In a 2011 survey of wealthy US households, over half of respondents indicated they would maintain their levels of giving over the next three to five years, while approximately one-quarter planned to increase their giving.[9]

2.1 Public recognition versus anonymity

Media outlets publicise and laud the efforts of prominent philanthropists. It is arguable that in general, public praise encourages more giving. American Ted Turner famously recounted how his fellow billionaires kept score of where they ranked against their peers in terms of wealth, and how they enjoyed tracking such rankings published in media outlets. He called on the media to start publishing the names of people who gave away the most money to charitable causes. And he accurately predicted that people's competitive nature would motivate them to get to the top of the philanthropy list.

Africa's richest person, Aliko Dangote, billionaire founder and chief executive officer of Dangote Group, attributes the increase in his giving to the example set by Warren Buffet and Bill Gates.[10] To date, more than 125 billionaire individuals or

---

3   *World Wealth Report 2014* (Capgemini and RBC Wealth Management, 2014).
4   A Sheth, *India Philanthropy Report* (Bain & Company, Inc, Mumbai, 2012).
5   *World Wealth Report 2014* (Capgemini and RBC Wealth Management, 2014).
6   *Next-Generation Philanthropy: Changing the World* (Forbes Insights, 2012).
7   A Richter and AK Gollan, "Germany" in AM Piper. (ed), *Charity Law* (European Lawyer Reference Series, European Lawyer, 2012) pp81-99.
8   N Sauvanet, "Philanthropy on the Up Among France's Wealthy", *Alliance*, Volume 17, Number 3, p11 (2012).
9   *The 2012 Bank of American Study of High Net Worth Philanthropy: Issues driving charitable activities among wealthy households* (Bank of America and The Centre on Philanthropy at Indiana University, 2012).
10   A Dangote, interviewed by L Kroll, L for Forbes.com Video Network (September 18 2012), at: www.forbes.com/sites/luisakroll/2012/09/18/africas-richest-person-aliko-dangote-on-why-hes-stepping-up-his-philanthropy/.

families have pledged to give away at least half of their wealth by signing the Giving Pledge, an appeal to the wealthiest American families and individuals to commit to giving the majority of their wealth to philanthropy or charitable causes either during their lifetime or upon their death.[11] Buffet and Gates are now appealing to their international counterparts to join the pledge. South African billionaire, Patrice Motsepe signed on to the Giving Pledge, and became the first African to do so.

However, not all philanthropists are interested in publicity. Some are intent on preserving their anonymity. In societies where risk of kidnapping is high, many wealthy individuals and families prefer to play down the extent of their wealth, and choose to give back discreetly or through their businesses. Others simply do not wish to draw attention to themselves or their philanthropy.

American philanthropist, Charles Feeney, co-founder of the duty-free shops located in international airports, established two grant-making vehicles in Bermuda, The Atlantic Philanthropies.[12] The Bermuda structures provided him with the opportunity to keep the details of his giving private – a privilege that would not have been available had he set up private foundations in the United States. His decision eventually to reveal his philanthropy was driven by necessity, due to a lawsuit over the sale of his business.

Further, certain cultural mores encourage modesty and discourage publicity of charitable giving: Chinese billionaire Chen Guanbiao was publicly criticised for the manner in which he publicised his philanthropy.

3.   Philanthropy developments

3.1   The evolution of strategic philanthropy

Philanthropy has evolved from passive, reactive cheque-writing practices that are essentially aid-focused and do not demand accountability, towards efforts to achieve systemic social change through collaboration across sectors and the empowerment of disadvantaged communities. While the traditional approach still persists, more and more industry players are working to identify how best to measure performance and maximise impact when tackling complex systemic problems.

Carlos Slim publicly shared his scepticism around traditional charitable practices. He advocates a hands-on approach to giving that is results-focused. While his own philanthropic activity has been criticised for a lack of transparency, his goals are to alleviate poverty through business, by investing in programmes he believes will build "human capital":

> We have seen donations for 100 years... We have seen thousands of people working in non-profits, and the problems and poverty are bigger. They have not solved anything... I don't like to talk about giving away money. That's not our purpose. Our purpose is to solve social problems.[13]

---

11   givingpledge.org.
12   www.atlanticphilanthropies.org/.
13   Carlos Slim, quoted in C Preston, "World's Richest Man Steps Up Giving Despite Wariness About Charity", Chronicle of Philanthropy (September 30, 2012),at: philanthropy.com/article/World-s-Richest-Man-Steps-Up/134714/.

Similarly, Swiss billionaire Stephan Schmidheiny's philanthropy in Latin America is focused on promoting small businesses. He refers to his donations as "investments" to highlight a long-term commitment and considers beneficiaries as equal partners.[14]

While current approaches remain imperfect, greater collaboration with stakeholders and commitment to improving upon methodology will move us toward greater philanthropic effectiveness and impact. As authors Paul Brest and Hal Harvey point out:

...Accomplishing philanthropic goals requires having great clarity about what those goals are and specifying indicators of success before beginning a philanthropic project. It requires designing and then implementing a plan commensurate with the resources committed to it. This, in turn, requires an empirical, evidence-based understanding of the external world in which the plan will operate. And it requires attending carefully to milestones to determine whether you are on the path to success... These factors are the necessary parts of what we regard as the essential core of strategic philanthropy – the concern with impact.[15]

These values are especially evident in younger philanthropists, who approach giving with a strategic, entrepreneurial spirit: they demand transparency and accountability, seek to improve efficiency and impact, and are also deploying capital at a faster rate than their predecessors.[16]

XPRIZE India funder and philanthropist, Naveen Jain, advocates an entrepreneurial approach to philanthropy:

The truth is, the most successful models in philanthropy are no different than those we apply in business. Entrepreneurs know that big, successful businesses rely on the size and scope of each market. I would never start a business that only reaches a potential market of 1,000 people, for example. Why should things be any different in philanthropy?[17]

Like the new generation of individual philanthropists, operating charities are striving to become sustainable, and less dependent on government funding and private donations. A Philanthropy UK study published in 2008 found that UK charities earned half of their total income through fees for goods and services provided.[18]

3.2   Strategic philanthropy models

(a)   Entrepreneurial philanthropy: social entrepreneurship and social enterprises

Social entrepreneurship and social enterprise are also growing trends. Social

---

14   Stephan Schmidheiny, interviewed by T Serafin, "Swiss Billionaire Stephan Schmidheiny on Philanthropy", Forbes (September 19, 2012), at: www.forbes.com/sites/tatianaserafin/2012/09/19/swiss-billionaire-stephan-schmidheiny-on-philanthropy/2/.

15   P Brest and H Harvey, *Money Well Spent: A Strategic Plan for Smart Philanthropy*, (Bloomberg Press, New York, 2008), p7.

16   *Next-Generation Philanthropy: Changing the World* (Forbes Insights, 2012).

17   N Jain, "Bringing Entrepreneurial Philanthropy to India with a New X Prize" (2013), at: www.fastcoexist.com/1681276/bringing-entrepreneurial-philanthropy-to-india-with-a-new-x-prize?goback=%2Egde_88635_member_212004886.

18   S Mackenzie (ed), *A Guide to Giving*, third edition (Philanthropy UK, 2008).

entrepreneurs develop innovative solutions to affect social change on a large scale. They use market-based approaches to deliver essential services to impoverished communities. Social enterprises apply commercial strategies and operate as conventional businesses with a social mandate to maximise social improvements.

Private philanthropy can enhance the success of social entrepreneurs and enterprise by providing access to capital to build the infrastructure needed for expansion and scalability.

(b)   *Venture philanthropy*

Venture philanthropy applies techniques from venture capital finance and business management to philanthropic goals. Through a highly engaged, hands-on relationship with the organisations they support, venture philanthropists focus on operations and capacity building over programme funding. They share skills and expertise with non-profit organisations, assisting them to become sustainable and to deliver measurable, scalable social impact. Measurement and accountability are priorities based on mutually determined benchmarks. Venture philanthropists measure impact using a social return on investment methodology that employs social, financial and environmental value measurement strategies to analyse the relationship between investment and results, illustrating the impact of change with a dollar value.

Venture philanthropy has taken root in the Americas, Europe and, most recently, Asia. Investments by European venture philanthropists are estimated to have reached more than €1 billion. Most investments are geared toward start-up non-profit organisations and social businesses, and while grants constitute the primary vehicle, debt and equity instruments are also utilised.[19]

Young high net worth individuals in India are notably interested in venture philanthropy. They invest in building the capabilities of operating charities with the goal of improving impact.[20]

3.3   Strategic philanthropy challenges

While collaboration between stakeholders is required in order to increase efficiency and maximise impact, advocates of social justice philanthropy argue that in order to be truly effective, philanthropists must invest resources in advocacy, influence public policy and engage the communities served.[21] This bottom-up approach establishes a collaborative forum, and empowers individuals to determine the best way of addressing the issues facing their community.

An example of cross-sector collaboration is demonstrated by XPRIZE India. XPRIZE India solicits submissions from community members to identify pressing local issues and to propose solutions. Upon selecting the top proposals, the donors

19   C Page, "EVPA conference creates roadmap for societal change through venture philanthropy", *Alliance Magazine*, (March 2012) at: www.alliancemagazine.org/en/content/evpa-conference-creates-roadmap-societal-change-through-venture-philanthropy.
20   A Sheth, *India Philanthropy Report* (Bain & Company, Inc, Mumbai, 2012)
21   N Jagpal and K Laskowski, *Real Results: Why Strategic Philanthropy is Social Justice Philanthropy* (National Committee for Responsive Philanthropy, 2013).

partner with the Indian government to identify which issues are best dealt with by private philanthropy – a collaborative cross-sector effort.[22]

(a)   Capacity building and operational efficiency

Often, operating charities concentrate their energies and resources externally at the expense of building a solid infrastructure and supporting their own capacity.[23] This approach is supported by public pressure to direct most if not all donated funds to programme support, as well as a resistance by donors to funding general operating expenses and overhead costs. Despite evidence demonstrating the necessity and benefits of general operating[24] and multi-year support[25] to the success of non-profit organisations, donors are reluctant to move away from annually renewed programme support practices.

(b)   Accountability and transparency

Systemic corruption in both the private and public sectors in certain cultures contributes to a pervasive lack of trust and confidence in the non-profit sector. In more developed economies, concern over inefficient expenditure of funds is a prevailing issue, while in general there is some confidence in the ability of operating charities to solve societal problems. Issues of public trust can be addressed through improved transparency and accountability to donors and the public at large for both operating and grant-making charities. Non-profit organisations would be wise to produce and disclose annual reports and audited financial statements on their websites, develop measurements to evaluate impact, and publish their findings in order to increase public confidence and encourage future investment.

The importance of accountability and transparency is illustrated by the case of Greg Mortenson. The Central Asia Institute (CAI) charity founder and author of best-selling book *Three Cups of Tea*, Mortenson was investigated by the Montana Attorney General's Office after allegations of financial and governance mismanagement of the charity. The Attorney General's probe focused exclusively on CAI's finances and operations and concluded in Spring 2012 that Mortenson mismanaged the organisation and misspent its funds. Mortenson was required to repay the charity approximately $1 million and to resign from the board, but remains a paid employee. Improved governance and greater transparency could have spared Mortenson considerable expense and embarrassment, and public confidence in the organisation may be difficult to recover.[26]

---

22   N Jain, "Bringing Entrepreneurial Philanthropy to India with a New X Prize", at: www.fastcoexist.com/1681276/bringing-entrepreneurial-philanthropy-to-india-with-a-new-x-prize?goback=%2Egde_88635_member_212004886.

23   G Ellis, D Hale Smith and R Wright, *The Little Green Book of Venture Philanthropy: How Business Hats and Volunteer Hearts Can Learn to Play Well with Each Other and Make the World a Better Place* (Social Venture Press, 2008).

24   N Jagpal and K Laskowski, *The State of General Operating Support* (National Committee for Responsive Philanthropy, 2012), at: www.ncrp.org/publications.

25   N Jagpal and K Laskowski, *The State of Multi-Year Funding* (National Committee for Responsive Philanthropy, 2012), at: www.ncrp.org/publications.

26   *Montana Attorney General's Investigative Report of Greg Mortenson and Central Asia Institute* (2012), at: dojmt.gov/wp-content/uploads/2012_0405_FINAL-REPORT-FOR-DISTRIBUTION.pdf.

(c)   *Evaluation and impact measurement*

Historically, non-profit organisations adopted traditional models of quantitative measurement by tracking volume of effort, or outputs, without evaluating outcomes. Performance monitoring focuses on whether the charity is doing what it agreed to do. Impact measurement and evaluation measures the extent to which the non-profit organisation succeeded in affecting the change it set out to make, and examines whether the outcome would have occurred without the project's intervention.

While many charities consider evaluation important to their organisation, impact measurement remains a key challenge. Many charities struggle to understand how donors define impact measurement, which suggests that greater upfront collaboration will help donors and charities understand one another's expectations.[27] In addition, a lack of consistency in the way organisations collect and aggregate data makes it difficult to compare results within the field. Although evaluation can be a costly and resource-intensive effort, donors should support charities' efforts by financing evaluation expenses.

In spite of these challenges, by outlining how change will occur and developing logistical models to assess the causal outcomes, organisations can track results consistently over the long term, enabling them to refine practices, develop greater expertise and increase efficacy. Impact measurement provides an opportunity to assess performance and modify approach, if necessary, to communicate programme success clearly to current and prospective donors, to raise the bar on accountability, to enhance credibility of the organisation, and ultimately to contribute to raising public confidence in the charitable sector.

Increasingly, philanthropists are using some form of impact measurement in their giving programmes.[28] From the grant-making perspective, it helps to educate donors on how to allocate resources more effectively in future.

4.   **Cross-border giving**

Globalisation, families with connections in multiple jurisdictions, international travel, global interconnectedness and sophisticated technology are all factors contributing to growth in cross-border giving. However, by and large, tax incentives are generally unavailable and the regulatory environment for cross-border giving is unfavourable. As a response to this, many donors are funding local intermediary charities that operate internationally in order to benefit from ease of administration and to maximise tax incentives. Foreign charities are also registering in multiple jurisdictions in order to attract international funding. Donors who wish to give directly across borders need specialised advice, as cross-border giving is complex and requires careful planning and oversight.

4.1   **Cross-border giving taxation**

Different taxes can arise in cross-border philanthropy, including capital gains tax on the value of the assets transferred, and gift tax, estate or inheritance taxes, corporate

---

27   *Charity Impact Measurement Survey Report 2012* (Third Sector, 2012).
28   *Next-Generation Philanthropy: Changing the World* (Forbes Insights, 2012).

income tax, and transfer taxes that may apply on certain types of property. Donors should confirm whether or not a cross-border transaction benefits from tax relief based on a double taxation treaty, declarations of reciprocity or other bilateral agreements entered into by the countries involved. While charity-friendly provisions in double taxation treaties tend to be the exception rather than the rule, the United States has entered into bilateral income tax treaties with charity-friendly provisions with Mexico,[29] Canada[30] and Israel,[31] as has Mexico with Barbados.[32]

4.2 Developments in facilitating cross-border philanthropy

Subject to few exceptions, cross-border gifts do not offer income tax incentives as gifts to national charities do. However, progress is being made: certain jurisdictions recognise that the world is becoming more interconnected and that economic inter-dependence is increasing, and are considering policies that facilitate cross-border giving.

Recent European Court of Justice (ECJ) rulings support equal tax treatment for cross-border gifts within EU member states incentivising cross-border giving.[33] In 2012, the European Commission presented a proposal to introduce a European Foundation Statute, which aims to facilitate cross-border giving among member states. The statute is designed as an optional tool to help foundations better to channel resources into improving the lives of European citizens. The legislation addresses the reality that donors are increasingly working across borders, and face a number of legal and regulatory impediments to their philanthropic efforts. The proposal was shared with the Council of Ministers – representing the 28 Member States – for review and approval, which is ongoing, and the European Parliament endorsed a resolution supporting the proposal in July 2013.[34]

In the United States, regulations applicable to private foundations desirous of making grants to foreign charities were considered cumbersome and expensive. The Internal Revenue Service and the Department of Treasury issued proposed regulations in September 2012 that would make it easier and more cost efficient for US-based private foundations to fund foreign charities via 'equivalency determinations'. The proposed regulations are scheduled for final action in December 2014.[35]

---

29   United States-Mexico Income Tax Convention, signed in Washington DC on September 18 1992, as amended by the protocol signed on September 8 1994, Article 22.
30   Canada-United States Convention with Respect to Taxes on Income and on Capital, signed in Washington DC on September 26 1980, as amended by the protocols signed on June 14 1983, March 28 1984, March 17 1995 and July 29 1997, Article 21(5).
31   Convention between the United States of America and Israel signed in Washington DC on November 20 1975, as amended by the protocols signed on May30 1980 and January 26 1993, Article 15A.
32   Convention Between the Government of Barbados and the Government of the United Mexican States for the Avoidance of Double Taxation and the Prevention of Fiscal Evasion with Respect to Taxes on Income, 2008, Article 22.
33   Case C-386/04 *Centro di Musicologia Walter Stauffer v Finanzamt München für Körperschaften*, ECJ, September 14 2006; Case C-318/07 *Persche v Finanzamt Lüdenscheid*, ECJ, January 27 2009.
34   European Foundation Statute; European Foundation Centre, at: www.efc.be/programmes_services/advocacy-monitoring/European-Foundation-Statute/Pages/default.aspx.
35   A Proposed Rule by the Internal Revenue Service: Reliance Standards for Making Good Faith Determinations (2012): www.federalregister.gov/articles/2012/09/24/2012-23553/reliance-standards-for-making-good-faith-determinations.

4.3 Practical challenges associated with cross-border giving

International giving increases the risk of misappropriation for non-charitable purposes. Donors are advised to adopt due diligence practices beyond those legally mandated in an effort to reduce these risks. Such steps might include: undertaking additional monitoring efforts including periodic site visits, adoption of activities to monitor compliance with expenditure use, mandating periodic narrative and financial reports, establishing an ongoing relationship with the recipient organisation, and monitoring terrorist watch lists in an effort to identify fraudulent charities and to mitigate the risk of funds being used to support terrorist activities. Board members of grant-making charities are responsible for the development of suitable governance practices ensuring fiscal responsibility, by introducing sufficient financial controls to trace the delivery and ultimate use of the funds. Staff and volunteers should be educated on the laws, regulations and best practices relevant to cross-border giving.

5. Modes of giving

Donors have an increasing number of options to create their philanthropic legacy. Independent legal and tax advice should always be sought in consideration of donor objectives, residency and domicile, and the location and nature of the assets to be donated.

5.1 Direct giving

Direct giving to qualified recipients is the most common form of philanthropy and can be as strategic and impactful as forms of indirect giving. In some instances, direct giving offers more attractive tax incentives. While direct giving requires due diligence on individual beneficiary charities, followed by monitoring and evaluation, it involves lower administration costs and affords donors the opportunity to develop direct relationships with the organisations they support.

5.2 Donor advised funds

Donor advised funds are funds that are in the custody of, and managed by, public charities, investment firms, community foundations or public foundations. They offer clients separate, tailor-made funds that give donors the option to provide immediate funding, or to build an endowment. The sponsoring organisation will monitor expenditures and report to donors on progress. Donor advised funds are increasingly popular in Canada, the United Kingdom and the United States. They are relatively inexpensive, as compared with private foundations, easy to set up and require minimal administration as they are handled by paid organisations and staffed with in-house experts. Typically, donors may recommend (rather than direct) where gifts are distributed, but the sponsoring organisation will only distribute to certain types of charities, which may narrow the pool of recipients. Likewise, donors typically choose from pre-determined available investment plans, but do not directly control investments.

5.3 Charitable trusts and foundations

Charitable trusts or foundations are independent entities that may exist indefinitely and deploy funds in accordance with their mission. Foundations can be set up as trusts or corporations depending on the governing laws of the relevant jurisdiction. Staffed or unstaffed, they are managed either by trustees or directors. Private foundations are distinguished from a public foundation because they are controlled by and receive funding primarily from one source – usually a corporation, individual or family. Conversely, public foundations receive funding from multiple donors and are governed by unrelated parties. They may carry out their own programmes, however the majority act exclusively as grant-makers.

Charitable trusts and foundations can provide a high degree of control to the donor over grant-making and investment management decisions, and provide opportunities for the family to build a legacy and work together across generations. However, these advantages can trigger higher costs.

Private foundations are subject to tight regulatory controls in certain jurisdictions such as the United States and Canada. Despite this, critics argue for greater stringency on the basis that private foundations diminish government revenue and can tie up capital in perpetuity.[36] Controls include mandatory distribution rules, investment regulations and restrictions, political activities, and operating business activities.

Where flexibility is desired and income tax deductibility is not relevant, setting up charitable organisations in a foreign jurisdiction with established charity law might be a suitable alternative. Independent legal and tax advice should always be sought prior to establishing a foreign charitable entity.

5.4   Giving circles

Giving circles are associations formed by groups of donors with similar philanthropic visions and interests that decide collectively where to direct funds. They can be set up in a number of forms ranging from informal gatherings to formal charitable vehicles such as charitable trusts or foundations to achieve maximum tax efficiency. Donors often commit to participate over the long term with a minimum financial pledge. Collaboration between donors sharing experience and expertise enhances learning and maximises the impact of giving.

6.   Family philanthropy

The returns on a family investment in philanthropy are – or can be – extremely high, both internally and externally. When such an investment is well executed, a family can achieve the cohesion that comes with a sense of higher purpose and cooperative effort. Family members report an excitement and fulfilment going far beyond what they had known as related (though often bloodied) members of a tribe.[37]

Family philanthropy can strengthen the family unit and build the capacity of the individual members – in particular the next generation. A recent survey of philanthropists from around the globe revealed that half expected their children and grandchildren to hold philanthropy as an important value, and more than two-

---

36   B Alepin, "Tax Incentives for Charitable Donations", brief submitted to the Standing Committee on Finance of the House of Commons Canada (2012); summary at: www.parl.gc.ca/HousePublications/Publication.aspx?DocId=5340612.

37   P Ylvisaker, *Conscience and Community: The Legacy of Paul Ylvisaker* (Peter Lang Publishing, 1999).

thirds expressed a desire for their descendants to continue their legacy through the philanthropic entities they established.[38]

6.1 The next generation

Many wealth generators are concerned that their wealth could serve as a negative force for their children, creating unproductive members of society who possess a sense of entitlement. Since the next generation grow up as a beneficiary of wealth, rather than a generator, there is risk of an imbalance between entitlement and personal responsibility to be productive and self-sustaining.[39]

Philanthropy can help the next generation to develop a more balanced view of the world and to develop the requisite skills to become independent, productive and responsible members of society. It offers them the opportunity to contribute to family affairs and teaches them to make responsible decisions regarding family wealth, while strengthening communication and dispute resolution skills. It also helps to develop an appreciation and respect for other family members as they deal with each other on a new and different level. The offspring of wealthy families report that they are driven by values they have learned from parents and grandparents.[40]

The younger generation of philanthropists seeks a balance between honouring their family legacy and assessing current social needs and the tools available to address those needs. They view themselves as more strategic and focused on impact than their predecessors. They play a hands-on role in giving, offering not only financial support to the causes they are committed to, but also sharing their skills with the organisations they support. They believe in the value of networking and collaboration, leveraging the collective knowledge and experiences of their peers to maximise impact. Their search for self-identity comes with the desire to establish their own legacy now, rather than waiting until their retirement years.[41]

In addition to employing different approaches, young philanthropists are supporting different types of organisations than their predecessors. While many older generations give to large, established, and prestigious organisations such as universities, hospitals and museums, the younger generation appears to be more focused on supporting smaller, grassroots organisations. Mark Zuckerberg, at the age of 26, pledged $100 million to Newark New Jersey's school system. EBay founder Pierre Omidyar and his spouse contributed $61.5 million to their philanthropies that support, in part, social entrepreneurship.[42] Japan's Chikara Funabashi helped to establish leadership training, mentoring and scholarships to Japanese secondary and post-secondary students orphaned by the 2011 earthquake.[43]

---

38   *Next-Generation Philanthropy: Changing the World* (Forbes Insights, 2012).
39   F Herz Brown and DT Jaffe, *Overcoming Entitlement and Raising Responsible Next Generation Family Members* (Relative Solutions, 2010).
40   *#NextGenDonors: Respecting Legacy, Revolutionizing Philanthropy* (Johnson Centre for Philanthropy and 21/64, 2013).
41   *#NextGenDonors: Respecting Legacy, Revolutionizing Philanthropy* (Johnson Centre for Philanthropy and 21/64, 2013).
42   M Di Mento and C Preston, "After a Frugal Year, 2011 May See a Jump in Top Donors' Giving", Chronicle of Philanthropy (2011) at: philanthropy.com/article/America-s-Biggest-Donors-Hit/126221/.
43   J Koppisch, "2012 Philanthropists from Japan and South Korea", Forbes (2012), at: www.forbes.com/sites/johnkoppisch/2012/06/20/2012-philanthropists-from-japan-and-south-korea/.

6.2 Entrepreneurial donors

Entrepreneurs who experience a liquidity event often look to philanthropy for their next venture. There is often a loss of identity associated with the sale of a company, and entrepreneurs can struggle with the transition to the next stage of life. Planned philanthropy may help mitigate the challenges many entrepreneurs face, as it provides a sense of purpose, community and structure.[44] There is opportunity for trusted advisers to help their clients plan for such transitions.

6.3 Giving through the family business

In certain economies, the majority of business is owned and controlled by families. In India families control approximately 70% of the top 40 business groups. These families give largely through their businesses, blurring the lines between individual philanthropy and corporate social responsibility.[45] The practice of giving through a closely held business is commonly seen throughout Asian and Latin American societies. Even though donated funds are technically assets of the corporation, often the principal shareholder(s) view such donations as an extension of their own personal generosity. Professional advisers may have the opportunity to offer support to clients donating through the family owned business.

Corporations undertake philanthropic activity to strengthen links with their consumers, suppliers and employees. Businesses demonstrate their commitment to local needs by investing in the communities they operate in. Companies that invest in corporate social responsibility initiatives that include philanthropy strive to achieve higher levels of public reputation, customer loyalty, employee retention and satisfaction, and market share. Executives see corporate philanthropy as a form of social insurance, to mitigate the impact of any negative publicity.[46] Leading corporations align their giving strategies with their business models, targeting social problems that impact their bottom line.

6.4 Family philanthropy challenges

Donors generally must deal with issues of governance, investment management, and impact. However, family philanthropies face additional unique challenges that stem from the family relationship. Pre-existing family dynamics – good and bad – will rear their heads, and can make reaching consensus difficult. Some family members may be ambivalent about the fact that part of their perceived inheritance is going to unrelated third parties. Determining who will participate in the family philanthropy, including the succession of leadership, is among the greatest challenges. Focusing on a commitment to shared values rather than differing interests may help to mitigate family conflicts. Establishing clear policies and procedures for participation and governance will also help avoid or resolve disputes.[47]

---

44   *Life after an Exit: How Entrepreneurs Transition to the Next Stage*, Entrepreneurs White Paper 03, (The Eugene Lang Entrepreneurship Centre at Columbia Business School for Credit Suisse, 2011).
45   A Sheth, *An Overview of Philanthropy in India* (Bain & Company, 2010).
46   J Hempel, et al, "The Corporate Givers", *Bloomberg Businessweek Magazine* (2004), at: www.businessweek.com/stories/2004-11-28/the-corporate-givers.
47   V Esposito, *The Power to Produce Wonders: The Value of Family in Philanthropy* (National Centre for Family Philanthropy, Washington, 2010).

A successful grant-making vehicle depends on good governance, which in turn relies on the commitment and skills of its leadership. Expertise in the areas of finances, legal matters, social issues and available tools is important when considering who to invite to participate on governing or advisory boards. Assessing performance can motivate members to remain productive. Hiring staff to run a private foundation or charitable trust is an option for families with limited time or skills.

7. Advisers

While strides have been made by advisers in recent years to promote philanthropic services, much discussion occurs on a reactive basis, initiated by the client. Today's philanthropists have increasing options to facilitate their giving. Many do not know where to begin, or wish to move away from reactive cheque-writing practices towards strategic, effective giving. While the topic of philanthropy is a personal issue, it can be raised in an unobtrusive manner. Philanthropy can strengthen the client-adviser relationship and help advisers to attract new clients by distinguishing themselves from competitors.

Most advisers and service providers offering philanthropy services focus on the initial phases of giving – namely the structuring of grant-making vehicles and tax advice. Certain private banks and multi-family offices have expanded their offerings to include educating clients on planning options and industry developments, facilitating networking events with fellow philanthropists and helping clients to define their philanthropic mission.

In addition to the planning and structuring phases, philanthropists also require support in the implementation phase, to identify the best partners and measure the impact of gifts. Advisers who feel this is beyond the scope of their expertise should engage or refer third-party experts to cover services outside the core offering.

7.1 Where do philanthropists seek advice?

Philanthropists are seeking advice from their financial advisers, accountants, estate lawyers, trustees and philanthropy experts. As philanthropy grows and evolves, it increasingly requires more sophisticated planning.

The next generation of philanthropists are partnering with multiple advisers, rather than one. Advisers may need to modify their approach with the next generation, and to focus on overseeing the use of multiple resources and experts rather than acting as gatekeepers or sole advisers.[48]

7.2 Family offices and philanthropy

The intimate knowledge that family offices develop about client businesses, family dynamic, succession and estate plans, and overall wealth management strategy may naturally extend to family philanthropy services. A recent study by the National Centre for Family Philanthropy looked at 400 family foundations connected to

---

48   L Philp, *Next Gen Donors: Shaping the Future of Philanthropy* (GrantCraft, 2013).
49   *Working together for Common Purpose: The First National Study of Family Philanthropy through the Family Office* (National Centre for Family Philanthropy Special Report, 2012).

family offices and published a report highlighting best working practices.[49] While this is a US-based study, its findings can be useful references for family offices globally.

Increasingly, family offices are offering philanthropy services to their clientele. There are a number of advantages to involving the family office in the management of a grant-making vehicle, such as a family foundation:[50]

- integrating a variety of key functions such as investment management, administration, tax strategy and compliance, and overall governance;
- alignment with family values;
- enhancement, by leveraging investment advisory services offered by the family office;
- economies of scale by receiving more services at a reduced cost;
- efficiency;
- communication;
- culture and synergy;
- next generation education.

Certain challenges may also arise when the family office is involved in managing the family philanthropy given its unique mandate. In order to be a successful joint venture, the family philanthropy must be treated with equal import to other areas of the family wealth plan and be viewed as part of the core offering. Clarity of goals and roles set by the family may mitigate potential conflict, and should be supported by structured reporting lines and forums for regular communication among staff and between staff and the family. Family office staff that support their clients in their philanthropy need to be trained and encouraged to engage in continued professional development.

A number of key legal issues may arise when a family office provides services to a family foundation. For example: self-dealing rules may prohibit a family foundation from engaging in certain transactions with disqualified persons; private foundation regulation may restrict large shareholdings of a single stock, and prohibits investments that jeopardise the foundation's purpose; and there may be investment adviser registration requirements that must be addressed.[51] Independent legal advice should be sought in the jurisdiction where the family office and grant-making vehicle are established to ascertain what, if any, issues arise before establishing a relationship between the family office and the family philanthropy.

The objectives of the family are not dissimilar to the goals of family philanthropy itself: to strengthen community and empower the next generation to become independent, productive contributors to society. Done with a view towards sustainable giving, philanthropy creates a lasting legacy that honours the family and its philanthropic founders.

---

50   *Working together for Common Purpose: The First National Study of Family Philanthropy through the Family Office* (National Centre for Family Philanthropy Special Report, 2012).
51   EK Fleishhacker and A Kosaras, *Key Legal Issues to Consider When a Family Office Provides Services to A Family Foundation* (Centre for Family Philanthropy Special Report, 2012).

8.   Conclusion

Charity in its classic form strives to alleviate suffering. It may succeed in providing temporary relief, but fails to address the sources of the suffering or affect systemic change. Charity is immediate, but its benefits fleeting. Conversely, philanthropy endeavours to improve the autonomy and welfare of the underserved and disadvantaged by tackling complex systemic issues through investment in change. Private philanthropy has the potential to empower its beneficiaries to become self-sufficient and move away from dependence on aid relief. Together with other forms of social investment, such as impact investing, philanthropy can enhance social equity within local communities and the larger global population.

The five challenges for wealth inheritors to develop a positive wealth identity

Dennis T Jaffe
Independent adviser

Inheriting wealth is supposed to be a wonderful and stress-free life opportunity. However, as financial professionals, we experience many short-sighted or self-defeating ways that our clients who have or expect to inherit substantial wealth respond to their fortunes. Inheriting wealth can be a source of conflict or difficulty. How can this be? What can we do to be helpful since we are often in the middle – between generations – and involved in planning for the transmission of wealth. In this chapter, I discuss the ways that inheritors can be prepared to receive wealth by developing what is defined as a positive wealth identity, which is the foundation for a young person to develop the internal capability to make optimal use of their gift.

Growing up in a wealthy household, the trappings of wealth are omnipresent. This reinforces a sense that they are 'special' in undefined ways, affecting expectations, questions and concerns about their future. This upbringing also provides inheritors with an unusual amount of freedom to define themselves. But this same freedom and privilege also offer challenges for how to make good choices and feel good about their fortune in a world where people with inherited wealth may feel devalued by others who have less and resent them. The way a young inheritor integrates the presence of money and wealth into his or her work, personal relationships and life choices, creates their 'wealth identity'.

How an inheritor relates to money is a distinctive part of personality that expresses deep anxieties, aspirations, choices and values. While every person can develop a positive self-identity in their lives, this chapter focuses on the special challenges facing the inheritor of significant family wealth. Some of the questions family wealth can pose include:

- Does the person see money as a path to fulfilment, a burden or something of an embarrassment?
- Is money the most significant thing in their lives or a minor aspect of their character?
- Does money lead to tension or conflicts in relationships?
- Do inheritors fear or avoid learning about and keeping up on what is happening to their money?

Most of the wealth amassed by global families is new, first generation wealth. Wealth creators are aware that such wealth rarely survives the second generation. They want to be among those who pass their wealth successfully to their children, but they also are deeply concerned that their heirs use the money intelligently and compassionately. Rather than bringing fulfilment, this gift can bring unexpected complexity or even distress to life. Money comes with tremendous potential, and the choices inheritors can make about how to use it are unlimited. But sometimes these choices can be surprisingly difficult, particularly if they are uncertain about, or lack the foundation of, the awareness, values and skills that can enable them to choose wisely.

Several challenges exist for the next generation: knowing they are wealthy and do not have to work, how to motivate themselves and what to do with their lives. They often live in the outsize shadows of their parents, and wonder what they can do that will be significant and important. The opportunities of wealth can be lost if spent on meaningless, self-defeating or destructive pursuits. It can be a source of confusion if inheritors are not sure what it means to them, what they want to do with it, or how it fits into their lives.

For many clients, money alone is not the issue. It is also the status and recognition that comes with wealth, leading to feelings of power and entitlement but also feelings of entrapment and isolation. It changes their lives. We now recognise that having and inheriting money has a marked impact on one's core identity – on the beliefs and values that map how we see ourselves as people as well as how others see us. Inheritors can experience guilt about what they inherit, or a feeling that they do not deserve these gifts, which complicates their ability to move forward in their lives with a positive relationship to their wealth.

At its best, understanding the place of money in one's life can represent a positive, mature life stage, offering many choices but still posing issues of meaning, personal empowerment and social responsibility. After sifting through what money means to them – its effect on their sense of self-esteem, personal relationships, work and community – inheritors of wealth will be better able to embark on new ventures with an invigorated set of priorities.

Inheritors must overcome five key life challenges to generate a sense of life purpose, meaning and positive and facilitative emotional connection to their money. Each challenge describes an important aspect of the psychological relationship to the saving, spending and sharing of wealth. To develop a positive wealth identity, heirs must resolve conflicts and overcome their vulnerabilities in each area. Advisers to a wealthy family will be called upon to help inheritors with these issues. As advisers become aware of the elements of wealth identity, and how they are formed by overcoming specific life dilemmas, they will seek opportunities to address these areas with their young clients. If they appear to be disabling or difficult, advisers may help them find coaching to develop themselves within each area.

1. Challenge I: financial awareness – what does the wealth I have inherited consist of?

Many inheritors avoid the issue of their wealth by using it unconsciously, without knowing anything about it. This challenge indicates the degree to which a person has actively become aware of money matters: how much they have, how it is invested, and how it is spent and shared. Not knowing about money is a way of denying it, or not being responsible for taking care of it. Just as a person must learn to take care of a prized possession, so people should take care of their money, to insure their future. Success in this area indicates a solid hold on one's finances characterised by the feeling of truly 'owning your money'.

Lack of financial awareness is seen in people who have difficulty claiming ownership of their wealth, or at worst avoid or deny responsibility for it. They may behave as if the wealth is really not their own, or believe that it is magically taken care of by others, and that it is infinite and always present. Such wealthy people are prey to all sorts of schemes that lose their money.

Many heirs and people who achieve sudden success are not really prepared to handle their money. It comes to them without preparation, sometimes seemingly out of the blue. The existence of trusts and family financial advisers designated to make decisions for them leaves them feeling like dependent children, reinforcing a childlike lack of awareness and empowerment. This dependency often leaves them feeling incomplete, undeveloped and vulnerable. To avoid entitling their children, many wealth creators do not speak about money or inheritance, leaving their children to cope with the effects of wealth on their own. But to develop a positive wealth identity, inheritors need to inform themselves and begin a learning process.

Sometimes, after a setback or huge loss, they finally take the reins. At other times they struggle to take control of their money against well-meaning but misguided financial advisers, behaviour they are told is foolish or selfish on their part. But taking control does not mean making all choices on their own or rejecting professional advice. It means being informed about what is happening and participating in or being aware of major financial decisions. This is part of being a mature adult. Many heirs feel like their inheritance is designed to keep them from experiencing any sort of personal maturity in relation to their money. They feel that they will never be trusted to take care of themselves.

Inheritors often suffer from difficulties with money awareness. Heirs are given money without necessarily being given the skills to manage it. Some heirs feel disconnected from their money, as if it still belongs to the family member who made the distribution. One variation on this theme are so-called 'trust babies', whose inheritance becomes an obstacle to growing up. Yet others feel guilty or ashamed about their bloodline's good fortune, hiding their wealth from others as well as themselves.

Success in this area comes when an heir develops a solid hold on finances characterised by the feeling of truly owning their money. While details of wealth management may be delegated to a team of professionals, the wealth-holder is keenly aware and in charge of saving, spending and sharing of money. They must develop special financial skills and capabilities that are not taught in college. Wealth advisers can steer young heirs to courses, workshops and programmes to help them in this area, but only after they understand the need and reasons for developing them.

2. **Challenge II: lifestyle management – how shall I live with the wealth I now have?**
    This element points to how people get pleasure from using their money: their spending habits and the nature of their life. Positive identity is seen in those who feel genuine pleasure and satisfaction from spending their money, who spend in ways

that are not ultimately compulsive or self-destructive. They buy things that have meaning and they buy things for fun. However, they also practise a values-based spending, balancing saving and sharing of money with spending. They enjoy spending without excessive shame or guilt, living according to an overall life plan.

The presence of money can be a resource, or a temptation to addiction and compulsive spending. Consider stories of people winning the lottery, or inheriting, and quickly spending it away. One might expect that they were not truly in control of their wealth and in the end it did not add to their lives. They buy lots of things that do not continue to bring them the pleasure that is expected.

People can feel out of control in spending along two extremes: they either over-spend and spend impulsively, resulting in a short-lasting pleasure, a sense of waste and potential negative financial consequences. Or on the other side of the spectrum: those who radically under-spend feel inhibited by a sense of non-entitlement and feelings of shame and guilt. They are afraid to get pleasure in their wealth, perhaps because they feel they do not deserve it, or it is not really theirs.

The challenge in developing this aspect of wealth identity is to get the inheritors of wealth to define their lifestyle within a set of life goals based on values about the use of their wealth, and how they fit with the kind of life they want to live. After they are aware of the extent of their wealth, their challenge is to define their values and what they want in life, and then to define a spending plan that will sustain their wealth and allow them to live with genuine pleasure.

3. Challenge III: stewardship – how do I use my wealth productively to make a difference in the world?

It is not enough for a person with wealth to just look to their own personal satisfaction. Having wealth means the opportunity to influence and help others, and studies show that the greatest pleasure and life satisfaction comes when one gives both to oneself and to others. A steward views wealth as a multi-dimensional resource that is preserved and shared for the benefit of both current and future generations. A healthy person will want to look around, and consider what can be done for other people and for the future.

The presence of significant money should lead a person to explore issues beyond their individual self. An heir may want to consider how his wealth can impact his heirs and community. An individual cannot possess a great deal of money and not listen to the needs that lie around him. A person who has acquired guilt about being wealthy can build a sense of self by defining a positive life mission beyond individual comfort, about what to do with his wealth. By having this broader purpose, wealthy individuals set themselves to live a life where they have a positive role in using their wealth for broader purposes.

People who view their wealth as primarily for their own use, who do not want or have a legacy plan, and who are not concerned about the future use of their money distributions are living in denial of the world beyond their personal sphere. They live in a bubble. Wealth is seen as a private resource for personal use and enjoyment. They feel no further responsibility. Wealth does not, and should not, make someone a saint; spending is not a sin. However, the presence of significant money should lead people to consider issues beyond themselves, how it can impact on heirs and on the community.

If one's life is no longer defined by having to make money, then the question will arise, what will one do to define who one is and what one stands for? Defining one's legacy and the meaning of one's wealth is a key step toward a full definition as a person of wealth. When heirs find a life purpose that involves doing something for the community or the future, and live in line with their values, they feel enabled to derive personal satisfaction from moderate use of their wealth.

Some wealth creators see their legacy as primarily to society, and foresee a more limited role for their children. Financier Warren Buffett famously has made it clear that he will leave his children enough to be comfortable, but that most of his wealth will go to a foundation. A common pattern is for the next generation to inherit some money, but more importantly to learn that their self-worth and life's work lies in philanthropy. The Rockefeller family, after the founding fortune accumulated by John D Rockefeller, has carefully cultivated careers of philanthropy and social activism in several generations of heirs. Newer families such as the US Gates, Moore, Hewlett and Packard families have defined their legacies along similar pathways. Families of more modest means set up a family foundation, and achieve purpose and meaning in their lives by using their time and energy in making a difference in society. This outward and expansive life focus can help heirs overcome conflict or ambivalence they may experience about coming into money.

Stewardship refers to the degree to which one's financial decision-making is based upon a family mission and set of values. Wealth is viewed as a multi-dimensional resource that is preserved and shared for the benefit of both current and future generations. While it is his or hers, a healthy person will want to look around, and consider what can be done for other people, and for the future.

Strength in this factor is reflected in people who have a 'future sense' in their money decisions, who desire to leave a meaningful legacy and who are thoughtful about the impact of distributions to future generations. They plan for how wealth can make a difference both in their own lives and in the larger community. Success in this element indicates a person with a plan for the utilisation of their wealth, who wants to leave a values-based legacy for future generations.

Vulnerability in this factor is seen in people who view their wealth as primarily for their own use, who do not want or do not have a legacy plan, and who are not very concerned about the future use of their money distributions. They see their wealth as only a private resource for personal use and enjoyment.

4. Challenge IV: self-esteem/personal Security – how can I feel good about myself and the good fortune I have received?

Money by itself does not make people feel personally secure or good about themselves. In fact, its presence may lead a client to feel an increase of anxiety. The element of self-esteem refers to how much an heir's sense of personal value, self-respect and personal identity is founded on wealth. How comfortable and secure do they feel in their own skin, which includes their inheritance and the role that it defines for their lives? Unless clients have a strong sense of personal identity, the fear of losing money may lead them to feel continually vulnerable. Strength in this element means an individual has a solid and coherent foundation of self-esteem and personal security that is not primarily reliant on net worth. They feel in charge of their lives, enjoying the advantages of money without feeling that it makes them a better or more worthwhile person, or an evil one.

Positive self-esteem comprises a multitude of factors, including the capacity to love and be loved, to be recognised and connected to family and community, and to be successful and productive. Certainly achieving financial independence, a symbol of success in our society, can enhance self-esteem. But what if one did not earn the money, but received it from one's parents? The impact of wealth on self-esteem can be even more problematic for inheritors than it is for earned wealth-holders. Inheritors may feel unworthy of their gifts and may suffer from doubt and guilt regarding their wealth.

Inheritors may suffer far more from shame, doubt and guilt than their earned-wealth counterparts. The luck of their bloodline does not automatically make for an increase in self-esteem or self-worth. The struggle to develop a sense of self-esteem for wealthy heirs is recounted in scores of moralistic life stories. Heirs can experience a difficult and multi-year struggle that lasts well into adulthood, as they seek to find a sense of purpose and vitality in their lives, and to overcome feelings of guilt, worthlessness and depression.

Achieving self-esteem is a task beyond defining a life purpose, in that the person has to take active steps to live within their values. This often means going on a life journey where they discover their own capabilities by living on their own, with no or minimal support, earning a living and doing something that is remunerative and useful. Sometimes this does not happen until the person has some sort of personal crisis, caused by self-destructive or self-defeating behaviour, which their money or their connections cannot solve for them. By resolving a life crisis on their own, they develop the strength of character that is the foundation for positive self-esteem. The family often inadvertently uses inheritance to keep their children from taking this life journey and developing themselves.

5. **Challenge V: trust in relationships – how can I trust and build lasting relationships with others who may not have the advantages that I have?**
A person's willingness to trust others in a personal relationship is affected by wealth. The presence of money can make it hard to trust others even as it attracts them. A wealthy person must learn how to select and trust special other people, or he will always feel that money undermines the nature of relationships. People can always wonder if someone likes them for their money, or for who they are. A mature person finds ways to find the personal friends who are genuine. When a person finds their personal comfort zone in handling the impact of money on personal relationships, he is able to trust other people and deal with money issues without poisoning or undermining his relationships. Vulnerability arises when intimacy, trust and stability are over-determined or undermined by money matters. Conflicts over money can contaminate relationships with loved ones, causing money-driven hardships and heartaches.

Vulnerability is seen in heirs who develop exaggerated fears about being taken advantage of by others. They are asked for money or loans and then feel the awkwardness of not being repaid. Some people develop irrational fears of contact with others of differing economic classes. Fears about how others may respond to money issues can result in secrecy or at its extreme, the 'Howard Hughes syndrome' of privacy with a paranoid edge.

Money must be managed in relationships. It is hard to overcome starting from a sense of distrust and vulnerability. But uncritical acceptance of others can also lead to being taken advantage of. Clients must accept that money will get in the way of relationships, and use personal skills to break through to resolve these issues in their most important relationships

Strength in this capacity indicates a person who has found his or her personal comfort zone in handling the impact of money on personal relationships. A person must learn to say 'no' to others, and to not feel guilty at having more than others. He is able to trust other people and feels both confident and trusting in handling the impact of money on relationships.

The value of self in a relationship is not determined by the size of one's bank account. Strength on this factor does not mean that the interaction of money and relationships is without difficulties, but it indicates that challenges can be handled without significant pressure on self-esteem or on the stability and involvement with important others. For example, in many close relationships, we see people grappling with differences between savers and spenders. Strength in this factor indicates the capacity to communicate in constructive ways in resolving or reconciling differences.

6.   Helping clients: counselling and consultation

There are several avenues that inheritors pursue to progress in their own development. First, and probably most easily available, there are workshops, groups and support networks that are sponsored by investment banks, financial service groups and philanthropy networks where people can combine discovering what to do to preserve their money and what to do with it. They offer several things. First, they offer the support of people who are struggling with similar issues, together with safe and confidential environment to explore issues. They also offer clear outlets where heirs can learn about issues from money management to philanthropy without feeling burdened by the pain and difficult choices that are put upon them by those in need.

Secondly, various types of personal and family counselling and coaching can help one discover a basis for making choices, develop understanding of one's mixed feelings and chart a course for the future. Family members have a chance to stop the action of daily life, truly take stock of where they are today and create values-based lifestyle action plans.

A third option is to meet as a family. Increasingly, families get together to explore the issues of wealth in their lives, and explore the choices facing their children and heirs. The family can gather informally, at the family home or at a meal, or they can have a more formal gathering, where they talk about specific approaches to money, whether investing, spending or giving. Meeting as a family, to discuss values, how money will be shared and used, and what is important to each member, is a key activity for coming to terms with wealth.

Using the "Wealth Identity and Preferences Inventory" (available online at no cost) can help clients assess the level of difficulty they have in each of these areas, and help them set personal priorities for their own development. By looking at the key areas of vulnerability identified in the inventory, a wealth heir can identify which of these challenges is a starting point for their journey to self-development.

This chapter has presented the most common challenges faced by young heirs as they grow up to be ready, willing and able to receive and use an inheritance in a personally and socially useful manner. As an adviser, one should be aware of these challenges, and alert to helping one's clients to face them and to take steps to support their own personal development.

The model and concepts in this chapter are derived from work in collaboration with Steve Goldbart and Joan DiFuria of Money Meaning and Choices Institute. The "Money Identity and Preferences Inventory" self-assessment tool that can be used to explore these five challenges is available without cost at our websites: dennisjaffe.com, and mmcinstitute.com. A guide to holding family meetings about wealth is available on the website dennisjaffe.com, and many other resources are available on both websites.

The golden rucksack – insights from qualitative research among wealthy heirs

Raimund Kamp
Marijke Kuijpers
Guidato Family Office (Amsterdam, the Netherlands)

In this chapter we present the main insights of our qualitative research on wealth transfer in the Netherlands. We have researched the upbringing of heirs in wealthy families, how they are prepared for the inheritance of family capital and their experiences with inherited wealth.

The existence of family wealth does not guarantee its perpetuation. This is consistent with the popular Dutch proverb *"verwerven, vererven en verderven in drie generaties"* ("acquisition, inheritance and destruction in three generations"). This famous saying illustrates how family wealth often dwindles over time. Every country has similar sayings, like the American "from shirtsleeves to shirtsleeves in three generations" or the old British "there's nobbut three generations between clog and clog". Besides our professional experience that many heirs experience obstacles with their inheritance, we were also intrigued by this phenomenon: why do some families retain their wealth for longer than three generations, and what do they do differently? What factors make family wealth resilient to the passage of generations? How do wealthy families prevent their capital from waning? Undoubtedly Dutch family culture has an impact on the way wealthy Dutch parents transfer family capital to their children, but many principles will be universal and therefore relevant for non-Dutch wealthy families and their advisers.

In this chapter, we will first discuss the how and what of our research. The second section focuses on the poor preparation of most heirs. We continue in section 3 with a look at the 'head in the sand' approach to upbringing. Section 4 deals with the expectations of future heirs. Next we discuss the pitfall of boundless opportunities (section 5) and look at the question 'to work or not to work?' (section 6). We continue in section 7 with wealth education: what every wealthy child ultimately should know and learn. Then we describe the objectives of family wealth and finish with the ideal wealthy family (section 9).

1.   Our research on wealth transfer in the Netherlands

As advisers we were curious about the success factors involved in preparing heirs. To that end, we conducted a qualitative study of 18 wealthy Dutch heirs, starting in December 2009 and running until April 2011. As far as we are aware, this type of research has never before been conducted in Europe. Our research aimed to gain insight into the issues and dynamics of capital transfer by inventorying and analysing these heirs' experiences.

The 18 wealthy heirs were from the second up to and including the ninth generation. This sample consisted of seven female and 11 male heirs, with ages at the time of our interviews between 40 and 70 years old. All respondents had been multimillionaires for at least 10 years, so they were able to reflect on their experiences as wealthy heirs. In order to get a better understanding of the family dynamics we interviewed brothers and sisters within one family. All 18 respondents have children so our interviews partly focused on their preparation of their offspring.

All sorts of goods are transferred from one generation to another: (family) businesses, estates, investment portfolios, real estate (companies), cash, paintings and so on. We recorded all the interviews and ended up with 600 pages of information that needed further analysis. Professor Ad Kil PhD of Nyenrode Business University assisted us with the analysis and theoretical building blocks to clarify the results.

Capital transfers can take place either through a gift while the donor is still alive, or through an inheritance after his death. In our research we took both forms into account. We focused on the personal experiences of heirs that grew up in wealthy families and received (a part of) the family's wealth. Our approach requires that subjects like upbringing, personal development and family relationships take centre stage. The theory we present brings the fields of pedagogy and psychology prominently forward. The results of our study were published in December 2013 in the Dutch book *De gouden rugzak – Handboek voor vermogende families* (in English: *The golden rucksack – Handbook for wealthy families*). The research and book do not address the legal and fiscal aspects of capital transfer, or any of the associated tactics used to pay as little tax as possible.

The book title, The golden rucksack, was inspired by a childhood experience of an heiress:

"Hey! Don't you have a golden rucksack?" said some middle school students in a teasing tone. I didn't know them, but apparently their parents worked at my grandfather's company. Riding my bike on my way home, I was quite sad about the things they had said to me.

It shows that more often than not, the outside world has a preformed opinion or prejudgement of wealthy people, independently of their age. As we mentioned earlier, wealth can be as much of a burden as an opportunity, which in our opinion, fits in perfectly with the image of a golden rucksack.

This is our contribution to a new world. In the old world, the sole focus of wealthy families and their advisers revolved around financial and estate planning, where fiscal and legal technicalities took centre stage during the transfer of estates. This was all to ensure that heirs would pay as little tax as possible, while creating as many opportunities for them as possible. In the new world, there is an additional element that comes into play, which is to prepare the next generation in the best possible way for the responsibilities that come hand-in-hand with wealth.

Not all aspects associated with the inheritance of substantial wealth are positive ones. The challenges can be of a diverse nature. Many heirs do not openly speak of problems and disadvantages of their inheritance, not even within their own social circles. To bystanders, it may sound rather ungrateful that the receiver of a large amount of capital has nothing but complaints about it. Who wouldn't swap roles with a wealthy heir? Why else do so many people play the lottery? The dream, of course, is to win the millions that would solve all one's problems at once. However, this is without a doubt a simplistic view of things. We would therefore like to examine how wealthy parents can ensure that their future heirs perceive their inheritance as more of an opportunity than a burden.

2. Poor preparation of most heirs

To our surprise only two of the 18 heirs in our study were properly prepared for the responsibilities of their inheritance. Inheriting a fortune did not change their lives very much. They were old-money heirs, which we define as fourth generation landed wealth. This means that 16 heirs were not properly prepared, or were even ill-prepared, and encountered obstacles, both financial and emotional.

For most of the ill-prepared heirs it was very hard to deal with the financial management of their wealth, speaking with different experts and advisers and making the right decisions. A second generation heiress from an industrial family received a legacy together with her sisters and their experience with advisers is illustrative:

> We understood that we had to make decisions within two years for tax legislation reasons. We used this entire period, because they gave us useless advice. They think you know what you want, but we did not know ourselves. We received a recital of tax advantages: you could do this or that, and that depended on this and that. We really had no idea! We might as well have gone "Eeny meeny miney mo!" Our notary did not ask many questions either. The accountant only had explanations of how to minimise tax. We asked him: "How did we get here?" And "What would you do if you were me?" It just was impossible for us to make decisions.

A second obstacle was related to emotional ramifications of the inheritance. Some of the heirs were even ashamed of their own wealth: "Why did I receive this inheritance? What will others think of me now that I'm so rich?" Many experienced issues in their relationships with their partner and friends, and had feelings of inferiority, guilt and low self-esteem. Finally, a number of heirs were confronted with philosophical questions about the sense of their own lives: "I don't work because I'm rich, but what am I going to do instead?" One heir was also delicately confronted with his empty existence by his wife:

> I really have money in the bank, debts repaid. This situation feels good. However, our children must go to school in the morning and my wife says: "You were never home, and now you are and what are you going to do today? Go to your mother? You were already at your mother's place the day before yesterday." And she opens the door to go to her work and then you're home alone again.

We conclude that, even in old money families, a proper pro-active, well-defined process to prepare the next generation is often lacking. As we will see later in this chapter, the desire to sustain family wealth for these respondents can be traced back to implicit messages from (grand)parents to their (grand)children. Unfortunately, very little practical guidance is being given, which frustrates many heirs who wish to adhere to the family objective of multi-generational wealth.

2.1 Fears and concerns as underlying cause of poor preparation

Just like all parents, wealthy parents also have fears and concerns for their children. A number of these fears and concerns are directly linked to the unique financial situation of a wealthy family. An heiress summed it up concisely: "It is terribly difficult for parents to let their children go in general, and in particular with wealth."

Three fears and concerns of parents came up during our research, those of relationships, their own initiative and materialism.

Wealthy parents' first and most frequently cited fear concerns the child's relationships, in general and specifically with their future (marriage) partner. The following quote from an heiress is representative of the situation of many females:

My father was always terrified that we would come home with a partner that was in it for the money, so to speak. That was on his mind a lot." The fear here is that wealth attracts the wrong kind of people; people that are not as interested in the individual as in the wealth behind that individual.

The second fear is that wealth may limit or destroy the child's own initiative. The child can come to think the family fortune is a great base to live off. The child fails to feel the need to give some substance to his life with a (professional) career. This train of thought can lead to low educational ambitions and little interest in ever becoming independent. An heir explains how in his father's generation, knowing about the wealth of the family completely destroyed their initiative:

They did that really badly in my father's generation. Those expectations about the family wealth: my grandpa was not able to subdue it. The pride, the arrogance, they all have it in them. You couldn't have done it any worse.

The third fear is that the children will become materialistic. Wealthy families often enjoy a luxurious lifestyle from which children could possibly conclude that material things are of utmost importance in life. An heiress finds it crucial to show her children that even though money provides opportunities, wealth is not unlimited:

As a child you live in a well-to-do environment, but that is different than living off your wealth.

Heirs mentioned this fear about their own children more often than that they think their parents had this same fear about them. This is undoubtedly linked to a societal change whereby consumption is now being given more thought than previously.

How do parents go about addressing their fears and concerns? When it comes to the fear of relationships, parents warn their children explicitly. These warnings can go to the point that the heir subsequently finds that his parents succeeded in their effort. One heir said:

It was those two things in my childhood: the words jealousy and profiting. Those two words. The thought that I would get friends that wanted to take advantage of it. They were a bit uptight about that.

Heirs that are warned like this by their parents find that having a general distrust for everyone outside their family can have very negative effects.

To continue in the context of fears and concerns about relationships, a number of parents went one step further. Some went as far as to have their child's partner investigated by a detective agency. One heiress had nothing but understanding for it:

> My parents had someone investigate my former boyfriend, through an agency. I only heard about it a couple of years later, but I get it. I would do the same myself if I was in a similar situation. The classic example: wealthy parents and a wealthy daughter.

It appears to be common practice for parents not always to tell their children (mostly women in our research) that detective services have been hired. This can come to light years later by sheer coincidence, as seen from our interviews with two other heirs.

3.   Upbringing: the 'head in the sand' strategy

Parents who are fearful of the negative influence of family wealth on, for example, the child's initiative use the 'head in the sand' strategy. The assumption here is: what they don't know doesn't hurt them. Parents are often anxious about their children's questions about the family capital. The common reaction is to give no answer or to talk around the subject.

What do parents want to achieve with these messages? By telling their children that they need to get going by themselves and not just wait for their share of the capital, parents try to have a positive impact on their children's lives. One heir narrates how this worked in his family:

> We were brought up with the idea that we should be happy if there was anything left at the end. Until then we could make use of it, through loans. You have to do it yourself. So that you are not watching the figures thinking oh, this much will be left over when my father passes away.

Toning down expectations and restricting financial expenditure are recurring themes for a number of families in our study. By not making too many financial resources available to children, parents put their money where their mouth is, so that children learn to cope by themselves financially. A number of heirs also saw this happen to the generations before them. One heir saw this restriction of the wealth as a sign of Calvinism:

> My grandfather had a Calvinist slant. Above all he made sure his children wouldn't get the feeling that there was a lot of money. So my father did receive money, but he was always relatively tight-fisted.

Parents see nothing but advantages in not talking about wealth and dampening their children's expectations of inheriting: the financial situation of the family remains unclear to the children for a period of time and it does not have an adverse impact on their behaviour. However, this lack of communication and/or lowering of expectations can in fact have negative effects on the heirs. The first negative consequence affects the mutual trust between parents and children. If it later turns out that the wealth of the family was far greater than the child believed, or than the parents had hinted at, the heir can come to believe that his parents did not trust him with that information. Another negative consequence is that parents fail to nurture their children's interest in financial affairs, and thus fail to prepare the next generation in the best way possible for their future responsibilities with the family wealth.

3.1 The paradox of the 'normal' upbringing

'Being normal' and giving children a normal upbringing are values wealthy families want for themselves and aspire to. Many wealthy parents try their best to give their children as normal an upbringing as possible, concealing material manifestations of wealth – in certain situations – so that the child is not troubled by them.

The 'normal upbringing' paradox comes into play in families that continually behave as if they were not wealthy. Children are almost always aware of their family's wealth because of material symbols (houses, cars, boats, holidays) and might even be held accountable for these by the outside world ("Hey! Don't you have a golden rucksack?"). Parents often tell them not to talk about the family's wealth, and even to put special effort into concealing it from the outside world. In short, they are told to keep their wealth a secret. Children that grow up in these circumstances can feel guilty or ashamed of their parents' wealth. If these feelings grow in intensity and frequency, they can have an impact on the development of their identity. They are faced with a challenging paradox: how to live and act normally when the specific circumstances of their upbringing are very unusual. If they become the target of attacks because of their parents' wealth, children can come to believe that they are flawed and be anxious that their secret might be discovered. Despite this, the parents act as if the family is as normal as any other, average family in the Netherlands.

The idea that wealthy families who want to hide their wealth can give their children a normal upbringing is a myth, an impossibility. If the financial situation of the family is extraordinary, there is no more to it, it is extraordinary. Denial of the actual situation does not change anything. The myth of the normal upbringing leads to complicated paradoxes that often burden the children with choices, expectations and secrets that are hard for them to bear.

Families that are open about their wealth are not as confronted by the normal upbringing paradox. Parents inform their children about the wealth of the family; they let them experience and get acquainted with that wealth, and give them financial responsibilities. In short, the parents themselves realise their family is not normal in its financial aspects, and they take that into account during their children's upbringing.

Both in our study and our work we have seen more secretive than open wealthy families. This explains why most wealthy families might have trouble preparing heirs for their future finances and wealth. Unfortunately this can lead to problems during the later stages of an heir's life.

4. Expectations of future heirs

Our research shows that the group of interviewees' parents had a mixture of high, low or unclear expectations of their children. Naturally, this had a varied effect on the children, which in some cases might even have impacted on them in their adult lives.

Parents with high expectations nullified their children's initiative. Fear of failure prevented the heirs from taking on certain tasks to avoid disappointing the parents. One heiress described how her sister dealt with her parents' high expectations:

My sister thought: I won't start this. I won't even try it once, in case I make a mistake.

We used to call our sister Switzerland: always neutral. A bit of this, a bit of that.

These high expectations could of course also function as source of motivation to perform better in some cases, even to this day. The personality of each individual heir plays a crucial role here. One heiress is very demanding with herself because her father emphasized that nobody should ever choose the path of least resistance:

If I don't immediately get how to do it, I hate myself.

We noticed that a number of heirs' parents had remarkably low expectations. Our interviews showed that the intention behind these low expectations was to protect the children from disappointment.

Besides high and low expectations, we talked to heirs who had parents with unclear expectations. When children have no idea what their parents expect but feel they are not meeting these expectations, they carry a mental burden. One heiress said:

I have a very strong feeling that I have to accomplish something, but I cannot describe what it is. But I am not accomplishing it, and my sister feels it even more strongly. And she carries the mental burden that she is not quite meeting the standards.

4.1 Areas of expectations

We have seen three distinct areas of expectations that apply to the personal, the social and the professional areas. In addition, there is a general expectation in wealthy families that wealth will be sustained and increased. We will focus on wealth expectations in section 8.

Personal	Social	Professional
• Tapping into talents	• Etiquette • Future (marriage) partner	• Studies and academic performance • Career and work

(a)   ***Personal expectations: tapping into talents***

The parents of a number of heirs want them to harness their talents. They expect the child to do his best to get the most out of his own capabilities. These capabilities are intelligence, talents and skills. One of the greatest fears of wealthy parents is for their children to use the wealth of the family as safety net, no longer putting any effort into doing things for themselves. Parents believe that harnessing their children's talents would contribute to their high self-esteem and a happy life. One heiress worded her wishes for her son in a way we often encountered during the course of this study:

What we really want is for our son to use his talents, so that he becomes proud of who he is and goes on to do whatever makes him feel good for himself. I would really like that. For him to believe in himself, I find that to be the basis of everything.

(b)   ***Social expectations: etiquette***

Expectations about etiquette have to do with the behaviour expected of wealthy people, and in particular how they spend their free time and how discreet they are with their money. In new-money families, there tend to be more expectations about leisure activities. Parents make sure their children practise certain sports like horseback riding, tennis and hockey, or that they receive music lessons. The goal of the etiquette expectations of new-money families is to find a connection to the higher social classes. The set of norms and standards of the higher classes is passed on by newly rich parents to their children. These will enable the children to find a connection to the higher social classes more easily when they are adults.

In old-money families, it is important to teach each generation anew the standards that will make them be considered good people. Etiquette expectations in these families tend to deal with discretion, in particular not speaking about money and wealth. An heiress from an old-money family mentioned that to her family, etiquette meant dressing neatly, having good table manners and writing thank you notes, among other things.

(c)   ***Social expectations: the future (marriage) partner***
Not a single male heir indicated there was any kind of expectation regarding his marriage partner. In our study, the most commonly cited expectation regarding daughters' spouses is that they needed to be brainy and well educated. These very features were behind the decision of some daughters to go and study, as it was an excellent chance to meet a fitting partner, as one of the heiresses said:

> We didn't have to get PhDs per se, but it was better to do so because that put us in a whole different category when it came to life partners. If at least the husband was it, you wouldn't see that the partner wasn't it.

The intention of the parents, and especially of the fathers, is for a daughter to find a good candidate. To these parents, 'good' often means with as high as possible a level of education. The higher the level of education of the partner, the higher his potential to be financially successful. If a man makes good money himself, there is less risk of an unequal relationship between the wealthy heiress and her husband. Another definition of a good candidate seemed to be that of a man who comes from an old-money family. When a wealthy heiress marries into such a family, her social status rises.

(d)   ***Professional expectations: studies and academic performance***
The differences in expectations regarding studies and academic performance were staggering among the families in our research. Some parents had planned well-defined schooling or study trajectories for their children, going far beyond school performance alone. This was the reason some girls were made to follow a particular programme, or sent to boarding school, so they could later get the right life partner to bite the hook, so to speak. In some of the families the standard was to reach a university level of education, even if the child struggled to achieve that level. One interviewee put it in a way that was representative:

> It was a given that I would study. My brother and I both did. I think that if you assume that your children will go to university, you are setting the bar rather high.

A small number of heirs found their parents' academic expectations to be too low. If the child struggled with certain subjects, he would immediately get private tutoring or perhaps be transferred to private school. In retrospect, these heirs believe their parents could have put more pressure on them to do better instead of simply arranging for private lessons or private schooling. Low academic expectations motivated some heirs to go the extra mile to prove they could achieve more than was believed of them.

(e)   *Professional expectations: career and work*
The parents of our interviewees had remarkably few specific expectations regarding the careers and work of their children. Children could follow their own passion. When there were certain expectations about career and work, they mostly tended to be related to the family business and entrepreneurship. If the family owns a company, there is a big chance that it will affect the children's career choices to a certain degree. Our interviews indicated that expectations for an heir to go into the family business tend to grow gradually. Both the parents and the child grow into the idea.

There were also families with family businesses who did not expect their children to take on the weight of the company. These parents encouraged their children to choose their own path when it came to work, outside the company. One interviewee said:

It was my father's business and not a family business. He also never brought it up at the time: if you drop out of school you'll have to come and work with me… On the contrary, I was to go and find my own path.

In addition to expectations regarding the family business, expectations of entrepreneurship were also mentioned during the course of this study. In certain families of successful entrepreneurs the younger generations were bottle-fed entrepreneurship from birth. Some (grand)parents would go as far as to tell their children that any career path other than entrepreneurship fell nothing short of a disqualification. One heir was strongly influenced by his grandfather's ideas:

On my father's side we come from a lineage of entrepreneurs and on my mother's side from an intellectual family. The atmosphere, especially around my grandfather, was that only independent people are successful, and the rest are just those who work for others. That was more or less the norm. My father and his generation really took to it as they grew up and they also passed it on to us. So that set the tone and determined to a large extent the choices that we made.

The drawback to parental expectations of entrepreneurship is that not everyone has the talent to become an entrepreneur. For heirs that lack this talent, or who have it in lesser measure, it becomes difficult to accomplish what is expected of them. Career choices are not determined by considerations of what family members may be good at or what their real passions are. As one of the heirs aptly remarked:

In such an environment, you are driven to make certain choices that aren't always the choices you would have made from the standpoint of who you are, what you know and what you are good at.

Our conclusion is that most parents want their children to focus on making their own life and career choices, without letting these be determined by the wealth of the family. When there are family businesses, the family's wealth plays a less obtrusive role in the choices of work and career. Expectations regarding entrepreneurship are much more difficult for heirs to fulfil because talent and passion determine the outcome to a much greater extent.

5. The pitfall of boundless opportunities

Some parents set no boundaries to the opportunities of wealth. Their motivation for giving their children all types of possibilities in terms of studies, career or hobbies can stem from the fact that they had little or no access to them themselves, or simply because it is customary family culture not to get in the way of children.

Our interviews reveal that unlimited opportunities can have a negative impact on children. This is especially the case when any of the child's problems are solved with money, for instance, paying for further schooling when the child has already dropped out of school. By solving problems with money and continuously saving the child, wealth becomes a safety net of sorts. An heir talks about the effects of the all-solving wealth of his parents:

> My parents should have just told me: you get an education and for the rest, go figure it out yourself. Then you can go work at the grocery store. I will say that to my child. Tally-ho. I didn't become happy from it. If I dropped out, they would just give me money and I would go on.

The safety net of wealth means that the financial need to make money and make a career is missing. Of course this is a potential blow to any sense of initiative. This safety net effect is more likely for unprepared heirs who have access to large sums of money. Some participants in the study had postponed crucial choices in life on study and work. There was family wealth and therefore it was not necessary to graduate and to arrange a job. One heir described wrestling with this issue very clearly:

> During my whole study time I seriously wonder why I would actually have to go to work. I have postponed my graduation as long as possible.

Another heir said he had trouble with his motivation to work when it became apparent that investing earned him so much money (on paper):

> I remember that I had a spread sheet with my investments and at the end of the day I had earned twice my annual salary. As I look back now I think: for your own ambition, to make something of your career, it is very destructive.

Postponing choices sometimes goes over into avoidance: postpone plans in life as long as possible and concentrate on side issues instead of things that really matter. This phenomenon was described by an heiress:

> My sister has a kind of avoidance urge. She is always busy with side issues. Shoes to the shoemaker, a massage, et cetera. For years she has been trying to set up an art studio. I think: is it still not ready? She defers everything that she actually wants to be doing.

6. To work or not to work?

This research shows that there is a clear link between having a positive role model in the parents and the work ethic and self-esteem at the next generation. The heirs who have worked only in a limited way, or have sustained a setback in their career, had in all cases not been encouraged by their parents to work. Their family often lacked a role model in the field of work. There was no expectation for the next generation to go to work.

In our society, our profession and those with whom we interact determine an important part of our identity. For the outside world, a successful job and career ensure status. If someone is not working, or only volunteering, outsiders find this a strange situation and difficult to understand. "How does he pay the bills?" is a possible thought of someone who does not know the heir personally. Many respondents said that they suffer from the judgment of the outside world and lower self-esteem. One respondent indicated:

A question like: what do you do? Well, you cannot get more annoying to me. I think that is terrible. What should I say what I do? Yes, you can say very faintly: "I manage my own wealth. Oh, you still have to work then?" But of course, I don't say that. Everyone is saying: "I work there and there" and then they are held in high regard.

One heir had not only suffered from prejudice from the outside world. Even within his own family the unhealthy work ethic with which he grew up attracted disapproval. He said:

In the family my little brother and I had a huge image problem because my father did not work. One of the few who did not work. And apparently we were also not very ambitious, so we were very quickly dismissed as losers.

The interviewees indicated that they are happier if they work. It is good for their self-confidence to earn money, regardless of the amount. The heir who has done nothing for his inherited wealth finds that a self-earned euro feels different. Work provides structure in life, offers a possibility of personal growth and spiritual meaning. We call this the extra dimension of work. Unfortunately, this important aspect was not mentioned by the respondents themselves, and the possibility exists that wealthy parents and their children may completely overlook this extra dimension.

7. Wealth education: what every wealthy child ultimately should know and learn

Every child needs to acquire financial knowledge and skills that lead to making sound financial decisions. Financial self-reliance is the goal of financial education, with an emphasis on learning to handle money matters. A wealthy child needs to learn to make good decisions relating to the family wealth. The offspring will inherit the family fortune, and additional financial knowledge and skills are required to manage this fortune properly.

Becoming responsible for the future inheritance requires more than just knowledge and skills. Learning to talk about money and wealth and the ability to make decisions are skills that any future heir incrementally makes their own, with help from their parents. We call this process wealth education. The ultimate goal of a wealth education is that every wealthy child becomes self-reliant in handling their (future) wealth.

7.1 Three phases of wealth education

Wealth education starts with informing the children about the origin, objectives and composition of the family wealth. In other words what we have built, and what can and should you do with the accumulated capital? The second phase will focus on practice and practical experience. The final phase is about (learning) to let go by the parents. It involves both letting go of the emotional grip and the transfer of financial baton to the next generation.

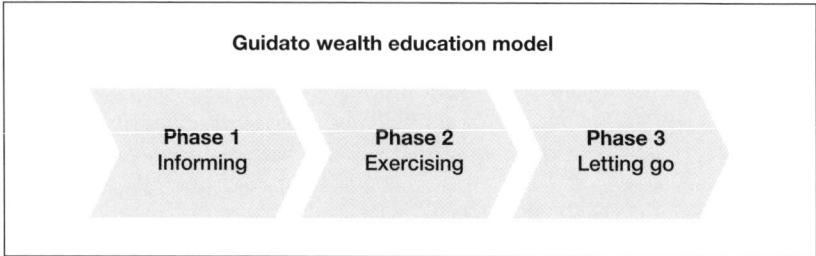

Guidato wealth education model

Phase 1 Informing	Phase 2 Exercising	Phase 3 Letting go

(a) *Phase 1: informing and a broader perspective of wealth*

In the first phase, information about the family wealth plays a central role. Wealthy parents provide information about the origin and objectives of wealth: where does it come from and what can you do or what are you allowed to do with it? Wealth will be placed in a broader perspective. Subsequently, the parents provide financial information: what do we have as a family?

Each family's wealth has an origin. The stories and events that are typical of the family and the assets acquired are important to transfer. This will show what sacrifices have been made, what risks (grand)parents took and what luck factors have played a role. Current and future generations will receive a good perspective on the source of the wealth through this history. Our research showed that most of the heirs know their family history and the origin of the family wealth well. A certain pride about what has been built in the past cannot be denied.

During their upbringing, parents do not want their children to embrace the family wealth and, in some families, even the family name. To feel superior – marked by one heir as "rich kid behaviour" – because the family is wealthy, or because you have a particular family name, did not score points with their parents.

(b) *Phase 2: practice, practice, practice*

Wealth management is a skill, and skills are built up by practising. Inheriting wealth does not automatically mean that an heir is interested in financial affairs. Indeed, we found both in our research and practice that many millionaires have little enthusiasm for wealth management. It is a mandatory task, almost like going to the dentist. The opportunity to practise in a family context, in order to become skilled in wealth management, is therefore not a general habit in most families we have spoken with. Nevertheless based on our interviews we concluded that parents undertook five actions to prepare their children for the future inheritance:

- donations;
- investments with family members;
- attending meetings with advisers;

- family meetings; and
- playing a role in family wealth matters.

Donations: All families in this study gave cash or shares to their (grand)children during the donor's lifetime. In old-money families, this was done from birth. What is striking is that the learning effect of these donations (in terms of financial education) was very limited for most heirs. One heiress had only one insight from her experience with lifetime cash gifts:

I have learned nothing from the gifts. Well, only the feeling that you have much more than you can spend.

Parents often do not tell the children that they have made a gift. This sometimes leads to comical situations, as illustrated by the following anecdote:

Because we were so badly brought up with money and we were all very bad with financial management, my sisters and I found out that my father had given us a sum. He once said: 'You still have not thanked me.' 'Thanked you?' I asked him. Yes, for the gift.

In addition to poor communication about the gifts, parents rarely explained what the children could do with it. Because most parents did not inform their children how they might use it, children found it very difficult to make decisions. This creates insecurity rather than comfort:

If I had made a trip around the world and it was gone, what would have happened? I did not ask, and my father did not say, but I'm not sure what would have happened.

It is therefore not uncommon for heirs to end up doing nothing with the money. It sits in the bank account and the heir barely looks at the bank statements:

Actually, I've never done anything special. I knew it was there, but I did not know exactly how much.

Many interviewees themselves give sums to their children. Their experience is that their children do not ask questions about these gifts and have little need to become responsible for the transferred assets. At one point an heir deliberately handed over the reins to his children:

When my children were 24 or 25 years, after they graduated and really could stand on their own feet, I said 'Guys, I am no longer interested in the financial management, so go ahead.'

After the transfer, his children handled their portfolio very differently:

One child still has the total amount and the other spent it all.

According to this heir, his children must learn how to manage their wealth at some point. It is a learning process.

Investments with family members: These are investments in the broadest sense of the word, ranging from a simple joint bank account to setting up legal structures, investments in private equity or real estate. By investing jointly with the family, children will practise under the supervision (or with the cooperation) of their parents. One heir enthusiastically told how his family and the next generation dealt with their investments:

The investments give the next generation the opportunity to work together. They do not have to make many decisions yet. They are in the process of learning how the roles of shareholder, executive board and management operate. And they find it quite all right. They are all very different characters, but they get along pretty well with each other. And they have to do it themselves. I'm busy enough.

In our research very few families used this method to educate their children.

Attending meetings with advisers: Some parents invite their offspring to meetings with advisers on investments or other areas relating to their capital. At the start the children are not involved in serious discussions, as an heir said:

I was in high school and joined my dad to visit our private bank to get acquainted with some people. That was about it, you know. It was just shaking hands and getting some insight in my investment portfolio.

In certain situations heirs are more actively involved in the meetings with advisers because they have a direct interest. For instance, an heiress visited a lawyer with her father:

We consulted a lawyer to find out what it meant financially if I would get married to my foreign national partner. My rights and obligations if I should emigrate and vice versa for my partner coming over here.

Through conversations with advisers, children gradually become familiar with the professionals who have a role in the family's wealth and the content of these technical conversations. It is great when the child makes a little progress at each meeting. In the end learning is a process that goes step by step.

Family meetings: Some families organised family gatherings on a regular basis around the topic of their family business or estate. These family meetings were held separately from corporate obligations such as shareholder meetings. The reason for the family to get together can be very practical in that something is going on, as one heir reported:

Recently I had a meeting with the next generation, led by a consultant, and that was about (the differences in) ownership and the transfer of the estate.

Our research shows that a family meeting in many cases will be held only in emergency situations, such as illness or after the death of a (grand)parent. The purpose of these meetings is very clear: informing all family members. One heiress who had a sick father at the time said:

At one point my father wanted to involve us more actively, because eventually we would inherit his estate. From that moment several family meetings were scheduled to inform us.

Role in family wealth matters: Some heirs have been asked by their parent(s) to manage investments. In all cases, these children had an interest in and talent for financial matters. The reason behind such requests is usually that one parent (often the father) is deceased and the child is asked by the remaining parent to help with the financial management of the estate.

Many heirs received shares or certificates in a family business during the donor's lifetime or inherited them from their (grand)parents. The study showed that teenagers gain their first experiences as shareholders in shareholder meetings. The guidance heirs experienced as young shareholders was very poor. One heir had to find out the mechanics of being a shareholder himself:

> *At the age of 16, I went twice a year to a shareholder meeting. But what was the very purpose of this meeting? I had no idea. For example, I did not like the experience that other people voted against me. Maybe these other people did not understand me. At one point, my sisters and I got the broader picture, but ultimately we did not talk to my parents about it.*

Wealth education and philanthropy: The interviews showed that philanthropy was used in only a very limited way to prepare children for their future responsibilities. Some interviewees are actively involved in philanthropy, but they do not involve their children in their philanthropic activities. One possible reason is that parents just like to establish a charitable foundation or carry out a project without their children. Alternatively, parents may not sufficiently realise that family philanthropy is an opportunity to get their kids involved. Finally, it is possible that parents do not want to show how much money they donate to charitable causes. Were the parents to disclose the amount given to charity, children might unintentionally get an indication of the magnitude of the family capital. This might be a step too far for many parents.

We can conclude that the use of practice as a way to acquire wealth management skills is below par in most families. If phase 1 – informing their children about the family's wealth – is for many wealthy parents already a step too far, the chances of them giving their children time to practise handling wealth are also limited. When opportunities were given, they were often too generic really to help the future heir to develop his skills.

(c)   *Phase 3: letting go*

The third phase of wealth education is about the parents learning to let go. At a certain point in time parents find that their children are responsible for (part of) the wealth themselves. They transfer the financial baton to the next generation because they have faith that the children are ready for it. However, some parents have become so intertwined with the assets that they have trouble with letting go, regardless of how much confidence they have in their own children. This is an obstacle that the parent(s) must overcome in order to transfer a substantial part of the assets.

Transfer of responsibility: A dominant fear of some parents is that wealth can ruin their children. In short, that they can become arrogant and lazy, with the wrong friends. Parents with such worries and concerns about their children will not be able to let go and transfer the family wealth. First they must have sufficient confidence that their children are capable of dealing with the family fortune in a responsible manner.

Several heirs informed us that they managed the financial affairs of their children for a long period. Sometimes until they were in their 40s. One heir would really like to give his children the responsibility, but they bat back the ball:

I'd like our children to be more involved in certain financial and wealth educational topics, and we are doing something in this respect, but to be honest it is all very marginal. The reaction of my own children is: 'Dad, can you please keep on managing our affairs.'

Only in the situation where financial responsibility is effectively transferred to the next generation will the children have the opportunity to develop the relevant financial skills. Otherwise it will always just be dry swimming.

Parents' identity issues: Some parents feel a great emotional attachment to the family fortune, and as a result their family fortune defines their identity. This sometimes makes it difficult for these wealthy parents to transfer responsibility to the next generation.

As we have previously described, quite a few families transfer wealth to their offspring during the parents' lifetime. If this is limited to annual tax-free gifts or to relatively small amounts compared to the family wealth, the question arises whether parents actually let go. What is the impact on their identity when a substantial part is eventually passed on to the children? And how do they feel when their wealth drops below a certain magic threshold? These feelings are often unconscious and form a barrier to success in the final phase of the wealth education process: the emotional release and consequent effective transfer of the family fortune to the next generation.

For the parent, looking into the mirror and reflecting on their own experiences can be a starting point for the required emotional release. One heiress gave her reflections on her role and connection to the family business in this way:

I am now 50 years old and I find that I cannot easily say, given what has happened, I am quitting my job as executive in our family business. At the same time, I realise: if I want to quit, can I leave it to another person? That is letting go according to my understanding. Can I transfer it to another individual? Or am I in the end so intertwined with the business, even though I always cried out that I would never work in our family business.'

8. Objectives of family wealth

What can you do and what are you allowed to do with your inheritance? The interviewees' parents had all kind of expectations for their offspring as we discussed in section 4. We have not yet described their expectations regarding the family wealth and how the heirs have dealt with this. The big question is what role the family fortune will play in the lives of the next generation. The respondents cited three objectives governing the use of their capital:

- preservation;
- facilitating their own lives; and
- sharing and giving it back (philanthropy).

8.1 Preservation

Almost all parents find it important that their children preserve the accumulated family wealth. The question is how they communicate this message. Our research shows that there are large differences between families. In the majority of cases, parents tell their children almost nothing, and the desire to preserve the capital is only communicated implicitly during the children's upbringing. The message that children especially remember is to not use the wealth for consumption. Perfectly illustrated by the following quote: "I've always felt that we were not allowed to 'consume' the wealth."

During the children's upbringing, some parents explicitly explain to them about the meaning and goals of the family's wealth. One heir said about the objective of wealth management:

It's a challenge if you get an inheritance. The purpose is to preserve this and pass it on. This is closely related to the way one has been brought up. I also inherited the wealth and try to pass it on in a responsible manner to the next generation. When they use their inheritance for an education, illness, care and better living, then it is not an issue, if done in a responsible manner. Like a good steward, ensure that the wealth is managed in a good way.

Preservation and the famous 'stewardship' clearly stand out in his words.

When a family business is involved, the message of preservation is a top priority and is always communicated explicitly. In a family business it is not so much about the value of the company, but rather its history and aspirations for the future. Because of the employees attached to the company, it is a logical idea to pursue preservation. In short, the continuity of the business is paramount and the individual wishes of the heir are of secondary importance. This is summarised in the following excerpt from our interviews:

I am damn sure that this business is something that should continue in the family, that I am just an administrator for a certain period. Yes, I'm a steward of the heritage.

The wish to preserve wealth for future generations is an almost crippling goal for heirs with limited financial knowledge and experience. As they have absolutely no idea how to achieve this important family goal, some of them just ignore their financial matters and hope for the best. During and after the financial crisis of 2008, a few of them became suddenly aware that their lax attitude needed to change. One heiress said:

It always went well so I thought it would be good forever. Only in the last few years with the crisis have I had a little more contact with the bank. Everyone does.

We have seen in some families that a financially talented family member picks up the ball and looks after the affairs of the untalented relatives. In some cases, these financial high fliers were not only able to maintain the inherited family wealth, but they also increased it substantially. This sounds like a perfect model to sustain wealth, but the drawback is the huge responsibility these financially savvy heirs feel for their untalented relatives. At the same time, some untalented heirs were unhappy with their overdependence on their sibling.

8.2 Facilitating the heir's own life

Heirs of old-money families are often used to a certain lifestyle. Parents strive to ensure that the next generation can maintain this level. The inherited assets may support their children's goal. It is implicitly or explicitly made clear that there is a difference between expenses associated with sustainable expenditures, such as houses, and consumptive expenditure. For the purchase of a house the family fortune should support the next generation (unconditionally). With respect to consumer spending there are limits determined by family rules: there are expectations that a family member will live within their means, and the expenditure must be really necessary.

In addition to purchasing a house, parents facilitate special life events that have a large impact, such as an education and starting a business. Children regularly get the opportunity to purchase an enterprise through a friendly loan from their parents. The wealth may also be used to change jobs or to work less.

It takes many heirs a lot of effort to spend (a part of) their inheritance, because emotionally they feel the wealth is not theirs yet, even when it is in their own name. One heiress had to get used to the idea too:

It took a while before I could enjoy it. I had a wish-list and I could have done things earlier, but one way or another I did not.

8.3   Giving back and sharing

The third and final objective in respect of the family wealth is about sharing it with other people and/or feeling the responsibility to contribute towards society. Some families have been active with charities for decades, often through their own family foundations. The next generation is familiar with this and aware that this is one of the objectives of the family fortune. If parents are no role model in giving back and sharing, it is more difficult for heirs to pursue this objective at a later stage.

The conclusion is that too often, parents communicate the three objectives for the management of the family wealth only implicitly to their children, which leads to confusion and ambiguity in the next generation.

9.   The ideal wealthy family

Well-prepared heirs are more able to maintain peace within the family, safeguard the wealth of the family for future generations and (which is often a goal of many families) lead meaningful lives. How can wealthy parents ensure that the inheritance is a benefit rather than a burden for the children? The following six steps are the road to successful wealth transfer:

- Do not pretend to your children that your family is not wealthy;
- Have realistic expectations of the next generation;
- Set boundaries for your children and do not try to resolve all issues with money;
- Encourage your children to live their own lives and develop themselves as individuals;
- Give your children a wealth education – be proactive and establish a process; and
- Organise family discussions about the objectives of the family wealth and how to fulfill these objectives in practice (which is especially relevant for the main objective: sustaining wealth).

Our experience is that many wealthy families find it difficult to establish wealth education and family discussions. An adviser or facilitator can play an important role in getting the family started. Through increased awareness of the dynamics and aspects of growing up in wealthy families, advisers can improve their understanding of both testators and heirs. Being able to look beyond the regular remit of a wealth adviser can make a positive contribution to their advising and to building a sustainable practice.

Next generation wealth and the future of the world

Aron Pervin
Pervin Family Business Advisors Inc
Jonah Wittkamper
Nexus Global Youth Summit

The millennial generation is the most global, transparent, interconnected and interdependent generation in human history. It is also the most aware of both its ecological footprint and the needs of the earth. As a generation it sees society at a crossroads. While social and environmental tensions are growing, technology has helped the members of that generation become a global village. People everywhere are seeking transformative ideas, new resources and new leadership to ensure a peaceful and sustainable future.

We, as part of the Nexus group (www.nexusyouthsummit.org) have asked young wealthy individuals these questions:

- What special role do you feel a wealth holder might have to society?
- Describe the best thing you have done with your wealth so far. What is the next thing you hope to do? Comment on your biggest setback or mistake.
- Describe some of the challenges/your experiences in having a normal life in a world that labels you.

And here are some of their responses.

1. Contribution by Joshua Thomas
CEO, crowdMGNT

I am the son of Basketball Hall of Famer Isiah Thomas. My father is the epitome of the American Dream. He was raised from nothing by his mother, Mary Thomas, in the violent and poverty-stricken west side of Chicago. Basketball, for my father, was never a means to fame and fortune, but it was an outlet for him to grow and gain access to things he would have otherwise not have been exposed to. The values that were instilled in my father from his parents have been passed along to his own children, my sister and me. As the son of a wealth-holder, I have personally seen the benefits that giving back to a community and society have had.

My father participates in the Peace Tournament, which is an effort to have rival gangs shoot basketballs on the court rather than bullets at each other. He has shown me that time can be much more effective and influential than money. He along with other National Basketball Association athletes has used his influence to achieve the unthinkable, getting rival gangs to participate and interact together in a nonviolent and peaceful basketball game. My father's donation of his personal time has inspired me to do the same. I have donated my professional skills as a DJ to many charitable events, most notably Many Hopes, which battles extreme poverty in Africa. Like my father, I believe it's best not to focus on monetary donation size but on the quality contribution of service, which is why I regularly donate my time to support causes I believe in.

I am gay, and at the age of 20 I made the decision to tell my family. Following my coming out, my parents showed me nothing but love and support as they always had. One of the most powerful and personal moments in my life was posing for the NOH8 campaign alongside my father. This was not just monumental on an individual level, but my father taking a stand and becoming the first Hall of Fame professional athlete to pose for this campaign showed me what a true role model can be. As a wealth-holder there is more to helping society than financial responsibility. Our ability to influence and motivate change has proved to be of great and measurable value. My father and I decided to pose for NOH8 because we believe that all hate and discrimination is wrong. We believe it's time for full equality and equal rights for everyone, regardless of race, sexual orientation, religion or gender.

The NOH8 campaign opened my eyes to how wealth can be interpreted by people. My father, along with financial wealth, also has influential wealth which was built along with his basketball career. He has shown me how to use influential wealth to benefit society, and I take that lesson to heart. I have personally seen the struggles people have had coming to terms with their own sexual identity. I want to become a role model for lesbian, gay, bisexual and transgender (LGBT) youth, by helping them come out and not let sexuality hold them back or define them. Like my father, I want to reach out and mentor struggling youth. I want to be a mentor to those who need help and motivation to be themselves and assure them that it does get better.

I acknowledge that I have been blessed with the life that is bestowed upon me. The affluence of my family has created opportunities for me that others are not privileged to. I plan to continue following my passion as a DJ and producer. My deep personal connections to the cities of Detroit and Chicago, where many musical legends have been birthed, inspire me. It reminds me to strive for that level of excellence in my own musical career.

2.   **Contribution by Gray Keller**
Writer, philanthropist

Now more than ever, extreme wealth lies in the hands of young people in their 20s or 30s. Some may have inherited it, made it in some tech company or other venture, or even married into it. What I find fascinating is how nosy most people are in wanting to know how a person so young has so much. Unless you're a professional athlete, pop star or the next social networking guru, it really is no one's business as to how so many young people are wealthy. And for the most part, many never feel comfortable talking about their wealth, even if they like to appear socially rich. I had the opportunity several years ago to attend a private wealth management class at the Wharton School of Business. At Wharton, many young wealthy individuals would actually have normal-looking jobs, being schoolteachers or art instructors or retail salespeople, just so that they would have a specific title to share that would not link them to their true economic status. Nevertheless, this is just one area that young wealthy people must navigate through in order to maintain a healthy dose of normalcy in life.

Another area that is often challenging to young wealthy individuals is through family dynamics. This sometimes entails a patriarchal and domineering grandfather or father, or it may entail the young person having the wealth, while his parents or other relatives do not. This is easily understood in the classic example of a young person becoming a professional athlete. After a big signing bonus, the next thing they are hit with is to buy everyone from their mother to their sister and their long lost cousin a house or new car, or both. From feeling obligated to help their family in financial matters, to feeling manipulation or even guilt if they do not help becomes an enormous relational and family burden for many. It even comes from friends who may need seed money for a start-up business. And like myself, most do not have an MBA or other degree in business or finance to enable them truly to understand all of the many complexities that wealth creates. But I am not sure even business schools really address the relational dynamics of wealth. Simply put, money impacts all relationships.

Even though you may not think money should not change one's relationships, it in fact does. Wealth changes everything – either for the good or the bad, the happy or the sad. Therefore, learning to understand wealth, and the stewardship and responsibilities that come with it, is a lifelong learning journey that is best experienced in relationships with soul care.

When pressures mount from friends who may want you to bail them out of a bad financial decision, or invest some money into their start-up company, or to give to a slew of different charities that you may or may not even believe in, the young wealth-holder generally responds in one of a few ways. One response is simply to please everyone by being a soft touch for money. Another response is being a jerk. Arrogance and wealth among the young are often closely related in the absence of the proper wisdom, training and relational healthiness. And even there are times when others perceive a young wealth-holder as being a hardass who lives by a set of predetermined rules for relating. But this only occurs when the wealth-holder is disciplined to live by a committed set of standards. One such rule is never to give money to friends, because it often hurts the relationship. Another wise response is to ask questions, probe deeper and really take the time deliberately to think through the impact of how giving may or may not be the wise and appropriate thing to do. As I have often said, if a wealth-holder only gives to charities because they are trying to buy their way into a relationship, then eventually it will never be enough. Thus, another response is to run and hide.

Sadly there are too many stories of the reclusive ultra-high net worth individual. Knowing who truly cares about you as a person and for your soul, and not for what they can get from you, may be one of the greatest ongoing challenges of wealth-holders. And yet many wealth-holders tend to find each other and associate primarily with other wealth-holders. This too may be comforting on one level, but it is not necessarily healthy. It takes an enormous amount of courage, humility, trust and love simply to be oneself no matter what the context. And if young wealth-holders only define themselves in economic terms, then they will surely suffer the loss of many relationships that would have otherwise been a transformational blessing. I have found that one of the best ways to experience this kind of transformational blessing is by serving others. Rather than isolate or insulate oneself with other wealth-holders, taking meaningful philanthropic trips to the developing world opens the doors to gratitude, new relationships and a desire to realise there is so much more to life than one's own personal wealth.

When it comes to seeking honest counsel from professional wealth advisers, my wife and I have the rule that we do not care to hear the company line. We want honest communication that is authentic and from the heart. Only when we know these people truly care about us and are not just protecting their interests, are we able to engage in financial decisions that may be more qualitative than simply quantitative. As one adviser asked: "How does wealth impact your emotions? Fear? You might lose it all. Pride? You might become arrogant. Envy? You might try to keep up with other wealth-holders in foolish ways." Thus, there are many other questions of the heart and soul that professional advisers should be able to help young wealth-holders navigate through.

For me, from my own personal experience, I have been on a major learning curve over the past decade. Learning everything from financial management concepts and best practices within philanthropy to understanding how wealth impacts relationships continues to be an ongoing journey. Learning is a constant if you desire to live a life of significance and purpose. As I often say, my role in life is not simply to sit back, play golf and sip on martinis. On the other hand, wealth provides an opportunity to be free and flexible as an investor in greater purposes than one's own pleasures.

As a lifelong learner, I also continue to engage in seminars and conferences on innovative philanthropy. Some of the greatest lessons learned come simply from sharing stories with other wealth-holders at these events. Whether it is the Nexus: Global Youth Summit or the Association of Small Foundations – which defines small not in terms of money, but rather staffing – different associations and networks continue to be a place where young wealth-holders relate in meaningful and significant ways to improve the world through philanthropic leadership.

The burdens also entail being asked for money on a regular basis from family, friends neighbours and a myriad of non-profit organisations. A year ago, my wife and I learned of a friend who was in a dire financial situation. This single parent mother working three jobs needed help. We learned that she was behind on her mortgage payments and the interest she owed was piling up high. In addition, we learned her mortgage was held at one of our banks. So we decided simply to transfer funds from one of our accounts into hers to bring her up to par. As a result of our generosity, because she received money as a one-time gift from us that went directly into her mortgage account, it then jeopardised her from receiving any government assistance and/or room to renegotiate her home loan. A year later, the bank foreclosed on her. If we had not helped, then she would most likely have qualified for either refinancing or government assistance. Our charitable gift actually brought more harm than help. These trials and errors of giving are never any fun, and it does require a philanthropic willingness to press on and healthy relationships that encourage you to continue to give and give wisely.

But if the wealthy simply practise blind cheque-writing to charities, live in isolation, insulated from the rest of the world, and do not share their values and heart and soul in a caring and authentic way, then they may actually produce more harm than help to society at large. Sadly, I cannot say that giving away millions of dollars to different charities has always actually been the best thing for society. The best thing that I have done with my wealth is to share what I have learned from my journey to know myself (as Socrates would say), and to take the necessary time really to think about and to engage with the many different issues that wealth and philanthropy entail. People with wealth do see the world differently than those that do not. But more importantly, when wisdom, life principles and leadership manifest themselves in a context of soul care, it really does not matter how much money one has or does not have. There are so many things that money and wealth cannot do, and those with great wealth only have different problems. Because all humans share in the journey of life, wealth and philanthropy are just a few blessings among the power of a loving relationship where human flourishing occurs. I have learned that the poor can teach the wealthy much about love, relationships and hard work. They too have hopes and dreams, fears and desires, and human dignity. Whether one is rich or poor, young or old, how we relate to each other is ultimately what life is all about.

Whether it is enjoying the everyday things in life like eating at Taco Bell or driving a Jeep rather than a high-end luxury SUV, normalcy is living out my values with the character and integrity of who I am, with or without wealth. For in the end, money may come and money may go, but you will be remembered for who you are as a person in relationship from those around you.

In conclusion, in order to live a life of character and integrity to one's values, it takes courage, faith, hope and love to stay the course when the many temptations, pitfalls and burdens of life hit. The philanthropic leader understands the importance of living one day at time, learning through all of life's moments, while sharing from a holistic, honest and humble heart. No one person has all the answers, and there are no guarantees in life, but you can choose to live to be a blessing.

3. Contribution by Katherine Lorenz
President, Cynthia and George Mitchell Foundation

All of us should make our mark on the world in whatever way we can. We should use the resources at our disposal to make a difference in the issues we care about, to fight for what is important. We all have resources that can be used to make a difference – it is about making the best use of those resources to change the world in the ways in which each of us wants.

Wealth-holders are uniquely positioned with a great resource at their disposal to make a difference. Money can fund great work. It can fund people's time and energy, which are the key ingredients to making change. But, often more importantly, wealth-holders typically have a voice that carries. They often have the gift of being listened to when they speak. They can open doors that many people cannot. They can make key introductions to get things done. For whatever reason, the public listens when the mega-wealthy speak. That is one of the most powerful resources wealth-holders have at their disposal, and it is a resource that should be used to make a difference in the world.

I have tried my hand at making a difference, and I have experienced both great success and great failure as I have walked along that path. Although my grandfather was very successful, I have not inherited vast sums of wealth; but I do have enough to pursue my personal dreams and passions without having to focus on how big my paycheque is. I guess my family followed Warren Buffett's advice: I was given enough to do anything, but not enough to do nothing.

Upon graduating from college, I wanted to understand rural poverty issues in Latin America better. I spent two months living in Guanacastal Norte, Nicaragua, a rural village with 300 people, no running water and no electricity. I lived with a family of six in a one-room shack. I walked 45 minutes to the well to fetch water each morning. I took bucket baths. I used latrines. I went there thinking that I would teach them how to live better, how to improve their health and sanitation. And, boy, was I mistaken! In the end, they taught me much more than I ever could have taught them. They taught me about the true joys of life. They taught me the meaning of community. They taught me that money cannot buy happiness. They taught me the value of listening. They taught me how most of the world lives.

When I was 24, I moved to Oaxaca, Mexico to co-found a non-profit organisation. I honestly had no idea what I was getting into at the time, but it was the greatest adventure I have ever been on, and certainly the most fulfilling work I have ever been a part of. Puente a la Salud Comunitaria works with subsistence farming indigenous families in rural villages, providing improved nutrition and economic opportunities through the consumption and cultivation of amaranth, an ancient grain native to the region. During the nearly six years I lived in Oaxaca, I spent countless hours in rural farming villages. I learned about the daily struggles of the rural poor. I learned how to run a non-profit organisation. I learned how to operate in another country, another language and another culture. I learned how to fundraise. I learned how difficult it is to make change. I learned how much people's livelihoods are affected by changing weather patterns. And, mostly, I learned how to listen.

Not a day goes by that I don't think about the people I grew to know and love in Nicaragua and Oaxaca. Those are the faces that motivate me to get out of bed in the morning – they motivate me to use all the resources at my disposal to try to make the world a better place.

While I do not have vast amounts of personal wealth, I am now privileged to be the president of my family's foundation. I am honoured to help make sure that my grandparents' legacy lives on well into the future, and I am grateful for the opportunity to work with my family to do philanthropy together. But, most importantly, I feel a great responsibility to make sure that we are using these philanthropic resources to make the most impact we can in the issues we care about. While the foundation enables us to deploy financial resources to address these issues,

I feel that money is only one of the tools in our toolbox. With great wealth comes great responsibility, and it is our duty to use all of the tools in our toolbox to make change. We must speak out publicly when necessary. We must stand up for what we believe. We must call upon our networks. We must be leaders in creating a movement to make change.

Financial wealth is a powerful tool, and those of us who are privileged enough to have access to it have a responsibility to use it to make the world a better place.

4.   Contribution by Zac Russell
Founder, Russallo

When I think of the fact that next-generation wealth applies to me I still find myself surprised. Surprised not with fear, but a moment of "Oh, yeah? Cool, I guess so." I think that much of what went into my family's success has been articulated to me. I had to accept, partner and feel comfortable with a label that was not my own. I've learned from my mentors and my family that the truth comes from knowing who you are, and where you are. That truth allows for the objectification of wealth to be secondary to what we bring to our community.

However on leaving that bubble, I find that it is inevitable that once the family story comes out, a wider assumption seems to dominate. As part of the next generation of a wealthy family its assumed that I am in an untethered world, where all the money is available to me, when in actuality it seems that the power that I've really been given is to listen, learn, share with my family, and ideally to generate and create my own enterprises with solid foundations and values, inspired by those set by my grandparents. When dealing with next-generation issues, the most important objectives are to be conscious, honest and open with the subsequent generations about what is expected, what wealth means and the power that it has, both to make life great but also to haunt and corrupt one's goals.

This is where the label I bear becomes most obvious; being labelled by others is limiting. My label, as the next generation of my family, is mine to create. And in creating this label, calling on the wisdom of temperance is the most crucial key to my success. So, I partner with my family, and forge my own relationships with our advisers, lawyers and network. I believe that the next generation has nothing to fear, as long as we are educated and inspired by the work that our forebears have achieved.

It is my story, and it is simple, but the fastest way I found to overcome the label of wealth was through open and honest communication with the source; be it talking with my grandfather or with his lawyers. I am also grateful to have parents who pushed me, kept me honest and inspired me to search for what made me excited. As they showed me, it needs to come from ourselves first, and secondly from how we articulate it in terms of the family. Thirdly, it comes from how we choose to appear in the world around us. We need accept it and let it empower us, in the context of what we expect. As such, I have always been in awe, motivated and inspired by the wealth creators in my family and the power that allowed their success, but also their honesty and openness, which in a way comes with the acceptance of the place they (and inevitably we as the family) have as a family with wealth.

5.   Contribution by Mary Ann Thompson-Frenk
Co-founder and president, Memnosyne Institute and John Philp Thompson Foundation

When Jonah Wittkamper of the Nexus Youth Summit asked me to answer his questions about the challenges and responsibilities faced as a young person of means today, I thought about how much I would have loved to receive direct answers to his questions before starting out on my own life's pursuits. Sadly, my father passed away when I was in my early 20s, warning me as he did so that, "Darl'n, you're going to meet the vultures and the wolves when I am gone. But you remember the things I taught you and you will do fine." He was right. I got bitten a few times along the way, but eventually learned, and am still learning, to become empowered by wealth as opposed to being a target for would-be users. It took a while to get here, so, I am going to share some of the lessons he taught me as well as some things I've learned on my own in the hopes that it can help empower you on your own life's journey!

The most important thing a wealth-holder can do to manage their wealth, whether it be inherited, married into or generated, is to get rid of the notion of personal entitlement. Others have helped to make your wealth possible and still do. That might be a grandfather, a staff, your current financial advisers, teachers from both formal education and informal mentorship, and the general public which has bought the product or service that led to your wealth accumulating. In today's world, especially, we are part of an interconnected web of social, economic, political, religious, cultural and other influences that literally span the globe. Our investments and humanitarian outreach therefore begin to overlap as the demographics we seek to affect for both our personal and societal benefit affect each other. We can either consciously orchestrate the nature of that interaction or we can ignore it indirectly, thereby causing harm to others and our target demographics in turn. As wealth-holders under the age of 40, we have an even greater responsibility to recognise the new realities globalisation has presented us with. This is because, due to the consistent growth of technological advancement, we are the first generation who has no excuse for ignorance. We can learn about exactly how the means by which we achieve our personal wealth is affecting others at the touch of a button, and we can hear it from multiple perspectives. Therefore, today's young wealth-holders have the special role in society of not only being among the most financially empowered, but also the most capable of effecting long-term systemic change. Learning of how all these factors overlap lets us become aware of where our influence lies and how we can cultivate it in a positive way. The diagram on the right is just one model for understanding our role in the world today.

This means that if we, as young wealth-holders in the 21st century, are going to achieve a personal legacy worthy of the financial legacy fate has given us, we must first recognise that we been entrusted with a unique task requiring an understanding of how globalisation is affecting humanity from a systemic point of view. Legacy is not something that is bestowed upon us via the money in our bank accounts; rather, it is something entrusted to us to continue, measured by our individual achievements today. The ethics of past generations are the intangible part of that

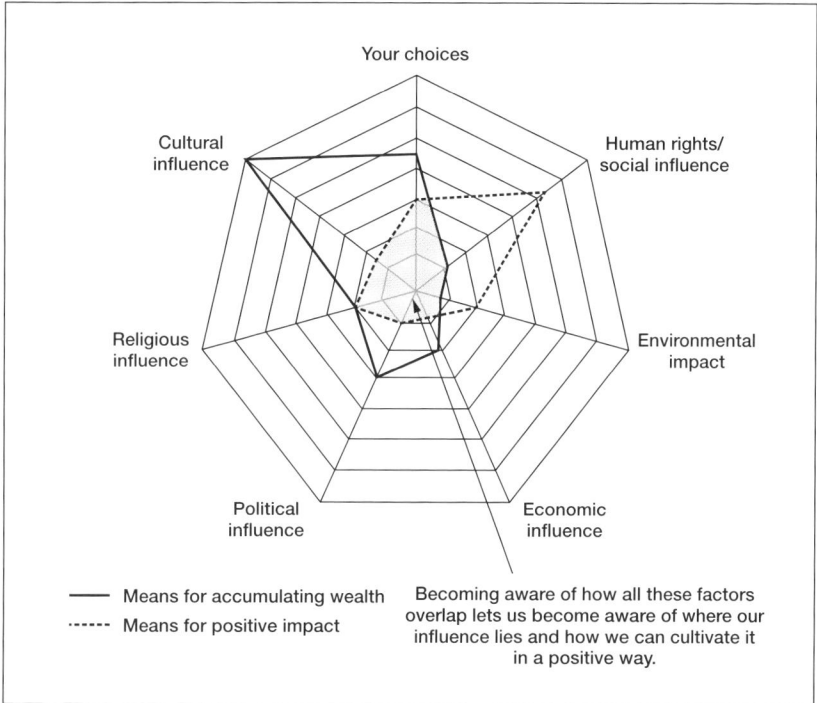

legend:
— Means for accumulating wealth
------ Means for positive impact

Becoming aware of how all these factors overlap lets us become aware of where our influence lies and how we can cultivate it in a positive way.

legacy, but are just as important. We add to that by either living up to the standards of past generations or trying to improve upon them in how we live our own lives. But the information age has made us more influential than any generation of wealth that has come before, due to globalisation's economic network. As the ones who have inherited part of that web, we are therefore given the responsibility of weaving it with strategic intent. Gone are the days when blind trusts relieved one of personal responsibility, as today avoiding personal knowledge requires a conscious decision on our parts due to the wide availability of information. Instead, a wealth-holder's responsibility to society requires becoming an active participant in how our part of the worldwide economic web we call globalisation is affecting humanity and the planet.

But with control over our investments in one hand and control over our humanitarian work in the other, we can leverage our influence in ways that no generation before us has been fully empowered to do. Today we can identify and track the relationships between financial causes and societal and environmental effects in a way our grandparents never dreamed possible. For example, when I was in fourth grade, my father brought home a stack of papers that contained a list of countries in one column and a list of manufacturing costs by the day in the other. When I asked him what this was for, he said 7-Eleven needed to manufacture a product and had authorised $7.00 a day for the individual worker. I then suggested that he select a country requesting anywhere from 15 cents to 25 cents and change their lives. My father, John Philp Thompson, Sr, chief executive officer of Southland

Corporation, which owned 7-Eleven, and a passionate philanthropist in his own right, just looked stunned for moment, then got down on his knees so he could match my height and replied, "Thank you for reminding me what my real job is in this world." Years later, I would learn that he did it and that a small village in South America now had schools, clinics and good roads, while he had stayed in keeping with his board's directives. Now magnify that by how many potential similar opportunities lie for those of great wealth to maximise our positive influence if we will pay attention. Then imagine how great that influence would be if such secondary effects were made part of the long-term strategic plan we carry in our minds: what would it mean not to just make decisions affecting the lives of hundreds of thousands via our awareness of their communities' needs, but also then to use our philanthropic influence to complement the positive effects our for-profit endeavours have set into motion? Doing this is maximising our financial resources. Maximising financial resources requires first recognising the interrelationships between existing challenges and, therefore, the holistic approaches necessary for creating sustainable solutions. The illustration below demonstrates this by using environmental challenges as an example.

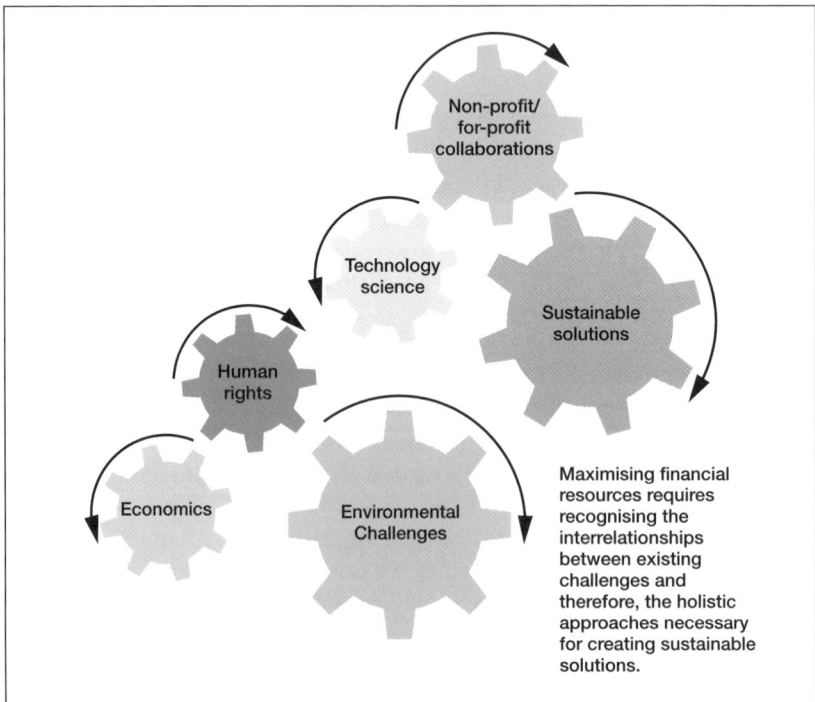

The best thing my husband, Joshua Frenk, and I have done with our wealth so far is to empower others, not just ourselves, to participate in our humanitarian endeavours, both via philanthropy and via socially responsible investing. While our private foundations, like the John Philp Thompson Foundation for Non-

Chemotherapy/Non-Radiation Brain Cancer Research, are about making grants for research, and our investments are likewise geared towards empowering others to achieve their visions of serving humanity, our life's work, the Memnosyne Institute, is about helping humanity to address the realities of globalisation strategically, by providing people with the means to encourage positive, peaceful collaboration across multiple areas of knowledge, cultures, geographic locations and more. To do this, we realised that by sharing the decisions regarding the strategy for our annual donations for creating sustainable solutions to the world's challenges, the diversity of others' perspectives would keep our vision broader and more detailed. The diversity of racial, cultural, religious and economic perspectives provides an invaluable asset because it creates a fuller picture from which to create cohesive strategies. We had to swallow our egos, but today, the things achieved by sharing the influence our financial blessings have provided us have far surpassed what we could have achieved either alone through a private foundation, or by surrounding ourselves with yes-people. While taking such routes can be tempting, it is immensely important to surround oneself with those who will speak the truth regardless of the wealth you bring to the table. Doing this will help you form trustworthy partnerships, develop a grounded outlook and learn to earn people's trust in your leadership capacity, as opposed to falling into the tempting trap of buying false respect. Respect that is bought is an illusion. Respect that is earned comes from how well you serve the interests of the team you lead. This is especially true when one is young, and can be achieved even faster when the ego is set aside to make room for collaborations.

Currently, I am excited about creating collaborations between for-profit and non-profit organisations aimed at avoiding reinventing the wheel and maximising funds. The urgency to pursue such hybrid strategies came about after seeing a presentation by Margot Brandenburg, the associate director of the Rockefeller Foundation, who explained that, "The cost of repairing and addressing the world's problems currently being faced far outsizes the combined budgets of philanthropy and governments to address." This means the numbers they crunched revealed that only by harnessing the power held in private hands, either by individuals or corporations, could the larger issues facing our species have a hope of being positively affected. In today's world, for-profit and non-profit organisations will have to create collaborative strategies in which they do not compromise their focuses, but wherein their focuses complement each other to achieve the goals of successfully addressing the challenges our species faces. As part of the millennial generation, we find it to be irresponsible to pitch humanitarianism against capitalism. One need not be in opposition to the other. There are plenty of examples where for-profit models can be major parts of the solutions badly needed. But only if they are run with strategies that take ethics into account. Do not think I am attacking conservatives in this, as I am very upfront with progressives who argue against capitalism altogether. Globalisation and capitalism are tools that, if harnessed strategically, can improve our world. But as of now, too few are doing so. I am proud of my family's legacy from 7-Eleven of demonstrating that it can be done through fighting to make profit-sharing legal, which increased employee loyalty and increased overall profit margins, and launching the first telethons, which provided marketing benefits surpassing traditional strategies. And I know that there are many others doing so as well. Entrepreneurs in their 20s and 30s want to find ways to focus on those types of modalities, so that a middle ground can be established where we can actually do something instead of reverting to either/or bickering. As leaders of a younger generation, we have that responsibility on our shoulders whether we want it or not.

One example of such a for-profit/non-profit hybrid project that our Memnosyne Institute team is overseeing is a collaboration called the "School Out of A Box Project" between for-profit organisations Green Habitat, Women That Soar Ltd and Oluvus, and the non-profit organisations the Club of Budapest International (COBI), Nexus Mexico, Centre for Human Emergence and the Carlos Slim Foundation's Casa TelMex, and led by the Memnosyne Institute, wherein we will be providing high quality high-school and college education for those who would otherwise not have access to it. Through COBI, leaders such as Desmond Tutu, Jane Goodall and others will take time to visit the students in the schools to encourage them as well as promote the project to their communities. Through Oluvus, led by the visionary Kosta Grammatis, access to the Internet will be provided to the schools, through Green Habitat, led by Tania Rodriguez. The architecture for the schools has been designed to be adaptable to multiple environments, enabling the programme to be scalable while using eco-friendly methodologies. Women That Soar has selected the programme to be the charity of choice for their annual wards, which will begin being aired nationally in 2015 with a telethon in 2016 or 2017. None of the things these for-profit organisations are doing would be achievable for a non-profit organisation to attempt all by itself. But by designing a business model wherein there is value for the for-profit organisations' participation through significant public relations and quantifiable marketing benefits, these organisations are able to keep the integrity of their focus while empowering the non-profit organisation, Memnosyne, to do likewise. Being able to create win-wins for both the for-profit and the collaborating non-profit partners allows us to maximise the dollar for everyone involved, allowing each partner to focus on what it does best, and thereby maximising the number of people served. The off-grid energy-independent schools will be able to go to places where there is the greatest need. We are currently exploring the prospect of the first four going to Mexico, Haiti, South Africa and Romania following their leaderships' requests for help in addressing great educational needs. Similar collaborative models we are involved in include FoodSourceDFW.org, which facilitates collaborations whereby for-profit food providers, such as restaurants, caterers, large sports stadiums and grocers donate surplus to food banks and homeless shelters within 24 hours, thereby streamlining connections that previously saw 30% of food spoiling in the Dallas/Fort Worth area. Such a solution would not have been possible without collaboration between for-profit and non-profit organisations. Lastly, I am especially excited about empowering others, like you, to create far-reaching collaborations of your own via GlobalCollaborationSource.org, which is aimed at empowering leading humanitarians, be they thinkers, entrepreneurs, activists, investors or philanthropists, actively to collaborate towards creating and implementing solutions serving humanity and the planet.

Things have not always come together so easily, as in the beginning, shortly after my father died, I thought the way to respect the elders in my family was to cater to their perceptions of how success should be measured. I spent a great deal of money and time focused on launching a line of fine china when my uncle told me he wanted me to use my talents to make money in a commercial venture. While my sculpture has sold at top prices, the dinnerware industry proved to be a major financial drain, leading me to spend money and time in a direction that was not towards my personal goals. When I was recognised with various awards for my humanitarian work or my fine art, he replied, "Awards don't make money." I realised in that moment that he shared very different values from my father as to what constitutes a successful life. I remembered my father had said:

> Peanut, don't try and do what I have done. I could not have built 7-Eleven in the midst of the depression like my father did. But he could not have grown it into an international corporation at the start of globalisation like I did. And I'm not the one capable of doing what you are destined to do. You say you want to create something to serve humanity. Now if I could sell an idea around the world that was about putting money in my pocket, don't you think you can succeed in selling an idea around the world that is about empowering mankind to help itself? In fact, I'd better see you already doing it by the time you're 30!

Great wealth will cause others to have expectations of you, but remember that whatever they demand of you is a reflection of their own values, and you have the freedom to claim those values for yourself or not. Allow your actions to speak for themselves, fully recognising that all money can do is give you a greater advantage to begin pursing your dreams. Greater advantages are not an excuse to slack off. Greater advantages are challenges to be set, achieved and surpassed. Greater advantages mean you have been given greater responsibility to ensure your impact on the world is as positive and far-reaching as possible. See this challenge as a privilege, and you will discover inspiration generating opportunities in your life!

6.   Contribution by Xiangchao 'Charles' Ling
Member, Silk Road Group Textile Company

What special role do I have as a wealth holder in society? Actually, I do not regard myself as a 'wealth holder'; instead, I identify as a young entrepreneur. I believe that both wealth holders and entrepreneurs have a big influence on the people around them. In China, I think people have to be low key. They should not show off wealth to friends (big house, fancy car, etc). For me, I always do one thing: I redirect eyes from my wealth to my spirit. I show them with my actions: I never buy brand-name clothing or fancy cars, but I always work hard for my job and take responsibility for the people who need help (if I know them). So I think the role of a wealth holder must be a social model – not a wealth model, but a positive role model.

The most important thing I have done with my life so far is come back to China after my education. I could have a comfortable life in the United States, but I decided to come back home to take the leadership of my family's company. The company was in a financial crisis and hundreds of workers were losing their jobs in 2011. Thanks to my efforts, the company is now operating in the right way.

Moreover, I do not live as a wealthy person; I earn a normal wage in the company. I can't donate money all over the world. Instead, I focus on the poor in my company. I always donate my annual bonus to a fund that supports helpless old workers.

As business owners, we are often mislabelled. We run a big company and have busy lives, but we are not focused on the profit – we focus on creating jobs for the poor. Currently, running big factories is not good business in eastern China – we are operating at a loss. My mother and I have often said to my father, "Please get rid of those factories!" But, my father responds, "The workers are all in their 40s or 50s. If I shut down those factories, who will hire them next? They would be poor again!" For this reason, I came back home to China from the United States to help. The challenge is that many people don't understand. The government continues to charge higher taxes and some workers still see us as a greedy capitalists. It disappoints us, but I feel as though I work for God. Taking this leadership is God's mission for me.

7.   Conclusion

As a generation, wealthly members of the millenial generation reject capitalism without a conscience. Young wealth-holders rely on advisers to help facilitate a global transition from heartless investing to higher touch and mindful impact investing; away from an unsustainable economy and towards one that relies on social and environmental profit as much as financial profit.

Advisers should not be afraid to be human and to give human advice. Even if your mandate is to make as much money as you can for your families, do not do it if it is unethical. Do not be afraid to tell your families that you disagree and think they are making a poor choice, if they are.

The life cycle of the family office

Leslie C Voth
Pitcairn

At its best, a family office works at the intersection of wealth and family. It focuses not only on achieving targeted financial results for its clients, but also on helping them understand how to use their wealth as a source of both individual strength and family connectedness. The ultimate goal is to empower family members to be responsible stewards of their wealth and heritage.

But like all organisations, family offices are affected by changes over the course of time and must evolve with the changes or lose their effectiveness. To survive and succeed, the office must engage in strategic thinking and long-term planning, communicating with, and helping to educate, family members as they make the transition to new generations.

1. The evolution of the family office

At its outset, the typical family office is usually shaped around the needs of the founder – the patriarch or matriarch who is the creator of the family's wealth. These founders normally expect the office to coordinate investments and philanthropic activities, and to manage the acquisition of assets like real estate and art. The family office may also provide personal accounting, legal and lifestyle management services. Whatever the exact details of the founder's requirements, the sole purpose is to serve the needs of the family. And of course as the wealth of a high net worth family increases, so does the extent of the family's needs, placing greater responsibilities on the family office.

Major changes invariably begin to occur when the family makes the transition to a new generation. During this transition, the family office team must serve the needs of more than one generation, and it must adapt to the needs of each family member's household, even when the needs differ greatly from individual to individual. One of the most important tasks of the family office during this period is to ensure that the next generation understands what it is inheriting – whether it is partnerships, foundations, private equity structures, or the family business – since it may well be getting a more complex and illiquid wealth structure than the previous generation dealt with. Education is, therefore, the key to empowering good decisions.

In some cases, members of the next generation may ask whether there is a reason for the family office to stay intact. They may question whether they need the same services as their parents or grandparents, whether they want to continue paying the fees, whether they want more (or less) income than their predecessors, or whether they want to give the wealth away.

Quite obviously, the family members need to come together to develop a shared vision for the future. A positive decision to keep the services of the family office is more likely to be made if the office is able to demonstrate that it can successfully serve multiple generations. This means fostering transparency and open communication, choosing financial advisors who are right for the family, and making a commitment to educating and mentoring young family members as they mature into decision-makers.

There are other key questions, too: what is the best way for many decision-makers to work together, and how does the power of decision-making get shared and then transferred across generations?

Ideally, the family office will create an open dialogue in which each family member feels empowered to contribute opinions and take part in decisions that keep the family intact and financially successful over the long term. The goal is a structure that will help the family office continue meeting the family's evolving needs.

1.1 Stepping back to move forward

Wealth preservation is always a major goal for both the family and the family office. But it's family preservation that leads to the greatest success. If family members can, so to speak, take a step back from the ordinary flow of events to think strategically about what their needs will be in five, 10 and 20-year timeframes, they've begun the long-term planning that is essential.

To develop these plans and then carry them out, family members will go through some of the hardest discussions they will ever engage in, because inevitably there will be different points of view and conflicts of opinion. Nevertheless, this process will provide them with the means to define individual roles and iron out the ways in which the different generations can work together.

For the patriarch or matriarch, this will usually mean giving up a degree of control, a development that can present challenges. But if the result is to instil future generations with the confidence they need to make critical decisions, and even make their own mistakes, the process will put them on the road to sustainability.

It is a powerful experience when the senior leaders of a family agree to assume the roles of mentors, as they step back and let the next generation take charge. Putting aside one's own needs and accepting the needs of the family as a whole can be difficult, to put it mildly, but it demonstrates a true desire to see the next generation thrive. That's why these discussions should begin as early as possible. In fact, the development of a good transition plan can stretch over a few years. During this long-range planning process the family office should be run just as a business would be, while carrying out its obligation to help create a shared vision for the future.

As the plan moves forward, it will be necessary over time to consider changes. For example, there may come a moment when some family members don't want their affairs managed by the family office any longer. Understanding their reasons for wanting to leave will be critical for the family office if the goal is to preserve the family as a whole.

There are various reasons why a family member would want to disassociate from the family office, or even want to dismantle it entirely. One could be the administrative costs they have to pay, which may seem onerous. There may be resentment if the patriarch or matriarch has structured the family office as a top-down operation that leaves the next generation with little or no say in decisions. And sibling rivalries, or at least sibling disagreements, are often a crucial factor. Finding a way to keep family members from falling out with one another and hurting their own best interests by dissolving the family office is often not an easy task.

Many of these conflicts can be avoided at the outset when the family office is set up if the first generation avoids locking it into a rigid mindset. Following generations will have their own issues and needs and ways of thinking, so it is important not to stay wedded to one patriarchal (or matriarchal) way of doing things. Instead, it's always good practice to begin with a multi-generation mentality.

2.   When the transition stages begin

Family offices, like the families they serve, go through changes too. It is a similar evolutionary process. In general, there are three possible outcomes for a family office. In dealing with each of these possibilities, planning for the transition is key.

A family office sits at the centre of a wealthy family's universe. Normally, its primary role is investing the family's collective wealth. When done successfully, this expands wealth for all the family members in ways they could not achieve as individuals; for example by allowing more risk-taking. In some cases, it also spurs family members who might otherwise focus strictly on the family business to take up exciting new interests. In any case, there is a greater pool of assets in play, with top professionals overseeing the investments.

The family office inevitably expands with the growing wealth to add alternative structures, new partnerships and other useful activities. When the wealth reaches a certain level, ancillary services are often added, including estate planning, paying the bills on time, tax accounting and real estate management. As financial affairs become more complex, most family members usually want these matters handled through the family office.

But as the family grows, different needs arise, and these needs change with time. This is when the family office's transition to a new phase becomes an important concern. For example, collective investing in the old way may no longer be acceptable because some family members want more of a say. The very existence of the family office may, therefore, be called into question.

When that happens, there are three possible outcomes:

- the family office may be restructured into a very different kind of operation;
- it may be merged with another family office;
- it may be dismantled altogether.

2.1   Restructuring: the Pitcairn story

The history of our organisation, Pitcairn, offers an instructive example of how a family office can be reshaped over the course of history.

When the three Pitcairn brothers decided to create a family office in 1923, the goal was to simplify their lives. The family had amassed enormous wealth in the early part of the 20th century under its Scottish immigrant patriarch, John Pitcairn, a passionate entrepreneur and private equity investor who ranked among the financial giants of his time, including the Rockefellers and Carnegies. One of Pitcairn's most famous investments was in a formula for plate glass that was so successful it led to the creation of the Pittsburgh Plate Glass Company (PPG). Following his death, his three sons wanted a family office to manage their wealth so that they would be free to explore their personal passions – architecture, theology and aviation.

The brothers saw the value of assembling all their advisers under one roof to coordinate the different aspects of their lives, including the management of PPG, which continued to flourish, management of their private investments, the accumulation of personal assets (real estate, aeroplanes, etc), support for their philanthropic initiatives and lifestyle management services.

As the Pitcairn brothers made the transition to the next generation, they selected an in-law as the new leader of the family office. He was a strong executive who, in keeping with the management style of the early years, centralised most decision-making, supported by a small board made up of key family members. He put together a professional investment team to give the family access to institutional investing opportunities. The team built good relations with the family and produced outstanding results over 30 years. Senior team members were even encouraged to co-invest with the family, which motivated them to stay with the family office as they built their own wealth. Over the years, however, this also led to a culture of entitlement and resistance to change.

Meanwhile, the family was getting bigger, and individual household needs were changing. A group of Pitcairns did not want to be tied together by commingled, illiquid assets. The only way to provide an exit was to liquidate the holding company, including the legacy investment in PPG. In 1986, the liquidation was completed and the family created a new private trust company. Simultaneously, they made the decision to convert the family office into a multi-family office.

We can learn as much from things that do not go well as from things that do. The lesson for the Pitcairn family leaders was that they needed a succession plan for key positions in the family office, which to this day is updated every alternate year. In addition, the leaders adopted a policy called 'free association' which allows family members to leave the family office with their trusts, even if the trust instruments technically do not allow it. That has proved to be a successful formula for maintaining family ties while allowing the individuals who want to go in their own direction to do so without creating conflicts.

Once the multi-family office was established, a new family leader committed to transparency and open communication took charge. He recognised that while the old command-and-control leadership had produced solid results for many years, it also discouraged the innovation and creativity that are critical to success in today's world. Equally important, the next generation of family members and employees did not respond well to top-down management that just parcelled out benefits. They wanted to understand what was going on, and they wanted a say in how it happened. Transparency was not only desirable, but necessary.

All these changes over the years have led to a very different kind of structure at the Pitcairn family office. As the current leader, I carry on the policy of transparency and open communications established by my predecessor while operating the office as a forward-thinking business and bringing in the best management techniques. Our goal is to use strategic thinking and continuity planning to ensure our sustainability far into the future. Pitcairn is a classic example of a successfully restructured family office.

2.2 Partnering with other family offices

The second possible outcome for a family office in transition is to merge with another organisation. There are several reasons why this may be the best option to pursue.

Not every family office has the capacity to offer a full array of services. In some cases, the office may have expertise in some specific areas but must look outside to meet additional needs such as investment advice, administrative capacity, customised education or fiduciary services. Therefore, sometimes a family office chooses to partner with another entity, like a multi-family office, enabling the management team to concentrate on business affairs while the new partner helps manage the added family needs.

Let us take the example of a family whose patriarch passed away unexpectedly. He had always managed both the family business and his family's personal assets through its family office. The family office also handled personal tax compliance, insurance, estate planning and household administration. The significance of the patriarch's death was much greater than his wife and children could have imagined, since no family members were involved in the financial affairs of either the business or the family office. Most of the family's assets were maintained within the holding company to support the growth of the business.

That meant that none of the individual household's needs were considered independent of one other. Everything was done collectively, which meant the adult children did not have a solid understanding of their financial picture. Not surprisingly, they began expressing a desire for greater control of their portfolios and an end to the family office's centralised control over their families' financial affairs.

The new president of the company, to whom the patriarch had given just about all his business and financial responsibilities, agreed that a new governance structure was needed. He also saw the need for individual family members to take responsibility for their households. On the recommendation of a business consultant, the president brought in a multi-family office to serve as an external chief investment officer.

Financial statements and projections for each family were created. Each of the adult children was given the tools to make his or her investment decisions. Forecasts were made on the business's capital needs over the next 10 years. The multi-family office, working collaboratively with the family members, the president, the consultant, and the family council, determined what each household needed to maintain its lifestyle over the next 10 years.

What arises from this process of merging the original family office with a multi-family office is future stability and growth, with individual family members now having a voice in their own financial futures.

2.3 Dismantling the family office

There may come a time when a family decides it no longer makes sense to keep the family office. Perhaps a new generation of family members concludes that the office does not serve any meaningful purpose in their lives. Perhaps the wealth of the family has been depleted and the cost of the office can no longer be sustained. Or the Dodd-Frank regulatory changes of 2010 in the United States that sought to clarify what constitutes a family office might lead to the dissolution of an office that cannot meet the standards.

One example is a family office that had been around for more than 50 years but was tied to an investment scandal that had significantly reduced the family's wealth. The scandal led family members to question the existence of the office, and since the office had been created by the patriarch and matriarch to meet their own needs, the children concluded that there was no point in funding it any longer.

It took two years and a well-crafted transition plan for the family office to be completely unwound. There was a lot involved: the disposition of real estate, artwork and furniture; scanning every record; building a website so the family could easily access everything; and reviewing the long-serving staff. One year was spent conducting the analysis and making tough decisions. The second year was the implementation of the plan.

What steps can a family office take to avoid being dissolved?

In some cases, the fate may be unavoidable; after all, it is the family that ultimately makes the decision. But the solution is to focus constantly on transition planning so that the office always keeps current with changing family needs. The family office has to be in sync not only with the founder, but also with each succeeding generation. The key is good planning.

It's not very different from strategic planning for a business. Typically, one would map out a three-to-five year strategic plan, test it, keep it up to date, and try to anticipate what might be just over the horizon. In the case of family offices, it's the same concept: Get the family and the office together to do a strengths, weaknesses, opportunities and threats analysis. Ask questions like: Where are we going to be in five years? Are there employees at the family office who need to be replaced? Is there anything we are not doing that we should?

Part of the process may be getting the patriarch or matriarch to think about a future that one day will not include them. That's hard for them, hard for the family, and hard for the family office. But it is crucial to think down the road.

3. Fostering open communication

As part of successful planning for transitions, we also emphasise the importance of fostering open communication. Wealthy families with multiple generations inevitably experience problems because of differing viewpoints on wealth management. The family office can play an important role in dealing with such conflicts by practicing transparency and encouraging open communication.

Keeping lines of communication open is not always easy, but it can be done. The Pitcairn family is a good example. By the fourth generation, consensus on how the family assets should be managed was impossible, but there was still agreement on preserving the family as a whole. That is what led the Pitcairns to liquidate their holding company in 1986 and implement the policy of free association, which allows any family member to leave the family office. The Pitcairns are now in their sixth generation of wealth management, a remarkable record, given that great numbers of American families have gone, as the old saying puts it, from shirtsleeves to shirtsleeves in three generations.

3.1 Educate to empower

Finally, we believe that one of a family office's major duties is educating and developing members of younger generations in family matters. They are the key to long-term family sustainability, so raising their level of awareness is vital. This is not always easy. When it comes to financial matters, for example, the conversations can be uncomfortable. Members of wealthy families tend to shy away from them; sometimes until it's too late. Yet another difficulty is when the patriarch has assumed total control, a situation that can discourage the open communication and educational process necessary for long-term growth. In fact, a top-down style of leadership can actually result in a loss of control, because nothing changes or moves forward. Transparency should always be an objective in the discussions, regardless of the issue.

Large families may want to consider creating a family council as part of the education of younger generations. The council can be a place where they learn what is happening within the family office and the family business, where they acquire the skills to work collaboratively with one another, and where they receive the training eventually to become members of the senior board.

Inviting in outside mentors and advisers can be beneficial, too. They bring a neutral perspective to controversial issues, and their specialised skills can help the family members identify unrecognised needs, locate resources they may not be aware of, and devise solutions to difficult challenges.

A family office's commitment to education is not only fundamental, it is crucial in empowering the members of the next generation and setting them on the path to success. It is a process that cannot start too soon and that never ends.

4. Conclusion

Managing a successful family office is in many ways like managing a successful business. It requires strategic thinking and long-term planning. The structure must be one that the founder is comfortable with, but it must also be one that accommodates change. That is especially true when it comes to the transfer of control from one generation to the next.

Succession planning for the family office's leadership is crucial, and this plan must be updated on a regular basis. Allowing some unexpected event to leave the office rudderless is a recipe for crisis.

The successful family office must assemble a team that has the skills to achieve the family's goals, whether they concern investments, the acquisition of assets, ancillary services like legal advice and tax planning, or generational transitions. The team must always be open to change and can never be allowed to settle into patterns of complacency and self-entitlement. Transparency, communication and education are the essential ingredients of the relationship between the family office team and the family members.

Every family office is designed to serve a purpose. But the process is organic and evolutionary; the only thing that is constant is change. The Pitcairn family office was created to manage the family's wealth, but it has been able to carry on into the sixth generation precisely because – despite all the ups and downs – it found ways to adjust to new demands and generational changes. Even as some family members have chosen to separate from the family office, many others, including an increasing number of non-Pitcairn families, have seen the value of the wealth-management and other services we deliver. And so, working collaboratively, we have kept our office aligned with the vision of the families we serve.

Australia

Keith Drewery
Drewery Consulting Pty Ltd

1.   Family offices in Australia

1.1   History

In Australia, the beginnings of the first family offices arose in the late 19th Century as wealthy landowners and settlers made rich by the gold rush decided to return to Europe, typically Britain, to educate their children. Fearful of theft and disputation, they created structures and legal frameworks to frustrate any attempts to dissipate their wealth and by doing so created the forerunners of today's statutory trustee companies, Australia's first family offices, and established as a cornerstone and key principle objective of a family office the preservation of wealth.

For the next 100 years, families of wealth relied on fiduciaries, trusted counsel and loyal retainers to assist in the management of their wealth. In keeping with other jurisdictions, family office services in Australia have evolved out of wealth-owners' needing to personalise their affairs rather than rely on the services offered by professional intermediaries to a broader population.

Trying to track down the first reference in Australia to the naming of an organised structure as a family office is difficult. The recognition that the way in which a family's affairs are organised may be defined as a 'family office' has been imported and adopted and only more recently been widely appreciated as a model for the professional administration and management of a family's capital in Australia.

During the current century, the recognition of the role of a family office and how service providers may develop services for a particular niche client set has accelerated to the point where Australia supports its own family office conference, increasingly looks to Southeast Asia to help influence and build global relevance, and its largest families have become truly global in the way they have organised structure and service delivery.

During that time the depth and variety of services offered by family offices have also increased as a broader appreciation of all that meaningful wealth management entails has been embraced by wealth-owners and advisers alike.

1.2   Specific caveats – dealing with an iceberg

Offering an opinion on family offices and the family office marketplace in Australia places one in a difficult position. Primarily, in Australia, the family office market is dominated by single family offices. Many are significant in size and influence, others are relatively unknown but no less interesting for that. Each is protected to a certain extent by their own networks and connections.

To purport to speak with any knowledge of the market place, when the vast majority is hidden, inevitably questions the validity of one's comments. To discuss more specifically the circumstances of several individual offices opens one up to an accusation of having committed the worst crime for a trusted adviser, the breach of privacy.

So to provide a chapter providing any benefit one must walk between superficiality and betrayal of confidence.

With that constraint, what follows offers a view of the family office market in Australia based on publicly available information and data, but hopefully also provides some interesting insights based on personal experience.

1.3   Australia – demographics as to wealth, age, family offices

Today, Australia's population is estimated to be approximately 23.5 million. This figure is quite striking when compared to the population from Australia's most recent census in 2011, which found that population had grown by 8.3% to 21,507,717 since 2006, with the largest percentage growth in population in the commodity-rich states of Queensland and Western Australia.

Like most developed western societies, that growth has been fuelled by a combination of skilled immigration and government incentives designed to reverse falling birth rates. Similarly, as with most western societies, the percentage of the population over the age of 65 increased to 14% in 2011 from 13.2% in 2006.

High net worth individuals by country – 2008

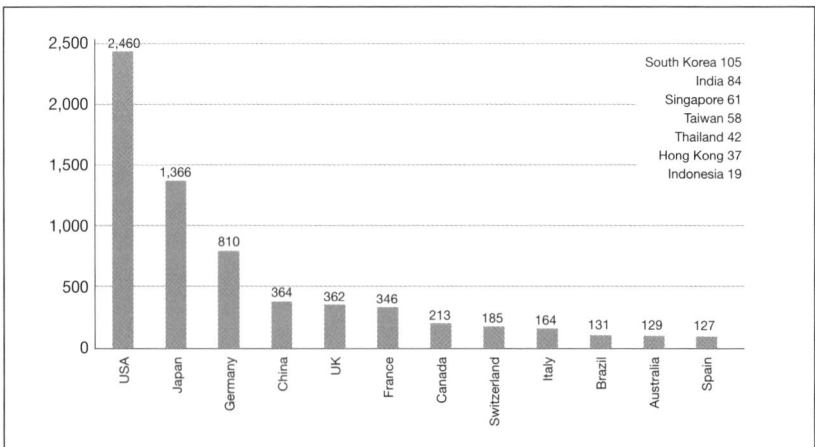

High net worth individuals (HNWIs) are defined as those having investable assets of US$1 million or more, excluding primary residence, collectibles and consumer durables. Sources: Capgemini/Merrill Lynch Wealth Management, World Wealth Report 2009, Asia-Pacific Wealth Report 2009; Austrade.

1.4 Distribution of wealth

Contained within the Australian Trade Commission's 2010 report, "Investment Management Industry in Australia", the table above suggests that Australia had 129,000 high net worth individuals in 2009, being defined as owners of more than US$1million in investable assets.

We also learn, again being a pattern familiar in other western societies, that the top 20% of households hold greater than 62% of the total of Australian household wealth.

Equalised household net worth quintile

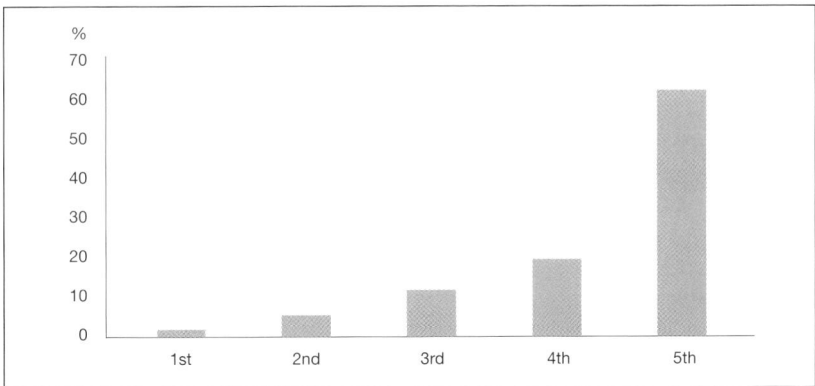

The average net wealth of this 20% is estimated to be $2.2 million although, as the following tables illustrate, the number of households whose net worth exceeds $2 million as a percent is closer to 1%, illustrating the significant wealth held by a small number of Australian households which has the effect of increasing the average for the top 20%.

Distribution of household net worth 2009-10

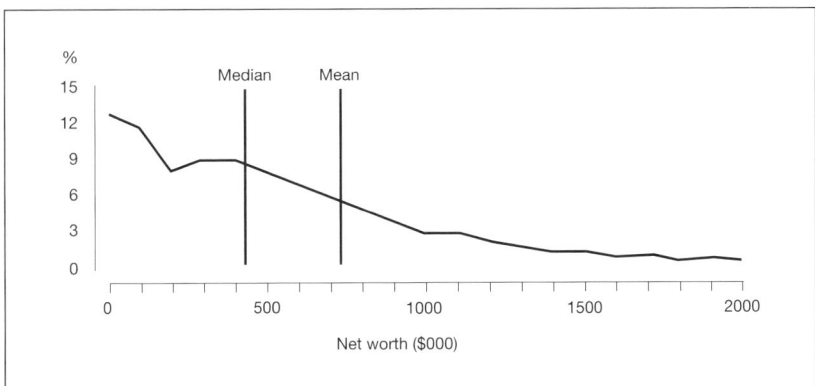

Note: Housholds with net worth between $150,000 and $2,050,000 are shown in $100,000 increments.

As with all multiple data sets, it is often difficult to validate one set of findings by reference to another; however, it is fair to surmise that Australia's population of affluent households as a percentage of the population is increasing in line with the relative growth of the country's GDP compared to western countries.

Australia's media, like that of many other countries, is fascinated with the wealth of its residents.

Australia's version of the Forbes Rich List or the FT Rich List, is the Business Review Weekly Rich 200 (BRW 200). Actually, when the list was first published in 1984, the cut off was merely A$10 million and the list contained only 144 individuals and 20 families. However, as wealth has grown and the powers of investigative journalism increased so the number of people mentioned has increased to the 200 limit today.

As an illustration of the growth of the wealth of the ultra-affluent, the annual survey of Australia's richest, the BRW 200 list had an entry point of net wealth of A$235 million in 2013. This list was headed by Mrs Gina Rinehart, with a net worth of A$23.5 billion, which the publication claimed made her the world's richest woman.

Her success is an illustration of how resources-rich Australia's proximity to China and Asia's economic growth has been the basis for a large increase in the wealth of those individuals that have benefitted from the ownership of raw materials and/or have been suppliers of services to the extraction industries.

1.5 The extent of the family office market in Australia

The extent of the market for the services of a family office requires some subjective analysis to determine at what level of wealth the provision of a family office service make sense for a family in Australia.

In common with other countries, the wealth management industry in Australia has segmented the market to position products and services better to meet the market needs. Commonly referred-to metrics within the annual Cap Gemini World Wealth Report refer to brackets of wealth as mass-affluent, high net worth (more than US$1 million of investment assets), mid-tier millionaires (between US$5 million and US$30 million) and ultra-high net worth (more than US$30 million investment assets).

In Australia, these definitions have been used by service providers to help clients self-select their service proposition relative to their own needs. However, it is fair to say that within the service providers themselves such boundaries are not religiously observed and instead value from a relationship perspective is often measured not in terms of assets but revenue and margin. Both these measures are now becoming tighter and tighter for financial institutions.

Such classifications are, however, relatively unhelpful in assessing the size of the family office marketplace, because the amount of wealth held by a client of a family office would ordinarily exceed the ultra-high net worth definitional cut-off but may not be sufficient to justify a separate independent single family office.

In its most recent Global Wealth survey, the Boston Consulting Group estimated that in 2013 there were over 236 households in Australia with a total net worth in excess of US$100 million.

On the basis that the BRW 200 research mentioned earlier is correct, this would suggest that the Boston Consulting Group's analysis may well understate the number of households with over US$100 million in net assets. While interesting to many, the figure does not necessarily assist in determining the size of the family office market in Australia, but merely offers some insight as to the number of people who may be inclined to consider their use.

If one assumes that the needs of the BRW 200 list are sufficiently complex to require specific personal assistance, it is probably not surprising that each person listed would have developed for themselves some framework to help administer their wealth. It is most likely that this would be in the form of a single family office style of structure, although it is also fairly common for several members of that list also to use the services of a multi-family office as either the supplier of a component part or as a full composite supplier.

A more comprehensive summary of the family office market has been provided by Family Office Connect, which estimated in its Australian Family Office Sector – Review 2011 that there were 350 single family offices administering a total wealth of A$226 billion as at December 2011.

Again, Family Office Connect's data is based on published information, which because of its nature does not necessarily reflect the true extent to which families with greater than US$100 million of assets may reside in Australia. It is quite likely based on the fact that many wealthy families value their privacy above all else, that the number of single family offices could well be closer to 500.

2.   Typical structure of family offices in Australia

There are essentially three main structures of family offices in place in Australia:

- the single family office – independently serving the needs of the wealth-owner with at least one member of staff employed by the wealth-owner for that purpose;
- the multi-family office – providing bespoke services to a number of clients, typically referred to the office, and in the case of Australia's two most well-known and largest multi-family offices (the Myer Family Company and Mutual Trust) created from an existing single family office framework; and
- the commercial multi-family office – established specifically to provide family office services, or operating as a separate division of an existing service provider.

Variants on each model exist, dependent upon the resources available to the office. Increasingly, models providing personalised, independent and objective points of view are being promoted by suppliers of complementary services looking to provide a virtual family office style of service to a lower wealth demographic.

Traditionally, the services of a family office have been based on the administrative framework, with a focus on the delivery of compliance-based services designed to deal with necessary evils. This is probably not surprising when one considers that the wealth-owner's position has typically been managed in-house by their businesses' accounting function while, to a large extent, the wealth-owner has outsourced the management of their passive wealth to private banks and other financial intermediaries.

Over time, as the focus of the wealth held across the generations changes, so the activities of the office may change by employing in-house investment expertise, typically as chief investment officers.

2.1 Single family offices

By far the largest group of family office style structures are single family offices. A single family office's organisation and structure remains heavily dependent upon the main focus of the wealth-owner's attention and the current phase of that person's relationship to their wealth.

Where the wealth-owner's assets have been converted from direct business ownership to investment-oriented activities, single family offices are increasingly seeking to outsource the compliance element, once the central core component of their service needs, in order to concentrate the resources and talent of the single family office towards investment management. Often they may turn to multi-family office providers to deal with these component parts of their service needs.

The expertise and sophistication employed by and demonstrated by single family offices varies: it is not always the case that the family's wealth is a pre-determinant to sophistication, but more and more Australian family offices look to become better educated not from the marketplace but from their peer groups. Many seek out channels for communication with like-minded families and share collective experience and wisdom.

The mistake that potential service providers can often fall into is to assume that the models and processes for offering services to one single family necessarily accords with the needs and wants of the single family office.

Experience has demonstrated that many single family offices, for example, operate with vastly different approaches to risk management, and that seeking to apply investment industry standard models in discussions around portfolio construction draws deep sighs and raised eyebrows from the audience.

Flexibility and being adaptable in the way that services are offered remain key where no two offices, like families themselves, are the same.

2.2 Multi-family offices

By contrast, multi-family offices provide a menu of services for their clients to order from. In Australia, the two largest providers of multi-family office services, the Myer Family Company and Mutual Trust, have traditionally focused on delivering compliance services by offering families the benefits of economies of scale.

It is only relatively recently that those providers have expanded their service offering to include specific investment advisory services, personalised to client needs, rather than offering a suite of manufactured products. This shift has been driven by the needs of a more diverse client group looking for enhanced investment offerings. The opportunity here is to capture investment margins from portfolio construction through to investment selection, and by doing so reduce the reliance of lower margin activity such as accounting and tax compliance.

Other firms have developed stand-alone multi-family offices offering a range of services to an ideally niche group without the provenance a family name provides. Common to this model is that they talk in terms of bespoke, tailored offerings and as a consequence many have struggled to scale their capability accordingly.

This paradox between trusted adviser status and a scalable business model is one which besets the family office industry in general but is felt keenly in Australia where the education and training sufficient to develop the people needed to create a scaled bespoke service is in its infancy.

2.3 Commercial family offices

The development of commercial family offices has followed from greater appreciation of and exposure to the models operating in both the United States and Europe and the influence of foreign investment banks, particularly Swiss banks.

However, interestingly, perhaps as a reflection of the difficulty asset-based fee service providers have faced in delivering services to the market, the Australian retail banks, in particular, have drawn back from labelling their services as being 'family office' services in their offerings to family offices.

Professional service providers, typically accounting firms, constrained by their firm's ethics and independence, or by reluctance to embrace financial market regulation, have positioned themselves as offering family office style services.

In doing so, they have sought to capture a market that has either not seen itself as previously requiring the family office style of services (mid-tier millionaires and mass-affluent clients) and have enhanced the manner and means by which existing services are offered beyond simple compliance-oriented solutions towards a more complete service capability with an enhanced reporting mechanism.

More and more, they have recognised that labelling their services as 'family office' services is difficult when you have a pre-existing market position as accountants, and therefore instead have sought to offer 'enhanced' services to pre-existing clients including wealthy families.

2.4 Specialist service providers

Interestingly, many more boutique service providers have also emerged specialising in offering specific service components, such as an outsourced private investment office or property-specific management services.

The private investment office model is expected to become more common for several reasons:

- an increased awareness of clients in alternative asset management models;
- the willingness of fund managers and suppliers to engage with mid–tier markets; and
- the move by retail managers into a wholesale environment using pre-existing frameworks as fees become harder to earn.

There is also a growing group of service suppliers that focus on particular elements of the family office model, acting as outsourced chief financial officers, for example, coordinating the delivery of services by several other providers.

Several of these providers work discretely for several family groups, having previously worked with the families as a service provider within a large organisation in the past. However, they do not specifically advertise their services and instead dedicate their attention to a small number of relationships.

3. The role of the family office

3.1 The family office as a civil service

In many cases the role served by a family office represents the administrative wing of the family's government, akin to the role of the civil service.

In the context of a family, the family office's function can be seen as a civil service so that its members enjoy the benefits of a coordinated supply of services. In much the same way as governments seek to deliver public goods and utilities, law and order and education, so a fully formed family office provides a framework based around how the family operates as part of a broad collective ownership structure and works across the family's generations to help develop its human capital by offering access to financial education and social networks.

Some of the family's needs may be provided by third parties, by for example, adopting a manager or a manager's approach to its portfolio, or by outsourcing back-office functions. In which case, the family office needs to take on the responsibility for ensuring proper regulation of such third parties.

Here it can often mean that a fine balance has to be struck to ensure that the benefits of the family office and the skill sets employed within the family office do not become overshadowed by the expertise of the third-party providers, thus leaving the family questioning the need for the family office's existence in the first place, or worse, that the family office ends up controlling the supply of knowledge and expertise to family members in such a way that the family's best interests are not being served – an internalised form of career risk management perhaps.

Successful chief executive officers of single family offices are consummate diplomats who offer an open mind with the capacity to understand and absorb new ideas, and are capable of embracing differing points of view and expressing an opinion that at the same time does not usurp or overrule the wishes of the family.

There is also a danger in larger family groups that the family office may also come to be perceived as being too focused on the needs of dominant family members rather than serving the interests of the family or community as a whole. In these cases a common complaint from family members is how much they pay for the services of the family office. In contrast, the family office executive may bemoan the extent of service creep that can occur; again not an uncommon complaint from civil servants reporting to department heads at budget time.

Due to the potentially broad multi-dimensional scope of even the most rudimentary family offices, the head of the family's civil service, be it a family member or third-party appointee, really needs to be capable of offering a far-sighted vision with the capacity to define the family's policy and strategy across a number of different departments and portfolios, including investment, compliance and education.

Due to the inherent complexity of wealth and families, the quality of the family's civil service should ideally be measured by a set of agreed deliverables and outcomes, and the heads of the civil service should on a regular basis communicate the costs and benefits associated with the operation of the family office to its client base.

3.2 Defining the services of family offices in Australia

The nature of the services provided by family offices to their clients can be widely different from office to office.

In the case of single family offices, it varies by reference to the needs of the family members and their ages. In the larger, well established offices serving several generations, the range of services that family members ask the single family office to provide can be as broad as full concierge travel arrangements through to next generation education and training. In this regard, the sustainability of the single family office can come under pressure as costs increase to meet needs but service creep is not rewarded with additional fees.

The way in which the single family office communicates its service proposition is vitally important, particularly for the larger single family offices as they strive to remain relevant to each subsequent generation.

The single family office's role must be clearly understood, particularly in matters of family governance and control. Is this the responsibility of the family office executive to organise, or is its role merely to act as the family's civil service, implementing decisions based on the directions of the government – the family itself?

In the case of multi-family offices, where clients typically order services from a menu, the client relationship often starts with an initial engagement, such as setting up a private philanthropic vehicle, which if executed well offers the chance to follow on to deliver further services.

The range of services offered by multi-family offices typically encompasses completing regulatory obligations and requirements as accountants and tax advisers through to more strategic planning. The extent to which a multi-family office takes responsibility for governance matters in general is a function of the extent to which the family requires an oversight of structure and control.

As an appendix to this chapter, we have included a template of the range of services that could be provided by a family office, including a multi-family office, on behalf of its client base.

Many multi-family offices may have a particular focus in their activities which then attracts a certain client. This is typically governed by the attributes and skill sets of the founders of the office and usually revolves around an expertise and capacity to offer opportunities based on a particular asset class. For example, Keystone Private, a multi-family office in Queensland, offers expertise in property portfolio management.

In competition with the general marketplace, the multi-family office's capacity to provide a full and complete range of services is both a clear differentiator and also potentially an impediment to significant commercial success. As more traditional service providers, accountants, financial institutions and wealth managers look to create a position in this marketplace, many have questioned their willingness to engage in a market which suffers significant margin contraction as competition increases.

3.3 Design of the single family office

The following template provides a basis for discussion with families as a means of evaluating their readiness to set up a family office structure.

Steps	Initial consideration	Objective	Outcome
Defining the family's goals and objectives	What does the family want to do and why does it want to do it?	Gain consensus as to the benefits of being a family whose affairs are managed collectively	Provides the basis for decision-making
Current position	What is the current position?	Articulate how service is currently delivered to the family	Defines what works and doesn't work, what fits and does not fit
Outline service needs as a family	What services does the family need? (You may use the template in the appendix to help with this)	Summarise the role that would be played by a family office	Highlights service requirements
Defining a new structure	How are the service needs of the family to be met?	To begin designing the structure of a family office	Enables a broad business plan to be put together
Setting goals and objectives for the family office	How is the performance of the family office to be measured?	Defines the family's expectations as regards overall costs of delivery and revenue performance	Helps develop a coherent strategy by defining the capacity of the family office to deliver services
Commence process of communication of strategy to stakeholders	How is the transition from the current view to the better view to be managed?	To develop a plan for implementation	Sets timeframes and allocates responsibility for moving to a new office

To help harness the benefits of success for future generations, wealth creators and their inheritors have used private family offices to manage the needs of the family.

Often, these private offices evolve from inside the business administration until they have an independent and separate objective.

Sometimes, they are formed as a consequence of a liquidity event converting the ownership of an active business into passive investable capital. However they are formed or evolve, at some point, either at inception or as generational change occurs, there is a need to contemplate the design of the family office.

The imagination that inspires the creation of wealth is typically fuelled by a passion and commitment to succeed. Success does not necessarily follow a defined path nor work within the confines of a tight framework. It is built on instinct, flexibility and resilience and often accompanied by good timing or good fortune.

Should the same imagination that created the wealth define its future administration? Or should the wealth-owner use their imagination to look over the horizon to determine how the future management and administration of their wealth should be undertaken for the benefit of future generations?

4. The future of family offices in Australia

It is at this point that some definition of terms around what constitutes a single family office may be important. It is quite often the case in Australia that the personal financial affairs of a successful entrepreneur may well be managed by administrative staff within the confines of the entrepreneur's business.

At the first generation, it is particularly common that such an individual's wealth may well be substantially represented by the equity interest in their business. As the business grows and passive capital is created, by way of dividend or increased access to capital, so the owner's pool of capital becomes more diversified and separate operational procedures are required to be implemented, giving rise to the separation of family and business interests.

None of this is of course unique to Australia, but what is perhaps more significant is the number of family businesses in Australia expecting to transition ownership and control from the first to second generation over the next five years. It is this change of government, the move from 'dictatorship' to 'democracy' that provides a useful opportunity for a family to take stock and re-consider how best to organise its financial affairs.

In the latest family business survey completed by KPMG in Australia in 2013,[1] 40% of the survey participants expected to be transitioning ownership to the next generation within the next five years. Coupled with the increase in the recognition of family office services in Australia from the start of the century[2] it suggests that the number of single 'family offices' and the providers of services to family offices, should increase markedly over the next decade.

Understanding how the family office can play a role in the management of family enterprises will be critical for successful family business owners who are keen to see the preservation of their family's capital.

---

1   KPMG and Family Business Australia, Performers: resilient, adaptable, sustainable (2013).
2   By way of illustration, the first Family Office Congress was held in Australia in 2006, organised by what is known as the Private Wealth Network, and has recently celebrated its sixth anniversary.

How the family office is placed in the context of a family business

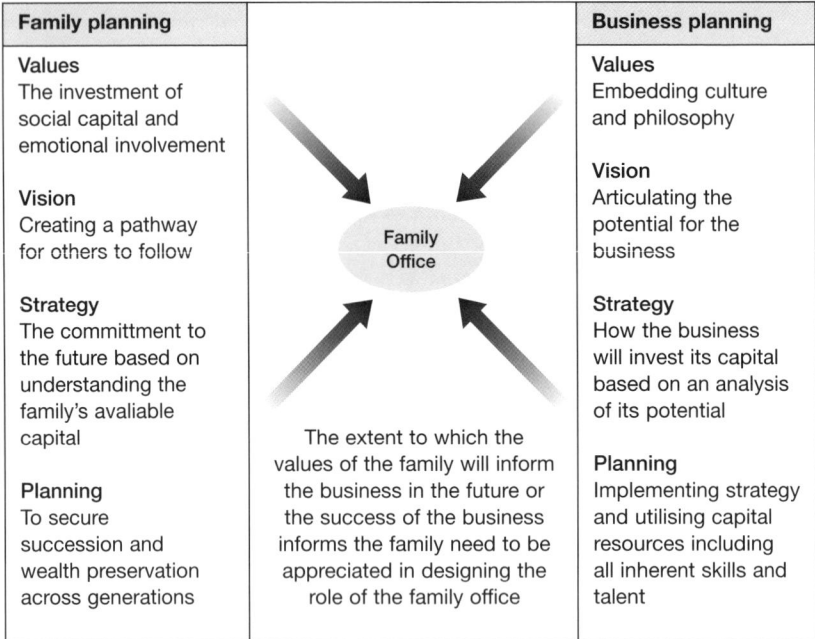

Family planning		Business planning
Values The investment of social capital and emotional involvement		**Values** Embedding culture and philosophy
Vision Creating a pathway for others to follow	Family Office	**Vision** Articulating the potential for the business
Strategy The committment to the future based on understanding the family's avaliable capital		**Strategy** How the business will invest its capital based on an analysis of its potential
Planning To secure succession and wealth preservation across generations	The extent to which the values of the family will inform the business in the future or the success of the business informs the family need to be appreciated in designing the role of the family office	**Planning** Implementing strategy and utilising capital resources including all inherent skills and talent

Extract from "Building a family office – presentation to private client group 2012".

Appendix: Defining the service needs of the family office in Australia

Using the attached template will help a family to understand their service needs in a way articulated by service providers. It will be useful to help understand the extent to which the family office plays a role in serving the needs of the family and also in helping to articulate which services should be outsourced and which can be administered successfully in-house. The range of services provided is by no means exhaustive and in several cases, is specific to the Australian context.

Broad service area categories offered as services by or to family offices in Australia				
Regulation and compliance	Monitoring and reporting	Structure and efficiency	Family unity and succession/ strategy and sustainability	Family business/ strategy and sustainability
Tax compliance and reporting including preparation of income tax returns	Financial health checks / monitoring and review functions	Tax planning and consulting	Setting the role of the family office	Business operations – strategy – alignment of family and business interests
Preparation of financial statements	Quarterly / monthly management accounting	Asset protection	Capital allocation – policy setting and goals	Business operations – market knowledge / innovation / competitive positioning
Quarterly lodgement of business activity statements and instalment activity statements	Cash-flow reporting • tax • lifestyle • capital needs Short to long-term funding requirements	Creation of entities – set up and registration	Alignment of family goals	Capital financing – liquidity and debt ratios

continued overleaf

Broad service area categories offered as services by or to family offices in Australia				
Regulation and compliance	Monitoring and reporting	Structure and efficiency	Family unity and succession/ strategy and sustainability	Family business/ strategy and sustainability
Preparation of fringe benefits tax returns	Outsourced finance capability – where client delegates responsibility for all financial administrative matters	Philanthropic services – structure / grant making / governance and control	Creating a family vision and mission	Corporate governance
Bookkeeping including assistance with data entry	Chief financial officer outsourcing	Budget preparation and monitoring – see cash flow management / goes to sustainability of capital	Family governance – decision making and rules for operation	Valuation services
Payroll and client payment/ administration of pay as you go	Asset recording and administration	Review of internal controls	Family education including business experience	Exit strategies – consideration of alternatives for realising value
Tax liability review consideration of appeals/ objections and direction as to payment	Consolidated reporting based on mandate and agreed objectives	Risk review and mitigation	Risk assessment and mitigation as they affect leadership and succession	Capital flows – business liquidity requirements and impact on passive wealth
Corporate secretarial including documentation /minutes	Performance reporting – movement in asset values period to period and year to date – comparison to benchmarks	Service provider contract reviews and service negotiations	Estate and succession planning	Meeting income requirements – dividend versus reinvestment

continued overleaf

Broad service area categories offered as services by or to family offices in Australia				
Regulation and compliance	Monitoring and reporting	Structure and efficiency	Family unity and succession/ strategy and sustainability	Family business/ strategy and sustainability
Trustee administration including documenting trustee decisions/pre paration of minutes	Investment manager – review and summary of performance		Philanthropic legacy and management	Participation options for family members/ management
Super- annuation – administration of self- managed super funds	Audit assistance			Vendor assist services
Cheque preparation and signing – liaison with financial institution and processing	Investment including capital gains tax data maintenance			
Sophisticated investor certificates				

Canada

Mary Anne Bueschkens
Miller Thomson
Lucinda E Main
Beard Winter LLP

1. Introduction

The concept of the family office is in its genesis in Canada and is not as advanced as it is in the United States and many European countries. Canada's minimal number of family offices is due, in part, to the country's relatively small population and its "less robust historical infrastructure for entrepreneurs to cultivate and pass on their family wealth."[1] This chapter will summarise the current status of single family and multi-family offices in Canada and the factors that have presented themselves which could lead to an increasing need for the services offered by such offices. However, while there are reasons to assume that family offices will become more prevalent in Canada, there are a number of reasons to believe that such growth could be thwarted. In addition, it is important that the family office industry in Canada should realise that because of the country's smaller population and fewer high net worth residents, the American and European concepts of a family office will need to be adapted in order for the family office concept to be successful in Canada and, therefore, a Canadian solution must be found and embraced.

2. The definition of a family office in Canada

The concept of a family office, single family or multi-family, is relatively new in Canada. In fact, if you were to ask 10 Canadians what a family office is you would likely receive many blank stares and perhaps one person stabbing a guess at defining the term. Tom McCullough, a founding member of Northwood Family Office, was once asked the following: "Is that like birth control and family counselling?"[2] The term has simply not yet become part of our vocabulary.

As a result of the continuing evolution of the business model in Canada, there is currently no commonly understood or accepted definition of a family office. The following are some of the definitions published for Canadian single family and multi-family offices to provide a sense of how such businesses are being marketed and portrayed in Canada:

---

1   Brent Barrie, "The Family Way: The Modern Family Office Deals with Many Issues", July 17 2013, at www.firstaffiliated.ca/media/.

2   Tom McCullough, "The Role of High Net Worth Family Offices for the Busy Practitioner" presented at the Toronto Lawyer's Association's Succession, Tax and Wealth Management in 2012 seminar, Toronto, October 2 2012 and *National Post*, "If you can't beat 'em, join a family office" at www.financialpost.com/story.html?id=55c4856b-deec-4394-8afd-ae9c6f1f57aa&k=24016.

- "A single family office is a private company that manages investments and trusts for a single affluent family."[3]
- "A family office acts as a Personal CFO [Chief Financial Officer] or Chief Adviser to wealthy families, with a dedicated team of professionals who oversee and manage the complete financial affairs of client families."[4]
- A family office is "… a commercial enterprise established to meet the investment, estate planning and, in some cases, the lifestyle and tax service needs of wealthy families."[5]
- "Family offices are essentially the quarterbacks who co-ordinate the activities of clients' other advisers and assist in tackling any financial issues that touch the whole family."[6]
- "A family office is an entity established or engaged by a single family or a group of families to manage all of their financial affairs. The focus of the family office is on managing, building and sustaining wealth for current and future generations. It also plays a major role in risk management, by building a diversified portfolio instead of one built on a single holding, and ensuring that this portfolio is properly managed and likely to be able to provide the funds to meet all of the family's goals and objectives."[7]

As the concept of the family office develops in Canada, the industry's goals and the services family offices deliver will become more consistent. In this regard, the way in which family offices are defined and marketed in Canada will become less vague and will better articulate the services offered to meet the wealthy family's business, financial and personal lifestyle goals.

3.   The future of the family office in Canada

3.1   Factors for potential growth
While family offices are still a relatively new phenomenon in Canada, there are reasons to believe that the foundation is being set for growth. First, the number of wealthy families in Canada is expected to continue to grow. Whether the funds are received as an inheritance or the result of the sale of a family business, such families are more likely than ever to need the services of a family office to manage the newly acquired funds and preserve their wealth. Second, the current trend of high net worth individuals moving to Canada is hoped to continue.

(a)   Increase in the accumulation of wealth
The number of high net worth individuals has been growing across the globe. In 1999

---

3   Sloan Levett, *Multi-Family Office – What Is It and Is It Right For You?* at www.fullerlandau.com/site/images/Articles/Multi_Family.pdf.
4   Northwood Family Office, promotional brochure, 2012.
5   "All in the Family", Forum magazine, September 2010, at /www.advocis.ca/forum/FMarchives10/FM-sep10/FM-sep10-all-family.html.
6   Jeff Beer, "Your Own Private CFO", *Canadian Business*, October 5 2011.
7   Tom McCullough, "Risk and the Role of a Family Office: What Entrepreneurs and Senior Executives Need to Know", *Ivey Business Journal*, November/December 2010.

there were 55,000 individuals with more than $30 million in investible assets. In 2010 that number had increased to 103,000. In 2013 that number had jumped to 187,380.[8] Wealth-X, in its *World Ultra Wealth Report 2012-2013*, estimated that over the course of the next five years this number will continue to increase an average of 3.9% every year.[9]

It has only been in the last three to four decades that Canadians have begun to accumulate significant wealth. Given Canada's relatively small population (33,476,688 in 2011),[10] the number of wealthy Canadian individuals and families and their total net worth are very often dwarfed by our neighbours to the south. According to Canadian Business's 2011 report, there were 61 billionaires in Canada with an average worth of $2.7 billion.[11] In comparison, the same 2011 report stated that there were 412 billionaires in the United States with an average worth of $3.7 billion. The Forbes list for 2014 stated that the number of billionaires in the United States had increased to 492 and that it is currently the country with the highest number of billionaires (out of 1,645 worldwide).[12] Growth in the number of wealthy individuals has continued in Canada too, and in 2014 Canada had 78 billionaires.[13]

Canadian Business annually ranks the top 100 richest Canadians.[14] The 2014 list ranks the Thomson family in first place with a net worth of $26 billion. The frozen food empire of the Harrison McCain family places 14th on the list with a net worth of $3.4 billion. In 19th place is Frank Stronach, founder of the car manufacturing company Magna International, with a net worth of $3.1 billion. All three have single family offices: Thomson family (Woodbridge Company Limited); the McCain family (GWF McCain Financial Services Inc); and Frank Stronach (Magna Management Inc).

As set out in greater detail below, only the ultra-wealthy can afford to sustain the operational costs of a single family office. The multi-family office is the more economically feasible option for the majority of wealthy individuals and families. However, there are still relatively few Canadians with the net worth necessary to join a multi-family office. In 2010, there were 594,000 households in Canada with $500,000 to $1 million in investable assets[15] with an average of $731,000 in assets. The same year, there were 562,000 households in Canada with investible assets of more than $1 million with an average of $3.1 million in assets.[16] It has been projected

---

8   Stephan Wessel, Carolin Decker, Knut SG Lange, Andreas Hack, "One Size Does Not Fit All: Entrepreneurial Families' Reliance on Family Offices," *European Management Journal*, 32 (2014) 37-45, p37.

9   Wealth-X, *World Ultra Wealth Report*, 2012-2013, at wealthx.com/wealthreport/Wealth-X-world-ultra-wealth-report.pdf, p20.

10 Statistics Canada, 2011 Census, www12.statcan.gc.ca/census-recensement/2011/dp-pd/hlt-fst/pd-pl/Table-Tableau.cfm?LANG=Eng&T=101&S=50&O=A.

11 Canadian Business, "The Rich 100" at www.canadianbusiness.com/article/48712--interactive-map-the-billionaires-of-the-world.

12 Pamela Heaven, "Forbes Rich List: More than 30 Canadians Ranked Among the World's Top Billionaires", *Financial Post*, at business.financialpost.com/2014/03/03/forbes-rich-list-more-than-30-canadians-ranked-among-the-worlds-top-billionaires/.

13 Canadian Business, "The Rich 100" at www.canadianbusiness.com/lists-and-rankings/richest-people-in-canada-2014/.

14 Canadian Business, "The Rich 100" at www.canadianbusiness.com/lists-and-rankings/rich-100-the-full-2014-ranking/.

15 Investible assets do not include the principal residence.

16 Noreen Rasbach, "High-net-worth Clients Demand More Face Time with Advisors", GlobeAdvisor.com, April 18, 2012, at secure.globeadvisor.com/servlet/ArticleNews/story/gam/20120418/SRWEALTH COMMUNICATION0418ATL.

that the number of Canadian households with more than $1 million to invest will double by 2020.[17]

Inheritance boom: With this increase in accumulation of wealth, Canadians have had to start considering how they will transfer their wealth after their death. It is speculated that there will be a significant transfer of wealth over the next couple of decades. According to a report by The BMO Wealth Institute "the biggest wealth transfer in history is set to take place."[18] The report stipulates that there will be an approximately $1 trillion transfer in the next 20 years. In comparison, the transfer in the United States is expected to be approximately $41 trillion. While there is uncertainty as to the plausibility of these exceptional numbers due to increasing life expectancy and escalating costs of health care, it is clear that there will be a transfer of some significance: "experts say that even if the anticipated tidal wave turns out to be a trickle collectively, it can still have an impact on individual's personal finances."[19] It appears that Canadians are more likely to pass their investments and assets to their spouses, children and grandchildren as opposed to making charitable gifts, at least in comparison to Americans.[20] Many Canadians – more than half surveyed for an Investors Group report – are expecting an inheritance (and many are relying on it).[21]

Business succession planning: The inheritance boom is not the only expected liquidity event to have much significance in Canada in the next couple of decades. It is estimated that 80% of all businesses operating in Canada are family-run.[22] A large number of family businesses expect to see an inter-generational transfer of management and/or ownership by 2017.[23] More specifically, over the next decade up to 70% of Canadian business are expected to see a change of ownership.[24] The same is expected in the United States: "private family businesses will transition ownership in unprecedented numbers over the next decade."[25] The concerns of such succession were well articulated by Sara Hamilton:

> *Many private family business owners aren't ready for the changes that are imminent as they transition leadership and/or ownership of their business enterprise. Some are in*

---

17   *Ibid.*
18   The BMO Wealth Institute, "Passing it on: What Will Future Inheritances Look Like?", Canadian edition at www.bmo.com/pdf/mf/prospectus/en/09-429_Retirement_Institute_Report_E_final.pdf.
19   Madhavi Acharya-Tom Yew, "Baby Boomers Set to Inherit $1Trillion", The Toronto Star, February 20 2012, at www.thestar.com/business/personal_finance/retirement/2012/02/20/baby_boomers_set_to_inherit_1_trillion.html.
20   Darah Hansen, "Canada's Pending Inheritance Boom Could Worsen Wealth Gap", Yahoo! Finance, April 9 2014, at ca.finance.yahoo.com/blogs/pay-day-/canada-pending-inheritance-boom-could-worsen-wealth-gap-183515296.html.
21   *Supra* note 19.
22   Samantha Garner, "Molson: A Canadian Family Business Success Story", GoForth Institute, July 31 2010, at canadianentrepreneurtraining.com/molson-a-canadian-family-business-success-story/.
23   KPMG, *Family Ties: Canadian Business in the Family Way*, 2012, at www.kpmg.com/ca/en/services/kpmg-enterprise/centre-for-family-business/documents/6530-kpmg-enterprise-canadian-family-business-report-v6-web.pdf.
24   *Supra* note 3.
25   Sara Hamilton, "Facilitating New Conversations in the Next Decade: Private Family Businesses Face Major Transitions", *Trusts & Trustees*, August 2013, p28.

denial, while others are oblivious. They may feel that their children aren't prepared to be in charge, or, perhaps, they haven't spoken to their children about handing over the reins because they love being in control. Maybe they say they can't find a successor who takes a long-term view or cares enough about the employees. No matter the reason, when it comes down to it, many clients can't see a logical transition path.[26]

Owners of such businesses essentially have two options: transfer the business to other family members or sell the business to a third party.

If the business will be transferred to the next generation, a family office can assist with the planning, tax structuring and creation of a workable corporate governance structure.

Where the business is sold to an arm's length party, the vendors will frequently come into a significant amount of liquid assets. Often they are not familiar with managing such a large sum of money. A family office can assist not only in creating and maintaining the investment strategy but also in preparing for the management of the money when it eventually passes to the next generation.

(b)   Immigration to Canada of high net worth families

Canada is a developed country with a high standard of living and good healthcare and education systems. It is a family-friendly and politically stable country.[27] Canada had the 11th largest economy in the world in 2011[28] and fares well in many international rankings, including placing 14th (out of 148 countries) in the World Economic Forum's *The Global Competitiveness Report 2013-2014;*[29] placing 19th (out of 189 countries) in the World Bank's "Ease of Doing Business" rankings for 2013;[30] and placing 11th (out of 186 countries) in the United Nations Human Development Report Office's "Human Development Index" for 2013.[31] Not surprisingly, Canada is a country that is appealing to potential immigrants. In 2012, Canada admitted a total of 257,887 permanent immigrants[32] from Asia and the Pacific (57.6%), Africa and the Middle East (13.8%), South and Central America (11.4%), Europe and United Kingdom (11%) and the United States (6%).[33]

---

26   *Ibid.*

27   For more fulsome discussion on the attractions of Canada for high-net worth individuals see Northwood Family Office, *Canadian Citizenship: The Wealthy Global Family's Safe and Tax-Efficient Alternative*, October 2009, at www.northwoodfamilyoffice.com/wp-content/uploads/2011/12/Canadian_ Citizenship.pdf.

28   The Economist Intelligence Unit, "Canada: Fact Sheet" at country.eiu.com/article.aspx? articleid=469708831&Country=Canada&topic=Summary&subtopic=Fact+sheet.

29   World Economic Forum at www3.weforum.org/docs/GCR2013-14/GCR_Rankings_2013-14.pdf.

30   International Finance Corporation and World Bank, "Doing Business" economy rankings at www. doingbusiness.org/rankings.

31   United Nations Development Programme, "Human Development Index" at data.undp.org/dataset/ Table-1-Human-Development-Index-and-its-components/wxub-qc5k.

32   The following is a list of the number of permanent immigrants admitted into Canada over the last decade: 2002: 229,048; 2003: 221,349; 2004: 235,823; 2005:262,242; 2006: 251,640; 2007: 236,753; 2008: 247,247; 2009: 252,172; 2010: 280,689; 2011: 248,748 (Citizenship and Immigration Canada, "Facts and Figures 2012 – Immigration Overview: Permanent and Temporary Residents" at www. cic.gc.ca/english/resources/statistics/facts2012/index.asp.

33   Citizenship and Immigration Canada, "Facts and Figures 2012 – Immigration Overview: Permanent and Temporary Residents" at/www.cic.gc.ca/english/resources/statistics/facts2012/permanent/08.asp# figure5.

The coveted Canadian passport: Many high net worth families are deciding to relocate to Canada. Northwood Family Office, a multi-family office in Canada, has summarised why wealthy families ought to consider Canadian citizenship when choosing a jurisdiction for their citizenship strategy:

Canada is one of the world's best kept secrets. It hasn't always showed up on the list of potential countries for wealthy families looking for additional citizenships or residences. The reason is its (partly unfair) reputation as a high-tax and chilly-weather destination, and also the perception that better alternatives might be available.

But things have changed and so have the perceptions. Canada is now recognized as a much more attractive destination for wealthy families... At the same time, the relative attractiveness of other destinations (such as the US, UK, Switzerland, Caribbean tax havens, etc.) has waned, for well-publicized reasons.[34]

Canadian citizenship is becoming a coveted status to hold. Many high net worth families are considering relocating to Canada, sometimes only temporarily, simply to obtain the Canadian passport. Having done so, they can return to their home country, which may be wrought with political and economic uncertainty, with the knowledge and comfort that they can return to Canada at any time and stay as long as need be. Moreover, holders of Canadian passports can travel to many countries without a visa.

As Canada levies taxes on the basis of residency, and not domicile or citizenship, once Canadian citizenship has been obtained the individual need not remain in Canada (and, therefore, can cease Canadian residency from a Canadian tax perspective) and can continually renew his passport without further residency requirements having to be met.

3.2 Factors that may prevent growth

Unfortunately, despite the above reasons for hope for, and anticipation of, the growth of the family office concept in Canada, in early 2014 the federal government unexpectedly announced three important changes that could very well slow down and impede the growth of the family office in Canada. In sum, the federal government took steps to make Canada a less appealing destination for wealthy immigrants.

(a) Termination of the Immigrant Investor Programme

The Immigrant Investor Programme had been created in the mid-1980s in an effort to entice high net worth individuals to Canada, and was sometimes referred to as the 'cash for citizenship' programme.[35] Immigrants had to invest at least $800,000 in Canada using an interest-free loan to the provincial government where the individual would reside. The individual would receive permanent residency status and could

---

34   *Supra* note 27, at p3.
35   *Globe and Mail* editorial, "The Immigrant Investor Program's Overdue End," February 12 2014, at www.theglobeandmail.com/globe-debate/editorials/the-immigrant-investor-programs-overdue-end/article16838689/.
36   Matthew McClearn, "Immigrant Investors to Canada Face Backlog," Canadian Business, March 19 2012, at http://www.canadianbusiness.com/investing/immigrant-investors-to-canada-face-backlog/.

thereafter eventually apply for Canadian citizenship. The programme brought in approximately 130,000 individuals to Canada[36] over the course of almost 30 years.

In early 2014 the government announced it was cancelling the programme.

(b)   *Change to the citizenship laws*

To apply for Canadian citizenship, an individual needs to reside in Canada for three of four years. The term 'residency' is not defined in the Citizenship Act.[37] The definition found in the Income Tax Act (Canada)[38] is not used. It has been, consequently, feasible to become a citizen without becoming a resident of Canada for income tax purposes.

In early 2014, the government proposed to make a number of significant changes to its Citizenship Act. If the proposed changes are made,[39] an individual will have to be physically present in Canada for four years in a six year period. In addition, he will have to be in Canada at least 183 days per year in those four years. This will very likely mean that the individual will become a tax resident of Canada too. This will require him to file Canadian income tax returns and report and pay Canadian income tax on his worldwide income. This requirement to file and possibly pay Canadian income tax may very well deter high net worth individuals and families from relocating to Canada, even if just temporarily to obtain a Canadian passport.

(c)   *Important tax holiday abruptly eliminated*

Canada is a high tax jurisdiction, and individuals are generally not known to relocate to Canada to save tax dollars. However, Canada offers an important tax benefit to immigrants: a step-up in the cost base of their capital property upon arrival. Paragraph 128.1(1)(c) of the Income Tax Act (Canada) provides that on immigration to Canada certain capital assets of the immigrant will be deemed to have been acquired at their then fair market value without the assets actually having to be sold. When the immigrant later sells or otherwise disposes of the assets, he can greatly benefit from this step-up in the cost base. Many high net worth immigrants benefit significantly from this provision in Canada's federal tax legislation.

In a more targeted and obvious effort to attract high net worth families to Canada with the hope that they remain and invest in Canada, the federal government allowed for a special tax holiday for high net worth immigrants to Canada. In the 2014 federal budget, however, the government, without warning, proposed to terminate this tax holiday.[40]

Since the late 1990s, Canada has increased its efforts to eliminate tax benefits for wealthy Canadians who use offshore trusts to shelter income from the Canadian taxing authority. These attempts have resulted in a long series of drafts of proposed legislation, the most recent of which was finally enacted into law in 2013.[41] These

---

37   RSC, 1985, c C-29.
38   RSC 1985, c 1 (5th Supp).
39   At the time of writing the recently proposed changes (Bill C-24) to the Citizenship Act had not yet been passed into law.
40   Budget plan, February 11 2014, at www.budget.gc.ca/2014/docs/plan/pdf/budget2014-eng.pdf.
41   For more see L Main, "Estates, Trust and Tax Law in Canada: Recent Developments of Interest", *Journal of International Tax, Trust and Corporate Planning*, Vol 20, No 4, 2013.

rules make it more difficult for a Canadian resident to establish, control or benefit from an offshore trust without the imposition of Canadian income tax.

The Canadian government, however, for many years continued to maintain a special exception for high net worth immigrants. While, like all other residents of Canada, immigrants must pay tax on their worldwide income or capital gains earned, Canada permitted immigrants to use a qualified non-resident trust – an 'immigration trust' – legitimately to protect income earned in such a qualified trust from Canadian taxes for up to 60 months. An individual who became a Canadian resident and who had previously not been a resident of Canada for more than 60 cumulative months could establish an immigration trust that would be exempt from tax on certain types of income earned in the trust. Thus, the immigration trust was a potentially very significant tax planning mechanism for high net worth individuals moving to Canada.

The policy rationale behind the immigration trust was to entice high net worth individuals to relocate to Canada to spend their money in Canada, invest in Canadian products and businesses and, in some cases, start their own businesses or set up a Canadian branch or subsidiary of a foreign business in Canada. It was expected and hoped that many would become intertwined in Canadian business and would set up a life and family in Canada such that at the end of the five-year tax holiday they would decide to remain in the country.

With the announcement in the federal budget of 2014 to shut down the immigration trust strategy, there is not much reprieve for immigrants who set up an immigration trust before February 11 2014. In such instances, the immigrant (so long as more funds are not contributed to the trust) can benefit from the trust only until December 30 2014, regardless of how far into the five-year tax holiday the trust found itself. Should the trust continue to exist, it will be taxable in Canada on its worldwide income commencing January 1 2015.

It is not yet known what effect, if any, the sudden termination of the immigration trust and the other measures referred to above will have on high net worth immigration to Canada. Some advisers are pessimistic: Kim Moody of Moodys Gartner Tax Law is quoted as saying that the elimination of the immigration trust "will certainly make immigration a more painful tax exercise for very wealthy immigrants."[42] In the same vein, Dave Rickards of Grant Thornton LLP has stated that "it's possible the elimination of the immigrant trust rule will be a disincentive for people who aren't used to Canada's high tax rates (like those from China or Hong Kong) to take up residence in here."[43] Kevyn Nightingale of MNP LLP explained that, combined with the two other recent measures taken by the federal government discussed above, Canada is sending a strong message to high net-worth immigrants: "If you really want to come here, we're going to make it hard and you're going to have to pay."[44] He goes on to say the following:

---

42   Suzanna Sharma, "No More Immigration Trusts? No Problem", February 13 2014 at www.advisor.ca/news/industry-news/no-more-immigration-trusts-no-problem-144733.
43   *Ibid.*
44   Kevyn Nightingale, "The Federal Budget 2014: A Hidden Trap for High-Net-Worth Immigrants", February 13 2014, at www.mnp.ca/en/media-centre/blog/2014/2/13/the-federal-budget-2014-a-hidden-trap-for-high-net-worth-immigrants.

The … measures will not really affect low and middle-income people because they wouldn't have used these tactics anyway. Since there are a lot more people in this average net worth category, the changes will be politically popular. Whether it is to Canada's advantage to hold up a 'STOP' sign to wealthy immigrants is a different question.

Conversely, Wilmot George of Mackenzie Investments remains optimistic following the termination of the immigration trust strategy: "It's not going to stop individuals from coming to Canada. There are other reasons to come here."[45] Some of these non-tax reasons were set out above. Another important non-tax incentive to remember is family ties. It is not uncommon for parents to relocate to Canada if their child moved to Canada for their education and decided to remain in Canada and start their career and family here.

It is far too early to determine if the elimination of this tax holiday along with the cancellation of the Immigrant Investor Programme and the proposed changes to the Citizenship Act will have the effect of reducing the number of high net worth individuals immigrating to Canada. It is hoped that the many non-tax factors will be sufficient incentives. However, these changes and proposed changes are important and must be considered when discussing the immigration of wealthy individuals and families to Canada. The message we are potentially sending cannot be ignored.

4.   Examples of current multi-family offices in Canada

While family wealth is growing in Canada and high net worth individuals are moving to and setting up in Canada, there are currently relatively few single family and multi-family offices in Canada. The three most recognised multi-family offices are Northwood Family Office, WaterStreet Family Offices (The WaterStreet Group Inc) and First Affiliated Holdings Inc.

Northwood was founded in 2003 and has stated that it has clients with a net worth in the range of $10 million to $500 million. Northwood assists families who have recently come in to a significant amount of wealth, perhaps following the sale of a family business. These individuals often have simply not needed to worry about investing money as they have spent most of their lives working to build a profitable business. Northwood also focuses on families who have a complex business and financial set-up and require assistance in simplifying and overseeing all business, financial and personal matters.

The bulk of Northwood's clients is around the age of 50 years[46] and composed of entrepreneurs with some high performing professionals (like investment bankers and lawyers) and athletes. Northwood provides a full range of investment, tax and legal services. It is a member of the Wigmore Association, a small group of family offices located in North America, Europe and Australia. The association's goal is to share issues, stories and ideas each family office faces in their own jurisdiction with a view to understanding and interpreting trends in the area of family offices.

WaterStreet has professional advisers located in five offices across Canada. Their

---

45   Supra note 42.
46   National Post article cited supra note 2.

advisers have a broad range of backgrounds and include lawyers, financial advisers and accountants. Where necessary, they will retain outside counsel and advisers for additional support. Similarly to Northwood, their clients include business owners, executives, athletes, entertainers and individuals and families who have inherited their wealth. The asset threshold is stated to be flexible but is targeted at a net worth of at least $20 million. They offer a full range of services including investment advice, tax and estate planning, tax filing preparation, accounting and bookkeeping, budgeting and bill paying. To remain competitive and offer additional value to their clients, they offer several additional services including career counselling and family conflict mediation.[47]

WaterStreet was purchased by a Canadian bank in 2010 in an effort for the bank to increase its services to its high net worth clients.[48]

First Affiliated was established in 1987 and is privately owned. They break down their client base into the following categories: family steward, business owner, freedom seeker, complex affairs and new wealth. They can offer their clients tax, legal, investment, philanthropy and insurance advice. They have three offices in two provinces.

5. Typical clients of the family office

Canadians look to set up or join a family office typically for one of three reasons. First, the family may have a keen interest in growing and preserving the family wealth for multiple generations. These funds may have already been accumulated over several generations, but now the family wants to ensure that the funds are in fact preserved and maintained.

The second reason is the sale of a business. As already noted, many family business owners are not sure how to invest or deal with the funds received on the sale of their business, and need assistance in determining how to invest and preserve it for the business owner's lifetime and to maintain the funds for future generations, if possible. A common story reads as follows:

> You're an entrepreneur who has worked for decades to build your business. Then someone comes along and offers you $30 million for it. After the last champagne bottle is drained, the new Bentley is in the garage and you're back from the Bora Bora vacation, you start to realize there's a big difference between running a company worth $30 million and managing $30 million in disposable cash. Taking care of that wealth is a business in itself.[49]

Finally, family offices can provide valuable help to surviving spouses, particularly if the surviving spouse was not the family member in charge of running the family business and/or the family finances. They provide one place for the surviving spouse to go to obtain all of the necessary help needed, including the preparation of a budget and guidance on investing.

---

47 WaterStreet Family Offices promotional materials, 2012.
48 Scotiabank Group press release, October 25 2010, at waterstreet.ca/data/PressRelease/English_Press_Release.pdf.
49 *Supra* note 7.

6.   Goals of the family office

Regardless of the source of wealth, Canadians considering setting up or joining a family office share many of the same goals as wealthy individuals in other parts of the world in similar situations. The main goals include the following:

- preserving family wealth for the current generation and, if possible, future generations; moreover, there is often a desire to provide continuity of investment and philanthropic philosophies over multiple generations;
- simplifying life – a family office can centralise financial matters and provide all the legal, investment and tax advice and planning under one roof and assist with maintaining all relevant bookkeeping and reporting, which can ensure that there is no duplication of efforts as all advisers work together and share information as they all work in the same office;
- as multi-generational wealth is relatively new in Canada, the goal of family offices is to assist families with the transition of wealth, which includes ensuring the proper tax and estate plans are in place. Moreover, there is often a need to teach the younger generation how to handle wealth properly.

7.   Services offered by the family office

To meet the goals of wealthy Canadians, the services of family offices in Canada are currently very wide-ranging. Family offices strive to leverage advisers (both within the family office and outsourced) with different expertise to work together for a family. In summary, the following services are offered by many family offices in Canada:

Planning
- financial planning
- philanthropic planning
- tax planning
- estate planning (eg wills, powers of attorney for property and powers of attorney for personal care)

Risk management and risk allocation
- review and management of assets and debts
- review and management of investment philosophy
- review and management of insurance coverage
- review and management of structures holding family wealth (eg trusts, corporations, partnerships, etc)

Financial
- financial planning
- selection of money managers
- consolidated reporting on investments
- managing expenses

Tax
- income tax return preparation
- strategic tax planning to minimise tax otherwise payable

- overseeing tax audits
- coordinating filing of tax returns in other jurisdictions

Accounting/bookkeeping
- renewal of insurance policies
- property management
- monitoring and reporting on outside counsel/adviser work
- assisting with the creation of a family and/or personal budget
- payment of bills and invoices
- overseeing contract/renovation work/projects

Philanthropy
- defining a family's philanthropic philosophy
- setting up and managing a charitable family foundation
- making charitable donations

Family
- managing a family's public reputation
- family governance
- family constitutions
- family mediations and dispute resolution
- arranging specialised healthcare services
- career coaching/counselling

Lifestyle
- managing day-to-day affairs
- holiday rentals
- private jet rentals
- travel arrangements
- social club and athletic memberships
- hiring childcare and cleaning services
- arranging for car service

To provide for greater services to their clients, family offices, both single family and multi-family offices, are determining ways that they can better provide for their clients. Given Canada's proximity to the United States and the fact that the majority of Canada's population lives close to the border with the United States, many families face cross-border tax and estate planning issues. In some cases, a child may move to the United States and take up residency or citizenship. In other cases, the family may purchase a vacation property in the United States. Such issues require particular attention in relation to the family's tax and estate planning as the family must now deal with potential US gift and estate tax issues. Canadian family offices are often required to advise on such matters and many are providing these specialised services to their clients.

Another example of family offices trying to provide more specialised services for their clients is to be able to act as executors, trustees and estate trustees of their client's living trusts, testamentary trusts and wills. In such regard, they can often provide independent and objective advice, as they are not beneficially interested in the assets. Having worked with the family for a number of years and having intimate knowledge of the family's financial situation and the family dynamics often makes the family office more suitable for the task compared to a more remote family member, friend, colleague or trust company affiliated with a bank. Moreover, the family office is more likely to have the expertise (or access to experts) than a more remote family member, friend or colleague.

In several jurisdictions in Canada, only individuals can act as executors, trustees and estate trustees. It is not always ideal to name an individual family office employee in the event they leave the employ of the family office, die, become incapacitated or otherwise choose not to act in such a role when the time comes. If a family office wishes to provide such services in Ontario, for example, they must establish themselves as a trust company in Canada with a licence to carry on trust business in Ontario. It is a rigorous, lengthy and highly regulated process.

Given the amount of work and costs involved in setting up a trust company that can carry on business in Ontario, it should not be surprising that many family offices choose not to attempt to travel down that road. In fact, as of August 2014, there were only 52 registered trust and loan companies operating in Ontario (a reduction from 56 in October 2012).[50] However, as the need for family offices and the desire to distinguish oneself from competitors increases, it may become a service family offices in Canada wish to provide.

8. Asset base required to operate a single family office

Neither a single family nor multi-family office will be appropriate for all wealthy families in Canada. The first determination is the costs of either operating a single family office or joining a multi-family office.

There is obviously no set minimum asset requirement to set up a single family office. It will depend entirely on the objectives of the family and what services the office will provide to the family in order to meet these objectives. It has been suggested that a single family office only becomes financially viable in Canada to a family with liquid wealth of more than $75 million.[51] However, Tom McCullough, the Chief Executive Officer of Northwood, has asserted that a single family office is really only economically viable when a family has a net worth in excess of $250 million and more realistically with a net worth of at least $500 million.[52] Tim Cestnick, the founder of WaterStreet, has stated that between $300 million and $500 million of net assets is needed to cover the operational costs of a single family office suitably.[53]

Some single family offices in Canada are simply a branch or offshoot of a larger international family office structure. These situations are typically the result of a

---

50   See Financial Services Commission of Ontario, "Loan and Trust Companies Registered in Ontario", www5.fsco.gov.on.ca/loanandtrust/loantrust.aspx.
51   *Supra* note 3.
52   McCullogh, cited *supra* note 2.
53   *National Post* article, cited *supra* note 2.

family creating much wealth several generations ago and, as the family has grown and the wealth has spread around, members of the family have relocated to other countries. There may be 20 to 50 family members in Canada who require the similar services of a family office, and there is a desire that all family members across the globe receive similar services and pursue similar investment and philanthropic philosophies so as to maintain the family wealth for as long as possible. Therefore, while it may not be economically feasible for the Canadian family members to establish their own single family office separately in Canada, by being a part of a larger international structure of family offices it is still possible to take advantage of some economies of scale.

9.   **Cost to join a multi-family office**
Multi-family offices often start out as single family offices, as was the case with Northwood. Some family offices are winding up and the family is joining a multi-family office to control and reduce costs.[54]

The multi-family office offers economies of scale and typically services families with a $10 million to $250 million net worth.[55] Most Canadian multi-family offices focus on families with a net worth of $25 million to $30 million.[56]

The fees charged by multi-family offices are typically on a percentage basis of the assets under management. Generally, clients are being charged between 0.5% and 1.25% of their assets under management for all services rendered.[57]

However, the view of charging based on the value of the assets is starting to change and an annual retainer is beginning to make an appearance.[58] Charging based on hourly rates or other billing structures is not yet overly common.[59]

10.   **Setting up and regulating a family office**
There is no particular legislation in place to deal with the setting up or running of a family office and no specific regulation of its work. Both single family and multi-family offices in Canada tend to be independently owned private companies. They are not typically part of an investment firm or bank. Therefore, the setting up of a single family or multi-family office simply requires the incorporation of a federal or provincial private company. The key to a successful operation is the staffing. Employees with the appropriate level of education and knowledge are needed. Further, a variety of expertise is necessary in the areas of law, tax, accounting and investment.

It is important to note that regulation is not required as Canadian family offices typically do not actually carry out any investing of their client's money. They will work with their client's current investment advisers, assist with selecting the proper money managers and/or consolidate the financial reporting. Those family offices

---

54   McCullogh, cited *supra* note 2.
55   *Ibid.*
56   *Ibid.*
57   *National Post* article, cited supra note 2.
58   McCullogh, cited *supra* note 2.
59   *Ibid.*

that are not affiliated with a bank or trust company pride themselves on their independence and consider this a strong benefit of using a family office over simply employing an investment firm or more traditional wealth-management firm. Single family offices will often pool together the family's funds so as to be in a position to leverage the best possible management fees from the money managers.

The management of funds is a highly regulated industry in Canada. The regulation of investment firms and individuals offering money management services is completed at the provincial level, with each province having its own regulatory system and rules. The Ontario Securities Commission's Compliance and Registrant Regulation Branch is in charge of regulating individuals and firms who provide investment advice and manage investment funds in the province. Ontario has legislation in place that regulates these activities.

11. Viability and future of the family office

Family offices are not yet commonplace or even commonly understood in Canada. There are reasons to believe that the concept of family offices will be embraced in Canada and become more commonplace. To this end, it is anticipated that:

- the number of wealthy individuals and families resident in Canada will continue to grow;
- there will be a significant transfer of wealth from one generation to the next in the following two decades;
- the ownership of many family businesses will be transferred to family members or sold to third parties in the near future, creating significant liquidity; and
- immigration, it is hoped, will remain steady and high net worth individuals will continue to relocate to Canada.

However, while the stage may be set for an increasing need for the family office in Canada in the next couple of decades, in 2014 the federal government dealt a series of blows to Canada's ability to entice high net worth immigrants to relocate to the country. The effects of the recently proposed changes to the immigration, citizenship and tax laws cannot yet be fully appreciated and understood. In addition to these new hurdles, the young industry needs to appreciate the differences between Canada and its neighbour to the south and Europe and adapt the family office model accordingly. If the industry fails to understand and deal with the differences (eg small population generally, relatively small population of high net worth individuals, shorter history of family businesses and wealth accumulation, specific objectives and needs of high net worth families, etc) and simply mimic the models currently presented in other countries, the concept of the family office will not take hold and will not proliferate in Canada.

The Gulf region

Barbara R Hauser
Barbara R Hauser, LLC

1. Gulf Region overview

This chapter will cover the member countries of The Cooperation Council for the Arab States of the Gulf (the GCC), which are: Bahrain, Kuwait, Oman, Qatar, Saudi Arabia, and the United Arab Emirates (UAE, whose seven member emirates are Abu Dhabi, Dubai, Sharjah, Ras al-Kaimah, Fujairah, Ajman, and Umm al-Quwain).[1]

The economy of the GCC is a fascinating blend of oil revenue and more traditional business revenue. The significance of its overall economy is quite important in the global market. The GCC economy has been compared to the size of the economy of India and of Russia,[2] both much larger geographic regions. All of the GCC countries are trying to increase their non-oil dependent revenue, with various challenges.

Growth in the GCC market has been impressive. The economy tripled in size from 2002 to 2008. The GDP of the region grew at rate of 28.9% to $1076.8 billion in 2008, which has been attributed to strong global oil demand (until late 2008), better geo-political environment, acceleration of reform measures, a strong boost in privatisation activities, the growth of assets of central banks and the strength of the GCC corporate sector. Nominal GDP decreased by 19.3% in 2009 due to the global financial and economic crisis, and the world oil market slump.[3]

In addition to the indirect impact of the global financial crisis of 2009, the region was also directly affected by the 'Arab Spring' protests throughout much of the region during 2011. More recently the increase in oil production in the United States has also caused some concern.

The 2012 International Monetary Fund's report on the GCC economy ("Economic Prospects and Policy Challenges for the GCC Countries") noted:

> *The GCC economies are growing at a strong pace. Output growth has in most countries been steadily increasing since hitting a low in 2009 in the wake of the global financial crisis. In 2011, overall real GDP growth for the GCC reached 7.5 percent – the highest since 2003. This occurred as oil production rose by over 10 percent and as non-*

---

1   For Israel, see the separate chapter by Alon Kaplan.
2   Article in *The Economic Times*, December 5 2012:
      The Gulf Cooperation Council (GCC) economy, which is growing at around 5-6 per cent, is almost as strong as that of the Indian economy, industry experts have said. "The GCC nominal GDP is 1.5 trillion; India's nominal GDP is 1.8 trillion, which means that as a very small economic block, the GCC has an economy size that is almost equal to India or Russia for that matter." (articles.economictimes.indiatimes.com/2012-12-05/news/35620562_1_gcc-indian-economy-economic-outlook).
3   www.gulfbase.com/gcc/aboutgcc?pageid=93.

hydrocarbon growth increased in all countries, except Bahrain where social unrest has taken a toll. …. In 2011, as governments responded to social pressures and took advantage of surging oil revenues, overall spending grew by some 20 percent in U.S. dollar terms, about double the pace of the previous two years. Much of the higher spending was in current expenditure, including from larger wage bills (all countries) and introduction of new benefits for job-seekers (Oman and Saudi Arabia). Capital expenditure also increased sharply in Saudi Arabia.[4]

In its 2013 annual report, the IMF updated its outlook as follows:

The growth outlook for the GCC is positive, but will be affected by global and regional developments. While growth has slowed from the exceptionally strong rates in 2010–11, it remains robust, and with confidence high and large infrastructure projects coming on stream, it should remain well-supported going forward. The path of oil prices remains the main uncertainty for the region, although countries would also be affected by increased volatility in global financial markets or broader unrest in the Middle East region. … In the region, growth converged in 2012 as countries that had grown relatively slowly in 2011 (Bahrain and the United Arab Emirates) saw stronger growth, and those that enjoyed very strong growth in 2011 (Saudi Arabia, Qatar) slowed. Strong growth in the non-oil economy has resulted in a large increase in employment, although this has been concentrated among expatriates in a number of countries.[5]

The IMF's predictions for 2014 were:

Regional growth will strengthen in 2014. Real GDP is projected to expand by 3.7 percent. Growth in the non-oil sector remains robust across the region as large infrastructure projects continue to be implemented and private sector confidence remains high. The Purchasing Managers Index for Saudi Arabia and the United Arab Emirates shows that output and confidence in the non-oil private sector are strong. In 2014, oil production is projected to increase, and with steady non-oil growth, overall GDP growth is projected at just over 4 percent.[6]

In September 2014 the IMF reported in its report for Saudi Arabia that:

The near term economic outlook is positive. Oil production is expected to be little changed from 2013, while non-oil growth will be underpinned by strong private sector activity and government spending on large projects in transportation infrastructure and housing. Inflation is expected to remain subdued. The main source of risk is the global oil market.[7]

2. Status of the family office market in the GCC

With such large and robust economies, and the prevalence of family-owned businesses, one would expect to find a proliferation of family offices in the Gulf Region. In fact there are very few at the present time. (By contrast, in the United States there are thought to be more than 8,000 family offices.)

The classic creation of a family office begins with a successful operating family-owned business, and this is true in the Gulf region but the evolution has taken place

---

4   www.imf.org/external/np/pp/eng/2012/100512.pdf.
5   www.imf.org/external/np/pp/eng/2013/100513b.pdf.
6   *Ibid.*
7   www.imf.org/external/pubs/cat/longres.aspx?sk=42355.0

more slowly than in the United States. Family businesses flourish in the Gulf region, yet there are few traditional family offices. That is likely to change: there is a growing interest in family offices.

In the Gulf region, estimates are that as much as 98% of the non-oil economy is made up of family businesses. Data is difficult to confirm, especially as the English and European studies tend to use the term 'SME' (small and medium enterprises) when in fact these family-owned businesses are often neither small nor medium.

As with all complex, wealthy families, these business-owning families in the Gulf region have a need for family office-type services. However, there are very few traditional full-service single family offices in the region. Estimates are that there are about 30 or 40, counting those whose offices are located in other jurisdictions, such as London. I think there are several reasons that family offices are not as prevalent as one might expect, based on my 11 years of working in the region.

One reason for this might be that the families and the businesses are much more closely intertwined, as an outgrowth of the culture that blends the two together. The families can seem to be much more close-knit than in the West, often living in large family compounds and marrying within their tribe, including to cousins. One example of the blending between the family and the business is a statement by the head of a large business in Kuwait, that the family member executive should be paid much more than a non-family executive due to the expensive expectations in the community – leading to more entertaining, larger weddings and larger homes. This assumption was well-understood.

There is an assumption that the family business will take care of all of the family members. This means that many traditional family office services are provided in practice, but without the formality of setting up a family office.

Another reason for the relative lack of organised single family offices is that the tax laws do not provide the incentive that they do in so many other countries, where it becomes difficult to justify claiming a business expense deduction from taxes for what are in fact very personal services to family members. For example, in the United States the tax laws would prohibit a company from deducting the expenses of an employee who provides personal services for a family member. One change that is coming, though occurs when the business begins to get ready for a partial initial public offering, and they need to professionalise the company operations. Outside investors will see the time spent providing personal services for family members as a negative. This could often be the impetus to create a family office to provide the personal services.

Finally, part of the reason may be that the businesses are fairly young in their organisational development. Although families speak with pride of the grandfather who began with nothing and built the business, in fact many of those businesses did not become the huge international conglomerates they are today until the oil boom in the 1970s. The sons who are running those businesses are well aware of global best practices, and I predict that the formation of many more formal family offices will soon take place.

3. Issues of concern to Gulf families in creating a family office

In this somewhat volatile region of the world, there are some specific priorities that are of more concern to families than in other parts of the developed world. The Kuwait invasion in 1990 was a lesson in the risk of privatisation. The Arab Spring of 2011 caused more uncertainty, particularly in Bahrain, which lost some of its global appeal as a safe financial centre. At the other end of concerns, there is the strong family culture, which means that extraordinary efforts will be made for the goal of keeping the family as a whole safe. Those risks and values result in a tailored set of issues for family offices in the region, in my opinion.

3.1 Location

It is not an automatic decision to locate the Gulf family office close to home. There are the geopolitical exposures, mentioned above, and difficulty in attracting and retaining global investment talent in some cases.

These concerns often lead to creating two parts of the family office. One part will be focused on investments. That location is usually chosen for reasons of safety combined with a desire for a location with a solid professional environment. Many families are willing to pay the extra expense of regulation (and in some case even taxes) for the assurance that their investments are safely monitored. In practice this often means that the investment division of a family office will be located in London or Geneva. Other contending locations, such as Singapore or the Caribbean, are usually seen as just too far away.

The non-investment part of the office is likely to be located close to, or even inside, the family's operating business.

3.2 Confidentiality

All families place a high value on confidentiality. But the very wealthy families in the Gulf have a higher than average concern for confidentiality. This is not based on physical safety (as in South America or Mexico, with the high risk of kidnapping) but more often on protecting the reputation of the family – the name of the family. There is a sensitivity to having others know the amount of wealth in a family. Homes are protected by walls and guards, so is the family's financial information. The family office has an important role in safe-guarding that information.[8]

3.3 Safety of assets (and consolidated management)

Any family office will be charged with the oversight of the family assets, to be sure they are safe in terms of location and of their management. I have seen many cases of very informal (poorly documented, if at all) investments, including casual but sizable co-investments with friends. A family office chief operating officer or chief financial officer can put procedures in place to be sure that all the investments are documented properly. Once that is done, they can also create (or purchase) a back-office system that will provide the family with consolidated financial statements.

---

8   The family offices mentioned later have all given their permission to the descriptions in this chapter, illustrating a generous willingness to share their experiences.

The chief financial officer can also be responsible for the selection and oversight of any external money managers.

3.4 Benefits intended for extended family

Given the high value placed on the closeness of the extended family, it should not be a surprise to find that a family office in the region is likely to include benefits for all family members. Those benefits range from company dividends to making travel arrangements. Most also include committees to plan regular gatherings of the full family, understanding how important it is to pay attention to nurturing those bonds. More examples will be illustrated in the selection below on samples of family office services in the Gulf region.

3.5 Pure investment office or full-service

In some cases what is called a family office operates in practice as a private investment company with the operations limited to investment management. In a few cases the inclusion of additional friends as co-investors makes these offices look somewhat like a traditional multi-family office, but they are not usually that rigorously operated.

One exception, which has been operated (from the beginning) as a professional multi-family (investment) office, is named The Family Office, located in Bahrain. It has been expanding during its 10-year existence, and now has branch investment offices in London, New York and Hong Kong. Its founder, Abdulmohsin Al-Omran, believes that the western model of family offices does not work in the Gulf region. His opinion is that families want to separate the business and investments from their personal service needs. Their office focuses on investments, including offering a number of educational programmes regarding investments, complete with exams. In fact, of their 64 employees, some 35% have been trained internally. Even though the office focuses on investments, Abdulmohsin says he does promote a club atmosphere, and wants the families to have a sense of belonging. They offer a number of client educational events.

3.6 Range of expanded services

In the Gulf region a family office might offer any or all of the following services:
- investment oversight and strategy;
- management of family aircraft and yachts;
- management of family homes, in various countries, and farms;
- hiring and supervising personal staff;
- planning regular family gatherings and off-site weekend retreats;
- coordinating the charity efforts of the family, including *waqfs* (religious endowments);
- building mosques, schools, hospitals, orphanages, and training facilities;
- caring for special assets: horses, cars, art, carpets, jewellery;
- creating a junior board for the next generation;
- creating a family venture fund to encourage family entrepreneurs;
- creating a family council with a family constitution;

- creating a holding company to oversee all of the family assets and businesses;
- encouraging an active board, in the family office and the holding company;
- creating special training programmes in the company for family members;
- testing and overseeing talent in the family;
- including bonding activities, such as ship-building or orienteering, in family gatherings;
- planning family celebrations, highlighting family history;
- creating a family investment committee;
- creating a family dividend distribution committee;
- creating an offshore trust as a safety net for future generations;
- sponsoring family competitions, such as competitive proposals for a sustainable initiative;
- creating a community award for achievement in areas relating to the family business;
- retreats for cousins, or by gender, or even for couples;
- teaching leadership skills, including public speaking and networking;
- having a committee for planning fun at the family retreats;
- hiring an outside team to create a family history book.

4. Examples of Gulf region family offices

This section provides an overview of a number of example family offices in the region. All of the following have agreed to sharing this information.

4.1 The A family

This is one of the largest and best-organised families in Saudi Arabia. The second generation consists of a number of brothers who own and manage a growing and diverse group of international companies. As with several other family businesses in the region, they have had a partial initial public offering but continue to encourage all family members to participate in the management of the business. The company head of human resources has put together a series of training plans for family members, which includes three years of rotating among the various companies. The family has engaged in best practices for family governance, including having a family constitution. Somewhat surprisingly, even this large family-focused group has not had a separate family office, until it was recently decided to create one. The primary goal is to begin to let separate family units separate and manage a portion of the group family wealth, for the smaller family units. They are in the process of considering where to locate the office and how to structure it.

4.2 The Al-Rajhi family office

The group currently exists to manage the wealth of one branch of the well-known Al-Rajhi banking family, and his immediate family.

The head office is located in the Eastern Province in Saudi Arabia, with two other offices in Bahrain and Geneva. Collectively, the three entities represent the private investment company encompassing those interests, both in Saudi Arabia and internationally.

The private investment company has a portfolio of investments, ranging across investment types, from public equity investments to private equity investments and real estate. The company has focused on strategic investments across various sectors, including financial services, real estate, infrastructure, mining, healthcare, telecommunications, utilities, oil and gas and petrochemicals.

In 2004, with the help of a consultant, the family spent two years working on a set of protocols (similar to a constitution), which were signed in 2006. Following that they were translated into Arabic and revised to comply with *Sharia* law and signed again in 2009.

The structure, role and scope of the family council is clearly set out in the family's protocols. The protocols also cover the family owners' vision statement, the overall group's governance structure, the principles on which the family chooses to conduct its businesses and refers to the family members' aspirations and goals in general. In addition, the protocols identify the formation of:

- the family office – for managing the daily family operations;
- the family development committee – for creating a platform for continuous improvement and employment for family members;
- the family charity committee – for governing the family *waqf*;
- the family finance committee – for advising on investment decisions for family members in respect of assets outside of the private investment company; and
- the family advisory committee – for conflict resolution matters.

Following five years of utilising the protocols and upon the request of the partners, the Protocols are again being refined.

The family office was formed in December 2007 to segregate the family from the business. The role of the head of the family office was particularly significant in the implementation of the family protocols.

The family office not only provides personal lifestyle management and concierge services, it is involved in philanthropic services and public relations as well. There is a vast focus on continuing education, training and development. They see it as crucial to train the younger generation and prepare them for the future as the group continues to flourish.

4.3 The Bin-Laden family office

Apart from its notorious terrorist member, the family is a large and successful family with a very good reputation, based in Jeddah. They have a very organised family office, including a detailed family 'university' programme for the next generation, which includes international faculty members.

4.4 The Al-R (FI) family office

The founder/father began as a trader walking across countries with camels to sell various goods. He saved enough to start the first bank in Saudi. He later invested in some large farm lands, which he left to his children under *Sharia* law. A son now heads their family office, and provides investment oversight and budget planning for a number of family members. He has 33 siblings, and the extended family has between 600 and 700 members. He convened a family gathering – 300 attended – and they agreed to form a family council that would act very much like a family office. The family office is named *Nal* (Arabic for receiving something). The family office itself became a closed stock company. The current project is to have a family website.

4.5 The Al-T family office (AI)

This is a unique family office in that it did not develop out of an operating business background. In fact, the founder was a corporate executive who was successful in increasing the wealth of another family group and who also benefited from the oil boom in Saudi Arabia during the 1970s. Successful local and international investments over the years were the nucleus of the wealth for this family. Since the establishment of this office in the 1970s, the founder has successfully handed over the leadership to the second generation and established strong governance. The office is managed by professionals (some of whom are family members) and utilises state of the art services (such as information technology) to report to a family board (which includes 30% independent members) on a detailed and consolidated basis (including personal assets). All of its decisions are scrutinised by an investment committee that has only one family member.

The family is extending its reach and is in the process of setting up a small office in New York to support its investments and to be closer to some of its portfolio managers.

In addition to managing its large and complex international and local portfolio, the office provides full concierge services to the family. Full-time dedicated resources cater to travel, personal and medical needs, among other things, for the family.

The family has committed to investing in the office's people and staff to provide the best services for the family, professionally and personally. A rule is to provide training twice a year to every member of its team, and family members, in relevant areas. The vision is clearly stated on their website:

> *God willing, we will increase the tangible value of our family portfolio of investments and business interests. We will provide for our family's current and future generations and for people associated with our family. We will also care for the wider good of our community and the Kingdom of Saudi Arabia as a whole.'*

4.6 The Al-A family office (Jarir Investment)

This is a very structured family office. The family head of the office says that over the years he has learned a lot from family offices in the United States.

They have two annual meetings. The second generation participates in the second part of each meeting and the girls are also included – all begin participating either after college or when over age 20. Each is given a small amount of money to invest at that time.

The meetings cover general family issues, such as ethics, public behaviour, risks, and how to learn not to depend on the money. The family head shares information about the new ventures (but does not tell them the total financial investments).

Their family office began in the 1990s as an investment office, and grew slowly. Born out of a need to diversify from their retail business, Jarir Investment grew from two people in 1992 to 40 people today. The family head was very influenced by the US lead in family offices, and learned a lot from the Family Office Exchange, based in Chicago, and the Institute for Private Investors, based in New York. He found them to be "extraordinarily helpful". He learned best practices and has incorporated them into his family office. The family office has developed a sustainable wealth management programme investing in the United States, Europe and Asia in different asset classes. The office has been largely investment-focused, but in the last several years it has been adding family services. The family office helps with education and schools, travel and family expenses. It has also created a family constitution.

In terms of supporting the next generation, the office has already funded some family ventures. There are now two girls training in the investment side and five boys are already working in different segments of the family business. The family likes the children to have between three and five years of successful work experience outside the family businesses. They also have a rule that a child cannot work for his or her father. If an uncle wants to hire them that is alright. Five children are now working in the company groups, and they had between three and four years' experience working on the outside. They are valued by how much they participate in the family and the business.

The head of the family office comments:

The key for success will be the next generation. They are clearly the most important. We are lucky in G-1 in that we are five partners, so we are already used to working together and respecting each other.

The family cooperation needs to be part of the DNA.

For the second generation, after they graduate and have a job, each one is given a small amount to invest. The office will help them only if they want the help. It is their decision. About three years later they are given a much larger amount. There might be more at six years. The hope is that they will co-invest in Saudi Arabia, and that they will encourage group thinking and cooperation rather than having selfish attitudes.

The family had a tradition of charity towards others. For 30 years they have been giving to a lot of small villages, especially the small town they came from. They do micro-financing with them, have supported orphanages and charities for the handicapped, and contribute to a lot of sports. They have also funded more than 30 computer clubs. They encourage the next generation to bring requests for funding for charities, and ask them to put in some of their own money.

The head of family office comments:

I see my job in the family to think ahead three to five years all the time, for the last 40 years, and to focus on navigation and visibility. We need to think ahead about who will be retiring, who will be the new leaders, and who might have influence on them. We could say: "the caravan is moving."

He sees that families in Saudi are much closer than most western families seem to be. Even so, he said they are realistic, that the whole family might not be perfect, so if just 70% of each generation is healthy that is terrific. They want to empower the kids and hope they will share together and protect their investments.

The advice he would give to other family offices, is to "develop slowly, and practice how it will work."

4.7 The Al-T-R family office

This family business is another one in the Gulf region that has not only grown into an international conglomerate – it has done so while investing in best practice initiatives. For example, the company's chief internal auditor, who leads their corporate governance and institutionalisation process, has also adopted a trade reporting and compliance code of conduct (against bribery and corruption). The company has also established a corporate social responsibility department based on international best practices and is planning to issue its first sustainability report at the end of 2014, which will be done by a specialised third party. They are also members of the Pearl Initiative as well as the GCC Directors' Organisation.

The founder started the business in 1973, and in 1975 formed the holding company. The company's portfolio consists of holdings in Saudi Arabia and in Egypt (operating companies). They have also institutionalised their private financial investment and real estate activities separately from strategic investments and operating subsidiaries.

In addition, this family has had an advisory office based in London since 1985, which is focused on global asset management in order to diversify its capital allocation away from the Middle East and North Africa region.

4.8 The Al-Muhaidib family office (Khair)

The family businesses began in 1946 and have grown to an international group with more than 10,000 employees.[9]

The extended family has been proactive in the family governance area. As one of the family members commented:

The Family Council serves as a legitimate forum for dialogue concerning the interests of the family. There are committees which work under the guidance of the council to:
- *Formalise communication*
- *Focus on organisational planning*
- *Strategic objectives*
- *Development initiatives*
- *Corporate social responsibility*
- *Philanthropy*
- *Women empowerment and education of its young generation. Right from the beginning, the group has encouraged the next generation of women to become valuable members of business.*[10]

Their family office is named *Khair*, Arabic for good will. At their annual retreat between 80 and 100 family members attend (about an 80% rate). They travel to a

---

9   See www.muhaidib.com.
10   Welcome address at a 2013 Pearl Initiative roundtable: www.pearlinitiative.org/tl_files/pearl/img/
      April%20to%20June%20Images%2013/Session%20Report%20Family%20Firms%20Riyadh.pdf

special location in a group bus, and have planned activities such as ship-building exercises, lessons in public speaking, orienteering and so on. The family council has existed for about five years and focuses on preparing the next generation, family education and a corporate social responsibility foundation. It includes males and females, and all family members of age 16 or older. A special event is the G-3 annual competition of creative proposals for self-sustaining business initiatives – called *Wasareou*, which in Arabic means let's run, let's go fast – where they have awarded winners each year. They have an impressive number of ongoing initiatives, all to engage the entire family, especially the next generation.

5.   Conclusions

The Gulf region has all the elements that lead to creating family offices. These include a healthy economy, a prevalence of family-owned businesses, a culture of very close families, a recognised need to professionalise their global enterprises in part by separating the personal services from the business services, a highly educated generation poised to take over the businesses, and a very strong dedication to preserving the welfare of the entire family.

I expect to see a rapid increase in the number of single family offices in the Gulf region.

Hong Kong

Christian Stewart
Family Legacy Asia (HK) Limited

Unless otherwise noted, the focus of this chapter is on the single family office set up to serve an ethnic Chinese family resident in Hong Kong, or another Asian family that has decided to base its family office in Hong Kong.

1.   Introduction

Asian families can be very private and secretive, inward looking and self-reliant. That makes it extremely difficult to obtain accurate statistics on the number and nature of formal family offices that have been established in Hong Kong.[1] A 2014 report by UBS and Wealth X estimates that there are 82 billionaires living in Hong Kong, and that there are now 190 billionaires in mainland China.[2] The Forbes list "The World's Billionaires" identifies 50 Hong Kong billionaires. Anecdotally, however, there might be no more than 50 formal single family offices in Hong Kong at the most – including family offices set up to serve families from other parts of Asia. In theory these figures suggest we should be seeing many more family offices being formed in Hong Kong. There is certain to be growth in this sector, but on the other side of the coin there will be many Asian families that are not willing to formalise the management of their family affairs through a formal family office or that are happy to maintain blurry boundaries between their family business and their private wealth.[3] Because of these cultural traits, it would be easy to over-estimate the potential for growth in this segment. The majority of Asian family offices are likely to be serving families that are in the first or second generation of wealth ownership. The characteristics of an office will depend on the generation of ownership of wealth. Hong Kong family offices can also be expected to be created and to evolve organically depending on the needs, interests and approach of the owning family.

1.1   Hong Kong's Confucian families

Much of Asian family wealth is still in the hands of the first generation wealth creators or the family patriarchs, though we are now in a time of transition. While not exclusively so, the majority of the billionaires (and other ultra-high net worth families) in Hong Kong are of ethnic Chinese origin. These traditional Asian

---

1   The Hong Kong Special Administrative Region of the People's Republic of China.
2   Reported in "The ultra-rich list: Number of billionaires in China and Hong Kong increasing", *The South China Morning Post*, Thursday September 18 2014.
3   A characteristic of Asian family offices is that there is often still a connection between the founding family and one or more operating businesses that the family control.

patriarchs typically attribute their financial success to their Confucian values and principles, such as frugality, hard work and perseverance, which they would like to pass on to future generations.

A traditional Confucian family will display the following characteristics:

- The family is the basic unit, not the individual; the individual will be called on to subjugate his or her personal interests to the interests of the family;
- Family harmony and togetherness are important values;
- The family will be hierarchical, and respect for elders is required;
- There may be gender differences within the family, with male heirs more likely to be expected to take on business roles and possibly receiving a greater share of the estate on inheritance than female heirs;
- There will be a communication gap between the generations;
- Siblings are not taught how to collaborate together, yet will expect to inherit equally. As such this is not a culture of primogeniture; yet elder siblings require that they be given 'face';
- The educational level of the family is likely to increase with each generation, with many of the third generation family members having received a top class western education. These western-educated family members often experience a values conflict when they come home to Hong Kong again.

As in other cultures, in Chinese there is saying that "family wealth does not survive for three generations". This is something that every patriarch is aware of and would like to overcome; they would like the success of the family to continue and they would like the family to remain together and united. Notwithstanding the equal inheritance rule mentioned above, the patriarch frequently has a vision of family wealth remaining undivided and jointly owned by all of his children, and in turn by the grandchildren.

Sadly there are also many high profile examples in Hong Kong of feuds breaking out among siblings – or between the families of different spouses[4] – once the patriarch has died. Articles in the press[5] also raise questions about how successful succession will be, in large part due to a failure of aging patriarchs to plan for succession or to let go and retire; and whether the personal connections and other "intangible assets"[6] that they possess can be passed on to their successors. The patriarch may contribute to the family feuds and succession failures that follow his death through his unwillingness to engage in formal succession planning and to adopt more formalised governance arrangements and family agreements, by failing to appreciate that the family will change once he is no longer around, and by failing to develop collaborative skills – the ability to share power together – among his children.

---

4   For Chinese families, polygamy was legal in Hong Kong up until 1971.
5   For example see Te-Ping Chen, "Aging Scions Stoke Concerns Over Transition", *The Wall Street Journal*, Friday August 31 2012.
6   In the words of Professor Joseph Fan from the Chinese University of Hong Kong.

1.2 A roadmap for the Hong Kong family office

In order for a family office to be able to help a successful Confucian family to sustain family wealth for at least five generations[7] while preserving family harmony and positive family relationships, that family office should be organised around and guided by the following roadmap:[8]

- First, it should be organised on the basis that family wealth has at least four separate dimensions and comprises family human capital, family intellectual capital, family social capital and family financial capital;
- Secondly, it will need to help improve trust and communication within the family, including by ensuring that the family hold periodic formal family meetings;
- Thirdly, it has to help the family members develop the ability to work together collaboratively and to become effective at joint decision-making together;
- Fourthly, it has to help the family to put in place more formalised family governance arrangements, including processes for dealing with conflicts, and agreements for dealing with the possible exit of a family member;
- Fifthly, it has to help the family address both the quantitative issues of managing family financial capital and the qualitative issues that family members growing up with inherited financial wealth have to deal with.

This chapter will be organised based on this roadmap.

2. Hong Kong as an international finance centre

Hong Kong is a well regulated international finance centre with a strong rule of law and an independent judiciary. In addition to families resident in Hong Kong, it can therefore also be considered as a location for establishing a family office either for ultra-high net worth families from other parts of Asia or for international families looking for a convenient geographical location to give them access to investment opportunities within China or elsewhere in north Asia.

2.1 The Hong Kong Special Administrative Region of China

Since July 1 2007, Hong Kong has been a special administrative region of China and is referred to as the "Hong Kong Special Administrative Region" or the "Hong Kong SAR". The Basic Law of the Hong Kong Special Administrative Region of the People's Republic of China is essentially Hong Kong's own mini-constitution.[9] The most prominent feature of the Basic Law is the underlying principle of "one country, two systems" whereby the socialist system and policies of mainland China shall not be practised in Hong Kong, and the previous capitalist system and way of life is to remain unchanged for 50 years.[10] This is not to say however that the capitalist system

---

7   The goal of beating the "three generation curse" by seeing family wealth in all its forms last for at least five generations is articulated in James E Hughes, Jr, *Family Wealth; Keeping it in the Family* (Bloomberg Press).

8   This roadmap is based on *Family Wealth; Keeping it in the Family*, and other works by Hughes.

9   Department of Justice website; see www.doj.gov.hk/eng/legal/index.html.

10 Department of Justice website.

currently practised in Hong Kong will suddenly disappear on July 1 2047.[11] China's national laws do not apply in Hong Kong except for a number of such laws relating to defence and foreign affairs.[12]

The Basic Law authorises Hong Kong to exercise a high degree of autonomy. Hong Kong enjoys executive, legislative and independent judicial power, including that of final adjudication, in accordance with provisions of the Basic Law. Although foreign affairs relating to Hong Kong are the responsibility of the Central People's Government, Hong Kong is authorised to conduct external affairs on its own in accordance with the Basic Law. Hong Kong has the capacity under the Basic Law to enter into international treaties and agreements.[13]

2.2 Taxation in Hong Kong

The taxation system in Hong Kong is a territorial system and a relatively simple system. It would not be correct to call Hong Kong a tax haven however. On the other hand, the taxation system should not be a deterrent to a non-Hong Kong family choosing to base a family office in Hong Kong. The Inland Revenue Ordinance (Cap 112) imposes a property tax, a salaries tax and a profits tax, and provides that, in general, tax is only imposed on income which has a Hong Kong source. Profits tax is imposed on any person who carries on a trade, profession or business in Hong Kong, and earns profits that arise in Hong Kong or that are derived from Hong Kong. The profits tax only applies to revenue profits and not to capital gains. Revenue profits from dealings in Hong Kong listed stocks will be regarded as having a Hong Kong source. In general the principles for determining the source of profits can be said to be well settled in Hong Kong. There is no tax on dividend income.[14] The current profits tax rate for corporations is 16.5%.

For the purpose of promoting Hong Kong's competitiveness as an international finance centre, there is an exemption for offshore funds from profits tax.[15] Under this exemption a non-resident person is exempt from profits tax in respect of assessable profits derived from specified transactions carried out through or arranged by a specified person. The specified transactions include transactions in securities, futures contracts, foreign exchange contracts, foreign currencies, making certain deposits and in exchange traded commodities. A 'specified person' refers to a broker, dealer or asset manager licensed under the Securities and Futures Ordinance. There are anti-avoidance rules to prevent this exemption from being used by resident investors.

The Basic Law contains articles that guarantee the independence of Hong Kong's taxation system from that of China. Double tax agreements entered into by China are not applicable to Hong Kong, and Hong Kong has the capacity to enter into both double tax agreements and tax information exchange agreements (see below) with

---

11 The future of Hong Kong in 2047 was a theme explored by Professor Anselmo Reyes of the University of Hong Kong in a keynote speech called "Hong Kong 2047" delivered at the STEP Asia Conference in Hong Kong in October 2014.
12 Department of Justice website.
13 Department of Justice website.
14 For an overview of the Hong Kong taxation system see the CCH *Hong Kong Master Tax Guide*.
15 Section 20AC of the Inland Revenue Ordinance, which was introduced by the Revenue (Profits Tax Exemption for Offshore Funds) Ordinance 2006.

other countries. Currently Hong Kong has entered into 27 double taxation agreements with respect to income taxes[16] with foreign countries. In addition, a comprehensive double taxation agreement was entered into between Hong Kong and China in August 2006.[17]

Hong Kong also imposes a stamp duty, which will be relevant in relation to dealings in Hong Kong stock, Hong Kong bearer instruments and Hong Kong immovable property, including leases of immovable property. Stamp duty measures have been introduced that are intended to prevent speculation in Hong Kong residential properties, including a 15% buyers' stamp duty, which applies when property is purchased by any corporation or individual other than a Hong Kong permanent resident, and a special stamp duty.

2.3 Exchange of beneficial ownership information

Hong Kong has entered into an agreement with the United States for the exchange of taxation information on request. This is effective from June 20 2014.[18] Hong Kong has also committed to enter into a model II intergovernmental agreement with the United States to implement the US Foreign Account Tax Compliance Act.

Under the Inland Revenue Ordinance the Inland Revenue Department has the power to collect and to disclose a taxpayer's information in response to requests made by countries with which Hong Kong has negotiated a comprehensive double taxation agreement, even when the information was not otherwise required for domestic tax purposes.

Hong Kong has also committed to adopting the Organisation for Economic Cooperation and Development/G20 common reporting standard for the automatic exchange of tax information, and for first exchanges of information to start to occur by 2018.

2.4 Anti-money laundering regime

Hong Kong is a member of the Financial Action Task Force. Hong Kong has an all crimes anti-money laundering regime. Under Section 25 of the Organised and Serious Crimes Ordinance (Cap 455), a person commits an offence of "dealing with property known or believed to represent proceeds of an indictable offence" if, knowing or having reasonable grounds to believe that any property in whole or in part, directly or indirectly, represents any person's proceeds of an indictable offence, he deals with that property. Indictable offences are more serious criminal offences.[19] Reference to indictable offences include conduct that would constitute an indictable

---

16   Hong Kong has agreements for double taxation relief and the prevention of fiscal evasion with respect to income taxes with Austria, Belgium, Brunei, Canada, the Czech Republic, France, Guernsey, Hungary, Indonesia, Ireland, Japan, Jersey, Kuwait, Liechtenstein, Luxembourg, Malta, Malaysia, Mexico, Netherlands, New Zealand, Portugal, Qatar, Spain, Switzerland, Thailand, the United Kingdom and Vietnam; source: Department of Justice website.
17   Before this there was a limited scope double tax agreement in place since February 1998.
18   Tax Information exchange agreements have also been signed with Denmark, Faroes, Greenland, Iceland, Norway and Sweden, but have not yet taken effect, as of November 2014.
19   Other legislation that is relevant is the Drug Trafficking (Recovery of Proceeds) Ordinance (Cap 405), which applies to drug trafficking, and the United Nations (Anti-Terrorism Measures) Ordinance (Cap 575), which applies to terrorist financing.

offence if it had occurred in Hong Kong. Tax evasion is an indictable offence in Hong Kong.[20] Under Section 25A of the Organised and Serious Crimes Ordinance, any person who knows or suspects that any property represents any other person's proceeds of an indictable offence is required to file a suspicious transactions report, as soon as it is reasonable for him to do so.

With effect from April 1 2012, Hong Kong introduced the Anti-Money Laundering and Counter-Terrorist Financing (Financial Institutions) Ordinance (Cap 615) which is applicable to financial institutions and money remitters and money exchangers.[21] Schedule 2 of this ordinance sets out the customer due diligence requirements that must be complied with by all financial institutions. If a single family office is dealing with any financial institutions in Hong Kong on behalf of the client family then those financial institutions will be required to collect from the family office the customer due diligence information specified by Schedule 2. If the family office itself were to be licensed by the Hong Kong Securities and Futures Commission (SFC) – which would clearly be the case for a multi-family office – then the family office would itself be a financial institution for the purposes of the Anti-Money Laundering Ordinance and would be required to comply with its customer due diligence requirements. If a family office is not licensed by the SFC, the family office and its staff and executives will still be required to comply with the Organised and Serious Crimes Ordinance provisions mentioned above, where applicable.

2.5 Family office regulation in Hong Kong

The SFC is responsible for regulating the securities and futures markets in Hong Kong. The SFC works to ensure orderly securities and futures market operations, to protect investors and to help promote Hong Kong as an international financial centre and a key financial market in China.[22]

The SFC is responsible for the licensing and supervision of intermediaries that engage in regulated activities as defined in the Securities and Futures Ordinance (Cap 571). There are 10 types of regulated activity,[23] which are as follows:

- Type 1: dealing in securities;
- Type 2: dealing in futures contracts;
- Type 3: leveraged foreign exchange trading;
- Type 4: advising on securities;
- Type 5: advising on futures contracts;
- Type 6: advising on corporate finance;
- Type 7: providing automated trading services;
- Type 8: securities margin financing;
- Type 9: asset management; and
- Type 10: providing credit rating services.

---

20   Section 82 of the Inland Revenue Ordinance.
21   The Anti-Money Laundering and Counter-Terrorist Financing (Financial Institutions) Ordinance (Cap 615) was introduced for the purposes of improving Hong Kong's anti-money laundering regime by "better alignment of the financial sector with prevailing international standards".
22   Securities and Futures Commission website; see www.sfc.hk.
23   Schedule 5 to the Securities and Futures Ordinance.

A multi-family office that carries on any of these regulated activities in Hong Kong will clearly be required to be licensed with the SFC for the relevant activities. If a single family office is formed in Hong Kong it will also be necessary to review its planned activities carefully, including whether it will have an in-house investment management team and the relationship between the family office and the investment-owning vehicles of the family, to ensure that the family office is not going to be engaging in any of the 10 regulated activities.

3. Providing support for family governance

If a family office has been created to help preserve family wealth, then it is critical that the family office is providing some form of support for the family governance activities undertaken by the family. The long-term preservation of family wealth, in all of its forms, comes down to whether the family can adopt a successful system for making joint decisions together with respect to their jointly owned family wealth.[24]

Family offices in Hong Kong are often responsible for arranging periodic family meetings and there are even some examples to be found of family offices that could be said to have the primary purpose of providing support for the family governance structures and processes of a family, as opposed to having a focus on investment management. Admittedly, these examples are more the exceptions than the rule.

One way in which the family office can help with family governance is to ensure that the family has spent time in creating its own written family constitution. The concept of having a formal written family constitution is now starting to become accepted among both families with significant financial wealth and business-owning families in Asia. Family constitutions have a number of benefits. One such benefit is simply that it helps to bring all family members on to the same page together. It helps to clarify the different roles that exist within the family enterprise system. A family constitution will normally also address the topic of how conflicts among family members are to be dealt with.[25]

3.1 What is the best family governance model?

When a family develops a family constitution, the question it has to address is what is the best system of governance for the family? What model is going to help preserve family harmony, avoid destructive conflicts, maintain positive family relationships, and otherwise ensure that it continues to be a successful family?

The family governance model that the Asian patriarch often has in his mind is one of leadership based on hierarchy or leadership based on competency, with limited scope for participation in decision-making by other family members, who are treated as outside shareholders. However research into the life cycle of Chinese-owned family firms has found that such family firms tend to fail by the third generation if not before, primarily because the family members at the ownership level cannot make joint decisions together, and secondly because the family member

---

24 *Family Wealth, Keeping it in the Family.*
25 For more information on family constitutions in general, see Barbara R Hauser, *International Family Governance, Avoiding Family Fights & Achieving World Peace* (Mesatop Press).

'outside shareholders' stop supporting the family members who are managing the family firm; the family's emotional commitment to the family enterprise breaks down.[26] When that happens, family members or family branches that are not involved in management roles will be left looking for a way to exit, and if this is not available then frustrations will arise.

The conclusion is that the patriarchal family governance model does not help to sustain the family enterprise beyond the first generation, and it does not help preserve family harmony and positive family relationships and avoid family conflicts. The family governance model for the family has to change[27] in the second generation if the family wants its family enterprise to survive beyond the third generation. From this point of view, the most important task for the Hong Kong family office will be to help ensure that the second generation family members have the ability to work together as collaborative decision-makers, at least with respect to ownership-level decisions.

3.2   The role of family elders[28]

It is very common to see family constitutions that make reference to both a family assembly, which generally refers to an annual meeting of all of the members of the family and a family council, which is a smaller committee with authority to represent the whole family. However, families that are developing their own family constitution should also consider including a committee or council of family elders, who then become the judicial arm of their family governance system.[29]

The idea of incorporating a role for family elders into the family governance system is one that is a good fit with Asian culture. A family elder has to be someone who is deeply trusted by both the older generation and the younger. They have to be a person (or persons) who will act in the best interests of the family as a whole. They need to bring wisdom to the family. Wisdom includes the ability to see the big picture. A family elder should be someone who has the capacity to help bridge the communication gap between generations. Therefore Hong Kong's Confucian families should be looking for their own equivalent of Lao Tzu – the archetypal elder from Taoism – to help guide their family.

Family elders can be given authority in the family constitution to facilitate when there are disputes among family members, or otherwise have responsibility for ensuring compliance with the family's conflict-resolution processes. They can also be given the authority to enforce the terms of the family constitution and any policies that are created in accordance with the constitution.[30]

---

26   Wong Siu Lun, *Family Business Review*, Volume VI, Number 3, Fall 1993.
27   The only exception to this is if a single beneficial owner can consolidate all of the share ownership in the family enterprise; in that event, the sole beneficial owner can run things in a patriarchal manner.
28   For an expanded discussion of the concept of family elders see Christian Stewart, "The Wisdom of Elders", *The STEP Journal*, July 2014, Volume 22, Issue 6.
29   The idea of family elders was first discussed in *Family Wealth: Keeping it in the Family*.
30   *Family Wealth: Keeping it in the Family*.

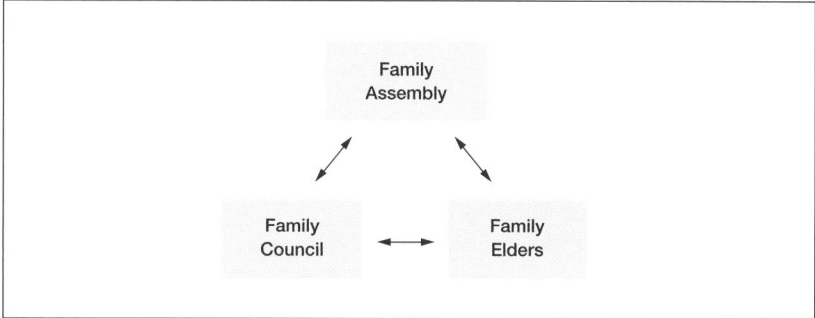

4. Helping to mitigate the impact of family conflicts

High profile family feuds are a common feature in the press in Hong Kong, and they usually break out following the death of the family patriarch or matriarch. There is a Chinese saying: "Parents in Heaven; children in court". The conflicts are typically intra-generational rather than cross-generational.

For Chinese families in Hong Kong, it is fair to conclude that family conflicts are a major risk to family wealth in all its forms.[31] If a family conflict occurs, this is damaging to the reputation of the family and can lead to the destruction of family relationships. If the job of the family office is to help preserve family wealth in all its forms, the family office has to be concerned with the issue of the management of family conflicts.

4.1 Causes of family conflicts

The origins of many of the conflicts that are seen among some of Hong Kong's ultra-high net worth families can be explained either purely in terms of a patriarchal family culture, or in terms of a conflict between the Confucian ideals and values of the older generation and the western values of the rising generation, many of whom have been educated overseas:

- The patriarch will favour setting up family trusts as a vehicle for keeping the family wealth consolidated and for designating one or more successors to have control over the trust structures (not as a trustee, but as a protector or through an investment committee for the trust) and with no easy mechanism for a family member beneficiary to exit if they do not want to be part of the joint family trust structure. If you are a mere discretionary beneficiary, you have no asset that you can sell back to the rest of the family. Therefore, an insistence on keeping the family wealth together when the heirs really cannot collaborate together causes conflicts.
- Having no mechanism to allow a beneficiary or shareholder to exit in return for some fair compensation causes conflicts.
- Family member successors who fail to hold themselves accountable to the wider family stakeholders cause conflicts.
- Lack of a mechanism for participative family governance, such as a family council, causes conflicts.

---

31   Barbara R Hauser comes to this conclusion in the context of international families.

- Conflicts can arise between the oldest sibling, who believes he should be entitled to lead the family based on the family hierarchy, and younger siblings who are more competent.
- Conflicts can also arise because the patriarch has multiple wives or concubines, which was an accepted part of Chinese culture until 1971.

4.2   The role of the family office

What role can the family office play to help prevent, or at least better to manage, family conflicts once the patriarch passes away?

- First, the family office can help by ensuring that all family members have appropriate estate plans in place, and ideally in the case of the patriarch that these estate plans, including the terms of any family trust structures, have been communicated to their family in advance;
- Secondly, the family office can help considerably by ensuring that periodic family meetings are held;
- Thirdly, it can ensure the adoption of exit plans and mechanisms in all of the family trusts and investment-holding entities, including a mechanism for opting out of the services of the family office;
- Fourthly, the family office can help the family by getting family members to agree in advance on the process by which they would seek to manage any conflicts should they arise.[32] This might involve committing to attempting first to resolve conflicts through negotiation, failing which through mediation,[33] using an appropriately qualified professional, failing which by arbitration,[34] and only finally, as a last resort, through litigation.

It should be noted of course that families can be considered to be emotional systems.[35] Conflicts among members of a wealth-owning family are often likely to be emotional, rather than rational, in nature. There will be cases where a family conflict is best resolved by professionals who can work with the family emotional system, and in extreme cases by appropriately qualified family therapists.[36]

It has to be acknowledged that implementing the recommendations set out above is easier said than done. Cultural resistance should be expected. The patriarch will say: "My family will never fight"; and "We don't need things to be so formalised". However, the fact remains that conflicts are a frequent reality for Hong Kong's wealthy families on the passing of the patriarch. It is therefore important for

---

32   See Ian Marsh, "Conflict management and dispute resolution" in the STEP-endorsed publication, *Business Families and Family Businesses* (Globe Law and Business).

33   Hong Kong has a Mediation Ordinance (Cap 620), which came into effect from January 2013, and which provides a regulatory framework for the conduct of mediation. The objectives of the ordinance are to promote and facilitate the resolution of disputes through mediation and to protect the confidential nature of mediation communications.

34   The Arbitration Ordinance (Cap 609) was also revised with effect from June 2011 with the intention of aligning Hong Kong's arbitration regime more closely to international practice, to make the law of arbitration more user-friendly to arbitration users both in and outside Hong Kong and to promote Hong Kong as a regional centre for dispute resolution.

35   See for example, in the context of business-owning families, David Bork, *Family Business, Risky Business: How to Make it Work*.

36   Kenneth Kaye, *The Dynamics of Family Business, Building Trust and Resolving Conflict*.

senior family office executives – and the family advisers – to be patient and culturally sensitive on the one hand, yet at the same time to keep gently pushing for greater transparency, accountability, planning and more formalised governance.

5. Managing family human capital

Many Asian patriarchs attribute their financial success to their Confucian values of hard work, persistence, frugality and keeping a low profile. They establish family offices with a focus on the quantitative issues of creating, protecting and preserving financial capital. Yet they fear that their grandchildren may not leave productive lives; that the family financial capital will create family members who feel entitled, who do not know how to work and who have lost the values that brought success to the family. In short, they actually fear that the family's financial success will lead to a failure of their family human capital.

While, today, most Hong Kong family offices are focused on quantitative issues, they are very quickly going to have to help the families that they serve address the challenging questions of how do you promote both individual and family flourishing in a family of great wealth, while on the other hand avoiding, or at least alleviating, negative family dynamics and the dark side of inherited wealth.

This will require Asian family offices to start to pay attention to qualitative issues, in addition to the quantitative issues they are already focused on. When thinking about the individual family members (the family human capital) the kind of qualitative issues to be taken into consideration include whether individual family members know themselves: know what their personal dreams are, know what work they are called to, whether they can successfully individuate and separate themselves from the shadow of the family wealth, whether they are mature or are maturing, whether they can successfully navigate the transitions in the adult life cycle, and whether they are free or whether they are suffering from an addiction.[37]

Hughes recommends that five specific issues should be addressed for each family member in order to help them fully participate in their family's joint decision-making system:[38]

- First, they need to know how, as individuals, they learn and take in information;
- Secondly, they need to know what is their own unique calling in life;
- Thirdly, they need to know their individual work style; how they prefer to work in a group;
- Fourthly, they need to know their own personality type;
- Fifthly, each family member must be taught the skills of having difficult conversations.[39]

---

37 See James E Hughes Jr, Susan E Massenzio and Keith Whitaker, *The Voice of the Rising Generation, Family Wealth and Wisdom* (Bloomberg Press).

38 The first four of these recommended steps are expanded on in the "Tools & Pathfinders" section of James E Hughes Jr, *Family; the Compact among Generations* (Bloomberg Press).

39 See Douglas Stone, Bruce Patton, and Sheila Heen, *Difficult Conversations, How to discuss what matters most* (Penguin).

If individual and family flourishing requires families to have access to qualitative advice, the question that follows from this is: what would be the best way to institutionalise the use of qualitative advisers by a family?[40] One approach is for the family office to retain advisers with expertise in qualitative issues. If the family has a private trust company, the board of that company can include a director with qualitative expertise, or a family committee or mentoring committee can be created within the company.[41] Access to qualitative advice can also be institutionalised through the family governance system by creating a family advisory board or a family "brains trust[42] of different kinds of family advisers. Great families need advisers who can help the inheritors find their own voice, and who can help them to integrate the inherited financial wealth into their lives.[43]

6. Managing family intellectual capital

The intellectual capital of a family is another critical topic for a family that wishes to continue its success across generations. It includes the knowledge level and understanding of individual family members, as well as the family as a whole, as to how to be effective owners of the family financial wealth.

In practice, family offices in Asia tend to start off with a focus on preserving family financial capital. They may be organised with an investment committee. The natural next step is for the family office to start to assist the family members with the family's charity and philanthropy. There might be a family philanthropy committee. But what role can the family office play in relation to family intellectual capital? Just like there will be an investment committee and a philanthropy committee, the starting point could be the creation of a family education committee.

The first task for the education committee will be the development of an education curriculum. Topics the education curriculum might cover could include:

- how a family can have shared family values while leaving room for each family member to have his or her own individual values;
- education on the family governance system;
- how to be an effective owner of the family's financial wealth (an essential topic);
- trusts, or more specifically the trustee-beneficiary relationship (another key topic); how can you possibly have a good relationship if the parties involved do not know the roles the relationship is based on?[44]
- ensuring that family members are developing the skills to be effective joint decision-makers (a further critical element of the curriculum).[45]

---

40 For a more detailed exploration of this topic, see Christian Stewart, "The role of trusts, trustees and protectors in supporting family flourishing", *Offshore Investment Magazine*, Issue 246, May 2014.
41 Lee Hausner.
42 See Lee Hausner and Douglas K Freeman, *The Legacy Family: The Definitive Guide to Creating a Successful Multigenerational Family* (Palgrave).
43 See *The Voice of the Rising Generation, Family Wealth and Wisdom.*
44 A useful text for this purpose is Trustworthy, New Angles on Trusts from Beneficiaries and Trustees by Hartley Goldstone and Kathy Wiseman. Trustworthy is filled with stories of successful trustee beneficiary relationships.
45 See the five steps recommended by Hughes listed under the topic of "Managing family human capital", above.

```
┌─────────────────────────────────────────────────────────────────┐
│                                                                   │
│         Family Assembly                            ┐              │
│                                                    ▼              │
│      Education and Development Committee        ┐                 │
│                                                 ▼                 │
│         Family Education Curriculum          ┐                    │
│                                              ▼                    │
│         Family Office provides support                            │
│                                                                   │
└─────────────────────────────────────────────────────────────────┘
```

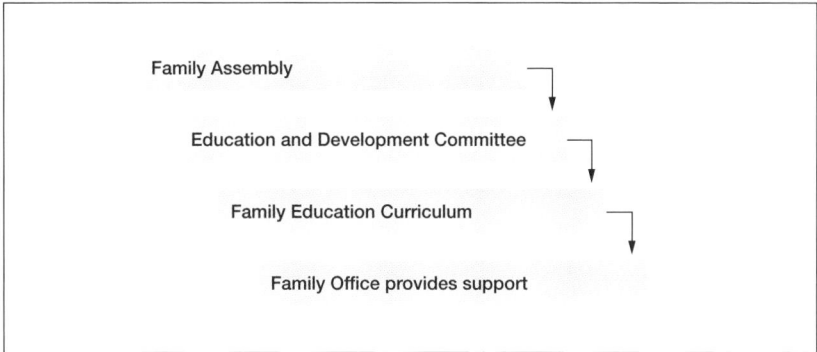

7. Managing family social capital

The Hong Kong family office will usually play a supporting role in helping to preserve or to enhance family social capital. An important component of social capital will be the charitable and/or philanthropic activities of either individual family members or of the family as a whole.

Under Hong Kong law, the term 'charity' currently follows the English common law meaning, as summarised by Lord Macnaghten in the 1891 case of *Income Tax Special Purposes Commissioners v Pemsel*.[46] In that case Lord Macnaghten listed four principal divisions of charitable purposes:

- trusts for the relief of poverty;
- trusts for the advancement of education;
- trusts for the advancement of religion; and
- trusts for other purposes beneficial to the community not falling under any of the preceding heads.

The Law Reform Commission of Hong Kong issued a report on charities in December 2013 which included a recommendation that a clear statutory definition of what constitutes a charitable purpose should be introduced in Hong Kong. Reform of Hong Kong's law on charities can therefore be expected at some point within the next several years.

It is common to see ultra-high net worth families and individuals in Hong Kong establish either a charitable trust or their own charitable foundation, that is to say a company limited by guarantee incorporated in Hong Kong for charitable purposes. A less established family office might be very involved in supporting the charitable activities of the family – in this case there are blurry boundaries between the family office and the family foundation – while a more established family office, one where there are more distinct boundaries between the family office and the family foundation, can still be expected to provide at least some degree of administrative support for the charitable activities of the family.

The charitable giving of families in Hong Kong is not driven by local taxation considerations. Rather, the common drivers for charitable giving in Hong Kong tend

---

46   [1891] AC 531.

to include pure altruism, Confucian values and a desire to preserve or enhance the family reputation or legacy. However an issue to consider will be whether to register the charitable foundation or trust under Section 88 of the Inland Revenue Ordinance.

The Law Reform Commission's report on charities considered whether Hong Kong should establish a charity commission as a sole regulatory body for charities. The Law Reform Commission concluded in its December 2013 report that a charity commission should not be set up "at this stage", but it should be a "long-term goal" for the administration to set up either a charity commission or a centralised regulatory authority.

It is not uncommon to find that a family will form its own charitable foundation, which will be housed in the same physical office as the family office but, certainly in the case of a more established family office, it is likely there will be a Chinese wall in place between the staff and management of the family office and those of the foundation. The foundation might be run by its own managing director who is not an executive in the family office.

The family office will likely be used to provide at least administrative support for the foundation, such as support with accounting, company secretarial, investment management and banking matters. However, where the foundation has its own staff and management, the family office would likely not be involved in setting the strategy, policies or processes for the foundation, nor would the family office be involved in due diligence on grantees, grant making or the ongoing review of foundation activities.

8. Managing family trust structures

In Hong Kong, the family office is not usually going to be the owner of the investments, rather it is a company providing services. It is common to see family trust structures set up as the ownership vehicle. Therefore the family office role will typically include having to coordinate with the trustee as well as with the family's external professional advisers if it is necessary to consider amendments or changes to the terms of the trusts.

The trustee of the family trusts is likely to be either an external professional corporate trustee or alternatively a private trustee company (PTC). One issue for a family office and its advisors to work through will be whether to set up a PTC structure for the family, or whether to continue to rely on the use of external professional corporate trustees.

8.1 External professional trustees

If the trustee is an external corporate trustee, the family office is likely to have its own staff or executives who will coordinate with the trustee. If the settlor and the beneficiaries are Hong Kong residents, then the trust deed might be drafted so that the trustee retains discretion over distributions of income or capital to beneficiaries (ie, it is a discretionary trust) but that investment decisions for the assets owned by the trust's investment-holding companies are to be made at the direction of the settlor, or of some form of investment committee constituted pursuant to the terms of the trust deed. In this case the family office will help to coordinate any distribution requests that are made to the trustee from time to time, making sure that the trustee has sufficient information and explanations to exercise an independent discretion. When it comes to investment matters, it can be expected that some degree of authority over investment accounts will be delegated to executives from the family office.

Where the trust is set up with an external corporate trustee, there is just as much chance that the trustee will be based in a reputable offshore trust jurisdiction, as that it will be located in Hong Kong (though it is very common for bank-affiliated international trustees to have trust relationship managers, but not trust administrators, based in Hong Kong). Whether the trustee is Hong Kong based or not, there is also a very good chance that the proper law of the trust will be the law of a foreign jurisdiction.

Hong Kong has incorporated the terms of the Hague Convention on the Law Applicable to Trusts and on their Recognition through its Recognition of Trusts Ordinance (Cap 76), which in general terms means that the selection of a foreign proper law for a trust established by a Hong Kong settlor during his life will be respected.

However, it is expected that there will now be an increased interest in the use of Hong Kong proper law trusts with the coming into effect of the Trust Law (Amendment) Ordinance 2013 as from December 1 2013. There are a number of interesting features introduced as a result of this 2013 amendment, including the abolition in Hong Kong of the rule against perpetuities and (except with respect to charitable trusts) the rule against excessive accumulations.[47]

8.2 The PTC structure

It is relatively common to see a family that has its own family office establish one or more PTCs. In practical terms, because of the Recognition of Trusts Ordinance, there is an option either to proceed with establishing a PTC in one of the traditional offshore finance centres, or to incorporate a company in Hong Kong for the purpose of allowing it to act as trustee of one or more trusts. When taking the offshore option, this typically involves the possibility of setting up a foreign law non-charitable purpose trust to own the foreign-incorporated PTC.

As part of the consultation process leading up to the Trust Law (Amendment) Ordinance 2013, it was considered whether Hong Kong should introduce into the Hong Kong Trustee Ordinance provisions allowing for the creation of non-charitable purposes trusts, which would then allow the creation of a vehicle that could be used to hold the shares in a PTC or otherwise to create orphan companies, but these proposals were rejected. Therefore, because Hong Kong trust law does not allow for the creation of a non-charitable purpose trust, in practice if a Hong Kong company is to be used as a PTC, it will either be incorporated as a company limited by shares (in which case the question of who can own the shares has to be dealt with) or more likely, as a company limited by guarantee.

---

47   For a full review of the Trust Law (Amendment) Ordinance 2013, see William Ahern, "Hong Kong's New Trust Law", *Trust Quarterly Review*, December 2013 (Society of Trust and Estate Practitioners).

There is currently no overarching regulator in Hong Kong for the provision of trustee services, nor are there currently any studies being conducted into the topic of trustee regulation as at this time.[48] Therefore, a Hong Kong company can be set up to act as a PTC without the need for it to have a trustee licence.

Where a Hong Kong PTC is used, again because of the Recognition of Trusts Ordinance, the PTC could be administering either Hong Kong law trusts, or it could be administering trusts with a foreign proper law.

In practice one might expect to see some overlap between the family office executives and the members of the board of directors of the PTC. However, it is also going to be very important to help ensure the integrity of the trusts administered by the PTC that the directors of the PTC have either ongoing access to trust law advice or at least one member of the board has trust industry expertise. With an in-house administered PTC, great care has to be taken to ensure that there is a clear boundary between the directors of the PTC and the family office executives. In short, the directors of the PTC have to have the capacity to say "no" to the family members and also to the family office executives. While the family office can help to provide administrative, accounting and secretarial support services to the PTC, it is always critical to remember that the PTC and the family office are separate and independent entities, both legally and in terms of control. There have to be clear boundaries between the family office and the PTC.

9.   Managing the family financial capital

As has been mentioned, the majority of Hong Kong's family offices have a focus on helping to preserve – if not actually to grow – family financial capital. Most likely the family office will be organised with an investment committee that has an oversight and approval role, and the office itself may well include its own specialised investment management team. The investments overseen by family offices in Hong Kong can be diverse in terms of asset classes as well as geographically.

The following statistics, taken from a study into the regional differences in structures and strategies of family offices by Robert Eigenheer,[49] are helpful in giving a snapshot of how Asian family offices tend to deal with investment management. Of the Asian respondents to the survey:

- the top reasons for using a family office were consolidated reporting, risk-monitoring/management and accounting services;
- 75% handled strategic asset allocation decisions in-house;
- 92% handled cash flow/liquidity management in-house;
- 67% handled risk management in-house;
- 67% handled traditional investment management in-house;

---

48   The Hong Kong Trustee's Association commissioned a report into the Hong Kong trust industry which was carried out by KPMG; see "Hong Kong Trust Industry: A cross sector perspective" June 2013. The argument was laid out in this report that Hong Kong based trustees essentially have their hands full at the moment in dealing with an avalanche of external regulatory changes, and would not be able to cope properly with having to deal with the introduction of local regulation at this time.

49   Robert Eigenheer, "New Data on Global Differences in Family Offices", *World Economics*, Volume 15, Number 1, January – March 2014. There were 61 respondents to this study of which 12 were from Asia, and nine of those were from Singapore. The study included both single and multi-family offices.

- 50% handled alternative investment management in-house;
- 37% reported investment performance to their clients on a weekly basis, and 37% reported to clients on a monthly basis;
- relationships with private banks and with brokers were rated more important by Asian respondents than those from all other regions;
- the report notes that "Asian family offices deliver both traditional and alternative investment management, more often in-house than their peers in the other regions".

10.   Looking at the roadmap

Returning again to the roadmap that has been the framework for this chapter, the key questions regarding the family financial capital will be how to make use of that financial capital to invest in the family human, intellectual and social capital, and how to ensure that family members have access to qualitative advisers who can help them to individuate and integrate the family financial wealth into their own lives.[50] Family members do not have to be taught how to manage family financial capital, but they do have to be taught how to be effective owners and stewards of that financial capital, which includes the ability to make effective joint decisions together at the ownership level.[51]

---

50   See *The Voice of the Rising Generation* (cited above) and James E Hughes Jr, Susan E Massenzio and Keith Whitaker, *The Cycle of the Gift, Family Wealth and Wisdom* (Bloomberg Press).
51   Hughes.

India

Aditya Gadge
Association of International Wealth Management of India

India is changing, and at what a pace! From being a socialist country where personal wealth was looked down upon to an era where Indians are celebrating their new-found riches, the country has indeed come a long way.

Economic growth, a liberal working environment, decisive and stable governance and exciting new opportunities have unleashed the entrepreneurial energies in the Indian economic system, resulting in the soaring fortunes of Indian high net worth families and an increasing number of first-generation dollar millionaires.

Despite old problems like lack of infrastructure, a tough tax regime and a lack of business-friendly policies and labour laws, the Indian market is too attractive to ignore. India's ultra-high net worth households have grown in number to 117,000 in 2013 from an estimated 109,000 in 2012-13. An ultra-high net worth household according to this report is one with a minimum of Rs 250 million ($4 Million) as net worth.[1]

With wealth exploding and the economy transforming from scarcity to prosperity, there is a huge demand for estate planning, wealth protection, taxation advisory services and more. As wealth managers look for ways successfully to engage with this customer segment, one concept beginning to gain currency among the rich is that of family offices. Family offices straddle the space between pure investment advice offered by financial institutions and the personal and family needs of high net worth individuals. A family office is a firm that takes care of the day-to-day administration and management of the funds of a super-wealthy family.

While the first family offices can be traced to Europe, it was in the early 19th century that wealthy families in America started taking professional help in handling their family wealth. The demand for family offices has been increasing constantly since then.

In general a family office accumulates and focuses resources to facilitate a common interest in asset protection, cost control, financial education, family philanthropy and a host of other needs.

Every family office is different and is customised to the needs of the family it is serving. Some are focused exclusively on managing the family's investments, or on its concierge and travel needs. Others provide professional support to the family, such as assisting with governance, financial reporting, project management and trustee and corporate services, and become the family's trusted advisers over time.

---

1   Kotak Wealth Management, *Top of the Pyramid Report 2014.*

1.   Why family offices?

Family as a collective unit is the bedrock on which the Indian society is built. Indian businesses are mostly owned and managed jointly across different generations by families, who have always functioned through a maze of cross-holdings to ensure that the wealth is kept within the family. Approximately 70% of all listed companies in India are family-owned. Prominent Indian communities in business are the Marwaris, Chettiars, Parsis, Gujratis, Muslim Khojas and Memons.

However, as is true around the world, Indian business families have been finding it difficult to keep their legacy together beyond the third generation.

With the younger generations going their own ways and the older ones becoming dated in their working approach, many Indian business families have been worried that their family-run businesses will not be able to cope in an increasingly competitive landscape. This raises a lot of questions regarding the survival of family wealth and social standing.

Unlike in the west, a lot of Indian families still retain operational control of the business empires they have built. This is another problem area, as not all members in a family may have similar capabilities or the inclination to run the business. India has had a long history of feuds in business families over family wealth, thanks to a number of factors like lack of succession planning, lack of capability and compatibility among new generations when it comes to running family businesses, or sheer lack of will or inability to separate out the professional management of an enterprise from an emotional attachment towards it.

Indian business families have been facing the following major concerns:

- Most family businesses do not survive beyond the third generation;
- Later generations born into prosperity suffer from a sense of entitlement;
- Members of the next generation who are inducted as managers (mostly at senior levels) are not aware of the nuances of the business that the older generation has built from scratch;
- Future exigencies are left to chance: there are no agreed criteria for future decision-making on family and business issues;
- There is often a lack of understanding of proper asset allocation and of long-term planning;
- There is often a lack of clear succession planning: an example is the case of Priyamvada Birla and how her entire estate of Rs 50,000 million was bequeathed to her chartered accountant, RS Lodha, an outsider to the illustrious Birla family;
- There is often a lack of clear division in business roles and responsibilities: the Ambani family dispute is testimony to this, where the absence of a clear succession plan for the business led to the conglomerate getting divided into two parts;
- Daughters are usually excluded from any succession plan;
- There is no blueprint for a family constitution;
- The judicial and legal framework are not conducive to speedy resolutions;
- The lack of uniform laws makes it difficult to manage geographically diverse assets; and
- Financing growth and retaining control of the business can be problematic.

A family office could just be the solution to these problems.

A family office is a personal operating set-up that can provide a single point of contact who deals with various matters on behalf of the Indian family. This is of particular benefit to families who are of high net worth and wish to have an efficient mechanism for dealing with all their personal and financial matters.

2. What is a family office?

Family offices are product-neutral unlike private banks, which may have conflicts of interest while managing the funds of private clients, in terms of pushing their own products. Family office service providers include private banks, lawyers, trust companies, tax firms, concierge service providers, alternative investment providers and private wealth management firms.

The biggest advantages of a family office are that it provides peace of mind and the concentration of efforts. So instead of a client dealing with different advisers for different services like investments, tax planning and succession planning, a family office combines all the functions in one place.

The first official family office was started by John D Rockefeller in 1882. It functioned both as a business office and an investment office, handling his personal investment and philanthropic work. Over a period of time, the family office also started handling the family wealth. In later years, the family office was carved out as a separate entity to handle the financial, legal and investment functions of the Rockefeller clan.

2.1 Functions of a family office

Family offices in India generally provide a combination of legal structures for protecting wealth from personal and legal risks:

- private wealth management;
- combination of various legal structures aimed at protecting family wealth from personal and legal risks;
- investing in alternate asset classes;
- international investments;
- creation of efficient succession structures and estate planning;
- inter-generational transfer of wealth;
- setting up and managing private family trusts and other holding structures;
- drafting and executing wills;
- family communication, involving setting up of family governance structures and a family constitution;
- consolidated reporting, monitoring of investments and accounting;
- administrative, legal and tax assistance, both domestic and cross-border;
- philanthropy advice;
- value added services, such as property management, concierge services and so on.

2.2 Benefits of a family office

The main benefits of a family office for the wealthy family are that it:

- provides a central source for information on, advice about, or oversight of, all of the family's financial matters (ie, it provides integrated financial services);
- creates pooled purchasing power across a family group, resulting in better service for a better price than individual family members could attain on their own;
- offers a dedicated team of professionals who are focused on client goals in a completely confidential manner;
- ensures continuity from generation to generation;
- provides access to professional advisers who can educate family members about their responsibilities of ownership and participative governance;
- facilitates management of substantial liquid assets generated through the sale of a business;
- sources customised credit;
- manages multi-generational needs, especially educating children and grandchildren to be responsible stewards of wealth;
- serves beneficiaries with diverse requirements and interests; and
- provides access to alternative investments, such as private equity, hedge funds and real estate.

2.3 Types of family office

(a) Single family office

Single family offices usually manage the affairs of a single family. Prominent single family offices in India include those of the Ambani family, Azim Premji, NR Narayan Nurthy, the Burmans, the Patni family, the TVS group, the Wadias, the Tatas and the Shapporji Pallonji group.

A single family office should have a net worth in excess of $250 million to make it cost-effective.

The key advantages of a single family office are:
- It is dedicated to and completely aligned with the objectives of a single family; and
- It can operate with a high degree of transparency and confidentiality.

The main disadvantages are:
- Recruiting, maintaining and retaining of quality professionals is a challenge;
- There is no scope to spread costs, and it will lack pricing power; and
- Managing the family office requires the time of family members, and it may suffer from lack of expertise.

Single family offices in India, although they differ in their investment preferences, mostly have two things in common: they are not in it for the short term, and they ring-fence deals to ensure proper exit routes. The average total investment being managed by a single family office in India is around $325 million, with some of the bigger ones like Premji Invest managing close to $1,600 million.[2] The average holding period for an investment is around 60 months.

(b) *Multi-family office*

Multi-family offices manage the wealth of multiple families. These are usually closely-held, boutique firms servicing the needs of high net worth clients. The net worth required of a client ranges from $25 million upwards.

The key advantages of a multi-family office are:

- They offer independent advice without any conflicts of interest, unlike private banks;
- They ensure the rationalisation of costs;
- A number of professionals with expertise in diverse areas are available;
- They have better reporting systems and risk management practices in place;
- The ability to pool investments from different clients means they can get better prices.

The main disadvantages are:

- They cannot provide bespoke services for individual families;
- Staff turnover could have an adverse impact;
- There may be transparency and confidentiality issues.

Prominent multi-family offices in India include Altamount Capital Management, Avendus PE Investment Advisors, Centrum Wealth Management, Client Associates, Karvy, Kotak Mahindra Bank, Metis Capital Management, Quant Capital and Waterfield Advisors.

International banks like Credit Suisse, HSBC and Standard Chartered Bank have also set up family office services to cater to the growing Indian market.

3.   The family office market in India

Unlike in the United States and Europe, much of India's wealth has been created in the last few decades. India has had a unique set of problems and opportunities during this time, and it is against this backdrop that the family office has started assuming a critical role in family businesses. The concept is relatively new in India, with only about 30 single family offices operating currently.[3] With the number of first-generation billionaires steadily increasing, the family office is gaining tremendous popularity. However, very few families have yet separated the management of their personal wealth from their business and set up a single family office.

The new complexities call for better regulation, as well as the need for family offices to be managed by people with strong professional capabilities.

Family offices are new to the Indian market, but the concept is catching on with the well-to-do very fast. The concept of the family office is, though, not fully understood by Indian families, but things will only get better as these clients get experience of best global practices.

Established firms that are already present on the Indian market are Kotak

---

2   *Business Today*, March 16 2014.
3   Based on research by the Association of International Wealth Management of India.

Mahindra Bank, DSP Merrill lynch, BNP Paribas, but market upswing has also given rise to boutique firms taking a share of the market, including firms such as Altamount Capital Management, Avendus PE Investment Advisors, Waterfield Advisors, Centrum Wealth Management, Quant Capital and Client Associates. Companies were originally targeting the high net worth individuals (those with investable assets of more than Rs50 million or $1 million), but the focus is now shifting towards ultra-high net worth individuals or families (those with investable assets of more than Rs450million or $10 million).

Globally, the minimum qualifying amount of investable assets is commonly suggested to be around $50 million to $100 million, but it varies from country to country and company to company. In India, various companies have their own qualifying amount for providing services. Client Associates have set it to minimum of Rs100 million ($1.6 milion) for their services, while Kotak Mahindra Bank and international firms DSP Merrill lynch and Barclays have a minimum amount of Rs1,000 million ($16 million).[4]

In addition to these multi-family offices, many of the top business families, like the Ambani family, the Shapoorji Pallonji group, the Wadia family, the Burman family, Azim Premji and NR Narayan Murthy, have set up single family offices or venture funds to manage their wealth.

So, although the market for family offices in India is still young, it is growing, with 100 multi-family offices expected in the country by 2017.[5]

India's ultra-rich, with increased global exposure and dynamic business needs, are now demanding specialised advice on business continuity, succession planning and philanthropy.

India's wealthy have traditionally been reluctant to share information on family wealth. This is leading many well-known Indian families to open their own family offices rather than going to private banks for wealth management services. India's rich are hands-on when it comes to managing their wealth and like to have full control over their investment decisions, which is another reason they prefer family offices over private banks.

Traditionally, Indian business families invested their personal wealth in their own businesses or in low-risk asset classes such as government bonds, fixed deposits, realty and even gold. Over the years there has been a marked shift in their investment preferences towards private equity and venture capital investments, which may be a bit risky but promise excellent returns. One reason for this shift is that the business families are worried about tying their family's long-term financial future to a single company in a single industry. They are increasingly investing in private equity deals, public stocks and venture capital.

The India family office space holds huge potential. Only around 20% of the high net worth market has been penetrated, according to MarketsandMarkets.[6] Further, it

---

4   Family Office Summit India 2013 conference.
5   Family Office Summit India 2014 conference, organised by the Association of International Wealth Management of India.
6   www.marketsandmarkets.com/Market-Reports/indian-wealth-341.html.
7   *Ibid*.

estimates that $128 billion of inter-generational wealth transfer will take place in India in the coming decade.[7]

4.   Setting up a family office in India

"I have a family office", "We offer family office services" – statements like these have of late become very fashionable in India, both with wealthy families' wealth advisers. But it is crucial for families first to understand whether they need a family office in the first place, and for the advisers to decide on whether they would like to be engaged in offering family office services.

Research says that most wealthy families lose their wealth by the third generation. So the most important reason families should consider setting up a family office is when they are looking beyond the current generation.

Such families need to give thought to what wealth means to them, what kind of wealth they want to leave, and what kind of legacy they want to leave. Inter-generational transfers of wealth in this case need not only mean financial wealth, but also all that goes along with it: social capital, human capital, family values and so on. In short, a mechanism to ensure that generation after generation are involved in the same thought process.

The concept of a family office in an unstructured form has existed for a long time in India. The concept of a structured family office is relatively new and is often confused with investment advisory services. Another problem is that like the term 'wealth management', 'family office' as a term has been used very loosely in India.

Family offices in India are not recognised as a distinct legal concept. They may operate as a separate entity or a group entity in any one of the following forms:

- private company, enjoying the status and tax benefits of a separate legal entity;
- Hindu undivided family – the term 'Hindu undivided family' is not defined under the Income Tax Act. It is defined under the Hindu Law as a family that consists of all persons lineally descended from a common ancestor, including wives and unmarried daughters. It has tax benefits for a joint family;
- private trust – there are many types of trusts used by family offices, and many purposes underlying their creation;
- limited liability partnership (LLP) – a corporate business vehicle that enables professional expertise and entrepreneurial initiative to combine and operate in a flexible, innovative and efficient manner, providing benefits of limited liability while allowing its members the flexibility for organising their internal structure as a partnership

Traditionally wealthy Indians families have been reluctant to share information on their family wealth with outsiders, leading many well-known families to avoid signing up with multi-family offices. But things are gradually changing, with an increasing number of wealthy clients outsourcing their financial, tax and accounting practices and succession planning to an outside agency.

The extraordinary growth in wealth of Indian business families, thanks to the exponential growth in the market capitalisation of their companies, has created a need for wealth management companies, professional trust companies, chartered accountants and lawyers specialising in estate and succession planning, family constitutions, family councils and the like. A family office perfectly covers all these services and has therefore emerged as a new-found favourite route.

Family offices in India have been investing in start-ups as well as listed companies. Sectors like technology, real estate, e-commerce, health care, education and financial services have been the preferred choices. India's high net worth investors are increasingly adopting the high-risk-high-return model as far as their investments are concerned.

The need for a family office is usually felt when:

- the family's liquid assets grow to such a size that professional management is required beyond what can be provided by current family business professionals;
- the family's business is sold, creating liquidity that needs to be managed; or
- the family has attempted to manage their personal financial affairs, but the business has suffered due to the time they have to spend in doing so.

Motivations for setting up a family office include:

- creating a family governance structure, thereby reducing internal disputes and smoothing wealth transfers between generations;
- professionalising the families' asset management activities;
- a younger generation's increased preference for formalised family office solutions;
- the prestige of the creation of a family office structure as it indicates a certain level of family wealth.

Monetisation of wealth has just started in India, and the needs of Indian families differ from their European counterparts. Indian families have of late started branching out after selling their ancestral businesses. A case in point is the Patni family. After selling off the controlling stake in Patni computers to iGate and flush with funds, Amit and Arihant Patni have set up a family office and are now investing in a diversified portfolio of companies. Many prominent business families like the Ambanis, Burmans, Jindals, Wadias, Godrej, Tatas, and Birlas have seen their wealth grow geometrically over the last few decades, thanks to a favourable business environment, strong governance and exemplary leadership.

Indian family offices face the following challenges:

- Indian business families do not like to pay for financial advice;
- the trade-off between an advisory role and a discretionary role;
- capital account restrictions means investments are predominantly spread within the country;
- more focus on wealth generation than preservation;
- motives are different in the absence of inheritance tax (India does not have an inheritance tax);
- cultural issues, as children have a natural sense of entitlement to wealth;
- families are still more trading-oriented, and are more tactical than strategic;

- A lot of business families still do not consider daughters in their succession plan.

There are certain must-haves for Indian family offices:
- professional expertise – family offices must hire top-notch professionals for different functions, including investments, taxes, law, succession planning and so on;
- discretion – the family office must engage highly discreet professionals who maintain client confidentiality;
- comprehensive services – family offices should ensure that they fulfil all the needs of their client families;
- trust – family office professionals will have to win the clients' trust before they are trusted with money.

5. Conclusion

Although the exact number of single family offices operating in India is not available, it clearly depends on how one defines it. Irrespective of that, it is beyond doubt that the interest among prominent Indian business families in setting up a family office is only bound to increase. One of the major factors generating this interest will be the need for better governance. As families become wealthier, and become more global, they will need efficient advice on estate planning, tax, legal matters, financial planning, succession planning and accessing capital markets.

It is an exceptional time for Indian business houses as they have found an able support in a stable and business-friendly government. The current government is expected to push the economy into a higher orbit by junking restrictive trade practices, archaic tax and corporate laws and prejudices. Business families now have the platform to help themselves grow globally, and setting up a family office just might be the right start to get the house in order.

Israel

Ori Ephraim
O Ephraim Multi Family Office Services
Lyat Eyal
Aronson, Ronkin-Noor, Eyal Law Firm
Alon Kaplan
Alon Kaplan Law Firm

1. Introduction

Israel is a democratic state founded 66 years ago with a Jewish population of approximately 600,000 and an economy based primarily on agriculture. Today, the population is about 8.37 million, 7.1 million of which are Jewish. During its 66 years of existence, the state has experienced three massive waves of immigration: at the start of the 1950s, during the 1970s and the 1990s. Each such immigration wave significantly increased the number of inhabitants.

Historically, the two powers that ruled over the land during the pre-state period prior to 1948, the Turks and the British, each left their mark on its legal system, based today on Anglo-American traditions. The State of Israel, via the Knesset (the Israeli Parliament), has since enacted independent legislation thereby creating the modern state's legal system as a common law jurisdiction. The highest judicial body is the Supreme Court, with 12 permanent members of the bench. It is responsible, among other functions, for interpreting the legislation passed by the parliament. While Israel does not have a formal written constitution, thirteen 'Basic Laws' effectively function as one.

While Israel is generally a secular state, there are areas in which religion imposes its influence. Israel has religious courts and judges, such as Jewish rabbinical courts, Muslim Shar'ia courts, and Druze tribal councils. However, in civil matters these religious institutions generally have the legal status of voluntary arbitrators. An important area in which the secular and religious courts overlap is that of marriage and divorce.

The significant legislation[1] relevant for this chapter includes the Trust Law 1979, the Law of Agency, the Succession Law 1956, the Tax Ordinance, Banking Law 1981, the taxation of trusts legislation of 2005 and the Law Regulating Investment Advisers, Investment Marketing and Portfolio Management 1995. A number of relevant governmental agencies include the Tax Authority, the Anti-Money Laundering Authority, the Israel Securities Authority, the Inheritance Registrar and the family courts.

1.1 The economic environment

Since its establishment, Israel has become a developed western country, with a well-

---

[1]   There is extensive legislation pending that, if passed, is likely to change much of the existing legislation. The information contained in this chapter may not be relied upon without independent professional advice.

developed economy, an advanced industrial sector and many high level high-tech industries when compared with other developed nations.

With respect to expenditure on education (7.3% of GDP), research and development (R&D) (4.2% of GDP) and defence (6.5% of GDP), compulsory conscription is in force in Israel and the majority of young people are conscripted into the military where they are exposed to technological systems, given responsibility that in civilian life is reserved for older people and, in essence, enjoy an informal education and develop mental maturity.

A significant portion of the defence expenditure is for military R&D needs and a portion of the military's investment in R&D constitutes the foundation for civilian R&D. This investment is both direct, through military industries, and indirect, in the form of young people who, after their military service, use the technological knowledge they gained during their military service to develop civilian technologies.

These factors result in over 100 Israeli companies operating in the fields of IT systems, algorithmic trade, firewall systems, cyber systems, optical systems, space and medicine, and traded in Israel and the United States. Israel holds the second place, after Canada, in the number of companies publicly traded in the United States. In addition, the Israeli biomedical industry has expanded tremendously, more so than the chemical and drugs industries, which receive government support.

In 2013, Bloomberg examined more than 200 countries and sovereign regions to determine their innovation quotient.[2] The final number was narrowed down to 96, and it then published a top 50. Innovation was measured by seven factors, including R&D intensity, productivity, high-tech density, researcher concentration, manufacturing capability, education levels and patent activity. Israel ranked first in R&D intensity, and seventh in high-tech density and in tertiary efficiency.

As a result, over the past 15 years, a broad range of professionals have developed in advanced technological industries and the associated areas of finance and law, and have become high net worth individuals. It is expected that the size of this population segment will expand in the coming years.

Israel is a young economy. The majority of businesses are still owned by the first generation, with only a few third generation businesses (primarily in traditional industries). The biomedical and hi-tech industries are developing industries and so, based on various indexes, Israel is defined as a developing nation. It exhibits, in practice, the characteristics of a developing nation when it comes to wealthy families and the expansion of this population segment.

1.2   Statistics: high net worth families

There are no formal statistics available regarding the number of high net worth individuals in Israel. A number of unofficial bodies have collected and published certain data upon which the information below is based.

According to Merrill Lynch's 2010 annual report,[3] a millionaire is defined as a person with more than $1 million in liquid assets. A multi-millionaire (or ultra-high

---

2   Bloomberg Rankings, "50 Most Innovative Countries, Innovation Index Revealed" (February 1, 2013).
3   TheMarker.com, June 22 2011.

net worth individual) is defined as one with over $30 million. In 2010 there were 10,153 millionaires in Israel, including 99 ultra-high net worth individuals.

According to the Wealth-X and UBS *World Ultra Wealth Report 2014*, the number and wealth of Israel's ultra-high net worth individuals grew in 2014 by about 7%, a rate higher than the global average. The number of ultra-high net worth individuals in Israel in 2014 was 385 (compared to 360 in 2013) and their total capital was $75 billion. The report mentions that more than 13% of these individuals have earned fortunes in the healthcare sector, and Israel is also a hotspot for technology, with 9% of its population involved in this sector. This report notes that only the United States has a larger share of its ultra-high net worth population in the technology industry. This suggests that there is scope for much greater wealth creation in Israel. 56% of the ultra-high net worth individuals have self-made fortunes, 30% got their wealth through a combination of inheritance and their own efforts, and just 14% of the ultra-high net worth individuals owe their wealth solely to inheritance, suggesting that a legacy of hard work is very much present in Israel.

According to a number of bank sources, it is estimated that there are more than 20,000 families with in excess of $1 million, and 500 to 1,000 with capital in excess of $50 million.

According to information recently published,[4] there are approximately 500 people with capital in excess of $50 million, and their total capital amounts to $110 billion, which includes 74 billionaire families.

In our estimation, there are, at least, an additional 250 families with capital in excess of $50 million who made their fortunes primarily from hi-tech, internet and healthcare industries. Additionally, there are at least 3,000 families with capital of between $10 million and $50 million.

It is safe to assume, in light of the scope of activity in hi-tech markets and innovation, that the number of high net worth individuals can be expected to grow at a faster rate than that expected in developing markets.

2. The family office

2.1 General background
Family office services in Israel are relatively new, having been available for only the past 15 years, with the exception of traditional single family offices. During the past five years, primarily since the start of the financial crisis in 2008, the family office market in Israel has grown, mainly due to clients' understanding that the field of financial investments is complex, together with the worldwide loss of confidence in the traditional banking system. Today, there are approximately 30 single and multi-family offices.

2.2 Macro-economic background
Until the start of the 1990s, the Israeli industrial sector was closed to activities abroad due to foreign currency and capital restrictions and the need of the government to

4   TheMarker.com, June 2014.

attract the public's money for its own benefit. From the start of the 1990s, the restrictions on the foreign currency market were removed, first for the banking and business sectors and later for investment funds. In 1998, foreign residents were allowed to invest in Israel and Israeli residents were allowed to hold foreign currency accounts in Israel and overseas, and restrictions regarding the amount of foreign currency permitted to be transferred abroad were gradually relaxed.

It was only in 1998 that Israeli households were allowed to make financial investments abroad and to invest in real estate abroad. At the start of the 2000s, the Israeli shekel became a tradable currency, and restrictions on long-term pension investments by financial institutions were gradually removed. In addition, as mentioned above, the development of hi-tech industries resulted in the creation of a new and large group of high net worth individuals.

The removal of restrictions on the export of foreign currency from Israel and the ability easily to execute foreign currency transfers through banks, along with globalisation, signified the start of the development of the family office market.

2.3   Development of family offices in Israel

As a result of the factors outlined above, the private banking arms of the world's leading banks identified the potential in Israel and set up Israeli desks, with the first banks beginning to establish offices in Israel from the late 1990s onwards. Over the years since, the scope of their activities has increased tremendously. The development of the family office market in Israel followed the establishment of Israeli desks within the banking sector.

There are a number of reasons for the development of a family office:

- the client's need for professional guidance relating to the bigger picture, such as finances, investments, consultation regarding asset allocation, tax issues, inter-generational planning, and assistance in the management and monitoring of the client's assets;
- the client's need for consultation and advice regarding investments, particularly international investments, which, in itself, is a complex area;
- the need to manage many assets including financial assets, real estate assets and other non-liquid assets;
- the complexity of the world of investments in the third millennium;
- the majority of financial investments being made through banks in general and foreign banks in particular. Banks suggest various types of investments, in different currencies, some of which are complex and difficult for the client to understand. Clients prefer to work with a number of banks and, as a result, each bank sees only part of the client's assets. The role of the family office is to oversee the client's complete investment portfolio and synchronise the various elements;
- banks' ceasing to be a neutral adviser with a view to the client's best interests, and instead becoming purveyors of products and financial services. The result is that the burden of investment decisions has fallen on the client. This has generated the need for a professional intermediary between the client and the private banking relationship manager;

- the complexity of domestic and international tax anti-money laundering laws, which has led to requirements for filing many reports with the authorities.

2.4 Professional background of family offices

The professional background of the majority of those active in the family office market is as set out below:

- former bankers who have worked as relationship managers in the private banking departments of international banks, or in institutional investment bodies in a variety of positions such as investment or risk management;
- traders who have worked in bank trading rooms in Israel or abroad;
- chief financial officers of public companies;
- certified public accountants and lawyers who have changed from their traditional professional areas to that of family office services;
- accountancy firms in which the main activities are in the traditional areas of the profession, such as auditing, and who began to assist their clients in the area of investments eventually leading to the establishment of family office departments; and
- law firms dealing with private client law, including trusts, inheritance matters, wills or individual taxation that have expanded their areas of interest to family office services.

The family office market can be divided into two main categories:
- the single family office; and
- the multi-family office.

2.5 The single family office

(a) The traditional single family office

Traditional companies that have developed over many years of activity will have financial managers or company accountants who have been working with the company owners for many years. They may also provide, alongside their regular activities for the family-owned companies, private financial services for the owner's family. They are the owner's business confidants and there is a long-lasting familiarity and relationship of trust. The financial advisers provide family members with a great deal of assistance in the family's financial activities, both business and private.

At present, there are many business owners working in this manner. In some cases, the company has become a public company, requiring the separation of the company's management and private financial management. As a result, some financial advisers began focusing on private activities and, in essence, created a single family office: an office for the management of the family's financial activities.

Many wealthy families, usually those with a fortune of hundreds of millions of dollars, have set up single family offices to provide services directly to and solely for one family. Needless to say, the structures are different from family to family, but usually include a person with financial or legal expertise who co-ordinates the family's financial activities, occasionally with the assistance of investment or real estate advisers. This person can also act as a co-ordinator between external service providers such as lawyers, accountants and others. In a limited number of cases, a number of professionals specialising in different fields may provide services to the family in a manner which is reminiscent of a company board.

(b) The single family office as a business

There are wealthy families who manage their family fortunes who have converted the wealth management office into a business venture providing investment management services for other wealthy families.

To the best of our knowledge, there are no families whose source of wealth is in Israel working in this fashion. But there are those who, over decades, have accumulated wealth abroad and transferred part of their activities, and even occasionally their place of residence, to Israel who own a financial or fund management company. This family office co-ordinates the family's activities and is used as a source of income for that family and as a hub for the identification of investment opportunities for the family (real estate, investments in private companies, and so on), while at the same time providing investment management services for other investors.

2.6 The multi-family office

The multi-family office market is one that began to develop about 15 years ago, and has gained momentum over the past five years.

Multi-family office clients are, primarily, families with assets of between $10 million and $150 million. Each family has different needs, which results in the wide range of different services provided by the multi-family office. Some families are interested solely in advisory or managerial services, while others seek wider services resembling those provided by chief financial officers of large corporations, such as consultation in all investment areas, co-operation with various professional advisers, reporting and accounts (including making the necessary filings to the authorities) and monitoring.

In Israel, there is no clear definition of 'family office', as the term is not a legal one. In fact, there are many who use the term as a marketing tool to attract clients. As a result, there is a wide range of service providers who define themselves as family offices and a number of models exist:

- portfolio managers who define themselves as a multi-family office;
- manager selection services;
- investment managers;
- family chief financial officer services;
- multi-family offices operating within the broader framework of financial management and marketing.

(a) Portfolio manager/investment manager

Portfolio managers and investment advisers are legal concepts. Both require a licence issued by the Israel Securities and Exchange Commission[5] to practise. Many portfolio management firms also manage investment funds in the Israeli market.

Over the past few years, portfolio management firms managing investment portfolios of between tens of thousands and millions of dollars per client have advertised themselves as family offices. These bodies manage, for the most part, a portion of each family's financial assets, and therefore their understanding and exposure to the client's assets is limited.

Some large portfolio management firms in Israel managing portfolios of millions of dollars who also manage mutual funds of billions of dollars have established family office departments which are, in effect, premium departments for their clients.

(b)   *Manager selection*
A number of companies operate in Israel as manager selection service providers. Manager selection service providers advise the client, once they have understood their needs and preferred risk avenues, as to the manner in which to distribute their assets between the various investment types; in other words advising on asset allocation, including currency allocation. Once this determination is made, (and it is updated periodically) the manager selection service manages the client's assets by placing them with portfolio managers, some at Israeli banks but primarily abroad, through recognised international banking institutions. The manager selection service allocates the available funds among the managers based on the relative advantages of each investment opportunity according to global investment areas determined by the asset allocation. This judgement is based on an evaluation of their past performance and experience with the bank's investment managers. The arrangement may be set up so that investments are made according to agreed risk definitions and in agreed types of investments at the manager's discretion, or in such a manner that the manager has to be given approval in principle for each investment type by the manager selection service. Often, the manager selection service instructs the banks as to specific investments.

The manager selection service collects and consolidates investment figures and results over a period of time and gives them to the client in the form of a consolidated report. Part of the reporting and the control mechanism includes supervision of asset allocation and risk evaluation as assessed for all the managed financial assets. In addition to consultation regarding financial investments, some of the manager selection services provide advice regarding real estate investments and locate supplementary consultants for issues such as intergenerational planning.

The majority of clients of manager selection services are high net worth individuals. Nonetheless, in many instances, the manager selection service may also manage some of the funds held by financial institutions or investment funds.

The majority of manager selection services operate within areas requiring

---

5   The law defines those areas in which portfolio management or investment management services can be provided without a licence. One example is that of a client who is defined as an 'eligible' client: for details see the Regulation of Investment Advising, Investment Marketing and Investment Portfolio Management Law 1995, discussed in section 5.3 below.

professional and independent consultation. They are generally compensated by their clients, although in certain circumstances they are also rewarded by banks or fund managers.

Manager selection service providers operate from their offices and it is customary to meet with clients periodically.

(c) **Investment managers**

In Israel, those primarily involved in multi-family offices are investment managers.

Investment managers either manage or advise high net worth individuals with regard to the majority of assets destined for investment. The investment manager is usually the client's trusted confidant and one who is familiar with the scope of assets intended for investment. The investment manager advises the client, after gaining an understanding of his needs and risk preferences, as to how to distribute his assets between various types of investment opportunities: in other words, advice on asset allocation, together with currency allocation.

Once this determination is made (and it is updated periodically), the role of the investment manager is to manage the client's assets as an investment manager or adviser to the client in relation to investments, while regularly analysing the client's portfolio and evaluating available investment opportunities. On occasion, some of the financial assets are transferred to the management of an external portfolio manager or private bank while the investment manager monitors performance. The investment manager coordinates communications between the bank and the client through the private bank's customer relations manager, and benefits from the advice and investment ideas provided by the bank. In addition to liquid investments, the investment manager examines various investment opportunities in areas including real estate, private equity, start-up companies and so on..

The investment manager consolidates investment and results data for a time period as determined with the client, formulating a consolidated report. Part of the reporting and control mechanism includes supervision of asset allocation and risk evaluation as regards all the managed financial assets. The main difference between the investment manager and the manager selection is that the former independently manages the majority or all of the clients' investments, or advises the clients and executes their decisions regarding investments.

In some cases, the investment manager recommends external consultants; mainly in relation to intergenerational planning, trusts, wills or management of the family's future activities. The majority of investment managers operate from their offices within practice areas that require professional and independent consultation, while they are compensated by the clients.

(d) **Family chief financial officer services**

Family chief financial officer services operate in a similar fashion to single family offices. Their activities include either managing or advising high net worth individuals with regard to all assets destined for investment as with investment managers and manager selection services. They also act as the coordinator between the client's accountants and lawyers, and assist in the consolidation of thinking and ideas relating to tax planning, both in general and specifically while using consultants in the fields of bookkeeping and the preparation of draft financial reports for tax purposes and for informing the client. They are also involved in the client's various legal agreements both in business and private matters, and are involved in the majority of the client's financial issues including private companies. Issues relating to intergenerational planning, taxation, wills or trusts are dealt with by experts in the relevant fields. Additional issues can include dealing with reports that family members with dual citizenship (for example, Israeli and US citizenship) are required to submit, such as foreign bank and financial accounts reports and annual tax returns. Thus, the activities of the family chief financial officer resemble those of a company's chief financial officer.

Usually, and as opposed to the other types of service provider discussed, the family chief financial officer is located in, and works at least part of the time from, the family's offices and not just from their own office. This allows for continuous communication with the client.

(e) *Multi-family offices as part of wider financial management and marketing activities*
There are a number of organisations in Israel operating in a wider financial area: investment management, portfolio management, the sale of financial products to private and institutional clients, fund management, hedge fund management, complex financial products or derivatives. In addition to their main activities, these bodies may also provide family office services to interested clients.

(f) *Remuneration*
There are a number of compensation methods in Israel:

- a proportion (normally between 0.15% and 0.4%) of the managed assets. This may, in limited circumstances, include success payments should the return be greater than the originally agreed percentage;
- commissions from banks, fund managers or portfolio managers (should be approved by the client), when the family office operates as a manager selection services; and
- a monthly retainer, derived from the scope of the assets and other services provided. This is acceptable primarily where the service provided is that of a family chief financial officer.

3.   **Banks**

Most of the commercial banking activity in Israel is concentrated in two large and three medium sized banks. Israeli banks successfully survived the most recent financial crisis, and at no stage was their stability in question.

A large scandal in the banking industry in the 1980s resulted in the establishment of a number of governmental commissions and in various legislative changes, changes to the industry and the formulation of operating procedures. The main result for the purposes of this chapter is the separation of the management of the bank from the management of investment funds, pension funds and portfolio management. Today, the banks only provide advice, and do not manage funds.

3.1 Private banking

There are no independent private banking institutions as in North America and Europe. Private banking activities are managed as a unit of commercial banks. In each of the five major Israeli banks, specialised departments serve high net worth individuals with a minimum deposit of between $1 million and $2 million. Some of the banks have a single, central unit operating in Israel, while others have a number of centres spread around the country. Over the years, bank trading rooms have been upgraded and have achieved excellent trading levels in world share markets, interest-bearing bonds, options, currencies and commodities, as well as in the field of product pricing. Working hours are very convenient, and cover the close of trading in Asian markets, and all trading hours in Europe and the United States.

Private banking in Israel has developed tremendously since 2000 due to the removal of prohibitions on foreign currency transfers and exposure of the capital markets to foreign investment. However, as mentioned above, banks may only provide advice relating to securities, with restrictions regarding foreign funds.

Departments providing advisory services in relation to international markets, as opposed to local markets, have limited manpower and resources for analysis and limited experience in international markets. The benefit lies in the objective advice they provide. At the same time, the level of advice and the potential scope of investments covered by Israeli banks are relatively low. As a result, most high net worth individuals bank with foreign institutions.

Israeli banks charge competitive commission rates in comparison to the accepted standards of foreign banks. As a result, foreign banks have reduced their securities trading commissions, which are now closer to those of Israeli banks.

Bankers in Israel contend that, due to global governmental activities to prevent money laundering and tax evasion, the 'secrecy premium' charged by some of the international banks for investment management was removed. As a result, it is expected that prices in Israel will continue to fall and, on the other hand, that Israeli banks will be forced to invest in and improve their investment advisory departments abroad.

3.2 International private banking

In the late 1990s, the private banking departments of the world's leading banks identified the potential in Israel and established Israeli desks. Over the years, this activity has increased significantly, and due to the rise in the number of high net worth individuals most of the world's leading banks active in this area have established an Israeli desk with some even opening a branch in Israel. Foreign banks view Israel as having great potential for a number of reasons, including the tendency of many Israelis to expend a significant proportion of their liquid assets on foreign investments. Israeli clients are characterised as having a more international outlook than is common in the world as a whole due to several factors: the active approach of Israeli clients, the restricted size of the Israeli economy, the geopolitical risk, the desire to reduce existing risks in the banking system and the desire to spread liquid assets between a number of banks.

Israeli clients seek a high level of professionalism and aim to find it in these banks.

International banks understand that there is a need to forge a long-term connection with their clients and the importance of intergenerational money transfers. Therefore, in addition to advisory service departments, the banks hold conferences and seminars specifically aimed at the next generation. Topics include investments, market risks, models for family behaviour and intergenerational asset transfers.

3.3 Additional needs of high net worth Individuals and associated services

The problems facing high net worth Israeli families are similar to those around the world. These include planning for the family's future, involvement of the next generation in the management and preservation of wealth, relationships between generations and family alienation from the third and fourth generations onwards. These are all studied and addressed in Europe and the United States, where professional and academic literature, methodologies and a wide-ranging industry of service providers is available.

Professionals claim that Israeli clients exhibit a number of unique characteristics resulting from the infancy of the state and the economy. Below are a few such characteristics:

- Most high net worth individuals are members of first and second wealthy generations, and are characterised by their enterprise and being more involved in increasing capital than in its preservation and transfer to future generations;
- Israel is a small country (both geographically and culturally). Families are large and members maintain close relationships. Meetings are exceptionally informal and a planned, formal meeting is a concept foreign to the Israeli experience;
- Formality and governance are less relevant. Therefore, concepts such as the family council or family representatives are less familiar to Israelis;
- Awareness of the need to use some of the associated services is low and in its infancy. It is reasonable to assume that within a few years, awareness of associated services will increase;
- Israelis, especially the founding generation, have a tendency to think that, as they are those who created the wealth, they will also know how to preserve it and to pass it on to future generations. Therefore, they feel that they do not require professional assistance;
- The speed of change in Israel is fast. However, Israelis are exposed to what is happening in the western world, and it can be expected that they will adopt a major portion of these western influences, including family and multi-generational behavioural patterns.

4. Succession planning

Inheritance matters are governed by the Succession Law 1965, which applies to individuals who were residents of Israel or owned assets in Israel at the time of their death. The fundamental principle guiding this legislation is to confer upon legally competent persons the right to bequest assets as they deem appropriate, based on a written document, a last will and testament, in accordance with legal formalities imposed by the Succession Law. An individual's freedom of testament is further evidenced by the lack of forced heirship laws, and even further expressed by the tax laws, which do not impose inheritance, estate or gift taxes.

Notwithstanding this guiding principle, the Succession Law grants certain rights to a surviving spouse, children (under 18 years old) and other dependants of the deceased, with a limited degree of protection where these dependants relied on the deceased for support during his lifetime.

Individuals residing in one jurisdiction owning assets in others should plan accordingly, and should sign separate wills in each jurisdiction in which they own assets, to govern the distribution of those assets upon their demise.

Israel does not recognise foreign probate court orders, and a petition for a court order must be filed with the competent authority in order to distribute estate assets located in Israel regardless of the jurisdiction in which the deceased resided prior to his death or to probate processes abroad.

4.1   Trusts

(a)   The Trust Law
The Trust Law 1979 governs the area of trusts. This law defines a trust as the duty imposed on a party to hold or to otherwise deal with assets under its control for the benefit of another or for some other purpose.

A trust is constituted under the Trust Law in circumstances where:
- assets are held by a trustee;
- there is a clear purpose, whether for an individual's benefit or for the attainment of certain goals;
- a trustee, who is empowered to deal with the assets is committed to act for the attainment of the goal of the trust.

A trust may be created either by contract or by deed.

A trust created by contract requires an agreement between the settlor and the trustee with no specific procedure necessary for its validity. Trusts created by deed must be in writing and signed in the presence of a notary public. A trust that is to be effective upon the settlor's death must comply with the formal requirements under the Succession Law for the signing of wills. These include signing in the presence of a notary public.

(b)   Underlying companies
Legislation on the taxation of trusts enacted the concept of an underlying company. In Israel this is viewed as a significant advantage, especially in light of global changes as well as by contrast to previous legislation relating to Israeli companies.

An underlying company is a company established by a trustee of a trust (or a foundation), in Israel or abroad, for the purpose of holding and administering the trust assets for the trustee. As the trust is not a separate legal entity in common law jurisdictions, unlike a foundation, assets may not be registered in the name of the trust. An underlying company is a separate legal entity, transparent for tax purposes, that holds the trust's assets for the trustee.

5.   Wealth Planning

5.1   General

The Regulation of Investment Advising, Investment Marketing and Investment Portfolio Management Law 1995 ('the Advising Law') was enacted following conclusions issued by two governmental committees. The purpose of the Advising Law is to regulate the investment advising market, portfolio management and investment marketing, which was unregulated until the enactment of this legislation.

5.2   The Advising Law: principles

The Advising Law is designed, as is globally accepted, to protect customers by regulating the relationship between the professional and the customer, including imposing ethical rules and obligations as to reporting to the customer, determining the licensing process and requiring professional training, as well as imposing a governmental monitoring system operated by the Israel Security Authority and the Israeli Anti-Money Laundering Authority.

The Advising Law requires a licence in order to conduct portfolio management, investment advising or investment marketing.

The Advising Law defines the fiduciary duty and duty of care of an investment adviser, investment marketing agent and a portfolio manager. These duties include, among other things, the requirement to adjust the services provided to the client's needs, the obligation for a written agreement, the requirement of adequate disclosure, prevention of any conflicts of interest, prohibition of preferential treatment, prohibition of financial incentives, obligations as to special risks, a duty of confidentiality, a duty of care and obligations regarding record-keeping and reporting.

5.3   Occupations that do not require a licence

Notwithstanding the above, the Advising Law defines limited circumstances where a licence is not required. A number of examples where no licence is required are listed below:

- only five clients – investment advising or investment portfolio management for no more than five clients during the course of a calendar year, by an individual who does not engage in investment advising or investment portfolio management in the framework of a licensed corporation or a banking corporation;
- family member – investment advising or investment portfolio management for a family member;
- accountant, lawyer, tax adviser – investment advising or investment portfolio management by a certified public accountant, attorney or tax adviser, when such activities accompany a service provided to a client within the field of their respective professions;

- investment advising, investment marketing or investment portfolio management for a qualified client (professional investor) – a 'qualified client' is defined in the First Schedule to the Advising Law, and includes:
- a joint investment fund, fund manager, management company or provident fund as defined in the Provident Funds Control Law, an insurer, a banking corporation, a licensee, a stock exchange member, an underwriter, most corporations with equity exceeding IS50 million (approximately $13 million); or
- an individual satisfying the following criteria (two of the three):
- the total value of the cash, deposits, financial assets and securities owned by the individual exceeds IS12 million(approximately $3.2 million);
- the individual has expertise and skills in the capital market field, or has been employed for at least one year in a professional position that requires capital market expertise;
- the individual has executed at least 30 transactions, on average, in each quarter during the preceding four quarters; for this purpose, the term 'transaction' does not include a transaction executed by a portfolio manager for an individual who has entered into a portfolio management agreement with him; or
- a corporation that is wholly owned by investors who are among those listed above, or a corporation incorporated outside Israel the activity of which has characteristics similar to those of a corporation listed above; or
- an individual who has consented in writing in advance.

This exception allows an unlicensed company to manage portfolios or to provide investment advice. Recently, the banks in Israel have requested that clients sign as qualified clients to facilitate the advice process.

As a result, qualified private clients are actually treated as institutional clients, which allows them to make investments that are defined as suitable for institutional clients, including participation in private issuances and participation in the institutional phase of public issuances, allowing them to purchase securities under better conditions.

5.4 Investment advising, investment marketing and investment portfolio management by a foreign service provider

The Advising Law went one step further, and permits foreign investment advisers, investment marketing and investment portfolio management professionals to offer services to Israeli clients, even without a licence, under certain conditions and subject to provisions set out in the Advising Law. There is a procedure for amending the law to allow marketing of foreign mutual funds to Israeli investors. The law is expected to be updated during 2015.

The logic of this provision is to improve the quality of the services and the know-how available to Israelis, by allowing them access to the top international investment houses.

The Law of Agency 1965 governs the legal relationship of principal and agent and may apply to agreements by which an asset manager, a portfolio manager or a person in charge of the management of assets provide services to clients.

6.   Tax

6.1   The Israeli tax system
This section outlines the Israeli tax system in general for the benefit of professionals such as family offices, tax advisers, attorneys and accountants, or of high net worth individuals. It refers specifically to Israeli residents or to those who have activities in Israel.

It should be made clear that Israel, like many other countries, is in a process of revising its tax laws and its anti-money laundering laws. The objective is to close tax loopholes that exist in the law and to expand the tax base. In this section we summarise the existing tax regime, but it is recommended to obtain updated professional advice prior to taking any action.

From 2003 on, the tax system has been revised to be a global, worldwide system. This amendment to the tax system results in Israeli residents being subject to tax on their worldwide income, and foreign residents being subject to tax on certain Israeli source income. Nonetheless, Israel encourages foreign investments, and grants tax benefits and exemptions to foreign residents. These include exemptions from capital gains taxes on part of interest payments or on the sale of shares of Israeli corporations.

6.2   Sources of Income
The Tax Ordinance differentiates between income and capital gains. This differentiation is very important as the tax rates and the loss deduction rates differ as set out below.

(a)   Personal income tax
The individual income tax rate is progressive, with a maximum marginal rate of 48% of the taxable income (capital gains are not included) over IS501,960 (approximately $130,000). However, some sources of income (dividends, interest and rent) carry a lower tax rate of between 15% and 30%, subject to some conditions and the source of the income. From 2013, individual rates include an additional 2% tax on taxable income of an amount over IS 800,000 (approximately $210,000).

(b)   Corporate taxes
The current corporate tax rate for Israeli companies is 26.5% for taxable income, including capital gains, interest income and dividend income that stems from income produced or accrued abroad as well as from dividends that originated abroad.

Income from a distribution of profits or from dividends that stem from income produced or accrued in Israel, received from another body of persons that is subject to corporate taxes, is not included.

Corporate taxes at the rate of 25% are imposed on the taxable income of a body of persons from dividends that stem from income produced or accrued abroad.

(c) Capital gains tax

As mentioned above, Israeli residents are subject to tax on a worldwide basis and foreign residents may be subject to capital gains from Israeli sources. The tax rates are calculated in shekels (the local currency) regardless of the currency of the transaction.

An individual is subject to tax on capital gains (including securities) at a rate not greater than 25%. Capital gains from the sale of securities of a body of persons, where the seller is an individual who was a substantive shareholder during the 12-month period prior to the sale, is at the rate of 30%. The Tax Ordinance defines a 'substantive shareholder' as a person who, directly or indirectly, holds at least 10% of the means of control of a body of persons. In addition, capital gains from the sale of debentures, commercial securities, state loans and loans that are not index-linked, are taxed at a rate of no more than 15%, or 20% in respect of a substantive shareholder.

A body of persons (corporation) is subject to corporate tax on capital gains at a rate of 26.5%.

(d) Real Estate Taxation Law

The taxation of capital gains from the sale of real estate in Israel is governed by the Real Estate Taxation Law, which follows the same general principles and tax rate.

Generally, individuals are entitled to an exemption from capital gains taxes with respect to the sale of one residential property (with a value of no more than IS4.5 million). Nonetheless, purchase taxes are applicable to purchasers.

Non-residents are subject to capital gains taxes on the sale of real property and to purchase taxes applicable to the purchase of real property in Israel.

(e) VAT

Israel imposes VAT (currently 18%) on business income and services provided in Israel.

6.3 Taxation of trusts

Legislation on the taxation of trusts legislation, which came into effect as of January 2006, was passed following the major revision to the Israeli tax system in 2003 from territorial taxation to worldwide personal taxation. The taxation of trusts legislation was revised again in 2013, with effect mainly as of January 1 2014.

The legislation distinguishes five types of trusts:

- A 'foreign resident trust' is a trust settled by a non-resident for the benefit of non-resident beneficiaries. This trust is subject to reporting and tax obligations in Israel only to the extent it receives Israeli source income.
- An 'Israeli resident beneficiary trust' is a trust established by a non-resident of Israel where at least one of the beneficiaries of the trust is a resident of Israel.

Two additional criteria must be met for the trust to be classified as an Israeli resident beneficiary trust. First, the settlor and beneficiaries must be immediate family members (ie, the settlor is a spouse, parent, grandparent, child or grandchild of the beneficiary), in which case it is known as a family trust. Alternatively, a broader family relationship (ie, siblings, nieces, nephews, aunts, uncles) will permit classification of the trust as an Israeli resident beneficiary trust upon the submission of evidence to the assessment officer of the Tax Authority that the trust was settled in good faith and the beneficiary did not provide consideration for the settlement in his favour. Secondly, the settlor must still be alive.

If either of these additional criteria is not met, the trust is to be classified as an Israeli resident trust (see below).

An Israeli resident beneficiary trust or family trust is subject to tax as follows:

- Distributions to beneficiaries will be taxed at the rate of 30% of the distribution amount unless the trustee provides evidence that the distribution consists of separate portions of income and of principal. Where the distribution is comprised solely of principal and no income, it is not taxable.
- The trustee may opt, under certain circumstances, to subject trust income allocated to an Israeli resident beneficiary to tax at the rate of 25% in the tax year in which the income is produced. This option requires the preparation of balance sheets, annual reporting and annual tax payments on realised gains. Once all of these requirements are met, the distributions to the beneficiary are not taxable. This route, once chosen by the trustee is irreversible.
- An 'Israeli resident trust' is a trust established by a resident of Israel for the benefit of Israeli resident beneficiaries. The trust is subject to reporting obligations and is taxable as an Israeli resident, on worldwide income, in accordance with the tax rates applicable to individuals.

The reporting and tax payment obligations are imposed by the legislation on the trustees regardless of the jurisdiction in which they conduct their business activities or have their residence. Once taxes have been paid, distributions are made to beneficiaries with no additional tax obligations.

- A 'foreign beneficiary trust' is established by an Israeli resident for the benefit of foreign resident beneficiaries. As the settlor is an Israeli resident, there are reporting obligations, both upon settlement and annually to ensure the identity of the beneficiaries as non-residents of Israel. This trust is taxed in a similar way to a foreign settlor trust, which is to say that there is no Israeli taxation where no assets are located in Israel and no income is derived from Israeli sources. The assets and income of this form of trust are regarded as external to the Israeli tax system provided a number of criteria are met:
- The trust is not considered an Israeli resident trust under the legislation;
- The trust is irrevocable;
- All of the beneficiaries are identified and are non-residents of Israel; and
- At least one settlor is an Israeli resident.
- A 'testamentary trust' is established under an individual's last will and testament in accordance with one of the categories outlined above.

6.4 Tax benefits to new immigrants and returning residents

A number of years ago, in 2008, for Israel's 60th birthday, Israel revised the Tax Ordinance in connection with tax benefits granted to new immigrants and Israelis returning to reside in Israel. As Israel is an immigration-friendly state, benefits have always been granted to such individuals, but the most recent amendments are extraordinary and in hindsight, have resulted in an immigration wave to Israel.

The law distinguishes between:

- new immigrants – those who have never resided in Israel previously;
- long-term returning residents – those who have resided abroad for a period of 10 years prior to returning to Israel; and
- regular returning residents – those who have resided abroad for a period of five years prior to returning to reside in Israel.

The law provides that the income of a new immigrant or of a long-term returning resident is exempt from taxes in Israel for a period of 10 years, from the time the individual becomes an Israeli resident, where it is derived from sources such as interest, dividends, royalty, rent or pension payments, or capital gains, as long as it originates abroad.

Under this revision, for the capital gains tax exemption to apply to new immigrants and long-term returning residents, assets no longer need to have been purchased prior to becoming Israeli residents.

Regular returning residents enjoy the benefits listed below in connection with assets purchased during their residence abroad once they were no longer residents of Israel:

- a tax exemption for a period of five years on passive income derived from assets abroad;
- a tax exemption for a period of five years on interest and dividend payments derived from 'preferred securities' which are defined as securities traded on foreign exchanges purchased while the individuals were non-residents of Israel; and
- a tax exemption for a period of 10 years on capital gains derived from the assets mentioned above provided that those assets do not themselves grant, directly or indirectly, rights over assets located in Israel.

6.5 Foreign residents

As mentioned above, certain tax exemptions and reliefs are granted to foreign residents:

- exemption from tax on interest, discount and linkage differentials paid to a foreign resident on debentures traded on the Israeli Stock Exchange issued by an Israel resident body corporate (under certain conditions);
- exemption from tax payments on capital gains from the sale of securities of Israeli companies traded on an exchange in Israel or an exchange abroad, provided that the capital gain is not realised by a permanent enterprise in Israel;[6]

---

6   This provision does not apply to capital gains from the sale of a share in a real estate investment fund, and short-term (under 13 months) State of Israel bonds or treasury bonds.

- exemption from tax payments on capital gains earned upon the sale of a security of an Israeli resident company, or upon the sale of a right in a foreign resident body of persons, the main assets of which are rights in assets located in Israel (subject to some conditions, including that the capital gain may not be realised in a permanent enterprise in Israel which at the time of the sale of the security is not traded on an exchange in Israel);[7]
- an individual working in Israel holding the status of 'overseas expert' can deduct expenses as defined in the relevant law.

6.6 Double tax treaties

Israel is a party to double taxation agreements with more than 50 countries. The agreements are based on the Organisation for Economic Cooperation and Development's model. The model includes double tax prevention in income categories including capital gains, interest, dividends and royalties.

Once an agreement to afford double taxation relief is ratified, the obligation to maintain secrecy imposed by the law shall not prevent disclosure to an authorised officer of the reciprocating state of any information that is to be disclosed under the agreement.

7. Conclusion

The family office industry in Israel is, as stated, still in its infancy, and therefore potential client awareness is low in comparison with the more mature western markets. In our opinion, a significant number of high net worth individuals operate and manage their assets alone while using portfolio management services for some of their capital.

There is potential in the family office marketplace, and the number of service providers and users is expected to grow significantly. It is reasonable to expect that within a few years the scope of the market will be similar to that seen in North America and Europe. There are those who claim it could be even larger due to the typical approach of Israeli clients, who tend to invest a major portion of their capital in foreign markets, requiring higher levels of professionalism.

Nonetheless, since this is a relatively young industry, professional levels and standards are still being created. These require an understanding of international markets, a familiarity with the various types of investments and a personal relationship based on honesty, confidentiality and discretion. We estimate that, given Israel's wide-ranging exposure to global markets, close relationships between the banks, the various product suppliers and family offices, awareness in this area both on the part of clients and of service providers will rise to those accepted as standard in the wider world.

In Israel there are no one-stop-shop family offices as it is a relatively small country and clients prefer to work with accountants, lawyers and others with whom they are familiar or that are known as specialists in the relevant fields. It is unlikely that such bodies will be established in Israel in the future.

---

7   This exemption does not apply to the capital gain if most of the assets held were real estate rights or real estate association rights.

Netherlands

Raimund Kamp
Marijke Kuijpers
Guidato Family Office (Amsterdam, the Netherlands)

In this chapter we first look at the demographics of the Dutch market for services for high net worth individuals. In the second part we focus on the Dutch family office landscape. We describe the tax implications for entrepreneurs and ultra-high net worth individuals coming to the Netherlands in the third part. The final part focuses on opportunities in the Netherlands for commercial multi-family offices and wealthy foreigners.

1. Millionaires in the Netherlands

Annual research by the governmental institute the Central Bureau of Statistics gives great insight into the prosperity, income and wealth situation of the Dutch. In early 2012, 2% of households had a wealth of €1 million or more. This corresponds to154,000 households. This was as many as a year earlier. After the sharp increase in 2007 and 2008, the number of millionaire households in 2009 was virtually unchanged. In 2010 the number of millionaires fell by 9,000.

The median wealth of millionaire households was about €1.5 million. In early 2012 it was more than 60 times the median wealth of non-millionaires: €24,000. Millionaires have relatively fewer debts than non-millionaires: 13% versus 47% (debt as a percentage of assets).

The definition of wealth is the difference between assets and liabilities. Assets consist of housing, banking and savings, securities, other real estate, movable property and business assets. Capital and pension insurance are excluded. Liabilities are any mortgage for the household's dwelling and other payables for consumption purposes, the financing of securities, debts for a second home or other real estate, and liabilities under the Student Finance Act.

Of all households in the Netherlands, 1.2% have investible assets[1] of €1 million or more. This corresponds to over 92,000 households. Of these 92,000, 61% have wealth between €1 million and €2 million, and around 28% have €2 million to €5 million. Only 3% of the millionaire households have a wealth of €10 million or more.

In an international study by Boston Consulting Group,[2] calculating the number of millionaires, in US dollars and including the value of pension rights and life

---

1 The Central Bureau of Statistics definition excludes the built-up value of any pension, the value of the home and any secured mortgage.
2 Boston Consulting Group, "Global Wealth 2014: Riding a Wave of Growth".

insurance, it appears that the number of Dutch with assets greater than $1 million was 2.6% in 2012 and 2.1% the year before (2011).

Based on an analysis of research by Wealth-X, the Netherlands is ranked as eighth in the European ultra-high net worth list. On the worldwide stage, based on the Boston Consulting Group international report, the highest density of millionaire households was in Qatar (175 out of every 1,000 households), followed by Switzerland and Singapore. The Netherlands ranked number 14. The United States had the largest number of billionaires, but the highest density of billionaire households was in Hong Kong, followed by Switzerland.

1.1 The Dutch rich list

Business magazine *Quote* publishes an annual rich list, the *"Quote 500"* which identifies the wealthiest Dutch individuals. Their information is based on various public sources, for example published annual reports and the value of floated stock. By no means is the list comprehensive, and most Dutch millionaires fear having their name published. The average wealth of the top 500 millionaires amounts to €166.6 million.

The 2013[3] and 2014[4] rankings list 20 billionaires, and for many years the heir of Dutch Brewer Freddy Heineken, Charlene de Carvalho-Heineken, topped the table. The 2014 list shows a new winner: Frits Goldschmeding, the founder of Randstad Uitzendbureau, a quoted employment agency. Goldschmeding tops the 2014 list with an estimated wealth of €3.2 billion. Famous media entrepreneur John de Mol ranks third, and is among the 'usual suspects' on this list. Ultra-high net worth individuals who reside outside the Netherlands, such as Charlene de Carvalho-Heineken, are now on a separate list. *Quote* estimates her wealth at €7.3 billion.

A few years ago the rich list started to make a distinction between individuals and families. For many years the entrepreneurial Brenninkmeijer family, founders of the C&A retail company and serial investors, has held a firm number one position in the latter category, with an estimated wealth of €22 billion.

1.2 Pen's wealth parade

"The parade of giants and dwarfs", a description coined in 1971 by the Dutch economist Jan Pen, is an eloquent way to map income or wealth distribution. He imagined procession in which people are marching in succession in order of the amount of wealth, with the whole population passing in one hour. The height of the people is in proportion to their wealth. People with wealth that is equal to the average are given a height of 1.74 metres, the height of the average Dutch citizen. People with lower wealth than average are pushed together, while people with higher incomes can assume gigantic proportions. All persons from a household walk along in the parade (of course all members of a household have the same height), or a household is represented by one of them.

---

3   *"Quote 500"*, November 2013.
4   *"Quote 500"*, November 2014.

(a)   **The average wealth passes at the 44th minute[5]**

Looking at the value of the wealth of households (as at January 1 2012) the first six minutes of the parade start below the ground. These are mainly employees of households with a home whose mortgage exceeds the value of the property. This group also includes a relatively high number of the self-employed with negative equity.

The next 10 minutes only dwarfs walk by. This group of households has a wealth of less than €2,000, and includes a relatively large number of households on social welfare benefits. It also contains many single-person households and single-parent families.

After half an hour, exactly half of the procession, there is a household with a wealth of €27,000. The household with the average wealth of €157,500 passes at the 44 minutes point. In the next quarter the parade grows to five times the average height. Two-thirds of the main breadwinners in this group are over 55 years old. Over 90% have their own property. In an increasing number of cases, without mortgage or with a substantial surplus value.

(b)   **True giants with wealth of €2.5 million or more**

In the last minute the first giants come by, with an average wealth of nearly €1 million. The last minute is dominated by the real giants. They have an average wealth of more than €2.5 million. In this group, more than four in ten are entrepreneurs, while one in three has retired. The wealth of the biggest giants accounts for more than three quarters of equities, bonds and real estate, such as second homes and retail property.

Pen's parade, wealth distribution of Dutch households, January 1 2012

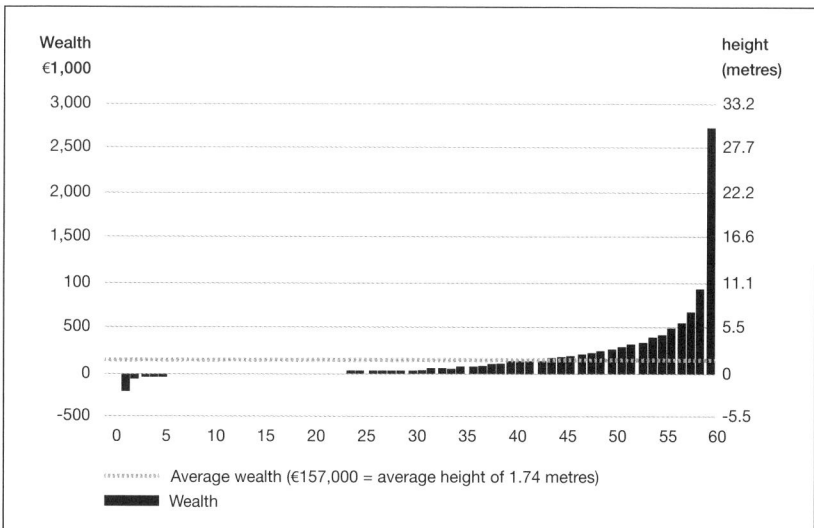

(c)   **Wealth inequality**

Wealth is unevenly distributed over Dutch households. The 1.2% that are millionaire households together own 40% of the total assets in the Netherlands. In addition, the

10% that are the most affluent households own three quarters of the total wealth. In the Netherlands, income differences are smaller than wealth differences. The Dutch fiscal regime plays an important role. Wealth is relatively lightly taxed, while income is taxed progressively and taxes on income are used to insure the social security system.

1.3 Is the Netherlands attractive for millionaires?

Currently nearly 16.9 million people live in the Netherlands.[6] According to the World Economic Forum, the Netherlands holds a strong eighth position in the top ten of the *Global Competitiveness Report for 2013-2014*.[7] Also the Netherlands was ranked in fourth place in the *Human Development Index 2013*.[8] The City of Amsterdam ranked seventh in the Global Wealth City Index[9] looking at six overall categories: economy, research and development, cultural interaction, liability, environment, and accessibility; with 70 individual indicators among them.

In 2011 there were 27 municipalities whose populations included 3% or more millionaires. The list is headed by Blaricum, where millionaires make up 10%, followed by Bloemendaal, Laren (NH) and Wassenaar.[10]

(a) The impact of family businesses

Family businesses play a very important role in the Dutch economy. Based on a research by Nyenrode Business University[11] there were around 260,000 family businesses in the year 2010 – almost 70% of all businesses in the Netherlands. At that time they created jobs for 4.3 million people – representing 50% of total employment. Family businesses accounted for 53% of the actual earnings of companies (after deduction of purchase costs and write-offs), resulting in a figure of €56 trillion. Since 2010 the absolute figures have changed, but the proportions have not. Due to the good achievements of family businesses the figures have improved since.

Business magazine *Elsevier* drafts an annual top 100 list of Dutch family businesses.[12] For their list they use the European Family Business definition. According to this definition the majority of voting rights (direct or indirect) must be in the hands of one or more individuals, or their next of kin, who founded the company or acquired the company through a gift or inheritance. *Elsevier* added two extra criteria: the second generation must at least be involved with the business, and it must be an actual business and not an investment company (buying and selling businesses).

Looking at the top 10 of the chart, the number one position is held by the Heineken family. The second and third positions are held by the dynasty of Fentener van Vlissingen, founders of the multinational SHV and BCD Travel. The Van Eerd family, founders of supermarket chain Jumbo, have secured the fourth place.

---

5   Central Bureau of Statistics, *Welvaart in Nederland 2014* (June 2014).
6   Central Bureau of Statistics, September 2014.
7   World Economic Forum at www3.weforum.org/docs/GCR2013-14/GCR_Rankings_2013-14.pdf.
8   United Nations Development Programme, human development reports at data.undp.org/dataset/Table-1-Human-Development-Index-and-its-components/wxub-qc5k.
9   Knight Frank, *The Wealth Report 2014*.
10   Central bureau of Statistics Welvaart in Nederland 2014.
11   RH Flören, L Uhlaner, M Berent-Braun, *Ondernemerschap en het familiebedrijf*, (2011).
12   *Elsevier*, April 12 2014.

(b) *Sources of economic prosperity*

In October 2014, *Elsevier*[13] published for the third consecutive year the results of the top 500 Dutch companies, giving an insight into current economic prosperity. The ranking is based on annual turnover figures, and the board of the companies must be based in the Netherlands. Therefore, Dutch holding companies that are only based here for fiscal purposes are excluded from the list. The number one position is held by oil company Shell, followed by Vitol Holding (another oil company), Unilever (food, toiletries etc.) and Aegon (insurance). Quite a few companies on this list benefit from the geographic location of the country being surrounded by water. Offshore oil and gas companies, shipping, raw materials dealers and tank storage are well represented. There are 90 family businesses in the top 500, and their performance is steady.

The conclusion of the *Elsevier* research is that the largest companies in the Netherlands overall hardly lost turnover in comparison with 2013, and net profit dropped only slightly. Moreover, 392 companies made a profit in 2014, in comparison with 375 in 2013.

2. The family office landscape

There is no legal or statutory definition of a family office. The job title 'family officer' is also not a qualified protected title such as medical doctor or lawyer. As a result, anyone in the Netherlands can start an enterprise and call it a family office.

If you ask the average person in the Netherlands if they have ever heard of a family office, the answer will very likely be no. Possibly they might think it has to do with family business or family planning. The answer to this question will be different if you ask wealthy individuals and entrepreneurs. Due to the increased attention in the (financial) newspapers and advertising campaigns by financial institutions the family office concept has become better known in the Netherlands. Although the awareness of the target audience has increased over the last few years, it would be interesting to research their actual understanding of and insight into the services rendered by family offices.

The Dutch landscape consists of various types of family offices: single family offices and multi-family offices.

2.1 Single family offices

Some entrepreneurial families set up a single family office to manage the family wealth separately from their operating (family) business, or after the (family) business has been sold (to a third party). The wealth requires professional financial management, which the owners prefer to arrange through a single family office.

The typical single family office is not always in line with how the family perceive it themselves. Most often the legal entity is a Dutch legal structure called an 'administration office' (*Stichting administratiekantoor* or STAK). In practice most of them operate with a low profile and are under the radar. Some of them were founded more than 100 years ago and manage the investments of old-money families. Other

---

13   *Elsevier*, October 18, 2014.

single family offices were established more recently and operate more in the public space, for example Cyrte, De Hoge Dennen and Navitas. These companies are professionally run investment vehicles for new-money entrepreneurs and even have websites.

One of the best known entrepreneurial Dutch families is the Brenninkmeijer family, and they also have a single family office. Their governance structure has its origin in one A4 page setting out the core (business) family values of the two founders Carl and August Brenninkmeijer. Their family office supports the executives of the family business and family members who are not actively involved in the daily business. It has evolved into a large organisation with lawyers, notaries, investment specialists and psychologists to serve the needs of national and international family members. Some years ago the family office obtained a formal banking status and complies with all necessary regulatory requirements accordingly.

Occasionally a single family office has transformed into a multi-family office and commercially exploited their investment resources, know-how and experience with other families. Of course the financial crisis had an impact on investment returns and therefore on the cost of running a professional organisation.

2.2 Multi-family offices

Over the last decade quite a few multi-family offices have been founded by professional advisers. Most of the founders are trained investment advisers, bankers or qualified (tax) lawyers and accountants. The companies are usually privately owned, although based on their business philosophy, some multi-family offices issued loyalty shares to key clients who played an important role at the start of the business.

The family office concept has also been adopted by a few large financial institutions. Private bank Van Lanschot created the private office concept to attract and introduce the bespoke services for its rich clients. Deloitte also introduced a family office tailored service to its clientele some years ago. At the end of the 20th century PwC was known for its advanced one-stop-shop private clients strategy, and packaged its services in a family office concept; however it has since abandoned this concept.

Looking at the multi-family offices marketplace in more detail, their business model can be divided into two core areas. The first and primary business model for the majority of multi-family offices is asset management. The fee that the clients pay equals a percentage of the assets under management. Clients might often pay an extra fee for additional services like administration or consolidated reports of their total assets.

A minority of Dutch multi-family offices have chosen a different business model: fee-based independent advice to their clients. The most common activities are consolidation and structuring of accumulated wealth, selection of banks/asset managers, strategic asset allocation advice, estate planning and drafting annual accounts. Also more specialised family-oriented services like financial education, preparing the next generation and transfer of the family business are being offered. These multi-family offices charge a retainer, a fixed fee or an hourly charge, and do not receive extra income from third parties.

A couple of multi-family offices have joined their forces and set up an association of independent family offices (Vereniging Onafhankelijke Family Offices, or VOFO) to share expertise and inform the Dutch public about the family office concept.

Based on the two approaches, form of ownership and type of services, we can picture the Dutch multi-family office landscape in a matrix. The horizontal X-axis represents the type of ownership of the family office, either privately owned or part of a large corporate institute. On the vertical Y-axis the services offered play a central role. Is the core business model investment services or other type of services?

The four types of family offices are:

Type 1	Type 3
• Privately owned multi-family office; • Core business: not investment management • Example: Guidato Family Office	• Owned by a large corporation; • Core business: not investment management. • Example: Deloitte Family Office
Type 2	Type 4
• Privately owned multi-family office; • Core business: investment management • Example; Box	• Owned by large corporation; • Core business: investment management. • Example: Van Lanschot private office

2.3   Setting up and running a multi-family office in the Netherlands

The process of setting up a multi-family office in the Netherlands is not subject to any specific mandatory legislation. The Dutch financial markets supervisory authority (the Autoriteit Financiële Markten or AFM) only requires a permit for qualified investment management services, like investment advice and asset management. A simple permit is required when a multi-family office advises clients as to which bank they should open a bank account at and transfer their monies to.

Certain future developments can contribute towards opportunities and growth for family offices focusing on ultra-high net worth individuals and their families.

(a)   Wealth transfer by the baby boomers

In the near future the baby boom generation will transfer its capital to the next generation. This means that all sorts of assets, including (family) businesses will change ownership. Based on our research *Wealth transfer in the Netherlands*, we conclude that future heirs need proper preparation to be able to manage their inheritance and to deal with the emotional impact of becoming a wealthy individual. Sustaining family wealth requires a proactive strategy prior to the actual transfer. This entails children becoming self-reliant in handling (part of) the wealth prior to the transfer and being able to make sound financial and legal decisions. Their having experience in joint decision-making with siblings also contributes to sustaining wealth. In short, services to help wealthy families to prepare the next generation will very likely be a growth area for the family office business.

(b)　　**Size and growth of the Dutch ultra-high net worth market**

Based on the research from Wealth–X[14] the future growth of the European market for services to high net worth individuals does not look very bright. In comparison to other parts of the world the proportion of new high net worth individuals in Europe is relatively small. At the same time Boston Consulting Group[15] expects a 3.3% growth in wealth in Europe between 2013 and 2018, a similar growth percentage as in North America.

Looking at the number of millionaires in the Netherlands, it looks like there are many potential clients that require advice from a multi-family office. A closer look shows that there is a substantial group that own assets that consist of real estate, property and shares in a company. A millionaire who has investable assets of €1 million or more is not necessarily a client for a multi-family office, because it more or less comes down to the complexity of the financial and family situation. Complexity is one of the foremost criteria in evaluating the need to hire the services of a multi-family office.

(c)　　**New legislation may lead to change in culture**

Dutch legislation on advising about financial products and services changed on January 1 2013. The aim of introducing new legislation was to give Dutch individuals insight into the costs of financial services, such as advice on investments, mortgages and insurance. Now all individuals must pay a fee for the financial advice they receive. The introduction of this new law has not been easy, because individuals now receive an invoice, whereas previously this advice was free of charge. However, it was not really free of costs, but these costs were hidden in product structures and therefore not transparent. Customers might have had the idea that financial advice was free. Looking at the Dutch culture, it is not in our nature to hire a professional financial adviser, in contrast to the United States where it is a more common practice that individuals consult a financial adviser and pay for (independent) advice. If that culture changes, the opportunities for multi-family offices will very likely improve.

(d)　　**Complexity of financial affairs and the trusted adviser**

For most people, financial affairs, markets and the industry are not very appealing. Many individuals have a low level of interest in their own financial situation. Apart from the odd person, not many high net worth individuals are keen on spending time on (managing) their investments. Due to the financial crisis, however, even the less financially interested high net worth individuals have needed to address the implications on their accumulated wealth. At the same time, the attention given in various media to scrutinising the business models of (private) banks caused a more critical attitude on the part of banking clients. The need for having a trusted adviser has increased, but where can you find these trustworthy advisers? A negative financial attitude might become a barrier to some high net worth individuals hiring

---

14　Wealth-X, *World Ultra Wealth Report* 2012-2013.
15　Boston Consulting Group, "Global Wealth 2014: Riding a Wave of Growth".

a financial adviser or a multi-family office, even if their business models are different from those of the (private) banks.

3. Tax implications for entrepreneurs and ultra-high net worth individuals coming to the Netherlands

We will highlight the most common and important tax topics for entrepreneurs, ultra-high net worth individuals and their families who decide to live and work in the Netherlands.

3.1 Residency and domicile

Dutch legislation does not make a distinction between concepts of residency and domicile. An immigrant wealthy individual will become subject to income tax and inheritance tax as of the date of becoming a Dutch resident. There is no clear statutory definition of residence. For tax purposes this is based on an evaluation of all the facts and circumstances of an individual. These include, for example, his place of work, the centre of his family and social life and the location of his dwelling. The criteria for establishing residence for inheritance (and gift) tax purposes are similar to those for income tax purposes.

3.2 Immigration of wealthy individuals

The immigrant wealthy individual who is considered a Dutch resident will be subject to income tax on worldwide income. For individuals who are still working (earning an employment income) there is an attractive income tax regime: the 30% ruling, which can reduce the tax bill through application for the expat regime. Certain strict conditions need to be met: for example the person's skills need to be scarce on the Dutch labour market. The tax benefit is a deemed 30% deduction from the Dutch salary, but the main advantage is the possibility to opt for deemed non–residency status for other sources of income. Through this election, income from portfolio investments and non-Dutch substantial interest shares can be exempt from Dutch taxation. This favourable tax regime applies for an eight-year period.

Non-resident individuals generally only become subject to tax on certain Dutch-sourced income, such as employment income, income derived from a substantial interest (at least 5%) in companies and income from real estate.

Dutch inheritance tax is levied on worldwide assets of a decedent who was a resident (or a deemed resident) of the Netherlands at the time of death. The tax is levied on the beneficiaries of the estate and the estate itself is not taxed.

There is no net wealth tax in the Dutch tax system, but income tax is levied on the value of the net wealth at an effective tax rate of 1.2% annually. An exemption applies for dwellings and substantial interests in companies.

3.3 Companies: an attractive participation exemption regime

The Netherlands is well known for its attractive regime of tax exemption for participations in companies and its large number of tax treaties. Quite a few shareholders in family-owned businesses structure their international business through a Dutch holding company. Capital gains and dividends received from qualifying participations are exempt if the regime applies, which it generally does if the following main conditions are met:

- The Dutch holding company holds at least 5% of the total nominal value of the shares of the company concerned; and
- That company is not a portfolio investment company in a low tax jurisdiction, unless it is involved in real estate activities.

Double tax treaties generally reduce the 15% withholding tax on profit distributions by the holding company to nil (zero).

3.4 Planning opportunities for entrepreneurs and wealthy individuals

Dutch-resident entrepreneurial families are able to transfer their business to the next generation in a manner that is advantageous from a tax perspective through the application of business property relief. This special business succession facility applies when business property is donated by means of a gift or bequest. This facility also applies to the acquisition of shares that constitute a substantial interest (5%, whether held directly or indirectly) in an active trading company. The total value of the business is fully exempt up to €1,045,611, and for the remainder of the value of the business assets an exemption of 83% applies. One important condition of this facility is that after the acquisition of the shares or the business property, the business must continue and the shares must be kept for at least five years. Additionally, in the case of bequests, the deceased must have been an entrepreneur for an entire year (a 12-month period) prior to death. For gifts this is a five-year period.

3.5 Trusts

The Anglo-Saxon concept of a trust is unknown in Dutch civil law. Dutch law is familiar with the distinction between real rights and personal rights, but is unfamiliar with a distinction between legal interests and beneficial interests in property.

Although the Netherlands has ratified the Hague Trust Convention, the Dutch tax authorities often used not recognise trusts for tax purposes. This often resulted in situations of 'floated wealth'. Since January 1 2010 new legislation has been in effect, and irrevocable discretionary trusts and other similar entities such as family foundations are now recognised for the application of income, gift and inheritance tax.

3.6 Foundations

For family estate planning purposes, the opportunities to use a Dutch foundation are limited. The concept of a Dutch foundation is known, but there is a provision in the Civil Code determining that an individual who sets up such a foundation cannot benefit from it, nor can any person who belongs to the board of directors of the foundation. Other individuals can only benefit from the foundation if the distributions from the foundation have a social character or are acknowledged to have an idealistic motivation.

In Dutch and international tax structures a Dutch incorporated foundation (Stichting Administratiekantoor or STAK) is frequently used as an asset protection vehicle. The STAK holds shares or other assets and at the moment of transfer of these assets to the STAK the former holder of the assets receives depositary receipts issued by the STAK. The main reason for this structure is to realise a clear separation between the voting rights (at the board level of the STAK) and the beneficial ownership of the assets by the holders of the depositary receipts. The STAK is considered transparent for Dutch corporate income tax. Any tax is only levied at the level of the depositary receipt holders.

4. Opportunities in the Netherlands for commercial multi-family offices and wealthy foreigners

The current multi-family offices in the Netherlands will probably be able to increase awareness of the benefits of hiring such an entity. The change in culture relating to paying for financial services will take some time, but will in the end be feasible. Looking at the size of the Dutch market for services to high net worth individuals there seems to be little room for new entrants. Only when a new entrant has a new business model or another competitive edge new to the Dutch market, will the company have an opportunity to set up a viable business.

For foreign ultra-high net worth individuals and their families the Netherlands has a very competitive fiscal climate. The key challenge is to overcome the current collision between Anglo-Saxon entities and Dutch civil and fiscal law. Obviously this needs to be addressed prior to any possible immigration to the Netherlands.

Russia

Maxim Alekseyev
Kira Egorova
ALRUD Law Firm

1. Background

These days, there is substantial awareness of and interest in family office services all over the world. The family office wealth management industry is growing faster than ever before. However, the family office as a set of services rendered to wealthy people has appeared in Russia only recently. This phenomenon can be easily comprehended by anyone who is familiar with the Russian history: for a long time the country subsisted in the form of the Union of Soviet Socialist Republics (USSR) where capitalistic values were denied and there was no place for private businesses.

Starting from the early 1990s when the USSR ceased to exist, the first Russians who could publicly declare their wealth began to appear. However, given a very unstable and not fully-fledged legal framework and the overall situation in the country, such people did not look to find ways to manage their assets properly as they were mostly busy with generating their wealth. Moreover, most of the new Russian millionaires were young enough and could tackle their problems without the need for permanent support.

In addition, they were marked with the negative '*nouveau riche*' label and associated with the criminal world, so the ethical side of it should also be taken into account. According to a survey undertaken several years ago, more than a half of those asked were still of the opinion that there is no way to become rich in Russia acting honestly. More than a third of the people interviewed adhered to the opinion that the capital of wealthy businessmen in Russia could only be earned through deception or speculation.

By the end of the 1990s, the legal framework had become more or less stable and predictable while Russian laws had become much more sophisticated. Russian high net worth individuals made their big money legitimate by investing in various businesses, which required new efforts to maintain, multiply and transfer the capital to their heirs. Furthermore, wealthy individuals were dealing with a lot of other issues not related to their businesses, such as vacation planning, education, travelling, visas, citizenship and so on. It became clear that there were opportunities for various institutions to assist high net worth individuals and wealthy families with most of the tasks associated with managing their wealth and lifestyle, and to help them define and achieve their personal and financial goals.

Now the average age of high net worth Russians has reached 50 and above, and the focus of their objectives is changing accordingly. They are aiming not only to preserve or spend their money, but also to ensure that the family's wealth is well-managed, to transfer the wealth to their children from generation to generation, and/or to involve other members of the family in their businesses. It is worth mentioning that this is the first generation of the Russians generating personal wealth. Therefore, the preservation of inherited wealth and education of the successors have become very important in Russia.

2. Current state of family offices in Russia

In Russia, family office services are still regarded as something exotic, and there is no clear understanding of what a traditional family office is and how it works. There is no universal model in Russia, not because of the peculiarities of the Russian market, but because most wealthy Russians are not ready to accept this new type of service in its traditional form and format. In general, the development of local services addressed specifically to private clients in Russia is still in progress. Family office services are obviously part and parcel of such local services, which opens new horizons and opportunities.

In most cases, when the patriarch and his family realise that they need and are ready to use a full range of traditional family office services they will still seek such services abroad. This approach is not a perfect one because it is only suitable for those with considerable wealth, assets located mainly internationally and families that already spend most of their time abroad. On the other hand, the market for family office services and an adequate range of professionals available in Russia are only now emerging, and it is difficult to find or to offer locally the range of services, opportunities and quality provided by foreign experts. In addition, Russians are obsessed with maintaining confidentiality and, therefore, they may seek assistance abroad irrespective of the price and availability of such services in Russia. With this in mind, the purpose of this chapter is to describe the current opportunities in Russia with respect to Russian assets.

Family offices' services as a separate business are usually not advertised in the Russian mass media. The use of such services locally is uncommon, but is in place (in one form or another) for high net worth individuals having their own businesses, successful business professionals or politicians. The need for local family office services may arise when the capital of an individual and his family exceeds between Rb400 million and Rb600 million (approximately between $10 million and $15 million). The scope of the services provided by Russian family offices or their equivalents are not as wide as they are globally. As a rule, they are confined to the legal and tax aspects of asset management, local real estate management and concierge services.

2.1 Regulation and types of family offices in Russia

Currently, there are no specific Russian rules or regulations in respect of family office services. Moreover, information on particularities of the family office services can be obtained only from very limited and fragmentary information in public sources and from the practices of consulting firms and banks that deal with private clients. We will therefore describe the current situation, available options and corporate forms used for the provision of such services to the extent known to us.

In Russia, the ways and corporate forms in which a family office can be established and operate depend on the type and location of the assets being managed, as well as the nature and number of users of such services.

As a rule, the family office in Russia as a separate unit providing such services is established as a limited liability company, a branch of a foreign company or a department of a finance institution, including banks, commonly with foreign shareholders.

In addition, it often takes the form of a virtual or isolated group of professionals (lawyers, accountants, financial managers) employed by the patriarch's firm but exclusively dealing with family matters. Such an in-house group can seek advice from outside professionals, including tax and legal consulting firms. Such firms may offer some family office services as well within the existing services offered to private clients. Banks tend to declare that they render private banking and family office services to their clients.

(a)   *Family office as part of a business group company*

Structuring services in this way is a standard solution for wealthy individuals who have a big business locally and are able to use its resources. At best, it can be formed as a separate department within an existing company of the business group. Another frequent practice is to vest certain employees with additional responsibilities, sometimes without extra remuneration.

Wealthy individuals usually engage different types of specialists in the operation of such departments. For instance, these can be accountants, legal and tax advisers, security service managers or investment experts. As a rule, a private assistant and a team of secretaries render concierge services.

Having a family office as part of an existing corporate unit has its obvious pros and cons. One of the main advantages is its cost, as it does not involve a lot of additional expenditures for a high net worth individual and his family. Therefore, employment costs will not be as considerable as they would be with a single professional family office. For many Russians (even high net worth individuals) cost still remains the principal criterion. Other important factors can be the minimum time spent on dealing with an in-house family office, because it is always at the disposal of the patriarch with a dependable staff.

The staff of such a department can be easily transferred from another company that is owned by a wealthy individual. More rarely, external specialists are employed to manage some particular assets.

The main disadvantage of having the family office as part of a business structure in Russia is the same as everywhere else – there is a high risk of failure to ensure confidentiality of information disclosed to the in-house staff. Obviously, it could be a problem to provide services within such a department on a highly private basis and under terms of strict confidentiality. The risk of disclosure is highest if a business is owned by several individuals. Members of the other families may be able to get access to the confidential information.

Moreover, in-house specialists usually do not have particular experience and expertise in family office services and private wealth management. There is also a problem of motivation of such staff, and conflicts of interest can arise.

(b)   *Family office services rendered by consulting firms*

In Russia, this type of family office can be compared to (but is not to the same as) the multi-family office concept found in international practice. Some consulting companies render family office services to multiple families. They provide wealth management programmes that are a combination of financial and investment advice, accounting and legal services as well as tax and estate planning. The management services offered may vary depending on the profile and resources of such firms.

The majority of Russian consulting firms also admit that families may have needs that extend beyond the tax, investment, estate and related services that a wealth management group or financial institution can offer. In these cases, they cooperate with other groups so as to render the fullest possible range of services to such families.

Russian consulting firms (and private bank departments) usually provide high quality services under terms of strict confidentiality. Where the consulting or legal firm is established as chamber of advocates, any information and documents provided by a client are privileged and additionally protected. Additional obvious benefits arising from providing family office services in this form are a high level of professional expertise, easy access to international experience and practice and independence. Such important aspects as succession planning are also taken into account by consulting firms.

However, Russian consulting companies do not usually focus on family office services. They render such services to clients in addition to legal and tax services, with only occasional support.

(c)   *Single family office*

The fullest range of asset management and family support services of the best possible quality can only be provided by a single family office.

In Russia, the most common services provided by a single family office are legal and tax support, wealth management, administrative and concierge assistance, and training of the younger generation. Usually a Russian single family office (as in international practice) is comprised of administrative, legal, accounting, investment and other professionals involved in providing single office services exclusively for the benefit of any particular single family. One of the primary advantages of a single family office is therefore the focus on the needs of one family and its representation. Each family member benefits from a group of professionals who can develop a deeper understanding of that family's needs and then offer an integrated approach to addressing the family members' targets. Having one consolidated group of professionals means that a family member needs only interact with one central source, this being the family office, and not a number of different service providers.

Even though most of the services that may be provided by a single family office are not licensed, some types of services such as securities management and brokerage are subject to licensing.

Therefore, apart from the permanent staff, the Russian single family office may also engage a number of licensed subcontractors. The other option would be for the family office as a legal entity to apply for such licences, but it will need to pass through a lot of formalities and fulfil all obligatory requirements. Due to the complexity of this procedure, it is more usual to engage licensed subcontractors.

It should also be noted that where one of the activities of the family office is managing the wealthy individual's foreign assets upon his instruction, certain tax risks (described in detail below) arise when such assets are effectively managed from the Russian Federation.

The obvious advantage of a single family office is the fullest control and privacy. In Russia, wealthy families tend to wish to exercise overall control over the experts advising them, which maximizes their privacy.

The main obstacle to having a single family office is the high cost. Separate premises, technology, highly qualified personnel and access to the best services and investment vehicles are very costly.

The minimum monthly expenses for a single office in Russia can be estimated at between $30,000 and $40,000. This amount includes only permanent staff expenses. Where it is necessary to engage outsourced services the expenses will be increased accordingly. In Russia, the sophisticated single family office may incur expenses in the amount of approximately $1 million annually. Therefore, if the scope of the services required is limited, it makes sense to utilise a multi-family office or to use any other options rather than to establish one's own single office.

In addition, because of its 'special nature', clarifications as regards the activities of the family office legal entity have to be given to the Russian tax authorities, which can be quite difficult to provide and may lead to additional business risks.

(d)   Family office as part of private banking services

Currently, there are a number of local banks and financial institutions in Russia that render special private banking services to large and prominent clients. Sometimes one may find on their websites information saying that family offices services are provided. But in practice it is primarily about lifestyle management services for very important clients (assistance in finding high-quality medical support or prestigious schools for children, arranging exclusive luxury journeys, acquisition of art objects and so on). Such services are indeed part of standard family office services, but not the most important ones.

Of course, private banks in Russia also provide wealth management services. These services usually relate to the clients' finances (such as asset management, investments, deposits and the like), but quite often private banks try to sell different investment products that are of no use to wealthy individuals or their families. It is a particular feature of Russian business that there is an exhaustive list of services approved by the head of the bank or specified in its internal politics, and there is no way of changing the scope or type of the services to cover the particular needs of potential or existing clients.

In addition, a bank saying that it offers wealth management services as part of a family office model is in most cases dependent on the choice of products and suppliers.

One of the main advantages of private banking services for the investor is that there is no need to obtain a separate licence regarding the services rendered because such formalities will already have been arranged by the bank.

The benefits of purchasing family office type services from a private bank or financial institution are a high level of confidentiality and the ability to have a wide range of services in one package.

In spite of the fact that banking services are evolving in Russia, a lot of Russian customers still prefer the products offered by foreign banks. This can be accounted for by the wider scope of the services and an individual and independent approach to each client.

3.   Ideal family office composition for wealthy Russians

Family offices are often global in their geographical presence and investments. A perfect set-up for a family office is the availability of separate single family offices in several target countries' being independent from each other and dealing only with the issues arising in each particular jurisdiction. The special nature of the Russian market requires a special Russian team to tackle problems arising in Russia and to manage assets in Russia.

If there are global or multinational tasks, it is vital to allocate them between different family offices in the jurisdictions in question. Moreover, there are considerable risks related to the management from Russia of foreign assets held by Russian high net worth individuals because in such a scenario Russia may be considered as the effective place of management of the assets, which leads to the possibility of consideration needing to be given to such issues as Russian tax residence. In practice, if there is no way of establishing a foreign family office for such activity, it is recommended to apply for the assistance of an independent foreign advisor or professional manager.

As mentioned above, most of the activities likely to be undertaken by a family office are not subject to licensing requirements in Russia. However, if a high net worth individual is in need of services in Russia that are subject to licensing (such as professional activity on a stock exchange, or the purchase and sale of securities), such operations may be executed by external contractors holding the necessary licences or the family office itself should obtain such licence.

Wealthy individuals and their families generally do not wish to make their financial status public, so all the services are of a confidential nature. Accordingly, a family office in Russia that is part of an international group should be established as a standard company in an appropriate corporate form.

3.1   Corporate form

As mentioned above, there are no specific rules and regulations for family offices in Russia, and a family office can be incorporated in any form provided for by Russian law. Due to the simplicity of incorporation and management, the most popular corporate form for a company in Russia is a limited liability company (LLC).

An LLC is a commercial organisation established by one or more founders, the charter capital of which is divided into participatory interests that certify the rights of the LLC's participants and are allocated only among its founders, who bear no personal liability for the company obligations but incur the risk of losses associated with the LLC's activities in the amount of the value of their respective participatory interests in the charter capital. So an LLC is the most common and flexible form of legal entity with the least burden and fewest statutory obligations.

The main features of a Russian LLC are the following:

- The minimum charter capital must be at least Rb10,000 (approximately $250);
- The charter capital may be composed of monetary contributions, securities, any other goods, property or non-property rights having a monetary value;
- The number of participants may not exceed 50 (or there may be a sole participant). Both individuals and legal entities can hold shares in an LLC;
- Data about participants, their participatory interests and any other information is contained in the list of participants to be kept and maintained by the LLC itself and in the Russian Unified State Register of Legal Entities.

The LLC's corporate bodies will have three levels:

- superior level – general meeting of participants;
- sub-superior level – board of directors/administrative council; and
- executive level – general director (chief executive officer)/executive board.

So an LLC can be easily incorporated and used for the provision of family office services.

In some cases (especially when the assets are located abroad or in the case of a diversified international structure), it may be feasible to organise a family office in Russia as a branch of a foreign company. A branch is not considered a legal entity. The head of the branch is appointed by the headquarters, represents the company and takes any actions in accordance with a power of attorney.

A branch is a subdivision of a legal entity. It is very similar to a representative office, but has wider powers. A family office as a branch would be established for the purpose of exercising some or all of the functions of its founder, including the function of a representative office.

3.2   Founder

As a rule, a high net worth individual establishing a family office does not wish to act as its founder or as a participant in the case of an LLC. Generally, the legal founder is a trusted person chosen by the wealthy individual. The founder may be appointed as the chief executive officer.

3.3   Staff

The number of employees in a family office depends on the scope, types of activity and complexity of services rendered by the office. To the best of our knowledge, the number of the personnel of such a company is not likely to exceed between 35 and 40 employees. More often than not, the staff comprises as few as 10 employees.

The team consists of corporate and fiduciary advisors, private lawyers, international tax consultants, financial advisors and administrators who take care of the affairs of the family on a daily basis. Most employees operate under a contract of emplyment; others are engaged on an occasional basis under civil contracts.

3.4   Services

As wealthy families and individuals wish to have a comprehensive solution to their day-to-day problems, a family office should offer a wide range of services. At the same time, in Russia there should be a contract for the services to be provided. Since all the services likely to be required cannot be listed comprehensively in a contract, the contract should contain a general description of the types of service envisaged, such as 'consulting services'.

Generally, family offices may provide the following services:

- Consulting services – in Russia, consulting services are rendered to wealthy individuals as regards different types of professional advice, including tax and legal support.

  Wealthy Russian individuals may have many types of assets, global assets, income and potential tax liabilities. To minimise the risk related to ownership and to preserve the capital, it is very important to be aware of the most recent developments and changes in Russian laws and to ensure that cross-border and international issues are also taken care of.

  For example, a tax adviser helps to improve the tax efficiency of the client's personal income, looking after tax liability, observing the deadlines for submitting tax returns and explaining the source of funds issue. A legal counsel takes care of ownership issues, provides risk management in corporate governance, business structuring and protection. First and foremost, a family office should ensure compliance with the local laws governing the client's activities on a consistent basis.

- Inheritance planning services – a separate type of family office project is the planning of business inheritance. In Russia, this involves of a wide range of services and multilevel operations on the part of a group of professionals. Some people in Russia prefer to plan the transfer of their business directly, but most of them search for a way to transfer their wealth in other ways because of the Russia's economic and market volatility.

  There is a complicated system of Russian laws and regulations in respect of the inheritance process, but there are no specific provisions for the protection of rights in respect of a transfer of business through inheritance other than those concerning wills and succession by law. It is worth saying that non-transparency is one of the main peculiarities of Russian businesses. A lot of businessmen arrange their business in a complicated form. In some cases their legitimate heirs have to search all over the world trying to find the inherited assets.

  Accordingly, the role of a proper family office is crucial for educating the next generation and providing protection against any circumstances of *force majeure*.

- Private investment management and planning – the Russian economy is very unstable. Wealthy individuals and families typically hold many different assets. Accordingly, effective capital management in Russia depends on a diversity of financial assets.

  Investment management services are among those that Russian family offices typically provide to their clients. Such services involve controlling the investments concerned using management, monitoring and reporting systems as well as the individual's interests on a day-to-day basis. These services can include the implementation of the client's investment plan or management of investment risks and cash flows. In other words, a family office provides services to manage investments in accordance with the individual's objectives.

In addition to investment management and portfolio management, some family offices recruit top risk-management experts and insurance specialists. Also, as mentioned above, in case of licensed activities either the necessary licences should be obtained by family office, or licensed subcontractors should be engaged.

- Administration and management of day-to-day needs – In practice, extremely wealthy people usually prefer engaging a special company to manage their everyday problems. Wealthy people are often too busy to make the necessary arrangements. Rich Russians are no exception. Family offices in Russia can offer life-management and budgeting services to help simplify the lives of wealthy clients and to ensure that their monthly budget is in line with their long-term wealth preservation goals.

Moreover, management of day-to-day needs in Russia can include such services as: planning of leisure and family events; secretarial services; planning of business trips; selection of the home staff (driver, housemaid, babysitter, cook and so on); assistance in purchasing and/or maintaining different types of luxury assets such as antiques, artworks, jewellery, cars, yachts, real estate and other assets that clients of a family office can afford.

3.5 Financing of the family office's activities

Generally, family offices are not profit-making and their income simply equals the expenses incurred, the largest portion of which will be salaries and wages. Payment for all services could be received as a regular fee from the main client of the office and as individual payments for particular services for non-recurrent clients. Rendering of services should be confirmed by the relevant acts of transfer and acceptance.

In the case of a branch of a foreign entity, the financing can easily be provided through a transfer of the funds from the head office.

3.6 Taxes

Tax liability of a family office depends on its corporate form.

(a) Tax liability of an LLC under a simplified tax system

Since a family office in Russia usually does not employ a lot of staff and has an insignificant value of fixed assets and income, it makes sense to incorporate the office in the form of an LLC under a simplified tax system.

Using a simplified tax system exempts a family office from the obligation to pay such taxes as value added tax (VAT), profit tax and property tax, and may provide for a reduced rate of social insurance contributions (to the Russian Pension Fund and other social funds).

Under Russian law, there are several preconditions for the application of a simplified tax system. Among the most important ones is the criterion that the annual revenue of such a family office should not exceed Rb60 million (approximately $1.5 million).

In addition, the following requirements must be met. Before commencing its activities under a simplified tax system, a company rendering family office services must choose the tax base. There are two types of tax base with different tax rates:

- a tax rate of 6% applied to income actually received;
- a tax rate of 15% applied to the margin between income actually received and expenses actually paid.

Accordingly, before choosing the preferred tax base it is necessary to calculate all the possible income and expenses and to decide which type of tax base will be more profitable for the planned activities.

If a company elects to choose the income minus expenses base, it incurs an obligation to account for both the income received and expenses incurred. Under Russian law, all expenses must be commercially justified and documented. Otherwise, there will be a risk of claims from the tax authorities and the corresponding non-recognition of expenses for tax calculation purposes. Before a company elects a tax base, it should note that the list of expenses that may decrease taxable income is limited and strictly regulated. Thus, it may sometimes be difficult for a company providing family office services to have clear proof of expenses claimed for the decrease of the taxable base. Therefore, for such type of services a choice of the income tax base may be preferred.

In addition, a company applying the income minus expenses approach (15% of the margin) has to pay the simplified tax even if the expenses incurred exceed the amount of income received. In this case the company is obliged to calculate and pay a so-called minimal tax. The amount of the minimal tax is calculated as 1% of taxable income received annually.

Tax accounting for an LLC under a simplified tax system is as simple as that: a taxpayer accounts for its activities in only one tax register – a book of income and expenses.

Therefore, the main advantages of an LLC under a simplified tax system may be as follows:

- Under a simplified tax system the family office activities are carried out in a clear and simple manner;
- The family office is exempt from profit tax, property tax and VAT. VAT exemption is very favourable for the family office's clients as they will not be faced with considerable VAT payments;
- Under a simplified tax system companies have simplified accounting and taxation responsibilities;
- Companies that use a simplified tax system attract less attention on the part of the tax authorities than organisations using a common taxation system;

- Also, if a company elects income as the object of taxation it bears no obligation to substantiate expenses incurred.

(b)   *Tax liability of a branch of a foreign company*
As an alternative, a high net worth individual can consider the option of establishing a branch of a foreign family office in Russia.

A branch of a foreign company in Russia is not a separate legal entity, but it must be accredited and registered with the state registration and tax authorities.

At the same time, a branch cannot apply a simplified tax system, and must pay all relevant taxes, including the profit tax, VAT and property tax, and must submit tax returns.

For profit tax purposes, the income derived by the branch may be reduced by the amount of expenses incurred. The final margin is subject to profit tax at a 20% tax rate. The branch established for family office services will always be of a commercial nature in Russia, and therefore will be subject to taxes on the services rendered with regard to Russian assets and residents.

The tax authorities pay a lot of attention to the issue of whether the expenses incurred by a branch are commercially justified and properly documented. If a tax representative considers that this requirement is not met then it will impose relevant fines and penalties with regard to the profit tax.

Moreover, with a branch being a VAT payer, the clients will have to pay VAT, which will create an additional non-recoverable 18% cost for individual clients.

So, the main downside in establishing a family office in the form of a branch is the liability to pay all taxes in full and to submit all types of tax returns.

In practice, the activities of a branch will also attract more attention on the part of the Russian tax authorities than the activities of a standard Russian legal entity.

From the Russian tax law perspective, the basic advantage of a branch is the ability to transfer cash flows from the account of the foreign company to the branch without currency control issues and any taxes.

3.7   Confidentiality
The family office industry is of a confidential nature. It is the family office's job to ensure the confidentiality of all aspects of the capital allocation and any other sensitive information. Thus, confidentiality of all types of information and protection of all documents and correspondence should be the key task of a family office.

In Russia, this task requires the taking of the following actions:
- Secure storage of information, documents, correspondence, databases and so on should be organised;
- All sensitive documents should be kept in specialised archive organisations under conditions of strict confidentiality;
- It makes sense to use safety mechanisms in respect of data exchange through the Internet;
- The premises in which the family office is located must be equipped with secure access systems.

4.   Conclusion

This chapter can be concluded by saying that wealth is always accompanied by a lot of responsibilities, such as the obligation to manage complicated local and international assets, invest wisely, protect the family and so on. Russian private wealth is one of the fastest growing in the world. While the first generation of Russian businessmen is in place, the next generation requires professional attention and care. So the need for professional family office services is apparent.

However, we cannot say that a family office is a standard set of services provided by numerous professionals in Russia and available widely. The principal source of such services offered in Russia is still foreign or international providers. But a growing need for domestic experts (first and foremost, with regards to local assets and affairs) will rapidly build up the market of family office services in Russia. The options, legal and tax opportunities described above constitute a very promising framework for such business activities.

Switzerland

Robert Desax
Baker & McKenzie, Zurich
Anne Gibson
Boston University School of Law
Marnin Michaels
Baker & McKenzie, Zurich

For Switzerland as a global wealth management centre, recent years have been characterised by ongoing upheaval. The past several years have seen expanding global trends towards transparency in the financial industry, and this trend has persisted over the past year. The United States has continued specifically to target Swiss banks, but this year also saw some interesting changes on the part of the Swiss government. In response to mounting global pressure, Switzerland has been taking internal measures to promote transparency.

In this chapter we discuss some of the recent developments that are impacting on Switzerland's wealth management sector, including family offices across the nation. With a disproportionate number of family offices based in Switzerland, it is especially important to understand the changes that have occurred, and to be prepared for those on the horizon. These developments include the US-Swiss non-prosecution agreement programme for Swiss banks, the implementation of the US Foreign Account Tax Compliance Act (FATCA) and potential changes to the United States-Switzerland intergovernmental agreement as a consequence, and Switzerland's participation in certain international exchange of information agreements. This year also saw several domestic legislative proposals regarding lump sum taxation, and a possible national capital gains tax. Finally, we discuss the recent developments regarding Switzerland's so-called white-money strategy.

1. The US programme for non-prosecution agreements or non-target letters for Swiss banks

In August 2013, the United States and Switzerland jointly announced a new component of the ongoing effort by the US government to address overseas tax evasion. This joint statement introduced the Program for Non-Prosecution Agreements or Non-Target Letters for Swiss Banks. The programme functions as an institutional equivalent to the Internal Revenue Service's offshore voluntary disclosure programme for individuals, allowing banks to come forward with specified information, certifications and penalties, in return for a non-prosecution agreement or non-target letter from the US authorities clarifying the bank's status under US law and its potential for criminal indictment. Banks that are currently under criminal investigation are not eligible for the programme.

The programme divides Swiss banks into four categories, indicating the treatment for which the bank is eligible. In order to be eligible for the programme, an institution must be categorised as a bank, specifically a "Swiss financial institution" as defined in the US-Switzerland FATCA intergovernmental agreement, but explicitly excluding investment entities or insurance companies. Category 1 banks are those that are currently under criminal investigation, and they are not eligible for the programme. Category 2 banks are those that believe they may have committed tax-related offences. These banks may request non-prosecution agreements. Category 3 banks are those that do not believe they have committed any tax-related offenses. Category 4 banks are deemed-compliant financial institutions under the intergovernmental agreement, specifically the category of "financial institutions with a local client base." Both Category 3 and Category 4 banks can apply for non-target letters. All categories must agree to certain requirements, including the production of certain information, record retention requirements, internal investigations at their own expense, cooperation with US government treaty requests and the closure of non-compliant US accounts. Category 2 banks must additionally pay penalties. Providing false or misleading information allows the US authorities to pursue criminal prosecution despite the non-prosecution agreement or non-target letter.

A key component of a Category 2 non-prosecution agreement request is the agreement by the bank to pay certain penalties. A penalty must be paid for US accounts open since August 1 2008, correlated to the maximum aggregate value of such accounts. The Category 2 bank must pay:

- 20% of the maximum aggregate value of all US accounts in existence on August 1 2008;
- 30% for US accounts opened between August 1 2008, and February 28 2009; and
- 50% for US accounts opened after February 28 2009.

This has the potential to result in extremely high penalties. The total amount can be reduced, however, by the value of accounts that the bank can demonstrate were either not undeclared accounts, or were disclosed to the US authorities either by the bank or with its encouragement. Exactly how this would be proven is not yet clear. The fact that the bank could benefit from disclosure by account holders, who would themselves then owe penalties, creates a potential for conflicts of interest between the bank and its clients.

The US authorities had received over 100 letters of intent to participate in the programme from Category 2 banks as of February 2014. Since that time, the October 31 2014 deadline for Categories 3 and 4 banks has passed, but no information on the numbers of applicants has yet been released. In October 2014, a draft version of a non-prosecution agreement was released by the US authorities, prompting a group of Swiss banks to ask for the revision of some terms they perceived as harsh. Swiss finance authorities also sought assurance of fair treatment for the banks.

The programme offers a way for Swiss banks to gain certainty regarding their position with the US authorities and, although it comes at a potentially significant cost, it seems that many banks have already determined that this cost is worth it. The fact that the Swiss government has approved of the programme, however, and that it has pledged resources for expediting treaty requests, suggests that this is another step towards a resolution of the ongoing US-Swiss tax evasion dispute.

2.   Implementation of FATCA and the United States-Switzerland intergovernmental agreement

On July 1 2014, the US Foreign Account Tax Compliance Act (FATCA) went into effect. Financial institutions in Switzerland have accordingly begun to implement the requirements put in place by this far-reaching legislation and the related intergovernmental agreement that was signed by the United States and Switzerland. FATCA imposes many due diligence burdens on Swiss banks in regards to accounts that are identified as US accounts or that refuse to be identified, and these are summarised below. Additionally, Switzerland has recently proposed switching its intergovernmental agreement from a Model 2 to a Model 1 agreement, as discussed in more detail below. This could mean a switch from the potential exchange of certain information on request to the reciprocal automatic exchange of information on an annual basis.

A brief summary of FATCA is helpful to understanding its impact on the Swiss wealth management industry. FATCA was enacted in 2010 by the US Congress to target non-compliance by US taxpayers using foreign accounts. The key provisions of FATCA focus on defeating tax evasion. Congress was concerned about US persons avoiding tax through the use of foreign financial institutions. FATCA essentially enlists these foreign financial institutions to assist the Internal Revenue Service (IRS) in locating and reporting on US persons who have accounts at that institution. FATCA requires withholding of 30% of any payment to foreign financial institutions or certain non-financial foreign entities, unless they identify and document US beneficial owners of accounts and US-source payments. Foreign financial institutions can enter into an agreement with the IRS to undertake certain identification, documentation, and reporting requirements in order to avoid withholding applying to payments they receive. Entering into and complying with one of these agreements categorises the institution as a participating foreign financial institution. FATCA is aimed not at raising revenue, but rather at obtaining information and forcing US persons to report their income, by enlisting the aid of institutions outside the United States.

The US government has negotiated intergovernmental agreements with other jurisdictions to ease the implementation of FATCA. It has released two types of model intergovernmental agreements to facilitate this implementation, Model 1 and Model 2. Foreign financial institutions in a jurisdiction that is treated as having an intergovernmental agreement in effect will be covered by that agreement. In jurisdictions that have a Model 1 intergovernmental agreement with the United States, foreign financial institutions will generally not need to enter an agreement with the IRS in order to avoid being subject to withholding. While they will need to register with the IRS, they will not be required to engage in the withholding or reporting requirements of participating foreign financial institutions. Instead, the jurisdiction's tax authorities will relay required information to the IRS. In Model 2 jurisdictions, foreign financial institutions will still need to enter into an agreement with the IRS and become a participating foreign financial institution to avoid being subject to withholding. However, the terms of the agreement applicable to them will be modified by the terms of the Model 2 intergovernmental agreement in place.

As it does for many jurisdictions, FATCA potentially imposes a large administrative burden and a great deal of complexity on Swiss financial institutions. In order to facilitate the implementation of FATCA and reduce this burden, the United States and Switzerland entered into a Model 2 intergovernmental agreement on February 14 2013. This agreement went into effect on June 2 2014. The Swiss national legislation implementing FATCA went into effect on June 30 2014.

As discussed above, the Model 2 intergovernmental agreement allows countries with local law impediments to provide information on US accounts held by foreign financial institutions. Thus, rather than providing a mechanism for Swiss financial institutions to report to the Swiss tax authorities that then pass the information to the IRS, the United States-Switzerland intergovernmental agreement provides for direct reporting from the Swiss financial institutions to the IRS. While no reporting deadlines have yet occurred, Swiss financial institutions have already begun the process of implementing due diligence requirements under FATCA and collecting relevant information.

On May 21 2014, the Swiss Federal Council adopted a draft negotiation mandate to be discussed by the relevant Swiss parliamentary committees and cantons. One recommendation of the council was to negotiate a switch from Switzerland's Model 2 intergovernmental agreement with the United States to a Model 1 intergovernmental agreement. The council indicated that the purpose would be to enable the automatic exchange of information on a reciprocal basis. Under a reciprocal Model 1 intergovernmental agreement, the United States would also be required to turn over to Switzerland the tax information of Swiss residents holding accounts at US financial institutions. This would be a major adjustment from the current Model 2 intergovernmental agreement, which does not allow for the automatic exchange of information between the two governments.

3.   Exchange of information agreements

In recent years, Switzerland has taken various steps in order to implement new standards on the international exchange of tax information. For example, Switzerland has signed tax information exchange agreements with Andorra, Greenland, San Marino, the Seychelles, Jersey, Guernsey and the Isle of Man.

In October 2014, the Swiss government began the domestic consultation procedure on proposed legislation providing for the unilateral application of the Organisation for Economic Co-operation and Development (OECD) standard on the exchange of information. If passed, the new law would allow Switzerland swiftly to amend those of its existing double taxation treaties that do not yet comply with the international standard for the exchange of information upon request. Additionally, the Swiss federal government plans to initiate negotiations to introduce the new global standard for the automatic exchange of information into agreements with partner states. The competent parliamentary committees and the cantons were consulted on the mandates in recent months. Negotiations with partner states should commence shortly.

In November 2014, the Swiss government decided that Switzerland should join the multilateral competent authority agreement on the automatic exchange of information in tax matters as put forward by the OECD. The Swiss government has reaffirmed its intention to pass legislation that would provide a statutory basis for the automatic exchange of information, and would thus allow Swiss financial institutions to commence collecting the account data of foreign taxpayers in 2017. The first exchange of such information could take place in 2018, subject to parliamentary, and possibly voter, approval of the necessary laws and agreements. It is expected that the proposed legislation will be presented in the beginning of 2015 for public consultation and subsequent parliamentary deliberation.

The upcoming two or three years will be crucial for Swiss financial institutions, custodians, brokers, insurance companies and others who will have to implement the OECD common reporting standard on the automatic exchange of information. Under the common reporting standard, they will have to carry out a due diligence process on existing client relationships (both individual and entity accounts) in order to identify reportable accounts. Financial information will then have to be reported annually for transmission to the relevant client's jurisdiction of residence.

4. Taxation

4.1 Lump sum taxation

Another recent upheaval in the Swiss wealth management field was a national proposal to repeal the lump sum taxation rules. Various cantons in Switzerland have laws in place under which wealthy individuals intending to reside in Switzerland can negotiate a fixed tax (known as a 'forfait' or lump sum tax), in lieu of paying ordinary income tax each year. Local residents have protested this policy in a number of cantons. A bill was proposed that would have required the repeal of lump sum taxation throughout the nation, and a popular vote was held on the proposal on November 30 2014. Although the proposal did not pass (59.6% of the voters rejected it), it exemplifies the ongoing changes in a part of Swiss public opinion towards lump sum taxation.

Lump sum taxation is seen by many as an important incentive and immigration planning tool for non-Swiss high net worth individuals. However, it has recently been the subject of controversy in Switzerland. Various cantons have begun to change their policies on lump-sum taxation in the last five years, with some abolishing the policy (such as Zurich and Basel), and others introducing stricter rules (such as Berne).

Despite the failure of the proposal to repeal lump sum taxation, there will be new national requirements on these policies. Among other changes, the federal government has said it will introduce a minimum taxable income of Sfr400,000 beginning in 2017. Previously, the federal authorities had not set such a minimum requirement on the lump sum taxation policies of the local governments. Currently, the specific requirements and thresholds that have to be satisfied by non-EU citizens in order to benefit from the rules in the various cantons are generally more stringent than those applied to EU citizens, and it is expected that this trend will continue.

Although lump sum taxation has not been abolished at the national level for the moment, the relative popularity of the proposal suggests that more individual cantons could abolish or place additional limitations on their own lump sum taxation rules going forward.

4.2 National estate and gift tax

There has also been a debate in the Swiss parliament regarding a legislative proposal for a national gift and inheritance tax in recent years. Currently, only cantons and communes have the ability to levy gift and inheritance taxes, and the impact of such laws in the jurisdictions that have them tend to be limited, in part due to the fact that spouses, registered partners and direct descendants are generally exempt. However, under the current proposal, first raised in 2011, transfers of property at death or by gift would be subject to a new flat tax of 20% of the actual value at the time of the transfer, with an exemption for the first Sfr2 million. Transfers among spouses and registered partners would be exempt, but no exemption would apply to others, including direct descendants. Cantons and communes would no longer have the ability to levy gift or inheritance taxes.

The proposal also contains a controversial retroactive effect. Based on the date that this initiative was originally launched, any gifts made after January 1 2012 would be included in the taxpayer's taxable estate at the date of death and subject to the tax. A majority in the Swiss parliament opposes the proposal. A popular vote on the proposal is expected in 2015.

4.3 Capital gains tax and an exit tax

In September 2014, the Swiss government issued a proposal for a comprehensive reform of the Swiss corporate tax system (also known as the 'corporate tax reform III'). The purpose of the reform is both to increase international acceptance of the Swiss corporate tax system and to enhance Switzerland's attractiveness for multinational corporations.

In order to offset some of the cost of this proposal, lawmakers included the introduction of a capital gains tax on the sale of privately held securities. Currently, there is no tax imposed on capital gains from the sale of privately held assets, with the exception of real property. Under the new rules, a portion of the capital gains from the sale of securities would be included in an individual's taxable income. Under the proposal, 70% of such capital gains and dividend income would be subject to individual income taxation.

Additionally, the proposal includes an 'exit tax', under which individuals giving up Swiss residency would be treated as if they had sold all of their securities just prior to exiting. Thus, abandoning Swiss residency would constitute a taxable event and could result in a substantial amount of deemed capital gain subject to tax.

Capital gains taxation has always been a highly controversial topic in Switzerland. It is currently uncertain whether such a tax would be kept in the proposed corporate tax reform bill as it might well jeopardise the entire reform. It is expected that the bill will be discussed and voted on by the Swiss parliament in mid-2016 at the earliest. If that happens, and if a popular vote on the bill is not required, the new tax rules could enter into force between 2018 and 2020.

5.   White-money strategy

A white-money strategy, or white-money policy, is an approach taken by various institutions and countries to address the use of such institutions or countries by non-residents as a means of circumventing their home country tax laws. In essence, white-money strategies compel financial institutions to obtain a declaration from clients that the funds at issue are properly taxed in the clients' jurisdictions of residence. Historically, such policies have only been needed in jurisdictions in which the evasion of foreign taxes is not a crime.

In jurisdictions in which foreign tax evasion is a crime under anti-money laundering rules, there is no need for a separate white-money policy because the existing anti-money laundering rules serve the same function. For example, within the European Union, the Third Anti-Money Laundering Directive, effective from July 2006, made foreign tax evasion a money laundering predicate offence. Thus there is no need to implement a separate, formal white-money strategy in the European Union.

However, in jurisdictions that do not have separate anti-money laundering rules that criminalise foreign tax evasion, white-money strategies are necessary to ensure that local financial institutions are not being used to hide undeclared funds. As a result of the global trend that started in 2008 towards increased attention on international tax evasion, and the change in attitude towards the issue of transparency and undeclared funds, many jurisdictions and financial institutions have decided that they would attempt to ensure that at least new funds, and possibly pre-existing funds, would be accepted only from declared sources. Switzerland is one of these jurisdictions, and has been exploring the possibility of implementing a white-money policy on the federal level since 2010. Below we discuss the developments regarding this policy in recent years.

In 2012, the Swiss government, specifically the Federal Council, began exploring a strategy for a tax-compliant and competitive financial centre. Part of this strategy aimed to prevent the acceptance of untaxed assets by requiring enhanced due diligence requirements, sometimes referred to as the 'financial integrity strategy', essentially a white-money strategy. This was in part motivated by Switzerland's acceptance of the 2012 revised Financial Action Task Force recommendations, which in part require jurisdictions to implement measures to identify the beneficial owners of legal entities and enhance transparency. The Federal Council also instructed the Federal Department of Finance to submit a corresponding draft for consultation by the beginning of 2013. Near the end of 2012, a report on Switzerland's financial market policy was issued by the Federal Council. The report contained a section on the financial integrity strategy, which included new due diligence requirements for financial intermediaries, and described how the strategy would be implemented.

On February 27 2013, the Federal Council launched two legislative consultations on combating money laundering and on enhanced due diligence requirements in the area of taxation. The proposals included:

- the introduction of a new predicate offence to money laundering in the form of qualified tax fraud in the area of direct taxation and the extension of the existing predicate offence in the area of indirect taxation; and

- the implementation of due diligence requirements for the acceptance of assets by financial institutions.

Under the current proposal, which was accepted by the Swiss parliament in December 2014, a qualified tax fraud (and thus a predicate offence to money laundering) would be constituted if it involves forgery of documents and evaded taxes of more than Sfr300,000 per tax year.

The Federal Council did not want to impose an obligation on financial intermediaries to obtain self-declarations from their clients in all circumstances. Instead, it proposed a risk-based approach, similar to the due diligence requirements that apply under anti-money laundering laws. Essentially this assessment would use pre-defined tax compliance indicators to undertake an assessment of the clients. If the financial intermediary came to the conclusion that the assets concerned were undeclared, it would be required to refuse to accept the assets. Pre-existing clients would also be evaluated, and if it were determined that their assets were undeclared, the financial intermediary would have to terminate the relationship unless such termination would expose the financial intermediary to a potential risk of criminal prosecution in the home jurisdiction of the client.

This proposal met with a great deal of criticism from various sectors, and in November 2013 the Federal Council announced that it would review and revise the proposal. It suggested that the new due diligence requirements would only be required for clients from those jurisdictions with which Switzerland did not have an automatic exchange of information agreement. The Federal Department of Finance was instructed to produce a revised proposal adhering to these guidelines, essentially putting the white-money strategy on hold. Subsequently, the OECD released what it described as a global standard for automatic exchange of information agreements, which contains reporting and due diligence requirements for financial account information. It is thought that the Federal Department of Finance's new due diligence proposal will incorporate the OECD standards.

6. Conclusion

There has been a big push globally for more transparency in the financial industry, and in wealth management in particular. Recent years have seen these global changes continue to have a practical impact in Switzerland. One trend in 2014 was the increasingly active role that the Swiss government is taking in these matters. This year also saw advances in several proposals and projects to which the Swiss government actively agreed, such as the non-prosecution agreement programme for Swiss banks, the multilateral competent authority agreement on the automatic exchange of information in tax matters and the continued development of Switzerland's own white-money strategy. Additionally, the willingness of the federal authorities to propose such things as the automatic exchange of information, a capital gains tax and an exit tax shows a shift in attitudes regarding taxation, moving more towards the prevailing global outlook. It seems that global developments and changing attitudes towards bank secrecy and tax evasion are having an impact on Swiss attitudes as well. However, the results of popular votes on tax matters generally suggest that changes of tax rules are difficult to obtain and therefore constitute a political challenge for those who would like to see them implemented (be it authorities, lobbies or political interest groups). These developments are forcing major changes for the wealth management sector, including private family offices, in terms of their legal obligations of disclosure and the extent of the discretion they can offer their clients. Regardless of where a family office is located, any of the family offices using Switzerland for investment purposes need to be aware of these extensive changes that have been taking place in the Swiss wealth management sector.

While the changes taking place in Switzerland that impact the wealth management sector will hurt for the next few years, this is not the first time a major industry in Switzerland has gone through such a change. Major upheavals occurred in the pharmaceutical sector in the 1950s, and the watch industry went through a similar crisis in the 1970s. However, both of these industries not only adapted, but thrived thereafter. The wealth management industry too will no doubt overcome this challenge.

United Kingdom

Grania Baird
Marianne Kafena
Alison Springett
Sarah von Schmidt
Farrer & Co

Someone's sitting in the shade today because someone planted a tree a long time ago. – Warren Buffett

People who create or inherit substantial wealth tend to want to preserve and grow it, to secure their families' future and, often, to fulfil philanthropic desires. Invariably, they also wish to maintain a distance between personal and business matters, while controlling their affairs flexibly and maintaining maximum confidentiality. The family office arrangement is one way of meeting these aspirations.

1. The United Kingdom and family offices: history and context

In the United States, during the 19th century, J P Morgan and the Rockefeller family established family offices with the express aim of managing family assets. The expertise was subsequently extended to other families and their legacy lives on today. According to the *Financial Times*, in an article published on November 25 2014, the Rockefellers' family office now has 259 clients.[1]

In contrast, the family office concept in the United Kingdom (UK) has grown incrementally over centuries. Medieval royalty and wealthy families would employ stewards to manage their domestic staff, household affairs and their wealth, including land. The steward's duties included, for example, preparation of accounts for review by the master of the house. This ethos of stewardship endures today in the management of private family wealth across the UK, whether or not that function is expressly labelled 'family office'.

Alongside this history of stewardship, London in particular has a long history of forming trade associations whose common themes are money, business and philanthropy. The origins of the livery companies of the City of London, for example, are rooted in Medieval guilds, and their remit extends far beyond aspects of training, maintenance of industry standards and regulation of the various trades they represent:

> *Each of them is a remarkable philanthropic fellowship… every Company has in its own way made its charitable work manifest either by supporting education, research and welfare or by nurturing the skills of those actively involved…*[2]

---

[1] "Expansion of family-office industry leads to blurring of distinctions", Financial Times, November 25 2014.

[2] Source: The Livery Profile leaflet, produced by the Mercers' Company and published on the City of London website.

Together, these traditions of stewardship, the organisation of trading assets and understated philanthropy still inform much of the advice provided by professionals to family offices in the UK today. The market is diverse and includes families with relatively recently-forged UK links as well as those born and raised in the UK.

2. The UK market today

2.1 What is a family office?

Once you've seen one family office, you've seen ONE family office.[3]

No doubt every submission to this publication will seek to answer this question and it will be interesting to compare, once compiled, the ambit of definitions by jurisdiction. In this section, we keep the definition brief.

The core activities of a family office arrangement involve the centralised management of wealth derived from one family, or a few, in an environment where family influence affects decision-making. Each family will add services to this core activity, in line with its requirements and ability/willingness to meet the costs associated with each activity.

2.2 Third-party providers

There is a range of providers of loosely defined family office services in the United Kingdom. Their remit varies according to expertise and can broadly be summarised as follows:

(a) Banks

Banks extend their expertise in investment and financial advisory services to third-party family offices. Some have in-house private investment offices acting as multi-family offices. In addition to investment management, services offered to families can include:

- financial planning;
- insurance planning;
- risk management;
- compliance and regulatory support;
- access to sophisticated banking platforms;
- global custody and consolidated reporting; and
- review and management of family investment philosophy and suitability of investments made.

(b) Consultancy firms

This group tends to support wealthy families by providing independent advice, often supported by research. Services include:

- acting as the main or trusted advisers;
- financial reporting;

---

3   Attributed to Patricia M Soldano, Chair of GenSpring Family Offices' Western region, in the following Forbes article: www.forbes.com/sites/toddganos/2013/08/13/what-is-a-family-office/.

- evaluation and consolidation of information provided by other service providers, such as accountants and wealth-management firms; and
- selection of money managers.

(c) **Law firms, accountancy firms and trust companies**

Each of these groups of professionals engages with wealthy families and family offices through the provision of services encompassing:

- advice in connection with establishing a family office;
- implementation of effective family governance;
- tax advice and reporting in relation to personal and business assets situated in the UK and overseas;
- trust and family office administration;
- advice in establishing a charity or philanthropic foundation;
- managing charitable donations;
- accounting and audit;
- expenses management;
- advice in relation to regulatory and compliance obligations of the family office;
- facilitating inter-generational change;
- immigration and employment law advice for family office staff and family members;
- wealth planning and matrimonial advice for family members; and
- review of overseas structures holding family wealth.

(d) **Independent advisers and boutique firms**

These firms provide specialist services, including:

- concierge services;
- lifestyle management;
- reputation management;
- security services;
- property finding;
- advice on schools in the UK;
- health services;
- insurance; and
- coaching.

2.3 Single-family offices and multi-family offices in the UK

As will be well-rehearsed elsewhere in this book, the nature, purpose and structure of family offices are dictated by the needs of the families they serve. Single family offices and multi-family offices will also be defined elsewhere, so here we focus on the main characteristics of each, by reference to the UK market:

	Single family office	**Multi–family office**
Client(s)	– One family	– A number of families
Structure	– The structure can be as informal or formal as a family requires – Staff tend to be employed either directly by the family or by a family–owned vehicle (eg a company or partnership) – The family remains primarily responsible for aspects such as premises, IT and managing staff – Family affairs tend to dictate the level of activity and nature of the work carried out – Changes in staff can disrupt service levels disproportionately	– These are organisations independent of the founding family/families – Family members may hold offices within the organisation, but its services are provided at arm's length – Service levels are less disrupted by changes in staffing – Day–to–day management of premises, IT and staffing is the preserve of the organisation, not the family
Accountability	– The closeness to the family can engender high levels of trust, a deep sense of responsibility for actions and a highly personal level of service – The same closeness can result in tension and conflict if poorly managed and staff can become over–identified with the family they serve. In turn, this can lead to behaviour aimed at pleasing the family, rather than focusing objectively on best interests. Longevity of service can present a particular challenge here: resistance to change must not be the price of continuity	– In serving a number of families, staff must bear in mind diverging interests – Potential conflicts of interest between founding families and other clients must be carefully managed where a multi–family office has recently evolved from a single family office – Conflict resulting from over–identification with one family is less likely

continued on next page

	Single family office	Multi-family office
Costs	– Costs are borne by one family – International families tend to want to base their London family offices in areas where the fixed costs of premises are high. This, in addition to other fixed costs, can be difficult to manage against unpredictable income – On the other hand, where asset management is carried out in–house, the high level of exclusivity, privacy and customisation can enhance returns in the absence of a product push	– Costs are shared among all the clients – Efficiencies of scale are easier to achieve – Situation of premises tends to be less of a personal choice for one family – Despite efficiencies on costs in other areas, some multi–family offices create and push their own financial products to help meet the cost of running the organisation

In terms of numbers, it is very difficult to say with any authority how many family offices there are in existence in the UK. This is partly because there is such a variety of arrangements falling within the concept (many of which may not identify themselves as family offices, though they function as such) and because one of the attractions of family offices is their discretion.

Recent research published by Ernst and Young states that "Family offices are arguably the fastest-growing investment vehicles in the world today... there are at least 3,000 single family offices in existence globally and at least half of these were set up in the last 15 years..."[4] Although this is not specific to the UK, it gives insight into the level of activity in this market in recent years.

In terms of the distribution of wealth as between single family offices and multi-family offices, in October 2013, Reuters reported that "Single-family offices managed about $1.2 trillion globally as of September 2011, while multi-family funds, which manage assets for several families, had assets of $777 billion in December 2012, a study by Boston-based Cerulli Associates showed."[5]

A third concept has been added over recent years to the traditional single family office and multi-family office: the virtual family office. In practice, this describes the situation where a family is starting to organise its wealth using technology and is not yet ready to commit to the cost of premises. It is, effectively, the business start-up phase of the family office. Family members often figure prominently, and the extent of success in transitioning to greater organisation and delegation of functions over time is often determined by the range and quality of their business skills.

---

4   Source: EY Family Office Guide: www.ey.com/Publication/vwLUAssets/EY-Pathway-to-successful-family-and-wealth-management/$FILE/EY-Pathway-to-successful-family-and-wealth-management.pdf.
5   Source: uk.reuters.com/article/2013/10/04/frontier-investing-families-idUKL6N0HS21J20131004.

2.3 A UK case in point: single family office to multi-family office

When his father died in 1984, and he had to take over running the family business, Mark Pears was 21 years old. He and his brothers, Trevor and David, are the third generation of a family that has organised and grown its wealth – most notably through real estate investment in the UK – discreetly and very successfully for nearly 60 years.

The Pears Foundation was established by the same family. Trevor now acts as its executive chair and its website consciously identifies the foundation with its founding family, stating: "We are a British family foundation rooted in Jewish values." The foundation recently made its largest ever donation, of £5 million, to support the efforts of the Royal Free Hospital, in Hampstead, North London, in building what is described as "a world class centre to research cures for cancer and HIV."[6]

In addition to building their own wealth and pursuing philanthropic activities successfully, the Pears family group comprises an investment management arm that started as the family's private investment office. Talisman Global Asset Management Limited was once the Pears family's single family office. According to its website:

> "Talisman was incorporated in 1998 as the asset management arm of a single family, following the sale of real estate assets which provided £50m of investment capital in 1994… The current Talisman structure was established in 2001 with [assets under management] of £250m…Today Talisman has [assets under management] of £2.4bn."

At the foot of Talisman's minimalist website is a link: "Commitment to the UK Stewardship Code". This code is one of many aspects of UK financial regulation that can affect family offices. It sets standards relating to institutional investment and its opening section declares that "Effective stewardship benefits companies, investors and the economy as a whole."[7] The same may be said for stewardship in a family office context.

In a rare interview given to the *Sunday Telegraph* in 2011, Mark Pears addressed the various concerns of anyone running a family business:

> A lot of them do struggle when they go past two or three or four generations. I hope that's not what's going to happen here…The way we've run it we have good quality people working here. If I were to get run over by a bus tomorrow, I think we've got very capable people who could run it already.[8]

As anyone running their own family office knows, capable people who work well together are the most important determinant in the ultimate success or failure of the enterprise.

2.4 Staffing the family office in London

One of the attractions of establishing a family office in London is the availability of people able and willing to take on the role of running it. There is, in addition, a

---

6   Source: Ham & High news report dated September 30 2014.
7   Source: www.frc.org.uk/Our-Work/Publications/Corporate-Governance/UK-Stewardship-Code-September-2012.pdf.
8   Source: James Quinn, "Pears Family Comes Out Of The Property Shadows", Sunday Telegraph, June 12 2011.

thriving network of family offices where exchange of information and shared experience contribute to the maintenance of standards and a sense of context.

Staffing the family office may, therefore, seem like a relatively straightforward proposition. In terms of roles, a relatively well established family office providing administration and financial services is likely to comprise people fulfilling some or all of the following senior staff functions (although the job titles may be different in practice):

- chief executive officer – often someone with an accounting, legal or financial services background whose role is to run the family office, taking account of the family's wishes on one hand and his/her legal, taxation, regulatory and corporate responsibility obligations on the other (the two often diverge);
- chief financial officer – core responsibilities include control and management of financial risk;
- chief operations officer – tends to be responsible for the day-to-day running of the family office. This role can be combined with that of chief executive officer or chief financial officer, depending upon the size of the family office; and
- chief investment officer – responsible for the investment aspects.

One of the relatively new challenges for senior staff concerns media and public relations. Online social networks and the incremental encroachment of cameras in public and private places together mean that privacy is under attack more than ever. Threats to the reputation and private lives of wealthy families are no longer the sole preserve of paparazzi. Senior staff would be well advised to include security and reputation management in their strategies.

This group of senior staff members requires administrative support from secretaries as well as colleagues providing general administrative support. This includes: payments processing; the effective marshalling and filing of information (particularly in terms of anti-money-laundering records and information exchange requirements); and general coordination and communication between family office staff, the family and external third parties, such as bankers and trustees.

In a family context, it is surprisingly easy for someone's role to grow wider and more challenging than the initial description envisaged. It can also seem artificial to impose formal boundaries around someone's role, in a context that feels personal and involves a family's most sensitive, private information. Nevertheless, the absence of objective management and focus on best interests often leads to employment-related disputes that can occupy a disproportionate amount of family and staff time and can be very disruptive to the operation of the family office.

It is, therefore, every bit as important that the family office team works well together as that each individual has the appropriate qualifications and skills to fulfil his role. Overlaid with family-centric interests, a good team is more likely to maintain objectivity and resist over-identification with the family than a dysfunctional team, where individuals can put self-interest or pleasing the family before doing the right thing.

As Casey Stengel once said in relation to baseball: "Finding good players is easy. Getting them to play as a team is another story."

2.5   **Family businesses in the UK**
According to the International Centre for Families in Business, family businesses based in the UK:

- account for two jobs out of every five in the UK private sector (9.2 million people);
- account for almost a quarter of the overall UK gross domestic product;
- contribute £73 billion of UK total tax revenues; and
- make up nearly 50% of mid-sized businesses in the United Kingdom (those in the range between £20 million and £500 million).

The same source also reveals that:

- approximately 60% fail to plan formally for succession;
- only 30% make it to second generation family ownership; and
- less than 10% make it to the third generation in the same family ownership.

3.   **Trends**
The financial crisis of 2007 and 2008 caused a loss of capital severe enough to cause wealthy families all over the world to start taking control of managing their own assets, and many looked to London to establish family offices. In August 2008, the *Financial Times* reported: "More than 300 ultra-rich families with assets over £100m each have set up their own private offices in London to protect and enhance their wealth in the financial services sector's newest trend…"

A parallel trend is the move away from one relationship with a private bank towards using multiple financial service-providers. This, in itself, prompts a need for tailored administrative support, co-ordination of information and expertise in the oversight of those financial service-providers, with a focus on the particular family's requirements. A family office arrangement tends to grow in response to these needs, whether or not the family is conscious of it happening.

The remainder of this chapter will assume that the model under consideration is the single family office.

4.   **Why establish a family office in the UK?**
Subject to its family's needs, a family office can fulfil a number of functions and can be tasked with providing some or all of the functions listed under the section on third-party providers above. The key aspect in a family office environment is that those services are delivered in a manner which, at its best, provides (among other things):

- centralised, highly tailored asset management;
- centralised management of assets such as art collections, yachts, real estate in multiple countries and private jets;
- effective co-ordination of third-party advisory relationships, often in different countries;
- a high level of confidentiality in relation to family information;
- streamlined reporting and quick decision-making;
- an environment in which a family with wealth can adapt to change privately, for example if the sale of a business yields significant additional wealth or a bad business decision erodes wealth;

- effective family governance support and implementation; and
- a means of facilitating generational change with little risk of dispute among family members.

The UK remains one of the world's leading centres for international services connected with wealth management and planning. The legal and accounting professions, in particular, are accustomed to advising families with inherited and business wealth situated in and outside the UK. For international families transacting business across continents, the UK can also be a particularly convenient place to do business in terms of time zone and proximity to European financial centres.

The wealth of experience and expertise available to family offices within the UK is a strong predictor for their success.

The UK is not, however, an entirely straightforward jurisdiction in terms of tax planning and financial regulation. International families often benefit from assets held within trusts and other non-UK structures. Often, these structures have been established with succession planning in mind, not the avoidance of taxation. Basing a family office in London tends to involve liaison between family office members and trustees of such non-UK trusts and their underlying companies. Unless this liaison is closely monitored and controlled, it can unwittingly bring a family's non-UK wealth within the UK tax net. In addition, family offices carrying out investment advice are likely to be subject to UK financial regulation and associated compliance obligations.

The next section summarises some of the essential considerations around good governance, UK tax and regulation. Appropriate professional advisers should be involved if these issues are relevant.

5. Good governance

There are two aspects to good governance: first, the putting in place of a sound process for decision-making and second: facilitating implementation of those decisions.

In a family office context, good governance affects both the family itself and the family office. In relation to the family, there are various names for a document that sets out a family's history, values and goals with the intention of minimising disputes and preserving wealth. It can be called a family charter, a family constitution or a family contract, for example. These kinds of documents are often not legally binding. They nevertheless share certain features with legal contracts and should be drafted with care. Their power lies in the family's collective will to abide by the terms to which they sign up.

Separately, there are more technical issues of governance where members of a family office situated in London interact regularly with trustees or directors of family trusts and companies that are not UK resident. These issues can be complex. The summaries below highlight the main concerns in this area.

5.1 Management and control of non-UK resident companies

Every member of staff within the family office, including family members, must understand and remain within the limits of his role. In a family context, it can seem artificial and awkward to insist on the clear delineation of authority in this way. It is, however, very important to get this right.

Over time, as working practices become more and more familiar, it can be easy to forget who has the authority to do what, how and where. There is a risk, for example, that decisions that should properly be made outside the UK start being made within the UK, because someone within the UK has become used to calling the shots.

Mohamed Al-Fayed found out the hard way why calling the shots in the UK in relation to non-UK companies is not a good idea:

> Her Majesty's Revenue and Customs (HMRC) benefits from wide powers to require taxpayers to provide information for the purpose of checking a taxpayer's position.
>
> In 2004, Mohamed Al Fayed (the former owner of Harrods) tried to avoid having to complete his tax return, on the basis that he had a special agreement with HMRC.
>
> One of the central issues in HMRC's case was 'management and control' and how that affected UK taxation. HMRC's affidavit stated: "...Mr Al-Fayed's perceived autocratic manner... directed my attention to the locus of central management and control of offshore companies. If the offshore companies are centrally managed and controlled in the UK, then it has taxing rights on profits..."
>
> Outcome: Al Fayed failed and HMRC was granted the right to launch a full investigation into his tax affairs.

There are numerous other cases concerning management and control of non-UK resident companies. The main risks they highlight in a family office context are as follows:

- If decisions concerning the management and control of an offshore company are made in the UK, the company will be taxable in the UK;
- Those responsible for the administration of that company will be accountable for the tax; and
- Anyone who deliberately misleads HMRC in relation to the management and control of a company may be guilty of tax fraud.

These risks can be controlled in a variety of ways. It is wise for family offices to put in place protocols that limit the risk of tax breaches. These tend to be practical, setting out a framework for how and where important decisions should be made, and most importantly, by whom. Advisers with appropriate expertise should draft these protocols.

In addition to putting in place documented protocols, it can be useful to ensure that staff and family members receive training, so that protocols are implemented properly in the day-to-day of office business. This often helps members of a family office maintain a higher level of vigilance, so that there is a conscious attention to the location of management and control of non-UK resident companies.

5.2 The residence of trusts

It is common for international family wealth to be held within non-UK-resident trust (and other) structures. These assets are often intended to benefit a number of family members and they may hold a range of assets such as residential property, valuable art, wine, yachts, aircraft or operating businesses. The trustees, directors and other professionals who run these structures are key decision-makers. They are also often, understandably, eager to maintain their relationships with families.

As any experienced trust professional will tell you: a good trustee is not necessarily the family's friend, acquiescing to all demands. A trustee's primary duty is to manage and exercise control over assets put in its care, with the beneficiaries' best interests in mind. This is not the same thing as agreeing to everything a beneficiary (or settlor) wants.

The family office would do well to remember that, unlike a company or foundation, a trust does not have its own legal identity. It is a legal relationship whose flexibility brings many benefits to families planning wealth over generations. Equally, this flexibility makes trusts vulnerable to poor governance. The immunity of a trust from UK tax – indeed, its very existence – can be undermined by the behaviour of families and their advisers.

A non-UK resident trustee can be treated as carrying on trust business in the UK through the agency of someone resident in the UK, if that UK resident person is allowed to make decisions on behalf of the trustees in the UK.

Again, such risks can be controlled with effectively implemented protocols that have been prepared with the help of appropriate advisers. The protocols do not have to be complicated and, when drafted properly, they are tailored to specific family needs and are intended to provide practical know-how for the family office.

There are two final aspects of good governance that a family should consider and address: marital contracts and non-disclosure agreements. Failure to address the effect of a marriage or its eventual dissolution on overall family wealth is a common mistake, as is the failure to control the dissemination of private information. Even when these issues are addressed, they are often forgotten and addressed too late, with adverse consequences.

One of the most common failures of good governance is less a legal issue than a practical one: remembering that the purpose of the family office is to serve its family. Regular (at least annual) reviews are necessary to ensure everyone involved stays in touch with the family's overall requirements. It is important to aim to balance required or advisable change against the reason a family office was set up in the first place. Asking leading family members what a family actually wants seems obvious, but tends not to happen regularly enough in practice.

6. Regulatory considerations in the UK

As noted above, family offices are all different and whether they will be caught by the UK's financial services regulatory regime depends on the nature of the activities they are involved in and the services they provide. Indeed, family offices may escape regulation altogether. If, for example, their services are limited to general administration, coordination and lifestyle management – as might be the case for some single family offices – it is unlikely that these activities will be within the scope of the UK's financial services regulatory regime.

If, on the other hand, the range of services provided by the family office includes financial services, such as investment advice and asset management in relation to certain investments, these are potentially regulated activities and the family office may need to be authorised by the Financial Conduct Authority (FCA) in order to carry out the activity.

The regulation of financial services in the UK is the preserve of the FCA. Anyone providing investment advice in the UK must be registered with the FCA, which is an independent, non-governmental body. The FCA derives its powers from the Financial Services and Markets Act 2000. These are wide-ranging and extend to investigation, rule-making and enforcement.

Common regulated activities that family offices may be involved in and for which the FCA's authorisation may be required, include:

- arranging for investments to be bought or sold;
- advising on the merits of buying or selling an investment;
- managing investments; or
- managing a fund

Unless a relevant exclusion applies, carrying on a regulated activity in the UK by way of business and without authorisation is a criminal offence. The FCA is one of two financial services regulators in the UK and, together with the Prudential Regulation Authority, the FCA is responsible for authorising and regulating businesses that wish to carry on regulated activities in the UK. The FCA also has responsibility for protecting the people who use financial services and it achieves this through wide-ranging powers which regulate, monitor and enforce how financial services are carried on in the UK.

For a single family office, there are typically two routes that might lead to FCA regulation: first, organic growth, where, for example, a single family office extends its asset management expertise to a broader family group; or secondly, where the family office makes a conscious decision to establish an independent asset management arm, as in the case of the Pears family when they started Talisman Global Asset Management Limited. In each of these cases, the entity proposing to carry on the regulated activity would have to apply to the FCA for authorisation before it could provide financial services in the UK.

In contrast to single family offices, most multi-family offices are likely to be carrying on a range of financial services for the families they serve, and they will need to be regulated by the FCA in order to do so.

A family office that is authorised by the FCA will be subject to on-going fees and to monitoring by the FCA. It will also have to file annual reports with the FCA on aspects of its business activities. Additionally, individuals within the family office carrying out key functions will need to be personally approved by the FCA.

A family office that is involved in any potentially regulated activity should consider, at an early stage, whether the UK regulatory framework will apply to them so that, where necessary, the family office can be structured to avoid coming within the regulatory framework or the appropriate authorisations can be put in place.

A recent example of the FCA exercising its powers: on September 23 2014, the FCA's website published details of a fine imposed on Barclays Bank Plc for "... failing to properly protect clients' custody assets worth £16.5 billion..." The FCA fined Barclays £37,745,000 in respect of this breach.

7.   Philanthropy

The desire to do good is a common aspiration for families with wealth. Often, that desire is expressed in the establishment of family foundations or charities, such as the Pears Foundation mentioned earlier, the Sainsbury Family Charitable Trusts and the Ashley Family Foundation (formerly the Laura Ashley Foundation).

The main issues in this area can be summarised as follows:

- Most families struggle to balance their wish to do good with making a profit. This is not an easy balance for the investment manager to achieve, in a context of tension between public and private markets;
- The nature of family wealth and families' aspirations tend to mean, together, that investing is undertaken more patiently. This sits well with challenges around philanthropic impact, because impact investing is typically illiquid and of long duration. Family wealth dedicated to philanthropy tends to be characterised as patient capital, where horizons for returns can stretch to between five and 10 years; and
- This longer-term investing sits well with stewardship.

A family giving serious consideration to investing with philanthropic aims should address these issues with appropriately experienced investment advisers.

8.   Costs

It is obvious that the costs associated with running a family office will be linked to the range of services provided, location and size of any premises and the number of staff, among other things.

Advice on costs must be obtained from the right professionals, with particular circumstances in mind. Each family office arrangement must take into consideration the comparative costs of fulfilling a function in-house, against the cost of outsourcing it appropriately. This analysis must be done against the background of the family context. In other words, the family office is not like any other small business. There are multi-generational time horizons that necessitate a longer-term approach to costs management. This is a particularly important balance when it comes to deciding whether to recruit staff or outsource certain functions.

In June 2014, the *Wall Street Journal* reported Pierre-Alan Wavre (head of Pictet's multi-family office) as saying that, "To really get the most cost-effective pricing on investment products and afford the best staff, half a billion dollars in assets is probably a good rule of thumb," when it comes to fixing a threshold.[9]

The same report detailed research carried out by Merrill Lynch and Campden Research, that showed the average cost of running a family office is approximately 0.6% of assets under management.

It remains important to strike a clear balance between controlling immediate cost

---

9   online.wsj.com/articles/SB10001424052748704002104575290462495992430.

and assessing the longer-term impact of intelligently-incurred cost, for the benefit of the family over time.

9. Sink or swim

If a family office is to succeed, no matter where it is established, everyone affected by it must recognise and accept that it has a key role in protecting, as well as serving its family/families. In 2006, Family Office Exchange published a "Thought Leaders Compendium" entitled *Recasting the Central Role of the Family Office as Risk Manager*. The analysis centred around the concept of the family office as an early warning system.

The research identified a number of risks that should be anticipated and controlled by any family office that is serious about protecting the family it serves. It is strongly recommended that family offices address these risks, to the extent that they have not already done so:

- the absence of a shared vision for the future
- lack of effective processes around decision-making
- absence of transparent communication within a family
- inappropriate ownership structure of assets
- lack of asset diversification
- poor focus on key family risks

Ultimately, the success or failure of a family office depends largely upon the behaviour, expertise and capabilities of the people within it, balanced against buy-in from the family and its members' willingness to accept change and guidance, where needed. This is particularly true when coping with generational change.

10. Conclusion

Family offices in the UK continue to thrive and there is no sign of contraction in the market. Each arrangement should suit the needs of the family it serves and everyone involved is well advised to remain conscious of the limits of their role.

Returning to where this chapter began: a family office arrangement is best implemented as a function of a family's circumstances. It makes sense only when a family has properly assessed its needs and the costs of meeting them. It is as important to know when a family would not benefit from one as when it would. There must be a vision shared by the family and implemented dynamically over time by anyone advising or working with the family.

Frank Stangenberg-Haverkamp is the chairman of the executive board of E Merck KG. He is also a member of the 11th generation of the family that controls the company. Here is what he has to say about family offices:

When a family has invested everything in their company and there is no money lying around in need of an investment then you are not in need of a family office.[10]

---

10   online.wsj.com/articles/SB10001424052748704002104575290462495992430.

United States

Mary K Duke
Independent adviser to families

1. US background

The family office community in the United States is distinguished by the number and variety of family office models that have developed there over the last few decades. The following discussion provides an overview of the most common models and an assessment of the inherent and potential strengths and weaknesses of each.

Each model has attributes that make it more or less suitable for the needs of an individual family. It is important to take these into consideration and plan accordingly. Being aware of the potential pitfalls of a model allows the family and its advisors to build in controls and counter-measures to offset them. For example, internal controls can often be lacking in a single family office. Knowing this, the family can work to ensure that more robust checks and balances are adopted in their office procedures, and will appreciate why enforcing them is important. (Let us not forget, it is often the family members themselves who enjoy the loose operating model and who might bristle at the idea of formal signoffs or procedures.)

This analysis is intended to provide insights into the considerations to be made before:

- establishing a family office;
- opening an existing family office to clients; or
- hiring a multi-family office.

2. The family office explosion of the 1990s

The functional grouping of resources, known today as a family office, has existed as long as there have been families with significant, complex wealth. In the United States, capitalists of the gilded age, such as Carnegie, Astor, Rockefeller and Vanderbilt, all amassed extraordinary wealth in an era before the United States had a tax code or anti-monopoly laws. Each had a private office to manage the attendant financial affairs. But it is worth noting that the term 'family office' is relatively new in the vernacular and only came into common use in the United States in the 1990s. Economies were expanding and the US capital markets favoured public offerings of private companies. A vast number of families and entrepreneurs sold their operating businesses into the public market or in strategic private transactions, creating liquidity events that fuelled an explosion in family offices.

Having a family office became a status symbol. A family office, a private jet and exotic investments were proof that one had truly arrived! But family offices were (and remain) very expensive, and only the most wealthy could afford to set up a true single family office, which required hiring the staff and committing the resources required to serve the family's needs exclusively. Suddenly people whose wealth did not rise to the level of supporting a family office wanted one, and so the wealth management market stepped in to meet that need. It is at this point the United States saw a proliferation of new types and styles of family offices being operated by very different players.

3. Family office functions

The United States is often cited as having a highly evolved and sophisticated family office community. But there is also an amazing universe of family offices in all regions of the world. And regardless of the regional variations in cultural, religious, social and political dynamics, the issues all family offices address fall within a surprisingly common framework. Family offices are tasked with unifying the wealth creation, wealth preservation and lifestyle management of a family under a defined family strategy. Typical activities include:

- managing the financial aspects of the family's wealth, usually relating to ownership and management of operating companies, interests in trusts, real estate, and pooled and individual investments;
- attending to tax, legal, accounting, reporting and regulatory implications of the above;[1]
- producing cash flows and budgets for the family's lifestyle;
- shielding private aspects of these interests from the public;
- overseeing the non-financial aspects of a family's wealth including generational transfer of wealth and the attendant preparation of the rising generation to flourish in its own right;
- fostering of entrepreneurship;
- implementing governance systems to support decision-making around jointly owned assets and collective activities;
- supporting philanthropy and social works of the family;
- managing family risk and security; and
- attending to the collection of activities often labelled 'concierge services', which involve taking care of any needs of the family from the proverbial

---

[1]   Two very significant factors setting US family offices apart are regulation and taxation. While most countries have some form of taxation and regulation, the United States can claim bragging rights for some of the most complex, exhaustive (and exhausting) regulatory and tax compliance regimes in the world. These two factors create a level of complexity that impact the role and focus of the US family office. The US family office invariably has a significant focus on tax planning – covering income, estate and gifts – and an increasing focus on regulatory compliance, as new and shifting regulatory bodies and rules draw more and more families into compliance reporting requirements. (And those who maintain their life outside regulatory regimes must document and prove their exceptional status – which takes resources and expertise as well.)

    There is a clear trend in the world today as countries seek to address their daunting economic realities. As a result, new and expanded tax and regulatory requirements are being added daily in other countries, and it is expected that family offices in the rest of the world will continue to add resources to address them – either through direct staffing or the use of professional accounting and legal resources. The bottom line is that tax and regulation will be an increasing focus in the United States and the world, and an increasing cost of running a family office.

walking the dog to medical care, managing household staff, insurance claims, school applications, vacation planning and so on.

Things were a bit simpler in the days of Messrs Vanderbilt and Rockefeller. There were fewer laws, fewer investments, fewer reporting requirements, and essentially no regulators. It was perfectly reasonable to expect that one well-educated and experienced lawyer, hired by the family and loyal to their service, could take care of all aspects of a family's needs. But as family wealth grew and the world grew exponentially more complex, family offices had to expand in their capabilities, sophistication and size.

4. Definition of models

Although examined elsewhere in this book, a review of the common models of family offices and the terminology associated with them in the United States will be a helpful foundation to analysing their relative strengths and weaknesses.

4.1 Single family office

The Rolls Royce of family offices is tailor-made to serve the needs of just one family. They are very expensive and very private. There is a very high premium placed on discretion and confidentiality in the single family office world. Operating under the radar and shielding the family from public attention is considered a defining attribute. Needless to say, the entire financial services world is looking for these families and targeting their family offices. Many families shun the term 'family office' in their organisation's name and will not refer to their office as such, preferring private investment company or holding company or a non-descript, generic name, instead. Remaining elusive has become harder and harder for careful family office executives.

It is not unusual to find single family offices in an incubator stage, often referred to as a 'co-located' (or 'embedded') family office. This model is a natural evolution of a single wealth creator with a privately operating company, where it is quite easy for the business owner simply to utilise the corporate staff for personal matters, comingling business and personal matters. The company accountant pays the bills and handles household payroll and benefits. The finance team handles home mortgages and investments. This situation usually becomes untenable when privacy, a second generation or proper segregation becomes an issue, or the sale of the company is contemplated. Corporate tax deductions in the United States for the personal services are also questionable.

4.2 Multi-family office

A multi-family office is a family office that serves more than one family. A single family office may decide to open to other families. But this is not the only source of multi-family offices. We also see professionals – such a lawyers, investment advisors or accountants – who work with large, complex family clients and develop an expertise in their needs, organising themselves into multi-client family offices. In addition, financial service providers – banks, trust companies, investment advisors and brokers – have moved into this space to extend their brand. The impact the origins of a multi-family office have on its business model are material and are explored in detail later.

As multi-family offices have evolved, some have moved toward a segmented multi-family office model, where multiple office locations are required, but expensive expertise (in areas such as investments, tax and philanthropy) is centralised in one location. Leveraging technology to communicate, execute and protect data security makes this type of model feasible.

One of the most flexible and adaptable models is the family alliance or affinity group. These are very fluid collaborations between and among a small number of families, and often formed for a specific purpose. Examples include two families collectively purchasing aircraft that they operate jointly and utilise collectively. The same occurs with hiring very special talent – such as investment or tax experts. Pooling buying power and spreading the carrying costs of required services without the onerous comingling of family financial and personal information, or the long-term commitment a traditional multi-family office requires can be an attractive solution for families.

Finally it is important to remember that not all wealthy families have family offices. But, with or without a family office, each has to tackle all the same issues. Often a family will work with an array of advisors and specialists and technology, creating a virtual family office. If a family's situation is not terribly complex, and they have the time available to coordinate all the pieces, this can be a viable model.

5. Assessment of models: the pros and cons

5.1 All family offices – in general
Family offices of all types share certain advantages:
- Holistic approach – the greatest benefit of a family office is the holistic and integrated management of all aspects of a family's wealth. Consideration can be made as to gaps and overlaps in all elements. The consequences of decisions and events can be assessed thoroughly. This is no small matter. Families rarely share all their facts with an independent advisor. In fact, it can take many years for anyone, inside or outside the family office, to become privy to and understand all the pieces of the vast empires these families often control.
- Pooled buying power – Wal-Mart is not the only organisation that benefits from buying in bulk. A family can access more sophisticated investments, structures and professionals, at a better price, by pooling their money and negotiating discounts.
- One-stop solution source – the convenience, effectiveness and efficiency to the family of centralising all aspects of its wealth management is one of a family office's greatest strengths.

Family offices also all share certain disadvantages:
- They are expensive! But any manner of attending to personal affairs costs money, and the failure to address these needs can be catastrophic.
- The structure can become dated. A family office can atrophy or become out-dated. As with any organisation, a family office needs to be monitored and

assessed against its objectives. (Its objectives, too, may need updating.) This is especially true in the United States, where many family offices were established more than 50 years ago.

- They may limit exposure to new and innovative ideas. Because of their clandestine nature, family offices can be isolated and insulated from new thinking, solutions or technologies. It is important to keep abreast of developments. This can often be achieved through participation in family office conferences, educational seminars and industry groups.

5.2 Single family office – service, service, service!

Beyond the general benefits of a family office, single family offices have specific positive attributes that define their offering:

- Loyalty to the family – the absolute best way to ensure that a system is in place to serve the family, with no other priorities or distractions, is the single family office. The overarching ethos of a family office is the service of the family. Staff become quasi-family members and are often deeply entrenched and committed to its service. They also acquire intimate familiarity with the family, its secrets and idiosyncrasies.
- Privacy – by managing all family wealth matters within a small, highly confidential setting, privacy is best maintained. The risks associated with personal information being maintained in large companies are significantly reduced. In fact, often only the family office knows all the details of a transaction or plan. The various advisors may only know the details required to complete their tasks, being kept in the dark with regard to the integrated effect of what they are doing. Names of holding companies can cloak personal identities from prying eyes. Families are often targets, not only of ambitious advisers and salespeople, but of kidnappers and extorters as well. Utilising a family office to diffuse this focus can be very effective.
- Prestige – because of their cachet and cost, family offices are an exclusive status symbol. While this may motivate some, many families are not at all interested in the prestige factor, but see their family office as a vital tool. Indeed, these families are usually bigger and more sophisticated, and often times, the lowest profile and hardest to see.
- Glue for the family – one of the really special attributes of a single family office, and one that deserves an entire book in its own right, is the role it can play in helping a family organise itself to be a legacy family. A legacy family is one that looks to the long-term flourishing of its members as the highest priority. Consider for example a family that has decided to sell its beloved family business that has been the central focus of the family for generations. This is a pivotal event for a family and can be highly emotional. Why? First, the family business has been a point of pride and often a reference of identity for the entire family. It defines the family in many respects, both among family members, and within the community at large. Family businesses can also be notoriously illiquid. This results in a family that is tied economically to the business's performance and valuation. Family members may not be

able to sell their interests, easily or at all. Working in the business is often a primary source of income for many family members. But these very challenges also serve to connect the family and hold it together. Once sold, a family is often left with a pile of very liquid, very fungible cash; cash that can be divided up and taken away. The bonding effect of the family business is lost, and a family once tightly organised and unified around the business may find its members quietly slipping away to do their own thing.

- Well prepared families will work to organise a family office in advance of (or in conjunction with) a major liquidity event. In so doing, they can create a new forum in which the family can come together to support each member towards personal flourishing. They will recognise that managing cash is a very different exercise from managing an operating company. It requires different skills and disciplines. They will need new expertise and tools to take the family forward. They will have new opportunities to participate in philanthropic and social causes; they will be able to dabble in hobbies, make exotic investments, and focus on the coming generations. A family office can support all these needs and activities.

- Total service model – single family offices are organised and staffed to provide exactly the services the family needs. They are built to support the types of activities in which the family is engaged and provide the specialist resources needed in that pursuit. There is no profit motive in a true family office itself: they are cost centres. While managing costs and justifying the services provided is always a part of managing the private family office, they are built to serve, not to provide a return on capital.

- Flexibility – because they are organised to service one family, and the costs are borne by that family, single family offices can be exceptionally flexible. They can drop and add services as needed. They can expand and contract. For example, if the family purchases a vineyard, the family office will ensure that specialists are secured to support the business. These might include accounting specialists (in the United States, viticulture is highly regulated and has its own section in the US. Tax Code, not to mention state tax rules applying to where wine is grown, bottled and sold), agricultural consultants, labour law specialists, marketing agencies and so on. If a wealth creator has children and wants to focus on their understanding of their role in the family and its wealth, a next generation specialist will be brought in and possibly philanthropy advisers also. The point is simply that the sophisticated wealthy family can bring whatever resources it chooses into the office to support its mission.

- Conflict-free advice – a key differentiator between a single family office and a multi-family office or any other family service provider is that the staff serve only the family and are in a position to give truly conflict-free advice – with one important caveat: even family office professionals may have conflicting motivations. The classic example often encountered is the family office executive seeking to justify their existence. Another is the executive who wants to exercise undue control over advisers and rather than filtering and integrating information for the family, in fact skews the information the family receives.

However, single family offices also have certain specific drawbacks:

- Expense – the biggest drawback and result of all this custom tailoring is the cost associated with it. Single family offices are incredibly expensive. Experience and various industry surveys generally peg the operating cost around 200 basis points for a family with assets of $200 million, or $4 million annually in operating costs. This would include costs of premises and staff, IT and legal and accounting fees, but excludes investment fees. Costs vary widely – and are often driven more by complexity than by asset size. But this cost level is a reasonable benchmark.

- Staff skills can become stale – another drawback of the single family office can be the atrophying of skills in the team. The hiring of a specialist lawyer can serve as an example. A family may decide they are spending a great deal of money on legal fees for a specialist in, say, real estate law. So they decide to recruit the lawyer who has been doing their work at a major firm. On the surface, it appears to make economic sense. The direct cost of employing the lawyer, even with benefits and a generous bonus certainly looks to be less than the legal fees. But in reality, one of the things that are hard to value is the exposure that such a lawyer has to two things while in the firm: extensive continuing education and experience garnered through exposure to many, many clients all with differing dynamics and issues. In practice, a lawyer might see multiple transactions in a month and learn several new techniques being utilised to address the latest economic realities. In a family, a lawyer might see a few transactions a year. Offsetting this is the benefit of having this specialist 100% dedicated and informed on the family's matters.

- Difficulty in attracting and retaining staff – this issue has eased over the years as family offices have become better known and understood, but there is still an issue for prospective employees who may fear being cloistered in a family office and out of the deal flow, learning and career progression they would have in larger or more mainstream firms. Compensation can also be a challenge for top talent, especially in the investment or private equity space. There is an entire body of experts who focus on building compensation models that will attract top talent without creating issues around equity ownership or profit participation, either of which might be impossible or unattractive for a family.

- Impossibility of firing clients/employees – it is simply one of the realities of a family office that clients cannot be dropped. Family members are footing the bill and the office is there to serve them. But the flip side of this can often also be an issue for a family. It can be very hard to get rid of staff. Whether the prospect arises because of downsizing, or needing different skills, or performance issues, families are often hesitant to dismiss staff. These staffing considerations can be addressed through good hiring and employment policies and by managing staff with the same professionalism as larger or more mainstream firms.

- No exit mechanism – often family offices are organised without providing a mechanism to wind them up when they have served their purpose, or the family's needs change. Also, individual family members may want to end their participation, but there is no clear path to do so. It is vital that the formation of a family office takes this into consideration and creates exits, for the family to withdraw or close the office.

- Oversight burden – a family office must be managed, which is a time-consuming undertaking. The family will have to play a role in the oversight of staff and decision-making. This can be a wonderful experience and a great living classroom for members who are interested, but if there is no family member with time and interest in this role, it will lead to failure of the system. At such a point, a family may be better served to work with a multi-family office.

5.3 Multi-family offices – it's a business

The critical difference between a single family office and a multi-family office is that a multi-family office has a profit motive (or a material cost-savings objective). It is a business. This is an essential difference compared to the single family office, and this fundamental aspect of the multi-family office informs the following analysis.

Further, the origins, or DNA, of the multi-family office will influence how it operates. As noted previously, there are a variety of entrants into the multi-family office market. One leading category of entrant is the financial services provider – banks, trust companies, investment managers and brokers. Often the appeal to this business category is to broaden their offering to existing ultra-high net worth clients, attract new clients and retain clients they would lose to competitors making the same move. It is a highly competitive landscape and it seems nearly everyone in this category has made a foray into the multi-family office space. It is vital to understand the ownership and ties back to the sponsoring entity. Is the family office just an asset-gathering and marketing office cloaked as a family office?

Another category of entrant into the multi-family office space is the professional – the law, accountancy or business management firm – broadening its offering to serve their clients. Both financial services firms and professionals benefit from the fact that they have been and continue to be profit-based operations. They often have corporate systems, products, infrastructure and cash flow to support the multi-family office through its start-up. But they face a real challenge in differentiating themselves and convincing families that their services are better. Multi-family offices face a real struggle with pricing power. Experience shows the hardest negotiations over fees are usually with billionaires. They drive a hard bargain!

One important type of multi-family office is the single family office that opens its doors to other families. They face unique challenges that are worth reviewing. It is easy to understand the intellectual (and financial) appeal of opening a single family office to other families. But cautious consideration is in order.

6. Making the transition from single to multi-family

6.1 Typical triggers to the transition from single to multi-family office

The death of a patriarch or matriarch can trigger the move to a multi-family office by the next generation as they begin to take responsibility for, and start to understand, the family office. Nothing has changed in the services and capabilities except that the parent is no longer paying for them. When faced with splitting the substantial costs of a family office with siblings, in the United States the next generation often considers the leap to a multi-family office.

Another factor that compels a family to evolve is an interest in leveraging a key strength of the family's business operating model. An example would be a family whose operating business involves the acquisition and development of oil and gas properties. Over the years, that family has developed a real competitive edge in this space. This type of expertise can be a core competency for the family with a family office and an attraction to other families interested in co-investing with the family in that field.

And sometimes a family office looks in the mirror and realises that, really, it is are already a multi-family office; that as the family has grown, it has served myriad family groups with widely differing members, needs and locations. So it seems natural to take the next step.

There are several key considerations involved in making this decision.

First, the central focus shifts from a total service model to a profit-orientated model. Once the family opens up to others, there will be a focus on money – and savings. There are difficult questions to answer about how fees will be charged and to whom. How will costs be tracked, both direct and indirect? Will staff now need to keep time sheets, like attorneys and accountants? Will all clients pay equally, both original family and new clients?

A second consideration is scale. The idea of opening up to more families is that with more families sharing the resources the cost can be shared, thus reducing the individual share. Unfortunately, families are often very different, and every time a new family is brought in to join a family office, there is an extraordinary effort and expense. This is not like building an assembly line for automobiles. Every car coming through this factory is unique!

The existing staffing often is not right for the new model. A multi-family office must run efficiently, but time management is often a foreign concept in a single family office where doing whatever it takes to get the job done is the clarion call. There are new roles and responsibilities to be filled. Sales people are needed, new client service people, and a layer of management is now needed as well. The office will need new people; or at least more people.

The services, reports and capabilities being provided to a family may not translate well into a commercially viable business model. Now suddenly there may be significant upgrades needed to the computer systems, consolidated reporting and accounting systems, investment styles and options. These too cost money.

There are a lot of new costs associated with this transition. To remain competitive, the business (and yes, it is a business now) must generate enough revenue to cover costs and to compensate new expensive employees, and also to reinvest in continuous upgrades of capabilities. This is a highly competitive business when it gets down to families paying for these services.

And finally, a family must really come to terms with some of the losses: the loss of privacy, the loss of flexibility and the loss of cachet that come with this move. New rules will be implemented, and the original family must adhere to them or it risks triggering animosities with the new client families. Sharing resources often does not come naturally to the originating family members. So experience shows that the transition can be made, but it is not a simple process; it requires careful planning and management and a commitment to investment of capital.

6.2   The pros and cons of the multi-family office

There are advantages to moving to the multi-family office model:

- Combined cost savings – probably the biggest driver in the decision to open a single family office to other families is cost savings. Corollaries to that include the desire to expand the services offered while spreading the cost among more clients, or the desire to pool more assets in order to increase buying power (again, saving costs). By sharing services and expensive resources across multiple clients, the rate can be lowered for each family. Experience, though, shows that the ability to achieve real scale in family offices can be very elusive! Families want tailored solutions, and finding a group of families whose needs are sufficiently similar so that solutions can actually be shared across family groups can be very difficult.
- Added capabilities – a multi-family office can leverage its scale to add functionality and sophistication, all of which are available to the original and new family clients' benefit. Often, the move to the multi-family office platform also raises the level of professionalism and discipline in the team.
- Quality of people – to some extent, the staffing issues that may be encountered in the single family office are alleviated in the multi-family office. They are often larger, have a higher profile in the industry and are run with more mainstream professionalism, providing more clarity around career growth and compensation. Staff can more easily participate in ownership. Exposure to multiple clients can provide a broader experience.

There are, though, also some downsides:

- Loss of privacy and cachet – a single family office cannot be rivalled when it comes to privacy, if simply for the lower number of people who have access to a family's information. If privacy is a critical priority to a family, there is generally some compromise in a multi-family office, again if simply from the number of people who have access to a family's information.[2]
- Less flexibility – as cost management is a key driver, and there is a profit motive, multi-family offices are less inclined to add new resources or services without assessing their potential to deliver to the bottom line. So, comparing the

---

2   While confidentiality has been an important hallmark of the family office, it is being eroded, even in the single family office. This can be attributed to various factors. Technology has expanded so rapidly that the entire financial world's data is electronic. Even if a family chooses not to leverage technology, their data is already out in what used to be referred to as the 'ether' but now, in fact, is the Cloud. As governments, the US government being at the forefront, press for incremental disclosure and reporting, more and more information is in more and more hands. Painful as it is, families are simply getting accustomed to the fact their information is less private than it used to be. (To be clear, this desire for privacy has absolutely no relationship to tax evasion, but to security and discretion.)

example of a single family office adding resources to support the acquisition of a winery, a multi-family office would not add these resources unless it could establish that they will not only be paid for by the client, but preferably have applicability to other clients (scalability) and the potential to be run profitably.

- Tension between legacy and new families – when making the transition from a single to a multi-family office, an interesting dynamic can arise between the original family members and new clients. Management is now focused on the bottom line and other clients, diluting the singular focus the family enjoyed when their office was private. Suddenly the office has imposed new rules. Conference rooms and offices have to be reserved. Advisors cannot drop everything to take a call or handle an issue. Controls are in place requiring approvals and signatures. The original family has some adjusting to do to live with the new approach. Interestingly, the opposite can also be an issue. New families can feel that the original family is getting special treatment. Animosity over the original family participating in the profits can also arise.
- Sustainability – in the United States, many, many multi-family office groups have formed, and disappeared over the last decade. It is a very difficult business model to sustain over time; and families should be interested in the sustainability and longevity of the platform because it is a difficult, time-consuming and expensive proposition to change to yet another relationship. It has been interesting to observe the US market. Some of the multi-family office platforms have been picked up by banks and brokerage firms, putting the family right back in the world they were likely trying to escape when they looked into a family office approach. It is certainly worth asking what the multi-family office owners' end-game expectation is for the business.

7. Alternatives to the traditional family office models

Technology has played a central role in the establishment of alternatives to the single and multi-family office models. Client investment, tax and accounting data can be warehoused electronically and accessed directly by the client, eliminating (at least in theory) some of the high cost for client service people. High-cost talent – like lawyers and accountants and investment specialists – can be centralised, which again will save costs. Communication technology, with video conferencing, intranets and data vaults for example, all provide tools for improving efficiencies in the family office.

This is the concept behind the segmentation model. Where high cost, high-IQ resources are centralised and the delivery model is local. A high cachet local office with a capped number of family members being served can be linked, along with other such local offices, to a centralised office containing the brains trust. This model is particularly useful for families with members in multiple locations. This allows the sharing of the expenses of these services, while delivering them in the traditional small, private office environment.

Technology is also helping to streamline many of the functions of a family office. More and more functions are capable of being outsourced, and are. There are increasingly powerful consolidated reporting capabilities, able to show in one report a family's assets and investments all over the world, in all currencies and asset classes.

There are more data services for investment due diligence, software solutions for philanthropy, socially responsible investing and even managing wine, fine art and automobile collections.

Another model emerging in the United States in the last decade is the cooperative or affiliate buying group. The idea here is that two or more families with similar needs for a specific service bond together and purchase it collectively. One of the overarching benefits of any family office, regardless of model, is the purchasing power of pooled assets. In the cooperative buying model, families join up for a very limited purpose to leverage that benefit, without folding their personal lives together in a family office. Consider a few of the ideas that work here:

- purchasing insurance;
- purchasing an aircraft (hiring the crew, housing it and them, and associated costs);
- pooled investments;
- personnel, including lawyers, investment managers and even family office executives.[3]

Outsourcing is a great way to improve quality of services in a family office. More and more top quality specialists exist in the market, and one function outsourced most often by the largest family offices with significant liquid assets is that of the chief investment officer. Large families that are looking for real investing performance often struggle with finding and retaining great investment specialists. This is often the case when investing is not the family's core expertise, as is the case with a newly liquid family following the sale of the operating business. Compensation can be an insurmountable issue between a family and a great investment professional. Moving to an independent investment advisory firm can be an effective solution. This is particularly true in families with a fiduciary responsibility for overseeing their wealth, such as those overseeing portfolios for future and unborn beneficiaries.

The combination of outsourced solutions with some cooperative purchasing and affinity group information-sharing, coordinated by a family member or a trusted family advisor – this is what is referred to as a virtual family office, and is probably the most flexible of the newly emerged family office models.

8. Conclusion

I have had the honour of working with families from all over the world, navigating many complex situations: an Asian family struggling with fairness between children in the family business and those who chose careers elsewhere; Indian and Saudi families managing the dynamics of a new generation with educated and capable daughters; a Latin American family struggling with the hard decision to prune the family tree; European families embroiled in text-book generational disputes; and families everywhere experiencing the liberating yet somewhat rudderless feelings

---

3   Two very important US families have just recently announced that they have hired a chief executive and a chief investment officer, both of whom will work collectively for the two families.

they face following the sale of their family's operating business.

As Jay Hughes has always emphasised, the issues these families face are truly universal. So while I have been asked to contribute a review of the US family office model, I am compelled to come back to this overarching message: the issues are the same the world over.

Families need to grow a system for tackling these universal challenges and a family office offers a powerful platform for developing solutions. When properly conceived, organised and run, a family office can ease a family's transition from the first generation wealth creator, through the second generation of siblings, the third generation of cousins and on through successive generations, helping to ensure that each family member flourishes as an individual and that the family manages its wealth as a springboard of opportunity and social good.

About the authors

Maxim Alekseyev

Senior partner, ALRUD Law Firm

malekseyev@alrud.com

Maxim Alekseyev is a co-founder and senior partner of ALRUD Law Firm, and head of the private client and tax practice areas. He specialises in private client, investment, corporate and commercial issues.

Mr Alekseyev has extensive experience in advising high-net-worth individuals on various issues to help them to manage their assets, business and family relations. He advises clients on all aspects of estate planning and administration, personal wealth management (trusts and other structures, financial instruments and models) and cross-border donations, as well as family business management, risk management in respect of foreign assets and taxation, including resolution of tax disputes. Mr Alekseyev is acknowledged as a leading Russian expert focusing on private wealth planning, including trusts and foundation, successions, onshore and offshore structures, private banking and individual taxation.

Clare Archer

Partner, Penningtons Manches LLP

clare.archer@penningtons.co.uk

Clare Archer heads up the London private client department at Penningtons Manches LLP. Ms Archer advises on a heavy caseload of capital tax planning, the administration of complex and large estates and trusts, will and trust drafting, and a wide range of asset protection and equity work, particularly for business owners and elderly clients with capacity issues. She has also developed a particular interest in family office work through her role as a trusted adviser to a number of high-net-worth families.

A member of the Society of Trust and Estate Practitioners (STEP), she chairs the editorial board for the England and Wales and UK entries for the *International Yearbook* and also writes the probate section of the STEP handbook. Ms Archer was a panel deputy of the Office of the Public Guardian for many years and is also a member of the Association of Contentious Trust and Probate Specialists.

Grania Baird

Partner, Farrer & Co

grania.baird@farrer.co.uk

Grania Baird advises asset managers, private banks, family offices and other financial services firms on all aspects of financial services law.

Her work covers both regulatory advice and advising on the structuring and set-up of investment funds and other products.

Ms Baird acts for both established institutions as well as start-up Financial Conduct Authority and Prudential Regulatory Authority-regulated businesses.

Linda Bourn
Executive managing director, Crystal & Company
linda.bourn@crystalco.com

Linda Bourn is executive managing director and leader of Crystal & Company's family enterprise risk practice. She holds an MBA and a BA. For the past 18 years she has specialised in advising family businesses and family offices on risk and insurance management.

Her experience includes managing director roles at Wilmington Trust, Family Wealth Group serving family businesses and delivery of insurance management, trust services, tax and accounting services, at a private family office that delivered integrated planning services to 25 family clients, and at Marsh, where she founded the Family Office Practice serving more than 60 family offices within the private client group.

Her board roles include Babson College Board of Overseers and Attorneys for Family Held Enterprises, while her advisory memberships include Collaboration for Family Flourishing, Risk & Insurance Management Society and Family Office Exchange.

Imogen Buchan-Smith
Associate
imobuch@hotmail.co.uk

Imogen Buchan-Smith is a senior associate in the private client team specialising in tax, trust, succession and estate planning. She advises a range of individuals – including non-domiciled individuals and entrepreneurs – on a variety of matters such as pre-immigration planning, as well as succession planning in the context of family-owned businesses. Ms Buchan-Smith also supports financial institutions (including banks, trustees and family offices) on fiduciary, tax and trust matters.

She is a member of STEP and was listed in the 2012 and 2013 'Top 35 Under 35' list of private client professionals by *Private Client Practitioner* magazine. Ms Buchan-Smith has also contributed to a number of publications including the *Trusts and Estates Law and Tax Journal*, the *PS Magazine* and *Private Client Adviser*.

Mary Anne Bueschkens
Counsel, Miller Thomson LLP
mabueschkens@millerthomson.com

Mary Anne Bueschkens is counsel based in Miller Thomson's Toronto office. A leading trusts and estates practitioner providing legal advice and expertise relating to the taxation, establishment and administration of domestic and offshore trusts and estates, Ms Bueschkens provides counsel to private clients, businesses, investment groups, trust companies, philanthropists and institutional and individual trustees and fiduciaries in the tax, estate, trusts and charities areas. She is often involved in multi-jurisdictional and contentious legal and tax issues.

Ms Bueschkens has written and lectured extensively on the areas of tax, estate, trust planning and administration. She has also been recognised as a leading trusts and estates practitioner in the 2011 to 2014 editions of *The Best Lawyers in Canada* (Woodward/White) and in Euromoney's *2011 Guide to the World's Leading Trust & Estate Practitioners*. She was recognised in the 2013 edition of *Who's Who Legal* for her private client work and in the 2014 *Canadian Legal Lexpert*.

In addition to her position with Miller Thomson, Ms Bueschkens is past chair of STEP. An elected academician, she serves on the Executive Council of the International Academy of the Estate and Trust Law. She also sits on the Board of Governors of the Royal Ontario Museum.

Ashley Crossley
Partner, Baker & McKenzie LLP
ashley.crossley@bakermckenzie.com

Ashley Crossley is head of the wealth management department and a member of the firm's global wealth management steering committee and chair of the European and Middle East steering committee. He is a coordinating partner for the firm's global banking relationships.

Mr Crossley's particular experience is in establishing private trust companies and providing advice on and establishing tax efficient venture capital and pre-initial public offering tax structures. His recent experience includes acting on one of the largest limited partnership structures in the Far East worth £5.3 billion, advice to some of the world's wealthiest Russian/ Commonwealth of Independent States entrepreneurs listing their companies on the London Stock Exchange and tax and trust planning for leading families in the Middle East.

Mr Crossley was recently named Lawyer of the Year at the Citywealth Magic 2012 Awards, as well as being included in the *Private Client Practitioner* 50 Most Influential Lawyers 2012.

Robert Desax
Associate, Baker & Mckenzie Zurich
robert.desax@bakermckenzie.com

Robert Desax is an associate in the tax department of Baker & McKenzie Zurich. He graduated from the University of Fribourg, Faculty of Law, in 2002 and passed the Zurich Bar exam in 2005. In 2006 he obtained an LLM in international tax law from the Vienna University of Economics and Business. From 2006 to 2010 Mr Desax worked in the international tax department of one of the Big Four audit firms. In 2010 he earned the diploma as a Swiss-certified tax expert. He speaks French, German and English.

Mr Desax advises corporations and private clients. He practises in the areas of national and international taxation, specialising in international corporate taxation, double tax treaties, tax aspects of wealth planning for private clients as well as tax controversy. Mr Desax is a regular contributor to various publications and a frequent speaker at events and conferences in the taxation field.

Keith Drewery
Director, Drewery Consulting Pty Ltd
keith@dreweryconsulting.com

Keith Drewery has worked for more than 30 years with wealth owners in professional services practices to help those families achieve financial goals and preserve wealth. His career included working in London and Sydney

He consults to wealthy families on issues of succession, legacy and philanthropy and for the last three years has worked as a director with KPMG's private enterprise division in Sydney. Originally working inside accounting firms as a tax specialist, Mr Drewery left the profession to work within funds management and between 2006 and 2011 he established and ran the Myer Family Company's Sydney office, Australia's largest independent multi-family office.

Through the last 15 years Mr Drewery has worked closely with founders and trustees of some of Australia's most significant foundations and private ancillary funds. He consults widely to the not-for-profit sector.

Mary K Duke
Independent adviser to families
mary.k.duke@thehighrd.com

Mary Duke helps families with significant wealth to leverage that wealth as a tool for family flourishing and social good. She focuses on empowering the next generations to recognise, receive and steward the family legacy, and on helping families adopt the practices and behaviours that foster individual growth while making family collaboration more effective and rewarding.

With over 25 years' experience she is an expert in trusts and cross-border transfer of wealth strategies, family business succession, family office architecture, next-generation mentoring, philanthropy, entrepreneurship and governance for families and their businesses. At HSBC Ms Duke spearheaded the private bank's award-winning Global Family Wealth Initiative and worked with many of the bank's largest and most sophisticated families and their advisors navigating the challenges of successfully transitioning wealth across generations.

Ms Duke is an author and international speaker. She has conducted next-generation and family retreats in Europe, Latin America, Asia, the Middle East and the United States.

Samy Dwek

Managing director, JPMorgan Chase NA
samy.e.dwek@jpmorgan.com

Samy Dwek is a banker at JPMorgan Private Bank in Boca Raton, Florida. With more than 20 years' banking experience in the investment bank, asset management and the private bank around the globe, he and his team focus on developing strategies for financially successful Florida-based families with complex wealth management needs, such as cross-border concerns, investment management and inter-generational planning.

His most recent role was head of JP Morgan family office solutions, Europe, the Middle East and Africa (EMEA) and member of the EMEA management committee for JP Morgan Private Bank. He also served as the head of emerging Europe for the private bank for six years. Previously he was a banker for the Turkey-Israel region and concurrently worked for JP Morgan Asset Management, covering institutional clients in Turkey and Israel for six years. Mr Dwek is a graduate of the European Business School in London.

Kira Egorova

Of counsel, ALRUD Law Firm
kegorova@alrud.com

Kira Egorova, of counsel at ALRUD Law Firm and head of the international accounting and corporate support department, plays a key role in the firm's private client practice.

Ms Egorova advises clients on all aspects of their estate planning needs, from wealth transfer advice to counselling on tax-related business issues. She acts as a project manager in a number of projects related to domestic and international probate, residential and other property and contentious trusts, and advises high-net-worth Russian individuals on the development of ownership and succession structures for diversified private and business assets, located in different jurisdictions. She represents families and individuals, family offices, closely held businesses, foundations, estates and trusts, and provides them with the spectrum of estate, succession, gift transfer and wealth planning services.

Ori Ephraim

Founder and manager, O Ephraim Multi Family Office Services
oriephraim@gmail.com

Ephraim MFO Services was founded in 2002 by Ori Ephraim. The firm's goal is to provide independent and trusted chief financial officer services to ultra high-net-worth individual clients in order to preserve the family's assets and multi-generational vision. The firm's services include comprehensive investment advice, tax, accounting as well as acting as a liaison between the auditors and lawyers of the clients.

Mr Ephraim holds an MA in economics and business administration (*cum laude*) and a BA in economics and accounting (*cum laude*), both from the Hebrew University in Jerusalem. In addition, he holds a diploma in international trust management from STEP. Mr Ephraim is a licensed accountant in Israel (CPA) and is a member of the Institute of Certified Public Accountants (CPA) in Israel. Mr Ephraim was an external lecturer in tax and accounting at the Hebrew University and at Bar Ilan University, and lectures widely in his areas of expertise.

Lyat Eyal
Partner, Aronson, Ronkin-Noor, Eyal Law Firm
lyat@are-legal.com

Lyat Eyal was admitted to the New York State Bar in 1998 and practised law at New York firm Faust & Oppenheim LLP until 2003. She has been admitted to the Israel Bar in 2005 and is setting up a new law firm in 2015.

Ms Eyal is a member of the New York State Bar Association Trusts and Estates Section and International Section and an academician of the International Academy of Estate and Trust Law. She has an extensive private client practice and advises on cross-border estate planning, taxation of trusts, pre-immigration planning and succession matters. Ms Eyal publishes in leading professional journals and lectures widely in her areas of expertise.

Joe Field
Counsel, Withers Bergman LLP
joe.field@withersworldwide.com

Joe Field is counsel to the private client practice at Withers Bergman LLP. He is resident in New York and has worked in the firm's London and Hong Kong offices. He is a graduate of Princeton University (*magna cum laude*) and Columbia Law School and is admitted in New York, California and the District of Columbia. He is a registered foreign lawyer in Hong Kong and the United Kingdom and was a *conseil juridique* in France.

Mr Field's practice is dedicated to international families, family offices and their charitable and quasi-charitable activities. He deals with tax and estate planning, but has increasingly devoted time to working with families to preserve both financial and human capital over generations. He has also been involved in family litigation.

He is a frequent speaker and contributes to trade periodicals, and has authored and edited a number of books on relevant topics.

Aditya Gadge
Chief executive officer, Association of International Wealth Management of India
aditya@aiwmindia.com

Aditya Gadge is the chief executive officer of the Association of International Wealth Management of India (AIWMI). AIWMI primarily takes the broad strategic role of developing a more robust and forward-looking training infrastructure for the private banking and wealth management sector in India.

Mr Gadge is a member of the Board of Directors of the Association of International Wealth Management, Switzerland and a member of the Advisory Board of Family Office Group, United States. He was a jury member for the inaugural WealthBriefings Asia Awards 2013, held in Singapore.

Mr Gadge has 10 years' experience in the financial services sector in disciplines such as wealth advisory, financial education, HR consulting, strategic planning, brand building, public relations, media planning and buying.

Mr Gadge holds master's degrees in human resources and economics, and is a certified financial planner. He regularly contributes to various business, financial and education publications, and is a member of the Editorial Board of *India Wealth Report*.

Anne Gibson
Course facilitator, Boston University School of Law
ahgibson@bu.edu

Anne Gibson is a course facilitator for the graduate tax programme at the Boston University School of Law, and a freelance writer on tax issues. She graduated from Harvard Law School in 2008 and was admitted to the Massachusetts Bar in the same year. She received her LLM in taxation from the Boston University School of Law in 2010. She worked as an associate in wealth management and US taxation at Baker & McKenzie Zurich from 2010 to 2012. In 2013 she taught estate planning and income taxation of trusts and estates as an adjunct professor at the University of Oklahoma School of Law. She writes on issues involving US income taxation of individuals, including residents and non-residents, as well as estate and gift taxation and estate planning.

Barbara R Hauser

Independent family adviser, Barbara R Hauser, LLC

brhauser@gmail.com

Barbara Hauser combines extensive experience advising families, family businesses and family offices first as a private client lawyer and later with a focus on governance. She helps families to develop their unique governance process, which may include a family constitution, a family council and a holding company board. She is a sought-after speaker and prolific writer, and is often referred to as a true thought leader in the family office field.

Her books include *International Family Governance, International Estate Planning, Trusts in Prime Jurisdictions* (advisory editor, Globe Law and Business), *"Mommy, are we Rich?": Talking to Children about Family Money* (co-author) and *Saudi-Girl Barbara*.

Her articles include "The Family Office: Insights into Their Development in the US, A Proposed Prototype and Advice for Adaptation in Other Countries," "Family Office Trends: Lessons from Dubai?" and "The Family Office Landscape: Today's Trends & Five Predictions for the Family Office of Tomorrow".

Håkan Hillerström

Independent family business adviser

hakan@hillerstrom.ch

Håkan Hillerström has been an independent adviser since 2003, providing family business and family office advisory services. These include succession planning, conflict management, building shareholder agreements, creating family constitutions, emergency planning, overall wealth management planning, financial education and all types of family office solutions.

Mr Hillerström previously worked in his family's own shipping business, for Banque Kleinwort Benson (private banking) and for PricewaterhouseCoopers where he created a European family business and family office service. He has worked with more than 130 families in 26 countries.

Mr Hillerström has an MBA from IMD Switzerland. He is frequently asked to lecture on his experiences and knowledge in this area, is the author of numerous articles in financial and business magazines and co-authored the book *Wise Wealth*, published by Palgrave Macmillan (December 2010).

Dennis T Jaffe

Independent adviser

djaffe@dennisjaffe.com

Dennis T Jaffe, a San Francisco-based adviser to families about family business, governance, wealth and philanthropy, recently completed the study "Good Fortune: Building a Hundred-Year Family Enterprise", published by Wise Counsel Research. This research project is entering its third phase this year.

He is the author of *Stewardship in your Family Enterprise: Developing Responsible Family Leadership Across Generations, Working With the Ones You Love: Building a Successful Family Business*, the management books *Rekindling Commitment, Getting Your Organization to Change* and *Take this Work and Love It*, and more than 100 management and psychology articles. In 2005 he received the Beckhard Award for service to the field from the Family Firm Institute. He has a BA degree in philosophy, an MA in management and a PhD in sociology (all Yale University), and is a licensed psychologist and professor emeritus of organisational systems and psychology at Saybrook University in San Francisco.

Marianne Kafena

Partner, Farrer & Co

marianne.kafena@farrer.co.uk

Marianne Kafena specialises in international private client work, with a focus on wealthy families with international links. Her work includes cross-border succession, the UK taxation of non-domiciled individuals, trusts and supporting family offices based in and outside the United Kingdom.

Ms Kafena speaks French and Arabic and grew up in Jordan. The families she advises tend to be based in Europe and the Middle East and are often concerned with succession, including family businesses, in a context of forced heirship. Ms Kafena also maintains her links with Bermuda, where her work is more focused on the concerns of professional trustees.

Raimund Kamp

Partner and co-founder, Guidato Family Office

raimund.kamp@guidato.nl

Raimund Kamp has studied notary and tax law at the University of Amsterdam. He has held tax adviser positions with Arthur Andersen in both Amsterdam and London, Ernst & Young and MeesPierson. He has advised Dutch and international entrepreneurial families on how to sustain their wealth and how to successfully transfer their companies and built-up wealth. For a number of years he has taught students financial planning education, and he also develops courses.

Mr Kamp has a robust, can-do attitude, and demonstrates sincerity and excellent communication abilities.

Alon Kaplan

Advocate and notary, Alon Kaplan Law Firm

alon@alonkaplan-law.com

Alon Kaplan was admitted to the Israel Bar in 1970, the New York Bar in 1990 and the Frankfurt Bar Association in 2010. He holds a PhD (Zurich University). His main practice areas are trusts and estates, international taxation, private client, corporate law, real estate law, agency and distributorships.

Dr Kaplan currently serves as the president of STEP and is academic coordinator and lecturer of the STEP diploma course at the Institute of Advanced Studies at Tel Aviv University's Faculty of Law. He also lectures on trusts in the LLM programme at the Faculty of Law of Tel Aviv University. Dr Kaplan is a member of the American College of Trust and Estate Council and an academician of the International Academy of Estate and Trust Law.

Dr Kaplan is general editor of *Trusts in Prime Jurisdictions* and is the Israel country correspondent for Oxford Journals' Trusts and Trustees. He has published many articles about trusts, estates and family wealth in professional journals.

Gray Keller

Writer and philanthropist

info@nexusyouthsummit.org

Gray Keller is a thinker, writer and philanthropist. He holds a doctorate in leadership (Regent University) and a certificate in professional development from the Wharton School. Mr Keller presides over the Leader Foundation, a private grant-making foundation helping public charities working on behalf of widows, orphans and the extremely poor. Mr Keller has served on the boards of many non-profit organisations, including donor-advised funds, and has held government positions with the state of Florida. Keller's writings range from articles in *The India Times* to his book, *Everyone Wants Your Money: Helping You Navigate Through Philanthropy*. He has travelled the world serving the poor, working with orphans and widows, and participating in everything from medical missions to constructing homes in the developing world. He has given millions of dollars to charities and understands the blessings and burdens of philanthropists.

Paul Knox
Managing director, JPMorgan
paul.f.knox@jpmorgan.com

Paul Knox is a managing director and head of wealth advisory services for the Europe, the Middle East and Africa region of the JPMorgan Private Bank. He is based in London and joined JPMorgan from Ernst and Young LLP where he was a director and head of the private client services group in London. He was also chairman and founder of the Ernst & Young international private wealth group. He has more than 30 years' experience in advising wealthy individuals and families on both domestic and international tax and estate planning issues. He also has wide experience in advising philanthropists on both tax and structuring issues in relation to charitable giving.

Mr Knox is a solicitor who is a graduate of Durham University. He is a member of STEP and has served as co chair of its International Committee and is also an adviser to its UK Technical Committee. He is also vice chairman of philanthropy impact.

Marijke Kuijpers
Partner and co-founder, Guidato Family Office
marijke.kuijpers@guidato.nl

Marijke Kuijpers studied business administration at Nyenrode and financial economics at the Vrije Universiteit in Amsterdam. She has more than 20 years' experience in banking, and since 1997 has held several positions at MeesPierson Amsterdam. Among her experiences with MeesPierson are investment consultancy and relationship management for ultra high-net-worth clients.

Ms Kuijpers has a strong sense of responsibility towards her clients and a renowned eye for detail. She is experienced in advising and assisting clients who acquire substantial capital unexpectedly. The family office business gives her ample room to work within her field of expertise. For several years she has been actively involved as volunteer for MamaCash, an international women's fund. Another of her passions is teaching finance and related topics.

Xiangchao 'Charles' Ling
Member, Silk Road Group Textile Company
info@nexusyouthsummit.org

Xiangchao 'Charles' Ling earned his master's in financial engineering at New York University and returned to China after interning at a Wall Street firm. Working for his family's company, he was initially responsible for marketing and development in Beijing. He then joined the company's headquarters in Zhejiang to manage operations of a high-end textile brand. In response to the Indonesian tsunami in 2004 and the Sichuan earthquake in 2008, his family donated millions from the company and established a special fund for poverty relief. Mr Ling also donates his own annual bonus to the fund.

Sandy Loder
Founder and chief executive officer,
AH Loder Advisers Ltd
sandy.loder@ahloderadvisers.com

Sandy Loder is a fifth-generation member of the Fleming family, dedicating his career and experience to helping other families establish secure structures for their future generations.

Formerly, he worked for both Robert Fleming and Fleming Family Partners, assisting in establishing one of Europe's largest multi-family offices. During his tenure he was also responsible for creating one of the leading next-generation education programmes.

With his long experience in the family business arena and having attended Harvard Business School, he has a wealth of knowledge and experience in setting up and running family offices. He advises and carries out reviews of family offices, as well working with families through the succession process. He has worked with over 500 next-generation members of families on a one-on-one basis or in workshops.

Katherine Lorenz

President, Cynthia and
George Mitchell Foundation
KLorenz@CGMF.org

Katherine Lorenz was elected president of the Cynthia and George Mitchell Foundation in January 2011. Before taking on this role, she served nearly three years as deputy director for the Institute for Philanthropy, whose mission it is to increase effective philanthropy in the United Kingdom and internationally. She now sits on the institute's board of directors. Ms Lorenz currently serves on the boards of directors of the Endowment for Regional Sustainability Science and the Amaranth Institute and was a board member of Resource Generation. Along with her family, Ms Lorenz is a member of the Global Philanthropists Circle (through the Synergos Institute) and is an active participant in the GPC Next Generation subgroup. She sits on the Council on Foundations Committee on Family Philanthropy and serves on their 2012 Family Philanthropy Conference Planning Task Force. Ms Lorenz holds a BA in Economics and Spanish from Davidson College.

Ian Macdonald

Partner, Wright Johnston & Mackenzie LLP
im@wjm.co.uk

Ian Macdonald is head of private client at Wright Johnston & Mackenzie LLP (WJM), based in Glasgow and Edinburgh, where he has been a partner since 1984. Mr Macdonald provides estate planning and tax advice to wealthy individuals, families and family offices, is particularly involved in capital tax planning and specialises in the use of trusts.

He has been closely involved in establishing WJM's own family office service which advises clients on the whole process of setting up a family office and carries out many family office management and advisory functions.

Mr Macdonald is accredited by the Law Society of Scotland as a specialist in trusts law, and is a member of STEP, representing Scotland on the STEP Council from 2007 to 2013. He is deputy chairman of the STEP Business Families Special Interest Group and was joint consulting editor of *Business Families and Family Businesses – the STEP Handbook for Advisers* (2009).

Lucinda E Main

Associate, Beard Winter LLP
lmain@beardwinter.com

Lucinda Main provides advice to her domestic and international clients on a wide range of estate, trust and tax issues. In particular, she advises on the Canadian taxation of various domestic and international trust structures and succession plans; assists in the setting up and maintenance of domestic and international trusts; drafts estate planning documents; and assists with the administration of estates. Ms Main is also regularly consulted regarding estate litigation matters and acts as counsel to not-for-profit and charitable organisations.

Ms Main has obtained her trusts and estates practitioner designation from STEP. She has written and co-authored publications and has spoken at conferences on various trusts and estate law issues. She is currently acting as an executive committee member of the Ontario Bar Association's Taxation Law Section and Trusts and Estates Law Section. She is also the Canadian representative for the International Association of Young Lawyers.

Ian Marsh

Founder and managing director, *family*dr Limited
imarsh@familydr.co.uk

Drawing on 40 years' experience of working with families as adviser, litigator and trustee, on his craft as a mediator and on the principles of interpersonal neurobiology, Ian Marsh works as a listener, communications and conflict coach, facilitator and mediator to enterprising families around the world.

He is accredited as a commercial mediator by the Chartered Institute of Arbitrators and as a general mediator by the Hong Kong International Arbitration Centre, and has been certified as an intercultural mediator (to International Mediation Institute Standards) by Mediation & Training Alternatives. He trained as a family mediator with ADR Group/Family Mediators' Association.

Mr Marsh studies interpersonal neurobiology with the Mindsight Institute and is a member of the Global Association for Interpersonal Neurobiology Studies. He writes and speaks regularly on communication, culture and conflict.

Ken McCracken

Consultant and joint managing director,
Withers Consulting Group
ken@withersconsulting.com

Ken McCracken is the joint managing director of Withers Consulting Group, which has advisers based in the United Kingom, United States, Switzerland and Hong Kong. He has specialised in advising complex family enterprises since 1995 when he helped found the first university-based educational programme in the United Kingdom for family enterprise owners and executives. His consulting work focuses on continuity planning and governance issues for family offices and family businesses. Mr McCracken is a regular speaker and writer on issues affecting enterprising families and provides strategic advice and training for professional associations, educators and trade bodies. He is, a member of the advisory board of the Institute for Family Business and is a past recipient of the Family Firm Institute Award for Outstanding Interdisciplinary Achievement.

Mark McMullen

Partner, Smith & Williamson LLP
mark.mcmullen@smith.williamson.co.uk

Mark McMullen is a partner in the private client tax services department. He holds a degree in natural sciences and qualified as a chartered accountant in 1989. He enjoys dealing with the complex challenges that face UK and international families, businesses and professional practices. He advises private clients, partners and their families on their financial and tax affairs and his specialisms include non-UK domiciliaries, UK direct taxes, UK property, limited liability partnerships and trusts.

Mr McMullen acts for several family offices, working with them on strategic and practical tax and financial issues. He has good experience of planning and administering offshore trusts and was on the board of a Jersey trust company from 2004 to 2006. He is a member of STEP, sits on its City of London branch committee and sat on its UK technical committee for many years.

Marnin Michaels

Partner, Baker & McKenzie Zurich
marnin.michaels@bakermckenzie.com

Marnin Michaels has been practising law for more than 15 years in the areas of tax and international private banking. He also handles insurance matters, particularly as it relates to tax investigations and wealth management. Mr Michaels has written extensively for many publications, including the *Journal of International Taxation, Tax Planning International, Tax Planning Financial Review, Private Client Business, International Tax Review, World Money Laundering Review* and The New York State Bar Association *Trusts & Estates Journal.*

Mr Michaels focuses his practice on international estate planning and taxation of trusts for families with connections in the United States. He counsels clients on US withholding tax and qualified intermediary rule, as well as money laundering avoidance legislation.

Charles Peacock

Director of philanthropy services, SandAire

charles.peacock@sandaire.com

As director of philanthropy services, Charles Peacock is responsible for managing client relationships and assists SandAire's clients in fulfilling their philanthropic objectives.

Mr Peacock is a graduate in law from Exeter University. He qualified as a chartered accountant with Price Waterhouse and worked for nine years in its corporate finance units in London and Frankfurt, advising on management buy-outs, company acquisitions and disposals and valuations. He then spent 12 years working in international equity markets in a number of companies, including HSBC and ABN AMRO, before joining SandAire in 2010. He is a trustee of a number of grant-making charitable trusts and a former trustee of Fairbridge, a national youth charity.

Aron Pervin

Owner, Pervin Family Business Advisors Inc

apervin@pervinfamilybusiness.com

Aron Pervin is an organisational consultant, social entrepreneur, mentor, counsellor, author and international pioneer in the field of family enterprise management and online assessment reports for the enterprise family marketplace. He works with multi-generational enterprise families and young wealth holders who wish to become effective owners and managers, foundation trustees and corporate directors. Mr Pervin serves on numerous local and global committees in associations such as the Society of Trust and Estate Practitioners, the Family Firm Institute, the Canadian Association of Management Consulting, the Institute of Corporate Directors and Nexus Youth Summit.

Gina M Pereira

Founder and principal, Dāna Philanthropy

gina.pereira@danaphilanthropy.com

Gina M Pereira is the founder and principal of Dāna Philanthropy and a practising lawyer. For more than a decade, Ms Pereira worked as a trusts and estates lawyer and fiduciary in private practice and in the international wealth management industry, servicing private clients from Asia, the Middle East, Europe and the Americas. Formerly based out of Zurich, New York, and The Bahamas, she currently operates in Toronto and Bermuda.

Ms Pereira established Dāna Philanthropy to assist her clientele to foster sustainable social development through strategic giving. Dāna Philanthropy is a donor advisory firm offering comprehensive advisory services to international private clients and corporations throughout all stages of the giving lifecycle, including: strategy development and planning, structuring, due diligence, negotiating gifts, implementation, monitoring, coordinating measurement and review.

MJ Rankin

Partner, The Rankin Group, LLC

mj@trgsearch.com

MJ Rankin manages the family office consulting and search practices for The Rankin Group. Her firm has been the leader in developing executive search techniques and related employee management resources for family offices for over two decades. Her prior professional experience includes management positions at Harris Bank, The Northern Trust Company and The Bank Marketing Association in Chicago. She started her career in management training and development for Honeywell in Boston, followed by roles in management and marketing consulting.

Ms Rankin is well known throughout the wealth management industry as an expert on family offices and family office management. Her clientele consists of wealth creators, Forbes 400 families and private investors who have or are considering establishing a family office to manage their complex needs. In addition, she works with multi-family offices and wealth management organisations that are looking to strategically position themselves in the family wealth market segment.

Amelia Renkert-Thomas

Joint founding partner, Withers Consulting Group
amelia@withersconsulting.com

Amelia Renkert-Thomas understands the complexities that family enterprises face. Not only from her experience as the joint founding partner of Withers Consulting Group – a consultancy dedicated to helping enterprising families make decisions, but also as a former lawyer, former chief executive officer of Iron rock, Inc, her family's fifth-generation manufacturing business and as the granddaughter of the founder of Fisher Price Toys.

Ms Renkert-Thomas works with families and enterprises of all shapes and sizes, from large multi-generational families with highly sophisticated business and investment structures, to entrepreneurs coping with the consequences of liquidity events. She has helped families to create more effective board structures, form and govern family offices, set up advisory committees and make trusts more functional.

No two jobs are the same for Ms Renkert-Thomas, as no two families are the same, but it always comes back to the same question: how can a family achieve its vision of success?

Kirby Rosplock

Founder and chief executive officer, Tamarind Partners Inc
kirby.rosplock@TamarindPartners.net

Kirby Rosplock leads Tamarind Partners Inc, a research, advisory and consultancy practice that works with families, advisers and institutions in the family office market. A recognised researcher, innovator, adviser and speaker, Dr Rosplock is the author of *The Complete Family Office Handbook* (Wiley/Bloomberg, 2014).

Dr Rosplock is part of an enterprising family, a co-trustee of her family's foundation and former board member of Family Enterprise USA. Dr Rosplock has a BA from Middlebury College, an MBA from Marquette University and a PhD from Saybrook University. She edited *A Thought Leader's Guide to Wealth* (GenSpring, 2009) and has authored numerous articles, book chapters and research reports. Dr Rosplock is a fellow at the Family Firm Institute (FFI), a board member of the FFI Practitioner and a faculty member of the FFI GEN Course in the Family Wealth Advisory Certificate programme.

Zac Russell

Founder, Russallo
zac.russell@gmail.com

Zac Russell has always been passionate about how to tell a story. He founded Russallo in 2013, a narrative consulting firm focused on listening, designing and implementing holistic communication and marketing plans for a wide variety of organisations. He is an advocate for next generation philanthropy, impact investing and global social entrepreneurship for non-profits and foundations. In the past, Mr Russell has worked in marketing for FOURPOINTS, a French international equities fund manager, and with One Nation, an initiative working with American Muslim communities to end discrimination. He has even worked as a Hawaiian cattle hand. He is a graduate of Sarah Lawrence College, where he concentrated on non-fiction writing and global economics. Mr Russell serves on the board of directors of the Russell Family Foundation as part of the investment committee.

Alex Scott
Executive chairman, SandAire
alex.scott@sandaire.com

Alex Scott is the executive chairman of SandAire, a company he formed in 1996 after leading the sale of his family's business, Provincial Insurance. SandAire is an investment office for families and foundations, managing several billion pounds for over 40 clients.

Mr Scott is a trustee of the Grosvenor Estate and a non-executive director of his family's investment holding company and several private companies. He is also co-founder and past chairman of directors of the Institute for Family Business (UK) and a former director of the Family Firm Institute Inc. He is also a trustee of the Francis C Scott Charitable Trust.

Mr Scott is a graduate of Oxford University and holds an MBA from the International Institute of Management Development, Lausanne.

Alison Springett
Partner, Farrer & Co
alison.springett@farrer.co.uk

Alison Springett provides tax and trust planning advice to UK-domiciled and resident individuals and foreign domiciliaries with international interests and worldwide assets. She specialises in developing and managing structures for international clients to hold business and personal assets.

The most common context for Ms Springett's work with family offices is acting as general legal counsel. In this capacity, her activities range from the more straightforward advice on administration and reporting to the more complex, involving the oversight of investment, corporate, property and commercial transactions.

Christian Stewart
Managing director, Family Legacy Asia (HK) Limited
cstewart@familylegacyasia.com

Christian Stewart founded Family Legacy Asia in July 2008 to provide independent advice to Asian families on family and family business governance issues. He works with enterprising families around Asia as a process consultant, coach and family meeting facilitator. He helps families to form their own family council, family constitution and family policies, often in the context of planning for succession.

Mr Stewart originally qualified and practised as a solicitor in South Australia from 1990 to 1994. He moved to Hong Kong in late 1994 where he joined PricewaterhouseCoopers in Hong Kong and was later promoted to be a partner in their tax practice and head of their trust and private client group. In July 2002 he joined JPMorgan Private Bank to head the bank's wealth advisory team for Asia, where he worked for six years before forming Family Legacy Asia.

Jonathan L Sutton
Partner, Dixon Wilson
jonathansutton@dixonwilson.co.uk

Jonathan Sutton is a partner in Dixon Wilson, a London firm of chartered accountants. He is a member of the Institute of Chartered Accountants in England and Wales and the Chartered Institute of Taxation. He holds an MBA from London Business School and has worked in London for 20 years.

Joshua Thomas
CEO, crowdMGNT
joshuathomas.zeke@gmail.com

Joshua Thomas got his first taste of business in radio, when he was the country's youngest assistant programme director at Hot 97.1 FM in New York City. From there, while maintaining his successful international DJ career, he received his bachelor's degree in business entertainment at Indiana University. His knack for entrepreneurship has lead to his partnership status with Dale & Thomas, the largest gourmet popcorn company in the country. Most recently, Mr Thomas has partnered with Edward Jamele to create crowdMGMT, a creative experiential marketing and media agency satisfying the needs of clients ranging from popular venues and hotels to leading accessories brands. At this pace, Mr Thomas has no plans to slow down.

Mary Ann Thompson-Frenk

Co-founder and president, Memnosyne Institute and John Philp Thompson Foundation
info@nexusyouthsummit.org

Mary Ann Thompson-Frenk is the co-founder and president of the Memnosyne Institute and the John Philp Thompson Foundation. She is a frequently requested international speaker, mediator, award-winning sculptor and board member for several organisations. She has been published in various books, blogs and magazines, including the Young Presidents' Organisation's *Real Leaders* magazine, which recognised her as a "real young leader to watch". Together with her husband Joshua, Ms Thompson-Frenk was identified by three-time Nobel Peace Prize nominee Ervin Laszlo as a "21st century visionary thinker" for her work leading innovative humanitarianism through her "social acupuncture" model.

Sarah von Schmidt

Partner, Farrer & Co
sarah.vonschmidt@farrer.co.uk

Sarah von Schmidt specialises in advising wealthy individuals and their families, entrepreneurs and land-owning families on personal tax, trusts and succession planning. She also advises executors and trustees on their duties and powers and works closely with family offices, wealth managers and private banks.

Ms von Schmidt is a member of the firm's entrepreneurs and family business group and has a particular interest in advising owner-managers of growing companies and family businesses on the personal wealth issues that affect those in these sectors.

Leslie C Voth

President and chief executive officer, Pitcairn
l.voth@pitcairn.com

Leslie C Voth is president and chief executive officer of Pitcairn, a recognised global leader in the specialised family office marketplace. A veteran of the financial industry with more than two decades of accomplishment, Ms Voth's industry experience and invaluable insights have contributed to the success of both the firm and its clients.

Ms Voth is directly responsible for overall corporate planning and strategic growth and oversees all client relationships. She has played a key role in Pitcairn's growth and expansion, spearheading development and implementation of an industry-leading 100% open architecture investment platform and developing a total wealth management strategy utilised by the firm's clients. She recently pioneered the creation of multi-disciplinary teams to meet the increasingly complex needs of the firm's clients collaboratively. Ms Voth was awarded the top honour of Women in Wealth Management at the *Family Wealth Report* Awards 2014 for her individual contributions to the wealth management industry.

Jonah Wittkamper

Global director, Nexus Global Youth Summit
info@nexusyouthsummit.org

Jonah Wittkamper is the co-founder and global director of Nexus, a global network of young leaders from several hundred of the world's most philanthropic families. Before co-founding Nexus, Mr Wittkamper served as the US director of Search for Common Ground and was part of Distributive Networks Inc, where he helped to build the text-messaging technology used by the Obama campaign. In 2000 Mr Wittkamper co-founded Global Youth Action, a global association of youth organisations that merged with TakingITGlobal to form the largest site on the Internet dedicated to empowering young leaders. Earlier in his career he founded two internet start-ups. An alumnus of Williams College and Camp Rising Sun, Mr Wittkamper lives in the Washington DC area.

William S Wyman
Chief executive officer, Summitas
bill@summitas.com

Bill Wyman is the chief executive officer of Summitas – a dynamic, secure and encrypted communications portal offering a virtual office, collaboration tools, a digital vault with iPad app and secure email. Summitas helps its clients – individuals, single family offices and advisory firms – to keep the dialogue open, yet address the real threats that they face in securing and keeping private personal correspondence and family communications. Mr Wyman has more than 30 years' experience working with single family offices, multi-family offices and registered investment advisers.

Mr Wyman was a senior director with BNY Mellon Family Office and managing director with Rockefeller. Previously, he was managing director of Deutsche Bank, vice president with JPMorgan, which included four years in Geneva, and Price Waterhouse.

Mr Wyman serves on boards and is a speaker at various conferences discussing technology-related issues, the risks of internet-based communications and operational efficiencies. He earned his BBA from the University of Notre Dame and his MBA (*summa cum laude*) from Fordham University.

Related titles

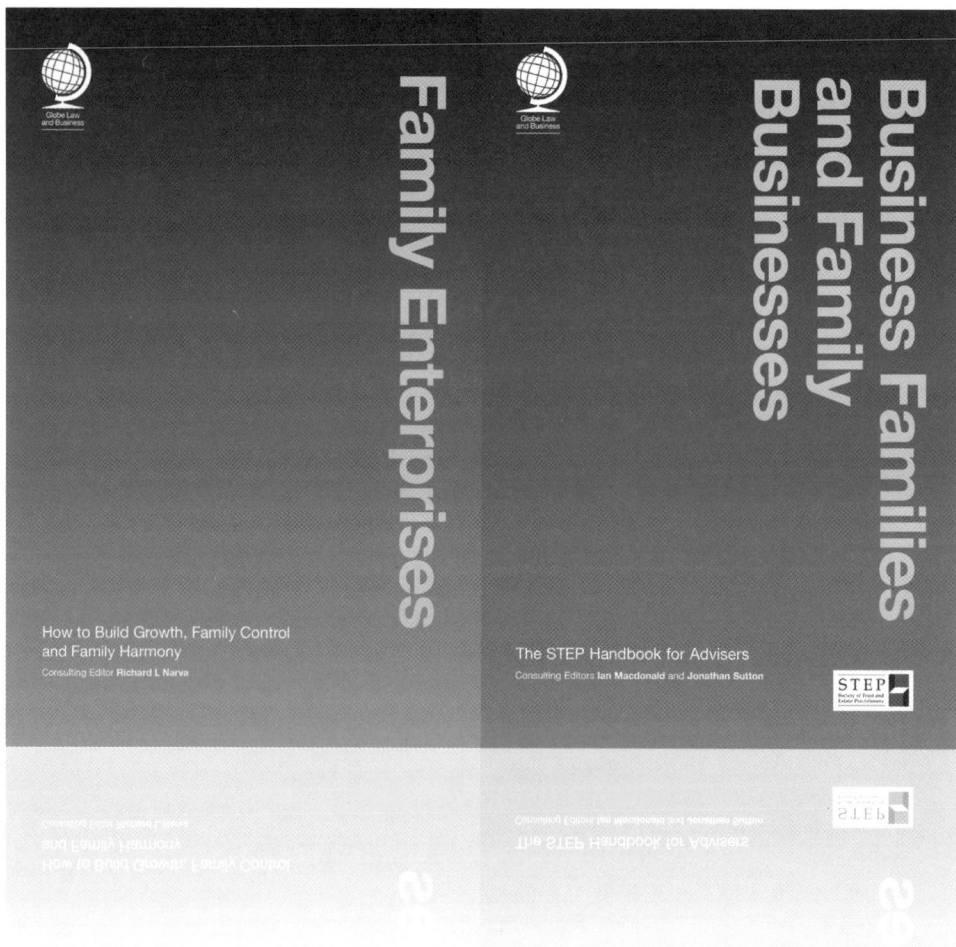

Family Enterprises

How to Build Growth, Family Control
and Family Harmony

Consulting Editor **Richard L Narva**

**Business Families
and Family
Businesses**

The STEP Handbook for Advisers

Consulting Editors **Ian Macdonald** and **Jonathan Sutton**

Go to **www.GlobeLawandBusiness.com**
for full details including free sample chapters

Globe Law
and Business